Sharia Law in the Twenty-First Century

Sharia Law in the Twenty-First Century

editors

Muhammad Khalid Masud
Supreme Court of Pakistan, Pakistan

Hana Jalloul Muro
Madrid Parliament, Spain

World Scientific

NEW JERSEY • LONDON • SINGAPORE • BEIJING • SHANGHAI • HONG KONG • TAIPEI • CHENNAI • TOKYO

Published by

World Scientific Publishing Europe Ltd.
57 Shelton Street, Covent Garden, London WC2H 9HE
Head office: 5 Toh Tuck Link, Singapore 596224
USA office: 27 Warren Street, Suite 401-402, Hackensack, NJ 07601

Library of Congress Cataloging-in-Publication Data
Names: Masud, Muhammad Khalid, 1939– editor. | Jalloul Muro, Hana, 1978– editor.
Title: Sharia law in the twenty-first century / edited by Muhammad Khalid Masud, Supreme Court of Pakistan, Pakistan; Hana Jalloul Muro, Madrid Parliament, Spain.
Description: Hackensack, NJ : World Scientific, [2022] | Includes bibliographical references and index.
Identifiers: LCCN 2021046138 | ISBN 9781800611672 (hardcover) | ISBN 9781800611689 (ebook) | ISBN 9781800611696 (ebook other)
Subjects: LCSH: Islamic law. | Law--Islamic countries.
Classification: LCC KBP144 .S5365 2022 | DDC 340.5/9--dc23/eng/20211109
LC record available at https://lccn.loc.gov/2021046138

British Library Cataloguing-in-Publication Data
A catalogue record for this book is available from the British Library.

For any available supplementary material, please visit
https://www.worldscientific.com/worldscibooks/10.1142/Q0344#t=suppl

Desk Editors: Christina Ramalingam/Michael Beale/Shi Ying Koe

Typeset by Stallion Press
Email: enquiries@stallionpress.com

https://doi.org/10.1142/9781800611689_fmatter

About the Editors

Muhammad Khalid Masud, MA and PhD (McGill), is presently an *Ad Hoc* judge, Shariat Appellate Bench, Supreme Court of Pakistan (2012–). Formerly, he was Academic Director, International Institute for the Study of Islam in the Modern World, Leiden, The Netherlands (1999–2003); Distinguished Visiting Professor, Kulliyah of Laws, International Islamic University, Kuala Lumpur, Malaysia (2003); Chairman, Council of Islamic Ideology, Government of Pakistan (2004–2010); and Director General, Islamic Research Institute, International Islamic University, Islamabad, Pakistan (2011–2013). His major publications include the following: *Shatibi's Philosophy of Islamic Law* (1977 [MKM1]), *Iqbal's Reconstruction of Ijtihad* (1995), *Islamic Legal Interpretation: The Muftis and their Fatwas* (1996) (co-edited with Brinkley Messick and David Powers), *Travelers in Faith, Studies of Tablighi Jama'at as a Transnational Movement for Renewal of Faith* (2000) (as the Editor), *Dini akhlaqiyat ke Qur'ani Mafahim*, Urdu Translation of T. Izutsu's book *Ethical Terms in the Qur'an* (2005) (as the Translator), *Nuqush-e Tagore,* Rabindra Nath Tagore's *Fireflies* (2012) (as the Translator), *Dispensing Justice in Islam, Qadis and Their Judgments* (2006) (co-edited with David S. Powers and Ruud Peters), *Atharwin sadi 'isawin men islami Fikr ke rahnuma* (2008) (as the Editor), *Islam and Modernity: Key Issues and Debate* (2009) (co-edited with Armando Salvatore and Martin van Bruinessen), *Shari'a Today, Essays on Contemporary Issues and Debates in Muslim Societies* (2013, 2019), and

Freedom of Expression in Islam: Challenging Apostasy and Blasphemy law (2021) (co-edited with Lena Larsen, Kari Vogt, and Christian Moe [MKM2]).

Hana Jalloul Muro earned a PhD from the University Complutense of Madrid at the International Relations and International Public Law Department. She received her Master's degree in European Union and International Relations. She was a Junior Expert on two European Commission projects in Lebanon for over three years. She worked as a Political Assistant for the European Union Election Observation Mission for the Parliamentary Lebanese Elections in 2009. She was a Lecturer, at the Department of Social Sciences, University Carlos III, teaching a dual bachelor's course in international studies titled, Politics: Political Theory and Ideologies, Introduction to Politics and Political Analysis I. She was also a Lecturer at the University of Nebrija till June 2019, teaching a course titled, The European Union: Culture, History and Institutions. She taught on the courses International Terrorism: Master in Geopolitics and Strategic Studies, and Comparative Politics at University Carlos III for postgraduate students till February 2020. She worked as an Adviser in the technical cabinet of the Delegate of the Government in Madrid till May 2019. From 26th May to 28th February 2020, she was a Deputy (MP) in the Assembly (Parliament) of the Community of Madrid. From February 2020 to March 2021, she acted as the Secretary of State for Migration of the Government of Spain. Following the election on May 4, 2021, she was elected Deputy (MP) and Spokesperson of the Socialist Parliamentary Group at the Madrid Parliament and served till 26 October 2021. She is now Deputy and President of the Socialist Parliamentary Group in Madrid. Recently, she was appointed Head of the Secretariat for International Politics and Cooperation for Development of the Spanish Socialist Workers' Party Executive. She is also a Member of the European Council on Foreign Relations (ECFR).

Most of her publications and conferences focus on key topics, including migration issues, preventing violent extremism and radicalization, Islamic law, moderate and radical Islamism, deconstruction of jihadist narratives, and international politics.

https://doi.org/10.1142/9781800611689_fmatter

About the Contributors

Rula Jurdi Abisaab is Professor of Islamic History at McGill University, with a focus on Shi'a doctrinal, legal and juristic developments from the medieval to the early modern period, and their political and socio-economic contexts. Another area of her research covers postcolonial Marxist Islamic thought, and the interface between the sacred and the secular in Lebanese and Iraqi Islamist movements. A third area deals with contemporary Arabic poetry and fiction, and compliments her own literary output. She has authored numerous articles and a book, *Converting Persia: Religion and Power in the Safavid Empire*, 1501–1736. She has co-authored another book with Malek Abisaab, *The Shi'ites of Lebanon: Modernism, Communism, and Hizbullah's Islamists.* Her forthcoming book examines the juristic and theological (*kalām*) foundations of the *akhbāriyya* (traditionist) movement in Safavid Iran, and its relationship with the new structure of power and social formations in the sixteenth century.

Abdullahi Ahmed An-Na'im is Charles Howard Candler Professor of Law, Associated Professor in the College of Arts and Sciences at Emory University, and Senior Fellow at the Center for the Study of Law and Religion. An-Na'im is the author of *What is an American Muslim* (2014); *Muslims and Global Justice* (2011); *Islam and the Secular State* (2008); *African Constitutionalism and the Role of Islam* (2006); and *Toward an Islamic Reformation: Civil Liberties, Human Rights and International Law* (1990). His edited books include *Human Rights under African Constitutions* (2003); *Islamic Family Law in a Changing World: A*

Global Resource Book (2002); and *Human Rights in Cross-Cultural Perspectives: Quest for Consensus* (1992). For more information, see https://scholarblogs.emory.edu/aannaim/.

Ana Ballesteros Peiró holds a PhD in Islamic studies from the Universidad Autónoma of Madrid. She is Associate Researcher at the Observatory of Politics and Elections in the Arab and Muslim World and Senior Associate Researcher at the Barcelona Centre for International Affairs CIDOB. Her area of expertise is International Relations in the Middle East and South Asia.

Kathleen A. Cavanaugh is a socio-legal scholar and the Director of the Pozen Center for Human Rights and Faculty at the University of Chicago (SSD/Human Rights). She holds a PhD in Government Studies from the London School of Economics & Political Science (1997) and an LLM (Distinction) from Queen's University of Belfast, Northern Ireland (1998). Her areas of expertise include nationalism, ethnic conflict, political violence, states of emergency, narratives on Islamic law and rights, freedom of religion, and militant democracy.

Mohammed Dahiri is Doctor of Philosophy in Literature, Professor in the Department of Arabic and Islamic Studies at the Complutense University of Madrid, and Coordinator of the Department of History and Civilization, Political and Social Sciences, Arabic and Islamic Studies, and EuroMed: Equality and Gender Studies at the Euro-Mediterranean University Institute (EMUI-UCM).

Mohammad Hashim Kamali is Founding CEO of the International Institute of Advanced Islamic Studies, Malaysia, and an international scholar in his field of specialization. He was Professor of Islamic Law and Jurisprudence at the International Islamic University Malaysia (1985–2004) and then Dean at the International Institute of Islamic Thought and Civilization (ISTAC) from 2004 to 2006.

He holds a 1st Class Honors Degree in Law and Political Science from Kabul University, Afghanistan, and an LLM and PhD in Islamic and Middle Eastern Law from the University of London.

Dr. Kamali was Assistant Professor at the Institute of Islamic Studies, McGill University in Montreal, and later a Research Associate with the Social Sciences and Humanities Research Council of Canada. He was a

Visiting Professor at Capital University, Columbus, Ohio, in 1991, and a Fellow of the Institute for Advanced Study, Berlin, Germany, 2000–2001. He served as member and sometime Chairman of the Constitutional Review Commission of Afghanistan in 2003. He is a Fellow of the International Institute of Islamic Thought and is currently on the International Advisory Board of 13 academic journals published in Malaysia, USA, Canada, Kuwait, India, and Pakistan. He has addressed over 230 national and international conferences, and has published 46 books and over 260 academic articles. His works have been hitherto translated into 13 languages.

Professor Kamali has been a member and Chairman of the CIMB Shariah Committee, Sunlife Takaful Malaysia, and Stanlib Corporation of South Africa. He is also Senior Fellow of the Royal Academy of Jordan.

He received the Isma'il al-Faruqi Award for Academic Excellence twice, in 1995 and 1997. He is listed in a number of leading Who's Who publications in the world. He has featured in the book The 500 Most Influential Muslims in the World several times (2009, 2010, 2016, 2019, and 2020). He is a recipient of the King Abdullah II International Award 2010 in recognition of his intellectual contributions toward serving Islam and Muslims. He has been a recipient in 2017 of the 24th Iran World Award for Book of the Year 2016 and in 2019 he received a Special Award, Halal Global Award, for Islamic Civilisation Studies.

Julio César Muñiz Pérez has degrees in History and Law. He holds a PhD in Ancient History from the University of Murcia (Spain) and a PhD in European Tax Law from the University of Bologna (Italy). He has written for more than 30 publications in Spain and abroad on comparative law, history of law, constitutional law, tax law and philosophy of law. His work involves academic studies, research, publications, patents, training, national and international conferences and seminars. His outstanding dedication to law and history has made him an interdisciplinary researcher, who has worked with international research teams. He has conducted research in Italy, Portugal and Germany. Currently, he is Professor at UNED, Faculty of Law.

Vrinda Narain is Associate Professor at the Faculty of Law, McGill University. Her research and teaching focus on constitutional law, social diversity and feminist legal theory. She is the author of two books: *Reclaiming the Nation: Muslim Women and the Law in India* (University of Toronto Press, 2008) and *Gender and Community: Muslim Women's Rights in India* (University of Toronto Press, 2001).

Mathias Rohe studied law and Islamic sciences at Tübingen and Damascus. Since 1997, he has been Chair for Civil Law, Private International Law and Comparative Law at the Friedrich–Alexander University Erlangen–Nürnberg and was Founding Director of the Erlangen Centre for Islam and Law in Europe. Rohe has numerous publications on the development of Islamic normativity, legal questions related to Muslims in Europe, and conflict resolution on a socio-religious basis; he has made numerous expert reports, participated as a guest professor, and given lectures on a national and international level.

Fatemeh Sadeghi is an Iranian political scientist and gender studies scholar. She is currently the O'Brien Visiting Fellow at the Faculty of Law at McGill University. She has published in both English and Persian. Her English publication is *The Sin of the Woman*: *The Interrelations of Religious Judgments in Zoroastrianism and Islam* (Claus Schwartz Verlag, 2018). Her Persian publications include *Gender in Ethical Doctrines From 3 to 9th Century Iran* (2013), *The Unveiling of the First Pahlavi: Rereading of a Modern Intervention* (2013), and *Gender, Nationalism, and Modernity in the First Pahlavi* (2006). Her translations from English into Persian include Leila Ahmad's *Women and Gender in Islam*: *The Historical Roots of a Modern Debate*, Agnes Heller's *A Theory of Modernity*, Asef Bayat's *Life and Politics*, Reza Aslan's *Zealot*, and Betty Friedan's *Feminine Mystique*.

Delfina Serrano-Ruano is PhD Tenured Researcher at the Spanish National Council for Scientific Research (CSIC). She specializes in the history of Islamic law and theology. In 1999, she published *La obra de procedimientos judiciales de Muḥammad b. ʻIyāḍ* (Madrid, CSIC). She is the editor of the volume *Crueldad y compasión en la literatura árabe e islámica* (Madrid, CSIC, 2011). Her publications also include the following: *Qadis and Muftis*: *Judicial Authority and the Social Practice of Islamic Law* (2019); *Redefining Paternal Filiation through DNA Testing: Law and the Children of Unmarried Mothers in the Maghreb* (2018); *Judicial Procedure and Legal Practice on Liʻān* (*imprecatory oath*) *in Andalus* (2017); *Forum Shopping in al-Andalus* (2016 & 2017); *Bringing Arbitration* (*tahkim*) *and Conciliation* (*sulh*) *Under the Gadi's Purview in*

Maliki al-Andalus (2016); *Later Ash'arism in the Islamic West* (2016); *Custom, Almohad Legal Ideology and the Development of Mālikī Maritime Law* (2015); *Later Ash`arism in the Islamic West* (2016); *Judicial Pluralism Under the "Berber empires"* (2014); *Malikis* (2014); *Ibn Rushd al-Jadd* (2013); and *Rape in Maliki Legal Doctrine and Practice* (2007).

Knut S. Vikør is Professor of History at the University of Bergen, Norway. He has worked on the topic of the pre-modern history of the Maghreb. His main areas of interest include Sufism in the nineteenth century, on which he wrote the book *Sufi and Scholar on the Desert Edge: Muhammad b. Ali al-Sanusi and His Brotherhood* (1995), and the history of Islamic law (*Between God and the Sultan: A History of Islamic Law,* 2005). He has also written on the history of the central Sahara and Sufism in Africa.

https://doi.org/10.1142/9781800611689_fmatter

Contents

https://doi.org/10.1142/9781800611689_fmatter

Introduction

Muhammad Khalid Masud[*,‡] and Hana Jalloul Muro[†,§]

[*]*Shariat Appellate Bench,*
Supreme Court of Pakistan, Islamabad, Pakistan
[†]*Madrid Parliament, Spain*
[‡]*khalid.masud@gmail.com*
[§]*jalloulhana@gmail.com*

This book, *Sharia Law in the Twenty-First Century*, offers a much-needed general introduction to the perspectives on studies of Sharia in the globalizing world. Globalism and Sharia have been challenging each other for more than two centuries. The book aims to highlight the significance that contemporary academia gives to the contextual diversity and multidisciplinary approaches in their analytical studies of Sharia laws. The co-editors began discussing the theme with the contributors to this volume in 2018. Hana Jalloul Muro organized an international seminar on "International law and Islamic law; Impact of two legal traditions in Spain" in cooperation with Casa Árabe, Complutense University of Madrid, and the European Mediterranean Institute on September 18, 2018 in Madrid. The participants in the seminar recalled how Spanish jurists from the Jewish, Christian, and Islamic legal traditions in Spain contributed to the mutual understanding of the legal challenges posed by the rising Mediterranean international trade and mercantile economy during the fourteenth to sixteenth centuries. These Spanish jurists laid the foundations of an international law beyond the laws of international relations. Among several scholars who participated in the above seminar, Ana Ballesteros Peiró,

Mohammed Dahiri, Muhammad Khalid Masud, Hana Jalloul Muro, and Delfina Serrano are contributors to this volume as well.

The contributors to this volume are well-known academics who have broken new paths for understanding the dynamics of Islamic law and society in their relevant fields; most of them have certainly influenced the current academic discourse on Sharia (see "About the Contributors," p. vii). The book aims to make their thoughtful contribution accessible to a wider public. The book follows the Chicago Manual of Style in references and for diacritic marks: (single opening quotation mark) for Arabic ʻayn and (single closing quotation mark) for hamza. There is no hamza at the beginning of words. The book offers an essential glossary at the end of the volume with diacritic marks and in the titles of the books where the authors regarded them necessary.

The fourteen chapters in this book analyze these challenges from multi-disciplinary perspectives. Accordingly, the chapters are arranged in three sections: Theoretical Perspectives, Historical Perspectives, and Contextual Perspectives.

Theoretical Perspectives

Studies of Islamic legal theory mostly deal with such topics as authority, sources of law, hermeneutic techniques, principles of interpretation, and maxims in Islamic literature (Weiss 2002). The four chapters in this section analyze Islamic legal theory from the following perspectives: political (Chapter 1), moral (Chapter 2), philosophical (Chapter 3), and theological (Chapter 4). These chapters explore issues relating human rights, law and morality, sovereignty, and theoretical challenges to Sharia and globalism.

As an academician and activist for more than three decades in the field, Professor Abdullahi Ahmed An-Naʻim examines the problems of understanding Sharia and international human rights in chapter one. He believes that genuinely mutual understanding is necessary for moving toward a globalized legal world, and that the human rights paradigm could have been a source for building such a mutually beneficial globalized world. In his critical study, "Contesting Sharia in Postcolonial and Geopolitical Contexts," he is doubtful that such an understanding is possible. He explains the two reasons for this failure: First, the human rights paradigm is seldom aimed at mutual trust and understanding and is rarely used for social justice and protecting individual freedom. Hegemonic geopolitics in postcolonial international relations invokes this paradigm to justify or rationalize their power, expecting others to conform to their epistemology and rationality in respective legal, philosophical, and cultural traditions—proving a real obstacle in building mutual trust. Second, the negative perception of the human rights paradigm led to a narrow vision of social transformation: interrupting states and societies and depriving existing local systems of moral and political authority undermined the universal legal force of international norms and institutions.

According to An-Na'im, Sharia is not a product of the sovereign state as in Western law. Historically, Islam, state, and society have been related to each other by constant contextual negotiations. Human agency has been central to the development of Sharia; human intent and intellect on an individual level are basic components of the concept of legal obligation in Islamic law.

In Chapter 2, Professor Mohammad Hashim Kamali, author of several highly valued academic studies on ethical issues, focuses on what he labels a more worrying question: Is there a crisis of values? Globalization, modernity, positivism, and science have challenged traditional values, and moral norms are now challenged in legal debates. Noting how moral precepts influence and interact with legal principles, Kamali explores whether this is a question about separation between law and morality, or if it is a question of understanding how Sharia regulates the relations between moral and legal components. He observes that the moral rectitude of conduct often provides the basis of legality in other legal traditions. Distinguishing between the concepts of "moral precept," "religious belief," and "legal norm," Kamali explains how the three are interconnected in the social and legal processes of normativity. The globalized world in which we live underrates global ethics; the environmental crisis has yet to find consensus-based solutions. Sharia, however, has continuously taken morality and law into consideration through the *usul al-fiqh*. The current interest in the *maqasid*, the higher purposes of Sharia, illustrates the process of elevating a "moral" into a legal principle.

In Chapter 3, Professor Rula Jurdi Abisaab, a poet, novelist, and historian with a special interest in the relationship between religious and political authority, focuses on the redefinition of Sufism as religious normativity to maintain the boundaries in the relationship between the religious and the political in Safavid Iran in the sixteenth century. Some Sufi orders, through their social influence within the public, had become a threat to Safavid political authority. Abi Saab explores the debate on religious knowledge and authority by Mulla Sadra, one of the most luminous Islamic thinkers in sixteenth- and seventeenth-century Iran. Challenges to political authority could be effective in a religious society because of the religious and moral authority claimed by some Sufis invoking spiritual authority. The Safavids resolved to define the boundaries between religiosity and heterodoxy on the one hand, and between religious and political authority on the other. This differentiation, which Abi Saab calls "sociolegal standardization," was considered conducive to greater administrative control and centralization during the process of empire-building under the Safavids. It did not mean elimination of Sufism but rather decreasing the public patronage and socioeconomic support for these Sufi orders. Consequently, specific Sufi groups were pushed outside public spaces of worship but allowed to continue their practices in private.

Mulla Sadra developed principles for distinguishing between legal and spiritual modes of religiosity, ethical values, and spiritual capabilities, and between hidden and apparent interpretations of Sharia texts. He considered it necessary to "cleanse" Sufism from such ideas and practices. Consequently, Abi Saab observes, by the late medieval period it was unlikely for a Sufi master to allow his disciples to enter the Sufi path before acquiring knowledge of the Quran and the *hadith* and expressing adherence to the Sharia. Sufi orders with no interest in socio-political mobilization and strong ties with textual tradition and Sufi scholarship fared better in Safavid Iran. Whereas the messianic-heterodox groups were suppressed, the Sufi brotherhoods were absorbed in the Twelver Shia devotional space. Sufi scholars increased emphasis on outward conformity to the Sharia, especially in a public space. Religious homogenization and sociolegal standardization played a decisive role in building the premodern state such as the Safavid Empire and privatizing Sufi religious practices.

In Chapter 4, Julio César Muñiz Pérez, a jurist and legal analyst specializing in conceptual history, stresses the need for comparative legal studies of Islamic and Christian theology. Specifically studying the concepts of justice, sovereignty, and laws of *kafala*, adoption, marriage, inheritance, and taxes in Islamic and Western traditions, he demonstrates how these are historically and conceptually rooted in dogma and theology. Pérez notes, however, that the interconnection between theology and law is often unknown to Western-style legal systems, mostly underestimated and even denied. Presently, jurists are primarily interested in the most recent jurisprudence and the latest legislative mandates. However, most authors interested in the "theology of law" are linked to the category of "believers," who discuss legal reality and consider it "standard rules of faith and life." This approach involves the risk of appearing biased or indoctrinated. According to Pérez, this phenomenon, motivated by the general secularization of Western society and modern judicial dynamics, has taken several forms. Islamic schools have particularly complicated this connection further and introduced cultural constraints for research in comparative law.

Pérez raises the following question: Is this evolution specific to Islam, analogous to Christianity, or an interpretation imported from Christian theological categories and as such foreign to authentic Islamic tradition? He answers that "it all develops from the assessment of historical objectivism so that the theological categories may be approached from a global perspective, without any theological purposes. In methodological terms, I seek to position myself in a more balanced position between the objective and the subjective element of all understanding."

Recognizing the theological connection with legal institutions is quite useful. First, it is a critical legal-social research method from the perspective of both the history and philosophy of law. Second, it helps to avoid conflicts in seeking to solve controversies more effectively. Third, it allows identifying differences that express possible dysfunction points, especially when Western society seeks to impose legal conceptions totally foreign to other societies. It also helps to examine the appropriateness of the extrapolation of Western society's legal model to the Islamic world to the detriment of Islam's traditions and legal institutions. Incorporating a Western model of governance based on the division of powers and founded upon a dogmatic basis may cause the dysfunction of Islamic legal traditions rooted in different theological principles.

Historical Perspectives

The second section on historical perspectives includes four chapters studying state practices and the institutionalization of Sharia and *ijtihad* (Chapter 5), nationalized legislation (Chapter 6), history of the legal interpretation of torture (Chapter 7), and the institution of modern *fatwa* (Chapter 8). Shaykh Muhammad al-Khudri (d.1927), probably the first Islamic modernist historian, divided the history of Islamic law into five Periods: that of the Prophet, his companions, *ijtihad*, the growth of schools of law, and ending in *taqlid* with the absence of *ijtihad* from the fifth Islamic century onward (Khudri 1967, 4). Analytically, al-Khudri explained that the Quranic injunctions were to be understood within a historical context. The verses revealed in Mecca differ from those revealed in Medina, the former dealing with moral and ethical aspects of Sharia and the latter consisting of detailed legal injunctions. The Quranic legislation is founded on three basic principles of removal of hardship, minimum legal obligations, and gradual legislation (Khudri 1967, 14–8).

While most modern historians of Islamic law, including Joseph Schacht, focus on *fiqh* in the classical period, N. J. Coulson argues that even though Muslim legal literature appears to show no interest in historical enquiry, Islamic legal history does exist (Coulson 1964, 62–73). The history of Islamic law is usually descriptive and based on periodization, generally focusing on schools of law. It is occasionally analytical, and rarely explores the conceptual and institutional evolution of Islamic law. Coulson historicizes Sharia as an Islamic law system evolving in three stages: growth (seventh to ninth centuries), classical Islamic legal tradition (tenth to nineteenth centuries), and legal modernism (twentieth century). In the classical tradition, the dominant concept was that law was eternally valid and binding for both state and society. The problem for Western legal history, however, is that as a divine command, reform in Islamic law could not be justified on the basis of social necessity. Islamic legal modernism, therefore, argued that divine commands were general principles, not expressed in rigid or comprehensive terms (*Ibid.*).

Unlike other scholars who limit the history of Islamic law to early jurists, Knut S. Vikør, with several ground-breaking studies on the history of Islamic law, includes *siyasa* and *qanun*, in addition to *fiqh* in the history of Islamic law. Recognition of the role of caliphs and sultans in the making of Islamic law allows him to view Sharia as a legal tradition. In Chapter 5, Vikør traces the history of the concept of the legal authority of Sharia from early Islam to the modern period of states and globalism. Legal scholars in early Islam resisted the authority of caliphs to influence the formation of Islamic law because they insisted that law was to be based on God's revelation: The Quran and the Prophet were the divine sources of authority. The issue of legal authority arose mainly due to different, and sometimes conflicting, interpretations of the Quran and *hadith* texts. *Ijtihad* for interpretation and *ijma*ʿ for validity existed, but they were not institutionalized. Legislative authority was, therefore, necessary for the formulation and application of law. This need was fulfilled by the evolution of schools, *madhhab*, which vested law-making authority in the founders of the schools, and *fiqh* literature, authorized by the consensus for validity of interpretation. The nature of legal authority in this system was autonomous, and the gates of *ijtihad* were open.

The conservative nature of law as a system, however, required institutional authority. This need led to the consolidation of schools by limiting *ijtihad* within the boundaries of school doctrines. Each school defined its own principles of interpretation, hierarchical codification of law texts, and strict adherence to schools by judges and courts. There were occasional calls for opening the gates of *ijtihad*, but which ended instead in the reorganization of states patronizing one of the schools for courts and codification. This development also led to the agreed-upon dual system of Sharia and *qanun*. The legal authority of the state brought legal pluralism in courts to an end. Islamic legal rule of exemption of non-Muslims from Sharia was reformulated in this period as capitulations or pacts between the Muslim and foreign states to exempt foreign traders from local taxes and laws. It not only confirmed Sharia law as personal and religious but also extended the authority of one state over persons in another state on a religious basis.

Vikør finds continuity in this quest for legal authority in the later periods under caliphs and sultans, Ottoman and colonial empires, and modern nation-states to the present globalized world. He points to various methods and interpretive tools like *talfiq* and institutions like capitulation pacts to solve the problems of authority after the decrease of *madhhab*'s legal authority in nation-states during the modern period.

In Chapter 6, Delfina Serrano Ruano, a specialist in the history of Islamic law, overviews the transformations experienced by Islamic law in the contemporary period. Her chapter uses a selection of outstanding studies to emphasize a number of continuities that challenge the view of Islamic law in the contemporary period as the result of a drastic break with the past. Serrano Ruano provides some updates that confirm or nuance such a view and tries to move away from the religious/secular divide. She finds the history of Islamic law and the shift of Sharia from classical non-state to a modern national law system to be a more complex historical phenomenon than the simplified and stereotypical image projected by Orientalist and Islamist scholarship.

Replacement of the classical Sharia structures and practices with new legal institutions and rules, the dissolution of the classical legal schools, and diversity in the revival of certain elements of traditional Islamic law reflect the changes that have taken place while Sharia remains an authoritative legal, ethical, and theological worldview strongly determined by the state and sociocultural norms. This relationship between Sharia, state, and society is the product of a constant negotiation that varies according to context, rather than the subject of a fixed formula of either total separation or complete fusion. The dissociation between law and religion in the legal systems of Muslim-majority countries has emphasized the association between Sharia and identity, be it individual, collective, or national.

Legislators tend to base laws on norms that enjoy widespread social acceptance. The adoption of a modern, unified national legal system with a division of power and the reform of personal-status legal matters were considered essential prerequisites for social transformation. Legal re-Islamization, since the 1970s, affected constitutional and family law, but it varied in the *hudud* punishments according to the specific contexts in which it took place. Serrano Ruano points to the emergence of "Islamic feminism" as an unexpected side effect of the re-Islamization wave. Muslim feminists fight for equal rights and the improvement of women's legal status within the framework of gender activism that intertwines Sharia with "human rights" claims.

In Chapter 7, Kathleen A. Cavanaugh, a critical sociolegal scholar of international law, examines how the politics of law has played out within the fields of international and Islamic law, specifically with reference to the prohibition on torture. The notion of international law as pre-political, fixed, and stable has been challenged in the legal narrative of the "war on terror." The "war on terror" discourse has shifted the boundaries of the legally permissible use of torture, invoking exception for the state. The question was whether torturing terrorists by the state to seek further information is subject to state law or entirely outside of it. The definition of torture, in Article 1 of CAT, suggests several constitutive elements of torture. Consequently, despite international and regional prohibitions, the very meaning of torture and of other forms of ill-treatment and the rationale for their absolute prohibition remain contested and uncertain.

Cavanaugh finds that politics is also visible in the contestation between the "textualist" and "contextualist" readings in Islamic law; Islamic legal scholars with the textualist approach believe that the law is fixed and immutable, while the latter approach reads the text within a specific historical context. Islamic discourses on various international legal norms and prescriptions, therefore, interpret and apply norms and principles of Islamic law with differentiated readings. Varying readings and interpretations of Islamic law challenge the notion that its content, scope, and application are fixed and stable. Legal practices specific to an individual country draw on a variety of sources that can shift over time in ways that are not identical to Western experiences and may not be consistent across Muslim cases (Mayer 2007, xiii). The three main Islamic declarations of human rights approach rights-based discourse in a variety of ways. With reference to the law on torture, she notes that "the gap in textual (and guidance) authority is most acute when we turn to Islamic criminal law and procedure."

Hana Jalloul Muro is a specialist in international relations and has particularly studied the Islamic legal institutions of interpretation, application, and adjudication. In Chapter 8, she studies the history of the institutionalization of legal authority in Islam in the absence of systems such as the modern state. In Islamic history, political and legal authorities were separated. It was a strong sense of religious community that held the people together. Legitimacy of political authority was entrusted by the people to the ruler with *bay'a* pacts of allegiance in exchange for responsibilities. This concept of pact—that continued despite structural changes in the formation of political systems—ensured the separation between legal and political authority.

Legal authority was secured by independence of legal education, autonomy of the jurists, and their authority of legal interpretation (*ijtihad*). Legal authority was exercised by the institution of *fatwa* which was collected in a somewhat codified form for the judges (*qadi*). *Muftis* also served as consultants to the courts. This system was reorganized under the Ottomans, who organized hierarchy in the *fatwa* by patronizing one school of law and by codifying Islamic laws. Christians living in the Ottoman Empire were governed by their own religious law under the authority of their religious courts. With Capitulation laws, the Ottomans allowed this authority to their co-religious European kings, thus accepting the international notion of personal religious laws in some areas. After the end of the Ottoman Empire in the twentieth century, most Muslim countries retained Islamic law personal status codes for Muslim communities. In countries like Lebanon, Egypt, Sudan, and Morocco, religious minorities may choose whichever faith codes they wish to apply to personal status codes.

Dr. Jalloul notes that the introduction of the modern state brought a new notion of national identity based on nation-states. It broadened and influenced not only political and social but also legal fields in local contexts. The religious confrontation between Shia and Sunni Islam led to ethnic tensions going back to pre-Islamic history. Thus, for example, many Shia in Iran include strong Persian elements within their religious identity, and many Maronite Christians in Lebanon identify themselves as Phoenician instead of Arabs.

Contextual Perspectives

This section reflects contextual diversity in geography, demography, legal frameworks, and religious affiliations, and, therefore, diverse problematization of legal issues. Six chapters in this section offer focused contextual studies of Sharia in the following selected countries: Morocco (Chapter 9), Germany, UK, France (Chapter 10), Iran (Chapter 11), India (Chapter 12), Pakistan (Chapter 13), and South Africa (Chapter 14). Contextually, the selected countries differ from each other in terms of modern legal frameworks: UK, India, and Pakistan follow the Common Law system and Morocco, Germany, and France follow the Civil Law system, whereas South Africa follows a hybrid Common and Civil law system. These countries also vary in Muslim population size: Morocco, Iran, and Pakistan are Muslim-majority countries, and Germany, France, UK, India, and South Africa have Muslim minorities. The populations in these countries also follow different schools of Islamic law: The Maliki school is dominant in Morocco, the Ja'fari Shia in Iran, the Hanafi in India and Pakistan, and the Shafi'i school is prominent in South Africa. The studies of Islamic law in this section are diversely focused; Chapters 9, 10, 12, and 14 study issues relating to personal laws, and Chapters 11 and 13 focus on constitutional issues.

In Chapter 9, Professor Mohammed Dahiri, with expertise in Arab and Islamic Studies, Comparative Literature and Translation, and focused studies in the fields of International Migration, Interculturality, Muslim Minorities, Interreligious Dialogue, and Conflict Resolution and Human Rights, offers an analytical overview of reforms in *Mudawwana*, the Moroccan Personal Status Code of 1957–1958 and why it took 47 years to review the Code. He studies how this Code inspired by the Maliki school of law came to be modified in 2004 and why public debates between the religious establishment and civil society groups continue.

According to Dahiri, the main problem of reform of gender inequality remains unsolved; changes are needed to create an independent judiciary, with judges and court clerks trained in the values of human rights and respect for gender equality. In his opinion, the Moroccan judicial system suffers from a structural problem; it is impregnated with a culture and mentality contrary to the innovative spirit of the *Mudawwana* and any possible future reforms.

In Chapter 10, Professor Mathias Rohe, a well-known German scholar of law and Islam in Europe and expert in civil law, international private law, and comparative law, discusses the place of religious law in Western societies. He explains that Christianity served as the state religion for centuries in most parts of Europe. Religious minorities were sometimes tolerated, sometimes persecuted, or even expelled. The state–church system broadly lost its political, social, and finally legal grounding in the nineteenth and twentieth centuries. The situation altered significantly after waves of mass immigration to Western Europe, particularly since the 1960s, for various reasons. Presently, Muslims are the largest group of "minority religions" in Europe, but Islam is much more widely distrusted in European public opinion than any other religion. The treatment of Muslims is considered a litmus test for the application of freedom of religion and equal treatment in legal practice, and thus for the credibility of the rule of law system.

In modern Europe, relations between state and religion are organized in three different systems: (1) strictly laic systems, (2) secular systems with a positive attitude toward religion, and (3) weak versions of state–church relations. In Europe, religious issues are regulated by the European and national constitutional provisions, including Article 9 of the ECHR, granting freedom of religion and state neutrality toward religions. State legal systems also differentiate between religious and legal issues. Freedom of religion includes private worship as well as adequate protection of religious needs like building mosques, forming religious organizations, and social security. Due to differing interpretations about the distance between the state and religion, Western European countries vary in their application of these provisions. The debates and demands regarding visible Muslim religiosity also influence the confrontation with Muslim needs and creeds. Often, democracy and the rule of law are simplistically equated, but the two might conflict with each other.

Contrary to religious rules, the application of foreign legal rules does not fall under the freedom of religion. That would amount to total equality of different legal norms within one state. "Legal pluralism," in this sense, would fundamentally contradict the existing constitutional orders in Europe. A few Western European states have introduced Islamic legal provisions concerning family matters that can be applied in Muslim communities on a voluntary basis. Mechanisms of conflict resolution outside state courts (ADR) are operating in the field of economic disputes. ADR systems fail because representatives of religious organizations often lack information about the scope and limits of European law regarding ADR as well as sound knowledge of Islamic law.

In Chapter 11, Professor Fatemeh Sadeghi, an expert in the fields of gender studies and political thought, particularly Islamic political thought and Iranian politics, explores the limits of constitutionalism on a universal scale, focusing on Iran as a symptomatic case. Sadeghi argues that rather than considering the guardianship of the jurist a particularity of Shiʻism, it needs to be studied in the general historical context of the notion of absolute authority (sovereignty) that goes back to the premodern contexts of Roman legacy and Ashʻarite Islamic theology and exists in modern political thought—from Jean Bodin to Carl Schmitt and the modern differentiation between sacred and profane. That is probably how in the Iranian Constitution, God as sovereign quickly transforms into Sovereign as god and is exemplified so in the doctrine of the guardianship of the jurist as well as in the absolute secular authority of the nation-state.

Sadeghi explores the concept of "sovereignty" in two contexts: general as well as specific to the Iranian Revolution of 1979. In the general context, sovereignty is the supreme authority with the ability to issue absolute and final decisions to be observed as law. The essence of sovereign power is "the [absolute] right to kill" (Foucault 2003, 240). The power of sovereignty comes from a potent mix of political and theological legacies (Martel 2012, 7). Building a constitution on the sacred and profane arches reveals the significant limits of the sacred/secular dichotomy for grasping how deeply violence is embedded in both orthodox Sharia and secular constitutional law. The sacred and the secular are not mutually exclusive, as is commonly believed. The ethical task is not to choose between secularism/atheism and religion; they are complementary. The chapter argues that a critical engagement with theology is required to question the simile of God as a sovereign ruler because it tends to justify political idolatry.

With reference to the specific context, Sadeghi observes that post-revolutionary developments led to the failure of the Iranian revolution. They were concerned more with the consolidation of power rather than with securing the rights of citizens. Ten years after the ratification of the 1979 Constitution, "an (un)constitutional assembly—whose members were no longer elected—modified the Constitution in 1989. As a result of this manipulation, people have lost many rights, while the absolute sovereignty of the *vali-e faqih* (the guardian jurist) became lawful," which possesses all authorities and forces equivalent to Schmitt's sovereign, who decides on the exception. The omission of "people" and their acceptance was a decisive change in the Constitution. Sovereignty was an amalgam of three intertwined types of divine, popular, and national absolute authorities. This theocratic notion of sovereignty that depicts God as a masculine patriarchal sovereign is disagreeable to the Islamic theology in which "God is neither masculine nor sovereign; it is rather a vision that promises the capacity of human beings to constitute a more equal and freer community."

In Chapter 12, Professor Vrinda Narain, an expert in constitutional law and feminist legal theory, examines the Supreme Court of India's decision on *Shayara Bano and others v Union of India and others* (2017) AIR SC 4609, which declared instantaneous triple *talaq* unconstitutional. The triple *talaq*, *talaq-e-biddat*, is the unregulated, unilateral right to divorce held by Muslim men. A husband pronounces *talaq* (divorce) thrice, and at the third pronouncement, the divorce becomes final and irrevocable.

The legal validity of triple *talaq* in India is a controversial issue, implicating minority rights, religious freedom, and gender equality. The contradictions inherent in the simultaneous existence of discriminatory Muslim personal law and constitutional equality pose serious challenges for Muslim women's equality in India. This contradiction between public equality and private discrimination, and the privileging of religious freedom and minority rights over gender equality, has meant that Muslim women's equality has been largely marginalized in Indian constitutional interpretation and jurisprudence. In this chapter, Narain examines the interface between religious personal law and constitutional law.

The chapter begins by contextualizing the situation of Muslim women and describes the multiple axes of discrimination they face. It also sets out the legal framework governing Muslim women's rights in the family and the constitutional provisions regulating minority rights. It details the facts of the Shayara Bano case, identifying the issues considered by the Supreme Court. It then assesses the Supreme Court's analysis of key issues, including the constitutional status of personal law, women's equality rights under Muslim personal law, the validity of the triple *talaq*, and the issue of whether the religious freedom guarantee disallows reform of personal law. It concludes by discussing the consequences and future implications of the Shayara Bano case for Muslim women's rights.

In Chapter 13, Ana Ballesteros Peiró, an expert on Islamic sectarianism and sociology of religion and politics in South Asia, analyzes the debates in Pakistan about Sharia, constitution, and identity of state. Explaining the context of this debate, she refers to the late colonial period when the British began the devolution of power to Indian nationals. Muslim elites were worried about their future political identity in India ruled by an overwhelmingly Hindu majority. The Independence Act 1947 provided a guideline for the Constitution of Pakistan that considered The Government of India Act (1935) the provisional constitution for independent Pakistan and India with dominion status.

Peiró finds that the question of national identity for state has been crucial to framing the constitution in Pakistan. The question about the definition of a Muslim further divided Pakistan. She explores sectarianism as the specific context in which the problems of identity, constitution, and legislation have been debated in the country. Identity is considered constantly threatened, not only because Sharia has been diversely interpreted by different sects but also because there is a constant debate on the definitions of Islamic state and nation. There has been confusion about other identity affiliations (linguistic, ethnic, provincial, religious) claimed by marginalized groups as being against the nationalist narrative.

In Chapter 14, Muhammad Khalid Masud, with research interest in Sharia debates, explores the debate on the specific issue of the recognition of Muslim marriages in South Africa. Public discourses on Islamic legal issues in the twenty-first century are usually labeled "Sharia debate" in academic studies on several Muslim countries and societies all over the world. Sharia became the most prominent subject for intense and even violent debates toward the end of the twentieth century. Debate as a formal discourse on a particular matter is one of the characteristic processes in the discursive traditions of Sharia. The rise of modern states was coeval with colonialism in most countries. While it introduced the modern concepts of a state's absolute authority and national law, it also shifted the focus of Sharia debates from the legal to political perspectives. Instead of adherence to specific schools, debates moved to Islamization of national laws in the twentieth century, and from pan-Islamism to Islamic globalization in the twenty-first century. Some academic studies notice this shift as a move from the interpretive to a discursive approach. Western Orientalist scholarship was fascinated by the textual growth of Islamic law, and considered these debates as a significant departure. Some scholars regarded them as gaps between the classical Islamic theory and practices; others viewed them as contestations between the modernist and Islamists.

Masud focuses on South Africa because while interpreting the universal values of freedom, equality, and justice, the differences in the four legal traditions of indigenous customary, Common, Civil, and Sharia laws in the country have generated debates on some basic issues. Sharia debates on the issue of the "recognition of Muslim marriages" are deeply contextualized in these differences. While the public debate is widely diverse and the Constitutional court is dynamically open, judicial reasoning seems highly inflexible and politically rigid. This chapter explores how we can learn from these debates about law reforms in general and Sharia in particular.

Muslim marriages are not legally recognized even today, and this most complicated debate is facing an impasse in South Africa. Sharia debates on this issue provide an opportunity to look critically not only at Sharia as a legal system in a modern secular state context but also to examine how Sharia and the Common and Civil law systems interact with each other while facing religious diversity and multiculturalism in the modern nation-state context. This chapter explores the issue in three local contexts: colonial-historical, Muslim minorities with cultural diversity, and legal politics.

The South Africa Act (1909) brought different British colonies and republics, racially and legally divided, into a united self-governing dominion within the British Commonwealth. Power was transferred to the white minority, excluding others from political participation. The South Africa Act (1910) declared independence under the name of Union of South Africa. The British and the other European settlers both had developed legal systems based on the philosophy of legal positivism. The British followed the Common law tradition, while others practiced Civil law. Three reasons may be discerned from the debates on this issue: (1) Common law restraints about custom, (2) negative perception of diversity as a threat to the modern state and the ensuing politics of law, and (3) positivist debates on the restrictive normativity of the religious as customary law.

Muslims have been diverse small groups, divided into various ethnic communities based on the countries of origin from where they were brought as prisoners and laborers by colonial rulers. They were also diverse in their affiliations to Islamic law. Even as a small minority, Muslims were conspicuous in business and other professions. They have featured prominently in the country's representative institutions since 1994. Since 1965, Muslim marriages enjoyed some statutory recognition, though subject to South African Civil Marriage laws. The courts have been reluctant to consider this indirect and limited recognition as a valid and full formal recognition of Muslim marriages. The issue remained under discussion with the South African Law Reform Commission.

The politics of recognition was shaped by the ideas of power and supremacy that believed in sovereignty rather than equality based on diversity. Most Muslims had the Islamic ceremony of *nikah* and registered it as civil marriage afterward. Some *ulama* declared civil marriages un-Islamic and advised Muslims to have only *nikah* marriage and not to combine it with the civil procedure. Sharia debates on Muslim marriages in South Africa emerged in 1993 and focused on two points: the status of Muslim women and normativity of Sharia in South African Law. Customary marriages came to be recognized in 1998, but religious, particularly, Islamic marriage is not yet recognized. To understand this legal issue, one must explore the historical background of the impact of the ideas of racial segregation as a determining factor of legal capacity and development of Constitutional law defining citizenship. Fundamental rights and legal systems informed the framework for legislation and codification of personal laws in modern states.

Most chapters in this volume point to theological and legal essentialism, the debating process, and politics of law as apparent causes for the impasse in these debates. These chapters stress the role of the judiciary and judicial authority in South Africa, Britain, Canada, and Pakistan more than the reforms through Parliamentary legislation and *ijtihad*. Sharia debates are often associated with legal pluralism that challenges the process of unification of laws in a modern state. Legal pluralism in premodern societies was commonly practiced on account of local ethnic, political, and religious diversity and plurality.

Globalism

The general theme of the studies in this book is the challenges that globalism and Sharia pose to one another. A brief introductory note on the theories of globalism and globalization of Sharia would, therefore, be helpful in understanding this theme. Historically, the first use of the term "globalism" was observed in 1943 (Merriam-Webster, "globalism") in the context of war-stricken Europe looking toward an imagined peaceful new world order without war and conflict. Most studies on the theory and history of globalism call these trends the three "waves of globalization" to underline diversity (Keohane and Nye 1972; Huntington 1993; Robertson 2003; James 2006; Steger 2010). Joseph Nye, however, understood globalism as transnational interactive connections, but later noted a huge shift of emphasis from globalism to a globalized world (Nye 2002). Steger

(2005) described these waves as the rise of different ideologies of globalization. Some studies (Nordregio.org, 2008) periodized the three waves as follows: the first wave (1860–1914), the second wave (1944–1971), and the third wave (1989–).

During the first wave, the ideas and theories of the global world reflected the dreams and anxieties of "the West." The ideal—"Western global"—in these theories was generally a Euro-centered, powerful society, shaped by the Kantian philosophy of the "universal citizen" (MacLean 2013,1). The United States emerged as a global power in the imagery of some American globalists like Joseph Nye—naturally because the US emulated Europe's imperialistic might before the 1940s. However, this vision of globalism was lopsided because the ideas of universal citizenship, civil society, and multiculturalism could not survive long with the ideals of the unique Western modernity and hegemonic globalization sculpted as colonial empires.

The second wave promised globalization based on a global economy. Referring to the role of capital mobility, multinational corporations, and economic interdependence between nations, theorists of this wave were associated with progress through constitutionalism, nation-state, modernization, and the establishment of international and transnational institutions and corporations. According to Luke Martell (2007, 9, 173), the three waves identified in most of these studies may be named respectively as globalist, skeptical, and post-skeptical. Skeptics argue that economic globalism in the second wave marginalized national economies and justified reducing the legal restrictions by some nation-states on global trade. It created uneven economies and unstable political structures.

Martell argues that the third wave that came toward the end of the twentieth century constructed a more complex and qualified theory of globalization (Martell 2007, 9, 173). The establishment of institutions like World Bank International Centre for Settlement of Investment Disputes (1966), United Nations Commission on International Trade Law (1966), United Nations Claims Commission (1991), and International Criminal Court (1998) illustrates how globalism transformed from an idea to reality. Now, it relies on law and inevitable judicialization for its sustenance.

Celebrating globalism, Fukuyama called it the "end of history." He was referring to global democracy as he wrote, "What we may be witnessing is just not the end of Cold War, or passing of the particular post-war history, but the end of history as such that is the end point of mankind's ideological evolution and universalization of the Western liberal democracy as the final form of the human government" (Fukuyama 1989, cited in Mazroui 1993, 512). He was, nevertheless, widely criticized, particularly on his "hegemonic" rather than universalist approach to the history of globalism. He defended himself in 1992 clarifying that his concept of history was misunderstood. He explained that history to him is the "single, coherent, and evolutionary process, considering the experiences of all people of all times." By "end," he meant the universal acceptance of the "Western liberal democracy" as the "final form of human government"; "final" and "universal" referred to the ideological universalization by all people (Fukuyama 1992). That is probably why he put a question mark at the end of the title of his article.

Referring to the Muslim world, Fukuyama explained that due to tribal and cultural political structures, Arabs and radicalized Muslims resisted global democracy. He explained that global democracy was free from such "fundamental internal contradictions." On the question of the concept of equality, he differentiated between absolute equality and broad equality to explain the problem of existing "incomplete implementation of liberty and equality." Fukuyama argued that equality and rule of law are religious and absolute values which are not pragmatically possible at the international level. Apparently, he was explaining "hegemony" with reference to absolute equality as universal normativity. He clarified that these were the radical Muslims who demand absolute equality, not the traditionalists. Global democracy is certainly an issue at the international level; Muslim minorities in Europe are invoking for themselves international human rights laws. American courts have been successful in dismissing the Muslim claims for exception by interpreting these claims in the framework of legitimacy claims as a state of exception (Fukuyama 1992).

While national laws in some Western countries posed their authority as coercive and hegemonic and claimed state exception at the international level, international human rights law evolved to be ethical and more comprehensive than national laws; it responded to concerns like the environment, international trade, human rights, refugees, disarmament, and cyberspace. Legislation on such matters was made at the international level because their enforcement was beyond the power of nation-states. Global law, nevertheless, had to depend on nation-states to rule the new "empire" of international law. Nation-states found issue with the perspective of universal normativity. Globalists defined the concept of law in international relations on the basis of right not might. Legal positivists suspected that this approach would revive moral, philosophical, and ethical values. As the concept of sovereignty was the central legal principle in constitutional law, nation-states feared that globalization would deprive them of their constitutional sovereignty in international relations. Some Western thinkers like Agamben (2005) even claimed exception for the state from basic laws in case of emergency and wars as states of exception (Humphreys 2006 and Cavanaugh 2012 and this volume).

Some studies on the ideology of globalism noted that the relationship between the legal and the political came too close to separate politics from law (Bartninkas 2014). Some political theorists note "hegemonic contestations" in the present discussions on international law (Koskenniemi 2004, 2006). Others find that law cannot be read as "divine," "unmediated," or "pre-political" when the space between law and politics is blurred (Cavanaugh 2012, 17, Koskenniemi 2004). Powerful states succeed in globalizing their own economies and cultures, and then transform their national laws to function as international law. Over time, international law has been reduced to a technique of hegemonic contestation and political supremacy of the powerful against weaker nations (*Ibid.*).

It was certainly not the "end of history" for the non-western countries who continued to suffer from internal and international wars, weak governance, illusive democracy, and growing poverty. The ideas of globalism and experiences of globalization were not the same between the various parts of the globe. In the non-Western countries, the first wave of globalism and globalization came with colonization in Asia and Africa. While colonialism brought new technology, and modern ideas of political organization and self-rule, because the colonial administrators also used law to establish hegemony on pain of subjugation and cultural humility, mistrust continued between the colonized and the colonial rulers. Muslim views were divided on modernity and globalism.

Islamic modernists, like Muhammad Iqbal (d.1938) and Ali Mazroui (d.2014), interpreted Islamic history as an "end of history" because Muhammad is the last prophet and with him the religion reached perfection (Iqbal 1982, 126 and Mazroui 1993, 513). The diverse Muslim responses to modernity and globalism were shaped by claiming finality of Sharia. Muslims understood modernity and globalism in terms of ethical and universalist perspectives. They disputed the hegemonic claims of Western modernity and globalism. Fukuyama calls this particular response "radicalism," also known as "Islamism" and "political Islam." Radicalism was, in fact, a continuation of the idea of the revival of pan-Islamic caliphate in the early twentieth century (Özcan 1997, Qureshi 1999), and extended to the ideology of the Islamic State and Islamization in the middle of the twentieth century (Adams 1983), emergence of Sharia and judicial councils for Muslim-minority communities in the Western countries (Al-Alwani 1994, 2004), and the proposal for globalizing the methodology of *fiqh al-aqalliyat* for application of Sharia to Muslims minorities today (Al-Alwani 1994, Ben Bayyah 2007). Islamic modernists disagreed with these responses and called for the reconstruction of religious thought (Iqbal 1930) and the transformation of Islamic law (Rahman 1982).

Globalization of Sharia

The term Sharia in this book is used inclusively for various expressions like Islamic law, *fiqh*, and *fatawa* and encompasses all the Sharia-related concepts, ideas, and institutions prevalent today. Established scholars of Islamic law assumed that Sharia, as a religious legal system, would not survive the challenges of globalization. Joseph Schacht was surprised when Islamic law was quietly superseded by codes of British inspiration in the nineteenth century and "no significant voice of dissent was raised" (Schacht 1966, 95). He concluded that "It showed that the idea of secular law had for the first time been accepted by the leaders of an important community of Muslims" (*Ibid.*). Wael Hallaq argues that the normative paradigm for Islamic law and state is moral, whereas for a modern state, it is the authority of state that coerces a person to obey the law. An "Islamic state" is, therefore, impossible to establish because "Islamic State" as a concept is a contradiction in terms of any standard definition of a modern state (Hallaq 2012, Introduction and 100). According to N. J. Coulson, Islamic law is a divinely ordained system preceding and not preceded by the Muslim state, controlling and not controlled by Muslim society (Coulson 1964, 2).

Coulson, however, disagreed with the assumption of rigidity. He observed that Western laws may have been imposed from above, but they are in "broad harmony with the temper of Muslim populations today" (Coulson 1964, 160). That is because Islamic political theory has always recognized the right of the ruler to supplement Sharia in the fields of public law and general civil law (*Ibid.*, 161). In his opinion, keeping family law as a stronghold of Sharia, separate from other spheres, created a sharp dichotomy between the Islamic and Western laws and led to growing emphasis upon the religious and Islamic significance of Sharia (*Ibid.*). Western powers ensured that their residents are governed by their own laws (*Ibid.*, 150). Vikør (this volume) also finds these observations about colonial concerns particularly important as they help in exploring why the British and French colonial policies laid stress on the religious and customary nature of Islamic law.

There were three concerns that colonials had about Sharia in the early period. First, that the legitimacy of their rule depended on continuing application of Sharia. Second, that the natives and colonial administrators must be governed by their own laws. Third, that the natives were not accustomed to modern laws. The Charter of George II (1753) allowed the application of English laws in their colonies only as an "exception" [to Mughal Farman]. The two reports of the Charter use two words, "reservation" (Grady 1869, xxxiii) and "exemption" (Fyzee 1963, 412). The notion of exception or exemption was understood as non-application of European laws to the natives in some specific matters. The Mughal Farman of 1765 bound the Company to abide "agreeably to the rules of Mahomet and the laws of the empire" (Wilson 1930, 25). Accordingly, Muslim judges (Qadis), first in Bengal and later in other parts of India, continued to administer Sharia laws until 1862.

The "exemption" later came to imply application of the Islamic laws limited to civil matters, including inheritance, which continued as personal laws because they were religious and customary and were applicable only to Muslims. Warren Hastings, Governor-General of Bengal (1772–1785), found problems working with Muslim judges who refused to pass death sentences on dacoits unless they had murdered someone during the robbery (Fisch 1983, 35). The Qadis argued, "The Muhummadan law is founded on the most lenient principles, and on abhorrence of bloodshed" (*Ibid.*). Hastings ruled that even though his proposed punishments were not in accordance with the spirit of the British constitution, the people in Bengal needed harsher penalties because they were not as perfect as the British people were (*Ibid.*). He wanted to abolish Islamic legal distinctions between the cases of murder based on the instrument of murder, the right of pardon, and *qisas*, the right of the heirs to execute the criminal (*Ibid.*, 34–5). Hastings assumed the title of Nawab (deputy) Governor-General Hastings to legitimize his authority as a deputy of the Mughal Emperor (Rankin 1946, 169). He justified his authority to amend the laws by invoking the Hanafi doctrine of Siyasa that authorized the ruler to make the exception to amend Sharia criminal laws in case of emergency. Hastings defined the objective of the 1772 Charter as "adhering as closely as we are able to their ancient uses and institutions." Metcalfs further described the following two points as principles of Hastings' jurisprudence: (1) "fixed body of laws" to be established by "lawgivers" and (2) distinct separate codes on religious grounds, laws of the Quran with respect to "Mahomedans," and the laws of the Shastras for "Gentoos" (Metcalf 2002, 56–57).

According to Joseph Schacht, the French colonial administrators faced similar problems. Qadis continued to develop Maliki Law in their competence as judges (Schacht 1966, 97). The development of Islamic law under French legal influence in Algeria was in some respects parallel to its development in India, "but widely different in its results" (*Ibid.*). Oussama Arabi's critical essay on Marcel Morand's (d.1932) Code provides relevant insights. First, Code Morand, prepared on the request of French government in 1905, completed in 1914, and published in 1916, was never promulgated as law (Arabi 2000, 43). Second, the code was more modern than the traditional Islamic texts which were restricted to one *madhhab*; the code was a synthesis of all of them. Third, the French policy had introduced a distinction between indigenous and naturalized peoples; the former were subjects, ruled largely by their own laws and customs, the latter were citizens governed by French laws. The code preserved Islamic identity. Morand explained that keeping Islamic law was a natural choice for Algerians. The reason was that when they were accorded French nationality in 1865 and French citizenship required opting into French laws, Algerian Muslims opted to be governed by Islamic law. In Morand's words, "Code gives more political and judicial power to Muslim legal culture," "Which is further step in distancing of Algerians from French Culture." Arabi concludes, "That is to say, the *Code Morand* could rightfully be considered one of the earliest heralds of twentieth century legal reform in the Arab lands" (Arabi 2000, 50).

Comparing Code Morand with Anglo-Muhammadan law, one finds that the Morand was more open to Muslim *ijtihad* tradition, not only in terms of adopting more suitable rules and principles from other Islamic law schools but also providing opportunities to courts to exercise contextual *judicial ijtihad*. In this way, the courts also had the opportunity to consult Muslim modernist jurists rather than being restricted by the classical legal texts which were treated as precedents in developing Anglo-Muhammadan law. Islamists, who opposed the Muslim modernist *ijtihad*, also came to an impasse when they restricted themselves to classical text without historicizing them. Contesting political theories debating separation or interdependence between religion and politics since the classical period show that Sharia has also been the arena for claiming final political authority and supremacy of law.

Like other laws, Islamic law and jurisprudence also have deep roots in theology. Concepts of sovereignty, command, sanctions, authority, and validity of the rules were informed by debates during the ninth and tenth centuries on God's sovereignty in classical Islamic theology. Later, twentieth-century authors like Uztaz Mahmoud Mohammed Taha (d.1985), the proponents of the "second message of Islam," argued that verses revealed in Mecca affirm religious freedom, spirituality, or gender equality, among other things, and prevail over those revealed in Medina, which he considered "subsidiary verses." While the Mu'tazili school proposed that good and bad actions are knowable by the human intellect, the Ash'ari school of theology rebutted arguing that good and bad are known by revelation from God. Al-Ghazali (d.1111), an Ash'ari theologian, held that human acts on their own have no legal value prior to Sharia, the revealed law; human intellect cannot decide what is good and bad (Ghazali 1904, 1:55). The point of discussion was theological, but the conclusion was taken from legal reasoning: legal obligation does not exist before the legislative declaration. This is like a legal positivist argument that theology, ethics, and morality do not create a legal obligation. Ibn Khaldun (d.1406) observed two major approaches in Islamic jurisprudence: theological and the Hanafi (Ibn Khaldun 1989, 455). The Shafi'i jurists followed the Ash'ri theology more than other schools. Consequently, Sharia and *siyasa,* the two basic legal concepts were defined, respectively, as theological and political and separated or combined from these two perspectives. The theological approach was strict and politically pragmatic (Masud 2001, 2018).

To illustrate the theological–political nexus, one needs to look at the development doctrine of *dar al-Islam*, House of Islam, in the medieval and modern period. It became the key doctrine in Sharia debates on the obligation of *jihad*, international relations, migration, and application of Sharia in Islamic political theory (Masud 1990). It addressed significant issues of Islamic globalism like the revival of the caliphate, *jihad*, Islamic State, and the status of Muslim minorities. Historically, these issues were formulated in classical Islamic legal theory with reference to the diversity of opinions on these issues, which does not allow a precise typology. During the modern period, three major groups may be described as traditionalists, Islamic modernists, and Islamists. The first group, mostly *ulama*, were nevertheless divided on whether Sharia could be applied in a non-Muslim or secular legal system (*dar al-harb*). In principle, Muslims could not stay in such a country and must migrate to an Islamic country. They demanded application of the whole of Sharia in postcolonial nation-states. They allowed temporary migration to non-Muslim countries, but Muslims must return to their countries if they were not free to practice Sharia laws. The second group, Islamic modernists, sought reforms in *fiqh* laws according to social and political needs in modern times. They dismissed the doctrine *dar al-Islam* and *dar al-harb*: The whole world was *dar al-'ahd* (House of Truce). They asked for reforms eliminating gender inequality, injustice, and religious discrimination. The third group, who viewed Islamic law as a comprehensive legal system, called for establishing an Islamic state to apply Sharia comprehensively. They insisted on Islamization of all the laws introduced in the colonial period. As for Muslim minorities, Islamists called for Muslim Judicial Councils in the Western legal systems to administer Sharia.

In the *fatawa* literature and legal texts, Muslim jurists debate the issues of *jihad*, migration, and application of Sharia. Three *fatwas* in the nineteenth century interpreted the traditional definition of *dar al-harb* in India: Shah Abd al-Aziz's (d.1824) *fatwa*, probably in 1803, Tariqa Muhammadiyah's declaration in 1857, and Karamat Ali's (d.1873) *fatwa* in 1870. Various members of the *jihad* groups, who took part in local revolts, like Farai'izi in Bengal in 1823, Mujahidin (in northern areas, present-day Pakistan in 1826–1831) led by Sayyid Ahmad Shahid, and some Wahhabi *jihad* groups (1837–1867), also wrote Fatawa in the name of Tariqa Muhammadiyya, calling for *jihad* in 1857 to restore *dar al-Islam* (Guenther 1998, 23).

Shah Abd al-Aziz gave three reasons: (1) The Imam lost sovereignty to Christians, (2) Taxes were collected by the Christians, and (3) Christian decided the lawsuits. Muslims had the freedom to carry on Friday prayers and slaughter cows (Guenther 1998). This *fatwa* is very academic and focused on the Islamic legal question of the status of Sharia law. Shah's approach is simply traditional Hanafi (Guenther 1998, 7). Shah Abd al-Aziz did not mention the obligations of Hijra and *jihad* in this *fatwa* (Masud 2008, 347–8).

Karamat Ali's (d.1873) *fatwa* in 1870 clearly declared India *dar al-harb*. He took a different position from others. Referring to Shah Abd al-Aziz's *fatwa* based on Hanfi rules, he argued that *dar al-Islam* required three conditions to be turned into *dar al-harb*: establishment of infidel rule, annexation to *dar al-harb* without a Muslim territory in between, nonexistence of true believers in the country. None of the three conditions existed. *Dar al-harb* may be restored to *dar al-Islam* by establishment of Muslim rule (Guenther 1998, 19).

To keep this introduction short, we have chosen to limit our of contemporary fatawa to an overview by Shaykh Yusuf al-Qaradawi on the issue of *jihad* (2009). The reason for this choice is that the classical and medieval jurists speak on these issues from the perspective of the law school to which they belonged. In the modern period, as mentioned already, two new perspectives have emerged in addition to the traditional: Islamic modernists and Islamists. Qaradawi belonged to the Islamists, but presently he leads the Wasatiyya group of jurists, who take a moderate position between the traditionalists and Islamists. This position is more post-Islamist than post-modernist and therefore distances itself from Islamic modernists. We find these views very important with reference to the rise of global Islam and global Sharia. The following is a summary of Qaradawi's analysis of these discussions on *dar al-harb*, *jihad*, and Sharia in the globalized world.

Regarding *dar al-harb*, Qaradawi mentions that the classical jurists differed about the binary division of the house of Islam and house of war. To clarify this distinction, the jurists formulated the following question: Can the *dar al-Islam* turn into a *dar al-harb*? Qaradawi lists the following five major views among the jurists (Qaradawi 2009, 2: 874–92):

1. *Dar al-Islam* can never turn into a *dar al-harb*. This is the majority view among the Shafi'i jurists, including Ibn Hajar al-Haytami (d.1567), al-Khatib al-Shirbini (d.1570), and Shams al-Din al-Ramli (d.1671). The first two held that *dar al-Islam* continues even when non-Muslims begin to rule a territory.
2. *Dar al-Islam* turns into *dar al-harb* when captured by non-Muslims. This was the majority view of the early Shafi'i jurists, including Imam al-Haramayn al-Juwayni (d.1085) and Abd al-Karim al-Rafi'i (d.1226).
3. *Dar al-Islam* turns into *dar al-harb* with the promulgation of non-Islamic laws. Abu Yusuf (d.798) and Abu Abdulla Muhammad al-Shaybani (d.805) among the Hanfi jurists, the Hanbali school, and some jurists of the Zaydi school held that as *dar al-harb* turns into *dar al-Islam* with the promulgation of Islamic laws, *dar al-Islam* does not remain so and turns into *dar al-harb* when Islamic law is no longer applied. Khamis ibn Sa'id Shiqsi al-Rustaqi among the Ibadi jurists qualifies this conclusion with certain conditions and stipulations.

4. *Dar al-Islam* does not turn into *dar al-harb* if the population continues to be Muslim. This view is held by the Maliki and Ibadi schools and some later Shafi'i jurists. The Maliki and Ibadi Schools and some later Shafi'i jurists hold the view that as long as Muslims can perform their Muslim rites publicly, like the call to prayer, and Friday and Eid prayers, the territory continues to stay as *dar al-Islam*. Muhammad al Dasuqi (d.1815) clarified that even if non-Muslims capture it by force, *dar al-Islam* does not become *dar al-harb* as long as rites of Islam continue to be performed.
5. *Dar al-Islam* turns into *dar al-harb* only under three conditions.

    a. The laws of the disbelievers gain supremacy so that no law of Islam can be executed.
    b. Muslim and non-Muslim populations are no longer governed by the original pacts that they enjoyed before the non-Muslim occupation.
    c. The land in question is adjacent to the territory of *dar al-harb* such that there is no land of Islam between them.

    Abu Ja'far al-Tahawi (d.933) and Abu Bakr al-Jassas (d.981), among the early Hanafis, reported that Abu Hanifa (d.767), the imam of the Hanafi school, held this view. Ahmad b. Yahya al-Murtada (d.1437) among the Zaidi jurists and Muhammad b. Abdullah al-Timartashi (d.1598), 'Ala al-din al-Haskafi (d.1677), and Ibn 'Abidin (d.1836) among the later Hanafi jurists supported it. The Hanafi jurist Sarakhsi (d.1090) added *dar al-'ahd* or *dar al-Sulh*, house of truce and treaty, to the binary division. Among the modern Hanafis, Abu Zuhra (d.1974) supported Sarakhsi.

Looking at these five views, one finds them to be nuanced legal clarifications of the issue with references to the respective contemporary political contexts. Qaradawi supports the Shafi'is and disputes the Hanafi and modern views. He finds the Hanafi jurists divided; some hold that *dar al-Islam* may formally turn into *dar al-harb*, but others qualify that if Muslims are free to continue practicing Sharia it remains *dar al-Islam* (2009, 2:891). Wahba Zuhayli (d.2015) said that such divisions are not found in the Quran and Sunna; they were inspired by the needs of time and context. Al-Qaradawi (2009, 2:874) disagrees with him and argues that they are certainly derived from the Quran and Sunna. He disagrees with the Islamic modernists who hold that "The world today, in the era of globalism, cannot be divided on religious basis" (*Ibid.* 893). He insists that *dar al-Islam* is continuing in the twenty-first century.

Regarding *"aggressive" Jihad, migration and Sharia for Muslim minorities*, Qaradawi disagrees with the terrorists who do not distinguish between *jihad*, and conventional wars. The Quran uses the term *harb* for conventional war and *qital* for fighting with sword; both are not *jihad.* Qaradawi clarifies that Muslim jurists do not regard the fight for the sole objective of domination as *jihad.* He finds that the terrorists claim a specific Quranic verse (9:5) and a specific *hadith* as the sword verse. Qaradawi argues that the context of the verse refers to a particular situation and refers only to the pagans in *Makkah.* It cannot be extended to all times, situations, and peoples. The cited *hadith* is technically too weak to be cited as authority (Qaradawi 2009, 1:336–44). This *hadith* is not acceptable also because it contradicts the Quran and Islamic history (Qaradawi 2009, 1:245–6). He argues that the ideas of aggressive *jihad* were developed by the leaders of Islamic political movements in the twentieth century (Qaradawi 2009, 1:31–3). According to Qaradawi, *jihad* is always defensive and is an obligation for all Muslim only when the enemy attacks a Muslim country. *Jihad* is not allowed with countries that have a pact or treaty with Muslims (Qaradawi 2009, 1:25–28).

Regarding migration, the questions changed in the nineteenth and twentieth centuries when Muslim began to migrate to European countries to study and work, and stayed for longer periods of time in non-Muslim countries. In a *fatwa*, even the term *dar al-harb* was translated as "enemy country." The Saudi *muftis* urged Muslims staying in the Western countries to return to their home countries because they were allowed only temporary stay in an "enemy" country (Baz and Uthaymeen 1998).

Qaradawi finds the following two views about migration from *dar al-Islam* to *dar al-harb*: (1) According to Shaykh Muhammad Ulaysh (d.1882) and Ahmad Abu'l Wafa, the Maliki School held that it is necessary to migrate from a Muslim country captured by the non-Muslim enemy (Qaradawi 2009, 882–3). Shaykh Nasir al-Din al-Albani (d.1999) issued a *fatwa* for Muslims in Palestine to migrate when Israelis occupied the territory (*Ibid.* 888). (2) Among the Shafi'is, al-Mawardi (d.1058), al-Rafi'i, Yahya Sharaf Nawawi (d.1277), Al-Haytami, and al-Ramli held that Muslims should not migrate from *dar al-Islam.* Al-Mawardi ruled that migration is necessary only when Muslims are not free to practice

Islam. If they have this freedom or if migration is not possible, then it is not obligatory. He preferred that people not migrate because if Muslims leave *dar al-Islam*, it turns into *dar al-harb*.

Qaradawi disagrees with Abu El-Wafa and clarifies that it is not the view of the Maliki school; the Maliki jurist Al-Dasuqi ruled that *dar al-Islam* does not turn into *dar al-harb* only by the enemy occupation. He refutes al-Albani because his *fatwa* supported what Israel wanted Muslims to do (*Ibid.* 888).

Muslim jurists held diverse views regarding Muslim minorities in Western countries staying long, taking residence, and seeking citizenship; some held it forbidden, some regarded it reprehensible, others allowed it unconditionally. Qaradawi disagreed with those who consider such stays forbidden even on the principle of prevented measures to avoid evil. He refers to the principles of universal objectives of Sharia, higher principles of Islamic jurisprudence, jurisprudence of reality, exception, dire necessity, and relaxation. Migration is allowed also for the purpose of education, financial needs, employment, medical treatment, trade, and asylum (*Ibid.* 931–8). Qaradawi mentions an earlier *fatawa* that opposed Muslims seeking citizenship in non-Muslim countries on account of lack of religious freedom in western countries or with reference to the principle of "loyalty (to disbelief) and disavowal (of Islam)." He discards such doubts. Instead, he stresses on the political, economic, educational, and cultural benefits to *dar al-Islam* that Muslims gain by staying and lobbying to strengthen Islam. He also clarified that Muslims have freedom, rather, facilities provided by the western countries, to ensure human rights. Muslims can claim exception from obligation such as participating in actions like war against Muslim countries (*Ibid.* 945–6).

With reference to the application of Sharia, he clarifies that Muslim democracies presently under Communism and Muslim countries governed by man-made laws all constitute *dar al-Islam*. The whole world today, constitutes *dar al-'ahd*, except Israel. *Dar al-Islam,* as a member of the organization, is bound by United Nations conventions, except those that are contrary to Sharia (*Ibid.* 895). He specifically mentions CEDAW because it contains sections that are in clear contradiction with the teachings of the Qur'an and Sunna, or they are known to be religiously essentials, for example, the difference between the shares of inheritance of a daughter and her brother or between the shares of a sister and her brother, or the prohibition of the marriage of a Muslim woman with a non-Muslim man, and legality of divorce and polygamy (*Ibid*., 896).

Global Sharia, as an idea, rather than as a term, originated with the migration of Muslims and their settlement as religious communities in non-Muslim countries. Conservative Muslims had built mosques and *madrasas* in Europe, but they discouraged political activities. Muslims were forbidden to participate in elections because such participation would support the infidel political system. Construction of a new branch of Sharia, *fiqh al-aqalliyat*, Islamic law for minorities, began to transform Sharia toward the end of the twentieth century. Islamists like Taha Jabir Al-Alwani argued that freedom of religion, according to International Human Rights, guaranteed freedom of belief and practice. In his *fiqh al-aqalliyat*, he developed new jurisprudence that was globally applicable (Alwani 1994). The Muslim Brotherhood issued an official statement in 1994 supporting Muslim participation in British politics and elections (Hussain 2004, 383). Islamists established Sharia Councils, *dar al-Qada*, and arbitration institutions for Muslim minorities in Britain, Canada, and the United States for regularizing marriage, divorce, succession, and consultations according to Sharia. We may call it Global Sharia, which allows exceptions to traditional *fiqh* and extended application of Sharia to Western countries (Alwani 1994, Qaradawi, 2001, 2002–3; Shavit 2015). Bin Bayyah (2007) welcomed this development as it encouraged Muslim countries to extend application of Sharia to penal and public laws where it was not applied after independence. Islamism pushed aside Islamic modernism during globalist waves. It is important to acknowledge that the political and religious hermeneutic that Islamism carries out rests on a politicization of Islam in general, with its own discursive and communicative techniques that favor the interests of Islamist groups and leaders; based on the idea that the main purpose of the Islamic creed is the construction of a political entity. And, while in Islam politics is innate to religion, the reality of religious texts does not clarify this unique and final consequence of this political goal in Islam (Jalloul Muro 2015).

In the twenty-first century, a new trend of post-Islamism is emerging, even though it is still Islamist in its understanding of gender equality and rule of law. Instead of reforms, Islamic modernism is "reconstructing Islamic law" (Masud 2019) that expands the principles like exception, necessity, and facilitation of *fiqh al-aqalliyat*. The new perspective of Islamic modernism is globalist as it invokes the philosophy of five basic rights and the purpose of law of the *Maqasid al-Sharia*; both doctrines are gaining popularity among the post-Islamists as well.

References

Adams, Charles J. 1983. "Maududi and the Islamic State." In Esposito, John L. (ed.). *Voices of Resurgent Islam*. Oxford University Press.

Agamben, Giorgio. 2005. *State of Exception*. University of Chicago.

Alwani, Taha Jabir Al-. 1994. *Muqaddima fī Fiqh al-Aqalliyāt*. Washington.

Alwani, Taha Jabir Al-. 2004. "Toward a fiqh for minorities: Some reflections." In *Muslims' Place in the American Public Square: Hope, Fears, and Aspirations*. Edited by Zahid H. Bukhari, Sulayman S. Nyang, Mumtaz Ahmad, and John L. Esposito. Herndon: IIIT, (2004): 3–37

Arabi, Oussama. 2000. "Orienting the Gaze: Marcel Morand and the Codification of Droit Algerien." *Journal of Islamic Studies*, 43–72.

Bartninkas, Vilius. 2014. "The pre-political and the political in Aristotle's politics." *Problemos*, 85 (2014): 18–29.

Baz, Ibn and Uthaymeen. 1998. *Fatawa Regarding Muslims Living as Minorities*. London: Message of Islam.

Ben Bayyah, Abdullah B. Mahfuz. 2007. *Ṣinā'at al-Fatwā wa Fiqh al-Aqalliyāt*. Jeddah.

Cavanaugh, Kathleen. 2012. "Narrating Law." In Anver M. Emon, Mark S. Ellis and Bejamin Glahn (eds.), *Islamic Law and International Human Rights Law, Searching for Common Ground?* Oxford University Press, 17–51.

Coulson, Noel James. 1964. *A History of Islamic Law*. Cambridge University Press.

Fukuyama, Francis. 1989. "The end of history?" *The National Interest*, 16 (1989): 3–18.

Fukuyama, Francis. 2006. *The end of history and the last man*. Simon and Schuster.

Fyzee, Asaf A. A. 1963. "Muhammadan Law in India." *Comparative Studies in Society and History*, Vol. 5, No. 4 (Jul. 1963), pp. 401–415.

Grady, Standish Grove. 1869. *A Manual of the Mahommedan Law of inheritance and contract, comprising the doctrines of the Soonee and Sheea schools, and based upon the text of Sir W. H. Macnaghten's Principles and precedent together with the decisions of the Privy Council and high courts of the presidencies in India*. London: W. H. Allen. p. xxxiii.

Guenther, Alan M. 1998. Dar al-Harb and Dar al-Islam, The Controversy regarding the British Presence in India, 1870–72. Academia.

Ghazali, Abu Hamid Muhammad al-. 1904. *Al-Mustasfa min 'Ilm al-Usul*. Cairo: Amiriyya Bulaq.

Hallaq, Wael. 2012. *The Impossible State: Islam, Politics, and Modernity's Moral Predicament*. New York: Columbia University Press.

Humphreys, S., 2006. Legalizing lawlessness: On Giorgio Agamben's state of exception. *European Journal of International Law*, 17(3), pp. 677–87.

Huntington, Samuel P. 1993. *The Third Wave: Democratization in the Late Twentieth Century*. Vol. 4. University of Oklahoma Press.

Hussain, Dilawar. 2004. "Muslim Political Participation in Britain and the 'Europeanisation' of Fiqh." *Die Welt des Islams*, 44, no. 3: 376–401.

Ibn Khaldun. 1989. *Muqaddima*, Tehran: Istiqlal.

Keohane, R.O. and Nye, J.S. 1972. *Transnational Relations and World Politics*. Harvard University Press.

Khudri, Muhammad. 1967. Shaykh. *Tarikh al-Tashri' al-Islami*. Dar al-Fikr.

Koskenniemi, Martti. 2004. "International law and hegemony: A Reconfiguration." *Cambridge Review of International Affairs*, 17, no. 2: 197–218.

MacLean, Derryl N. 2013. *Cosmopolitanisms in Muslim Contexts*, Edinburgh: Edinburgh University Press, pp. 1–2.

Martell, Luke. 2007. "The third wave in globalization theory." *International Studies Review*, 9, no. 2: 173–96.

Masud, Muhammad Khalid. 1990. "Obligation to migrate: Formulation of the doctrine of Hijrah in Islamic Law." In Dale F. Eickelman and J. Piscatori, *Muslim Travelers: Pilgrimage, Migration and the Religious Imagination*, London: Routledge and University of California, Berkley.

Masud. 2008. *Atthārwīn Ṣadī 'Īsawīi men Barr-e ṣaghīr men Islami Fikr ke rahnumā.* Islamabad: Islamic Research Institute.

Masud. Muhammad, (ed.) 2009. *Islam and Modernity: Key Issues and Debates*. Edinburgh University Press.

Masud. 2018. *The Dimensions and Phases of Globalization: An Islamic Perspective*. Islamabad: Iqbal Institute for Research and Dialogue.

Masud. 2019. "Modernizing Islamic law in Pakistan: Reform or reconstruction?" *Journal of South Asian and Middle Eastern Studies*, 42, no. 2: 73–97.

Masud. 2001. "The doctrine of siyasa in Islamic law." *Recht van de Islam*, 18: 1–29.

Masud. 2018. "Religion and State are Twin Brothers: Classical Muslim Political Theory." Ali Salman, Muhammad Hashim Kamali, Mohamed Azam Mohamed Adel. *Democratic Transitions in the Muslim World*. Selangor: Pelanduk Publications (M) SDN BHD, pp. 3–23.

Mayer, Ann Elizabeth. 2012. *Islam, and Human Rights: Traditions and Politics*, Avalon Publishing, p. 211.

Mazrui, Ali. 1993. "Islam and the end of History." *American Journal of Islamic Social Sciences*, 10, no. 4: 512–535.

Merriam-Webster.com. *Dictionary*. s.v. "globalism," Accessed January 26, 2021, https://www.merriam-webster.com/dictionary/globalism.

Nordregio.org. 2008. Accessed September 1, 2021, https://archive.nordregio.se/en/Metameny/About-Nordregio/Journal-of-Nordregio/2008/Journal-of-Nordregio-no-1-2008/The-Three-Waves-of-Globalisation/index.html

Nye, J. 2002. "Globalism versus Globalization." *The Globalist*, 15.

Özcan, Azmi. 1997. *Pan-Islamism: Indian Muslims, the Ottomans and Britain (1877–1924)*, Brill Academic Publishers.

Qaradawi, Yusuf al-. 2001, 2002–3. *Fiqh al-aqalliyāt al-Muslima* Cairo: Dar al-Shuruq.

Qaradawi, Yusuf al. 2009. *Fiqh al-Jihad.* Cairo: Maktaba Wahba.

Qureshi, M. Naeem. 1999. *Pan-Islam in British Indian Politics: A Study of the Khilafat Movement, 1918–1924*, Brill Academic Publishers.

Rahman, Fazlur. 1982. *Islam and Modernity: Transformation of an Intellectual Tradition*, University of Chicago Press.

Rankin, George Claus. 1946. *Background to Indian Law*. Cambridge: The University Press, p. 169, citing *Parliament Papers*, 1831–1832, 12, p. 696.

Robertson, Robbie. 2003. *The Three Waves of Globalization: A History of a Developing Global Consciousness*. Zed Books.

Schacht, Joseph. 1996. *An Introduction to Islamic Law*. Oxford: Oxford University Press.

Shavit, Uriya. 2015. *Shari'a and Muslim Minorities, The Wasati and Salafi Approaches to fiqh al-aqalliyyāt al-Muslima*. Oxford University Press.

Steger, Manfred B. 2005. "Ideologies of globalization." *Journal of Political Ideologies*, 10, no. 1: 11–30, 25

Swatscheno, Janet, and Patricia Denci. 2009. "Napoleon Bonaparte's Proclamations, speeches and letters during his campaign in Egypt." pp. 9–16.

Weiss, Bernard G. (ed.) 2002. *Studies in Islamic Legal Theory*. Vol. 15. Brill.

Wilson, Sir Roland Knyvet. 1930. *Anglo-Muhammadan Law: A Digest Preceded by a Historical and Descriptive Introduction of the Special Rules Now Applicable to Muhammadans as Such by the Civil Courts of British India, with Full References to Modern and Ancient Authorities*. India: W. Thacker & Company.

Part I

Theoretical Perspectives

https://doi.org/10.1142/9781800611689_0001

Chapter 1

Contesting Sharia in Postcolonial and Geopolitical Contexts

Abdullahi Ahmed An-Na'im

Charles Howard Candler Professor of Law,
Emory University School of Law, Atlanta, GA, USA
aannaim@emory.edu

Introduction

I have been working on issues of Islam and the state, Sharia, and human rights since the mid-1980s,[1] on the premise that humanity at large is moving toward a globalized legal world that requires mutual understanding in the field of legal and philosophical traditions. Recently, however, I have come to doubt the possibility of a genuinely mutual understanding in view of the realities of postcolonial power relations. In realistic, pragmatic terms, the obstacles facing possibilities of mutual understanding include the tendency of members of each tradition to project the epistemology and rationality of their tradition onto whichever cultures or traditions they presume to understand. It is not that mutual understanding cannot be achieved, but that our approach to mutuality of understanding is more likely to be realized if our attempt is deliberate and strategic, instead of

[1] My first relevant book chapter was titled "A Modern Approach to Human Rights in Islam: Foundations and Implications for Africa" (An-Na'im 1984).

expecting the legal and philosophical traditions of other cultures to conform to our own assumptions and expectations about them.

From this perspective, I call on the proponents of mutual understanding between legal and philosophical traditions to seek to promote conceptual and methodological tools to that end, and to draw up practical strategies. Large-scale socioeconomic and political transformations tend to happen with the support of changes at the global and regional level, which push for as well as sustain the structural changes achieved by social and political forces in each society. In other words, it seems to me that large-scale and sustained social transformations are achieved by a combination of social actors who interact through ethical and intellectual forces over extended periods of time. This view does not exclude or marginalize the role of the contributions of individuals who are active and effective at various levels of agency and resources. In this process, I see it as my role, as a Muslim from postcolonial Sudan, to engage in good faith and avoid apologetic or defensive discourse—regardless of what others do or fail to do—to promote mutual understanding.

For instance, and from the perspective of the tentative theory of Islam, society, and state I am briefly proposing here, I see deterministic attitudes of so-called Western and Islamic legal cultures[2] as highly destructive *mis*-understandings. These are likely to follow when human actors assume that since the role of Sharia in Islamic cultures is "similar to" the role of law in Western cultures, Sharia must follow the normative or empirical qualities of law in Western cultures and vice versa. Instead of adopting such simplistic equations, I recommend keeping each normative system true to its own nature, epistemology, and methodology. For instance, the "role" of law or Sharia is not the same when it is *politically* determined and coercively enforced by the state, on the one hand, or believed to be *divinely* ordained, though coercively or socially sanctioned, like the role of tribal structures and power relations for customary law, on the other.

It should therefore be possible, for example, to achieve mutual understanding in the fields of legal and philosophical traditions, *provided* due

---

[2]I use the terms "Western" and "Islamic" as shorthand, subject to serious reservations about the fallacy of possibilities of geopolitical uniformity. The most destructive wars in human history, particularly the First and Second World Wars in the twentieth century, were fought among Western powers. Muslims fought "civil wars" for a couple of decades after the death of the Prophet and continued to experience imperial conquests throughout their histories.

regard is given to the realities of postcolonial power relations and terminological and methodological concerns are clarified. These factors should be included in the comparative analysis and evaluation by all sides in domestic debates about the role of Sharia within a postcolonial "nation-state," as well as in international geopolitical discourse. This is not to suggest that conflicts and tensions among different constituencies can be permanently and categorically resolved through debate and discourse, but such strategies can help in *negotiating* agreement through peaceful means. While I can try to formulate some potential principles and guidelines on these processes within Muslim communities and in their relations to others, I will emphasize the historical and contextual nature of the process and its outcomes.

The human rights paradigm could be an important source of such principles and guidelines, but that paradigm is frequently invoked by the former Western European colonial powers and North America to justify or rationalize their exploitative geopolitical hegemony, instead of being used as an approach to globally inclusive processes for promoting social justice and protecting individual freedom. Negative perceptions of the human rights paradigm are also partly due to the inability of the system to provide effective and sustainable protection of human rights on the ground. Another source of negative perception is the view that the system is colonized by what I call "liberal relativism," because official representatives of states, officers of international organizations, practitioners of nongovernmental organizations, and scholars all tend to routinely define and apply key concepts and institutions of the human rights system in liberal terms.

I call this *liberal relativism* to counter the charge of *cultural relativism*, which advocates of the present international human rights system frequently raise against proponents of a more globally inclusive system. In fact, every conception of human rights, anywhere in the world, is necessarily *relative* to the culture and worldview of the person or group. The universality of some norms and institutions may evolve over time, as a product of overlapping consensus, but never through "proclamation" by any state, group of states, or international organization (An-Na'im 1993). The present international system's limitation to liberal conceptions of rights as the judicially enforceable entitlements of individual persons renders the entire system only regional (so-called Western) and not universal. The lack of universality deprives the present system of moral and political authority, thereby undermining the legal force of international norms and institutions.

Perceptions of Sharia as socially and politically problematic constituted an imperial "self-fulfilling prophecy" by European colonial administrators, as often happened throughout human history to justify the domination and exploitation of the inferior by the superior. As European imperialism sought to found its superiority on claims of "scientific methodology and rationality," it strove to attribute the civilizational inferiority of Islamic communities to the tenets of Muslims' religious and cultural systems, conveniently embraced by the vague and iconic notion of Sharia (Said 1978, 1993). Respectful belief in the civilizational inferiority and superiority of both sides of the imperial equation requires a common framework, like modernity or human rights, which imperial discourse claims is universally determined, while it is in fact relatively defined and anchored.

If implemented effectively, this colonial stipulation would seem to vindicate the so-called "civilizing mission" of the European colonization of African and Asian territories and populations. However, the nature and development of Sharia defies the simplistic characterizations and expectations of current debates in the late twentieth and early twenty-first centuries. Part of the problem is due to competing claims of Muslims to self-determination and concerns of both Muslims and non-Muslims about political violence and instability, which do not understand or address the underlying causes of those phenomena. Instability and political violence are most likely to follow from frustration with the lack of social justice and effective self-determination at home and abroad. These two dimensions reflect histories of colonial and neocolonial relations, current hegemonic, geopolitical ambitions, and assertions of self-determination to demand social justice. Poor and disempowered Muslims also seem to believe that they should exercise their self-determination by applying Sharia in order to restore social justice, which they believe existed in much of Islamic history. It should be noted here that beliefs of populist leaders are more effective in mobilizing and motivating mass movements and populist politics than the carefully reasoned and well-documented analysis of scholars.

On further reflection, however, Muslims should also realize that Sharia itself authorizes only relative equality and justice for Muslim men and discriminates against Muslim women and non-Muslims. These and other serious problems with traditional Sharia are structural and methodological in traditional interpretations of Sharia and cannot be redressed without a paradigm shift in the (organization of) fundamental sources of Sharia, as I have discussed in detail elsewhere (An-Na'im 1990,

Chapters 2, 3, 4, and 6, 2011). I would also emphasize here that redressing the fundamental limitations of Sharia interpretations in the modern context should be achieved through exercising the *equal* right to self-determination for all human beings, men and women, Muslims and non-Muslims alike. Muslim men are not entitled to the right to self-determination unless they are willing and able to grant the same right to all other human beings.

This obvious principle does not seem to be appreciated by Muslims at large because of their unfounded assumption of the religious sanctity of traditional interpretations of Sharia. Any interpretation of Sharia—past, present, or future—is always a human endeavor and not divine command as such. In other words, since the norms and institutions of Sharia reflect the human interpretation of relevant texts of the Quran and Sunna (*hadith*), they remain open to critical reflection and reinterpretation. The human quality of Sharia is obvious in view of the wide diversity in opinion among the founding scholars of Islamic jurisprudence and their schools of Islamic jurisprudence (*madhahib*), although they applied the same methodologies of interpretation (*usul al-fiqh*). As Ibn Rushd explained, all interpretations of Sharia are suppositional (*zanniyyan*) and not categorical (*qat'iyyan*)—i.e., they are outcomes of speculation and not divine command as such (An-Na'im 2008, 47).

One point to emphasize for this purpose is that Sharia norms defy codification or legislative enactment, because that would change the religious nature of the norm and deny Muslims the inherent religious freedom of choice among different interpretations of the Quran and Sunna (*hadith*) established by traditional Sunni or Shia schools of jurisprudence. Since Muslims are religiously accountable for compliance with Sharia, they must have the freedom and responsibility to decide which interpretation of the sources and methodologies of Sharia they accept (Coulson 1964; Weiss 1998). Moreover, arbitrary and harsh outcomes were bound to follow when the rich diversity of views among Muslim scholars was reduced to the extreme selectivity of the language of codification that characterizes the modern state's positive law. The claim of ruling elites in monarchies as well as republics that they can specify which Sharia norms state authorities should impose on the entire Muslim population of their countries violates Muslims' freedom of religion and inhibits possibilities for positive social change in their communities. This analysis confirms, in my view, that the mediation of competing factors in the practical governance of historical Muslim communities was consistent with the purpose and rationale of constitutionalism and democratic principles.

Whatever judicial system or manner of resolution of disputes prevailed among Muslims in the precolonial era no longer exists (Vikør 2005, 140) but remains most instructive on the nature and development of Sharia. The historical theory and practice of Sharia emphasize the importance of the political and social context of modern political regimes' pre-bureaucratic organization. In those polities, the caliphs and sultans had on the one hand apparently absolute military and political power and authority, and on the other hand needed the legitimizing authority of scholars and religious leaders of the communities (Hallaq 2009, 131, 147). The political and legal history of Muslim societies consists of interaction and negotiation between rulers and scholars/jurists. The rulers needed the legitimacy of the knowledge and interpretation of Sharia by the Muslim scholars/jurists, who in turn needed the political authority of the rulers to implement Sharia. Rulers needed to respect the integrity and autonomy of scholars in order to preserve their legitimizing competence, and the scholars needed to protect their integrity and autonomy in order to maintain their moral standing among their communities.

The integrity and autonomy of the founding Muslim scholars of Sharia were structurally safeguarded by the independence of the informal educational system, which consisted of circles of learning (*halaqas*) usually convened in mosques, where Muslims go to pray five times a day. Throughout Muslim history, these informal circles of learning remained the established forum of legal education and retained their autonomy by receiving funding not from the state ruling elites but from religious endowments (*waqfs*) established by private individual benefactors (Hallaq 2009, 140). In addition, more institutionalized colleges (*madrasas*) emerged at the end of the eighth century when endowments and salaries became available to professors. Ironically, it was through the funding of these institutions that the ruling elites gradually co-opted scholars/jurists and influenced the legal profession. By the seventeenth century, the state employed most jurists, and those who insisted on maintaining their autonomy still had to rely on state funding through their colleagues who did accept state patronage (151). The autonomous role of Sharia and its scholars started to decline before the rise of European colonialism in Africa and Asia, but the impact of colonialism seems to have been more effective and sustained in diminishing the role of Sharia in the transition to the nation-state.

To conclude this section, a central role in the daily practice of Sharia was played by the jurist/scholar (*mufti*), whose task was to consult a whole host of Sharia sources in order to produce a legal opinion (*fatwa*), which became the basis of rulings by judges (*qadis*) in specific cases. The authority of the mufti was based on his reputation as a learned and pious scholar, while the authority of judges was derived from either official appointment by the ruler or voluntary submission by individual litigants in the case at hand. The fatwa established the connection between relevant principles of Sharia and the particular facts of a case and was in theory valid only for the case for which it was formulated. Judges were not obliged to seek a fatwa for every case they had to rule on. They could seek it only when unsure of the legal basis for determining the case or if they felt the need for a more authoritative ruling due to the nature of the case or the public attention it attracted. The roles of both judge and mufti were limited to identifying and interpreting the law for application to specific cases, and never included creating the law. The tasks of a judge included resolving conflict, adjudicating rights and obligations, and representing the community in maintaining law and order in the market and in public life (*hisba*). In order to perform his functions, a judge was supposed to investigate not only the facts of the case but also information about the integrity of the litigating parties and the history of their interactions. He had to consider social customs and strive to resolve the dispute in ways that preserved social harmony and stability (Vikør 2005, Chapters 8, 9).

Transition to Legal Systems of Nation-State

European colonialism transformed the preexisting nature and manner of Sharia's role in the administration of justice in Muslim communities across the world, even in regions that were not formally colonized, like the Arabian Peninsula and Iran. European colonialism has been spectacularly successful not only in its scale and scope but, more importantly, also in transforming the political and legal institutions of colonized societies and integrating them into the global economic and trade systems. These transformations were initially prompted by attempts of the Ottoman Empire to modernize its political and legal institutions during the nineteenth century to meet the challenge of rising European powers. The symbolic significance of the Ottoman concessions to rising European powers culminated in the abolition of the caliphate (symbol of Islamic unity and sovereignty) by 1924. This event signified the irreversible shift to European models of the state and its legal system, which came to prevail throughout Ottoman regions in the Middle East and North Africa. Concurrent processes were taking place in Iran and South Asia, which culminated in similar outcomes.

A combination of colonial European challenges and accommodation and adaptation by Islamic societies during the nineteenth to the first half of the twentieth century resulted in the establishment of "nation-states" from North and West Africa to South and Southeast Asia. When the Islamic societies of Central Asia were finally released from the grip of Russian/Soviet colonialism by 1991, they also opted for the nation-state model, which has become the established global order. The same process resulted in the full incorporation of all Islamic societies into the global, state-centric economic, political, and security systems of today. Secular state courts applied European statutes during the colonial era and since independence in almost all Islamic societies; the domain of Sharia became limited to family law. Even in the family law field, the state continued to regulate the role of Sharia as part of broader legal and political systems of government and social organization within the framework of postcolonial European models.

While this process unfolded in different ways among Islamic societies, the experience of the late Ottoman Empire has probably had the most far-reaching consequences, because it set the model for similar effects of European colonialism on preexisting, indigenous legal systems. In particular, the Ottoman Majalla—enacted by the Sultan in the early second half of the nineteenth century (1867–77)—set the example of a highly selective combination of European codes and Sharia principles of contract and tort according to the Hanafi School of jurisprudence. This process simplified a vast part of the relevant principles of that School, making them more easily accessible to litigants and jurists. While it was a total innovation in form and substance, the Majalla was highly authoritative because it represented the earliest and most politically significant example of an official promulgation of large parts of Sharia by the authority of a modern state. In the circumstances of its promulgation, the Majalla successfully claimed to transform Sharia into positive state law in the modern sense of the term, although it dealt with only a small section of the jurisprudence of one of four Sunni schools. The principle of selectivity (*takhayyur*), allowing believers to choose among equally legitimate doctrines of Sharia, was not new to Muslim communities, but the Majalla transformed the practice by representing it in statutory form for the centralized and bureaucratic administration of justice by the state.

This trend toward the selection of sources and a synthesis of Islamic and Western legal concepts and institutions continued to develop and became irreversible. The most influential work in this regard is that of the Egyptian jurist Abd al-Razzaq al-Sanhuri (d.1971) (Bechor 2007), who applied this approach when drafting the Egyptian Civil Code of 1949, and that of Iraq in 1951, Libya in 1954, Kuwait in 1960, and others. This process made the entire body of Sharia norms and institutions more accessible to judges and other actors in the process of incorporating these principles into modern legislation. The process of mixing some general or partial principles or views from one school of Sharia (*madhhab*) with those derived from other schools was selective, without due regard to the methodological basis or conceptual coherence of any of the schools whose authority was being invoked. The ironic outcome of the entire process was that it exposed the extreme diversity among and within different schools of Islamic jurisprudence, which should undermine rather than promote the enforcement of Sharia as the law of the modern state.

In addition, the process of civil education and professional training of officials of the modern nation-state introduced a range of secular subjects that tend to create a different worldview and expertise among young generations of Muslims. The monopoly on intellectual leadership held by Islamic scholars in societies that had very low literacy rates has been drastically eroded by the fast growth of mass literacy and growing higher education in secular sciences and arts. In relation to legal education, for instance, the first generations of lawyers and jurists took advanced training in European and North American universities and returned to teach subsequent generations or to hold senior legal and judicial offices (Hallaq 2009, 445).

Sharia, Society, and the State

According to Islamic religious doctrine, every Muslim is personally responsible for knowing and complying with what is required of him or her as a matter of religious obligation. The fundamental principle of individual and personal responsibility that can never be abdicated or delegated is one of the recurring themes of the Quran (6:164, 17:15, 35:18, 39:7, and 53:18). In practice, however, when Muslims seek to know what Sharia requires of them in any specific situation, they are more likely to ask a trusted Muslim scholar (*'alim*, plural *ulama*) or Sufi leader than to refer directly to the Quran and Sunna themselves. Whether done personally or more usually by a scholar or Sufi leader, reference to the Quran and Sunna necessarily happens through the structure and methodology one has been raised to accept. This would normally happen within the framework of a particular school (*madhhab*) and its established doctrine and methodology, but never in a totally fresh and original manner, without preconceived notions of how to identify and interpret relevant texts of the Quran and Sunna.

In other words, whenever Muslims consider these primary sources, they cannot avoid the filters of not only layers of experience and interpretation by preceding generations but also of an elaborate methodology that determines which texts are relevant to any subject and how they should be understood. Human agency is therefore integral to any approach to the Quran and Sunna at multiple levels, ranging from centuries of accumulated experience and interpretation to the current context, in which an Islamic frame of reference is invoked. The next question to briefly clarify is how an Islamic frame of reference can be invoked from an institutional perspective of state policy and legislation. As a political institution, the state is not an entity that can feel, believe, or act. It is always human beings who act in the name of the state, exercise its powers, or operate through its organs. Thus, whenever a human being makes a decision about a policy matter or proposes or drafts legislation that is supposed to embody Islamic principles, this will necessarily reflect his or her personal perspective on the subject, and never that of the state as an autonomous entity. Moreover, when such policy or legislative proposals are made in the name of a political party or organization, such positions are also taken by the human leaders speaking or acting for that entity. It is true that specific positions on matters of policy and legislation may be negotiated among significant actors, but the outcome will still necessarily be the product of individual human judgment and the choice to accept and act on a view that those actors agree about.

For instance, a decision to punish the consumption of alcohol as a *hadd* crime defined by Sharia is necessarily the view of individual political actors, taken after weighing all sorts of practical considerations, and the language used in drafting legislation and the measures taken when implementing it are similarly the product of human judgment and choice. For my purposes, the point here is that the entire process of formulating and implementing public policy and legislation is constantly subject to human error and fallibility, which means that it can always be challenged or questioned without violating the direct and immediate divine will of God. This is part of the reason why matters of public policy and legislation must be supported by civic reason, even among Muslims who can and do disagree on all such matters without violating their religious obligations.

The structure and methodology known as *usul al-fiqh*, through which Muslims can comprehend and implement Islamic precepts as conveyed in the Quran and Sunna, was developed by early Muslim scholars. In its original formulations, this field of human knowledge sought to regulate the interpretation of these foundational sources in light of the historical experience of the first generations of Muslims. It also defines and regulates the operation of such juridical techniques as *ijma‘* (consensus), *qiyas* (reasoning by analogy), and *ijtihad* (juridical reasoning). These techniques are commonly taken to be methods for specifying Sharia principles, rather than substantive sources as such. However, *ijma‘* and *ijtihad* had a more foundational role beyond this limited technical meaning. This broader sense can form the basis of a more dynamic and creative development of Sharia now and in the future.

The consensus (*ijma‘*) among generations of Muslims from the beginning of Islam that the text of the Quran is in fact accurately contained in the written text known as *al-Mushaf* is the underlying reason why that text is accepted by Muslims at any time and place. The same is true of what most Muslims accept as authentic reports of what the Prophet said and did (Sunna), though that took longer to establish and is still controversial among many believers. In other words, our knowledge of the Quran and Sunna is the result of intergenerational consensus since the seventh century. This is not to say or imply that Muslims manufactured these sources through consensus, but simply to note that we know and accept these texts as valid because generation after generation of Muslims have believed that. Moreover, consensus is the basis of the authority and continuity of *usul al-fiqh* and all its principles and techniques, because this interpretative structure is always dependent on its acceptance as such among the generality of Muslims from one generation to the next. In this sense, *ijma‘* is the basis of the acceptance of the Quran and Sunna themselves, as well as the totality and detail of the methodology for their interpretation.

For Muslims, the significant difference between the Quran and Sunna, as distinguished from the techniques of *usul al-fiqh*, is that there is no possibility of new or additional texts because the Prophet Muhammad is the final prophet and the Quran is the conclusive divine revelation. In contrast, there is nothing to prevent or invalidate the formation of a new consensus around techniques of interpretation or innovative interpretations of the Quran and Sunna—which would thereby become part of Sharia—in the same way that existing techniques or principles came to be part of it in the first place. The safeguards of separating Islam from the state and regulating the political role of Islam through constitutionalism and protection of human rights that I am proposing are necessary for ensuring freedom and security for Muslims to participate in proposing and debating fresh interpretations of those foundational sources.

Any understanding of Sharia is always the product of *ijtihad*, in the general sense of reasoning and reflection by human beings as ways of understanding the meaning of the Quran and Sunna of the Prophet. Practical questions, such as who decides the Sharia rule on any issue and which methodology is used, are all resolved through human judgment, regardless of the specific outcome in a given situation. It is therefore illogical to say that a specific matter or issue is beyond *ijtihad*: this is a contradiction in terms, because that determination itself is the product of human reasoning and reflection. It is also dangerous to limit the ability to exercise *ijtihad* to a restricted group of Muslims who are supposed to have specific qualities, because in practice that will depend on those human beings who will set and apply the criteria used to select who is a qualified *mujtahid*. To grant this authority to any institution or organ, whether it is believed to be official or private, is dangerous because that power will probably be manipulated for political or other reasons. Since knowing and upholding Sharia is the permanent and inescapable responsibility of every Muslim, no human being or institution should control this process for Muslims. The power to decide who is qualified to exercise *ijtihad* and how it is to be enjoyed by every Muslim, as a matter of religious belief and obligation, cannot be censored or controlled. In other words, any restriction on free debate by entrusting human beings or institutions with the authority to decide which views are to be allowed or suppressed is inconsistent with the religious nature of Sharia itself. This reasoning is one of the main Islamic foundations I propose for safeguarding pluralism, human rights, and citizenship for all.

In concluding this brief overview, it is clear that there is an urgent need to continue the processes of Islamic reform to reconcile the religious commitment of Muslims with the practical requirements of their societies today. In my view, the main premise of a viable reform process is as follows: while the Quran and Sunna are the divine sources of Islam according to Muslim belief, the meaning of these sources for and their implementation in everyday life is always the product of human interpretation and action in a specific historical context. It is simply impossible to know and apply Sharia in this life except through the agency of human beings. Any view of Sharia known to Muslims today, even if unanimously agreed on, necessarily emerged from the opinion of human beings about the meaning of the Quran and Sunna, as accepted by many generations of Muslims and the practice of their communities. In other words, opinions of Muslim scholars became part of Sharia through the consensus of believers over many centuries, and not through the spontaneous decree of a ruler or the will of a single group of scholars.

Ends and Means of Social Transformation

The transformation of Muslims' attitudes to the relationship among Islam, Sharia, and the state involves the arena of state action, as governmental policies and constitutional and legal reform ensure the separation of Islam and *the state*. There is also the domain of *society*, at the individual as well as communal level, where the objective is to incorporate the values of religious neutrality of the state, constitutionalism, and human rights as at least consistent with, if not required by, Islam. These two dimensions of transformation through official institutional as well as civil, societal change are in fact interdependent and mutually supportive. Each objective may require different actions and strategies that will vary from one social and cultural context to another, but the two kinds of transformations are deeply connected in that each is both the cause and outcome of the other. For this dynamic transformation to happen in Islamic societies, we also have to clarify and transform the permanent and desirable relationship between Islam and *politics*, as suggested earlier.

The proposed transformations, therefore, recognize the multifaceted relevance of Islam to Muslim communities across the globe, as religion and—more broadly—as culture and the basis of social practice. This indicates a third dimension of my proposal, which is the question of how to root social change in culture or endow it with cultural legitimacy. The separation of Islam and the state does not mean the exclusion of a role for Islam in public policy, legislation, or public life in general, provided it is supported by what I call civic reason and subject to constitutional and human rights safeguards. Thus, Sharia does indeed have a most important future in Islamic societies and communities for its foundational role in the socialization of children, sanctification of social institutions and relationships, and shaping and development of those fundamental values that can be translated into general legislation and public policy through the democratic political process. But it does not have a future as a normative system to be enacted and enforced as such by the state as public law and public policy. The claim may of course be made that a certain policy or law is Sharia, but such claims are a necessarily human attempt to invoke the sanctity of Islam for the political will of the ruling elite.

Cultural legitimacy may be defined as the quality of being in conformity with accepted principles or standards of the culture in question, thereby drawing on the authority and relevance of its internal validity. A culturally legitimate norm or value is respected and observed by members of the particular culture because it satisfies certain needs or purposes in the lives of individuals and their communities. Recognition that this is true of the newly introduced or modified norm or institution is therefore necessary for the success of this process. This is not as difficult or unlikely as it might seem, because a similar process is always happening within every culture through internal contestation and transformation. Because there may be conflicts and tensions between various competing conceptions of individual and collective needs or objectives, the norms and values that are accorded respect and observance are constantly changed and adjusted in any culture. The proponents of change must not only have a credible claim to being *insiders* to the culture, but also use internally valid arguments to persuade the local population. In this way, the presentation and adoption of alternative perspectives can be achieved through a coherent *internal discourse* within the culture. The internal validity criteria for any initiative to secure cultural legitimacy for change will vary from issue to issue within the same culture or society and across societies, but can be questioned and reformulated as well.

While this approach raises the possibility of local culture being invoked as the basis for violating or rejecting the existence of a human right, I am unable to see an alternative to a basic methodology of cultural legitimacy that can be constantly improved through practice and over time. For example, culture may be used to justify discrimination against women or the use of corporal punishment against children as being in their own "best interest." Rejecting the cultural argument presented in support of such views is unlikely to work in practice. Indeed, women themselves are likely to support their own repression if they believe it to be “the will of God” or the immutable tradition of their communities. In contrast, an approach that acknowledges the underlying value of respecting the will of God or local tradition and then proceeds to question what that means under present circumstances is more likely to be persuasive. As a Muslim, if I am presented with a choice between Islam and human rights, I will always choose Islam. But if presented with an argument that there is in fact consistency between my religious beliefs and human rights, I will gladly accept human rights as an expression of religious values and not as an alternative to them. As a Muslim advocate of human rights, I must therefore continue to seek ways of explaining and supporting the claim that these rights are consistent with Islam and indeed desirable from an Islamic perspective, though they may be inconsistent with certain human interpretations of Sharia.

Second, since the individual person is dependent on his or her society, which has a powerful capacity to instill or enforce conformity in its members, public policy and action are more likely to accord with ideal cultural norms and patterns of behavior than private actions. Changes in public behavior are likely to take longer because of the tendency of individuals to conform until the new norm is widely accepted. In other words, open and systematic nonconformity gravely threatens those who hold authority in society: the elite who have developed a vested interest in the status quo. In suppressing nonconforming behavior, such elites would assert the imperative of preserving the stability and vital interests of society at large, rather than admit the reality that it is their own interests that they seek to protect. It thus becomes a question of who has the power to determine what is in the public interest, and the substance of the issue being debated becomes a proxy for that permanent struggle. These factors emphasize the desirability of seeking the support of the cultural ideal for any proposition of public policy and action, because that is less likely to be successfully resisted by the self-appointed guardians of society’s stability and well-being.

My emphasis on the role of internal actors and discourse in the cultural legitimacy of social change does not preclude the role that can be played by those who are cultural outsiders in promoting acceptance of change. But external actors can best influence an internal situation through engaging in internal discourse on the same values within their own societies, thereby enabling participants in one culture to point to similar processes taking place in other cultures. External actors can also help support the right of internal participants to challenge prevailing perceptions, while avoiding overt interference since this will undermine the credibility of internal actors. Advocates of change in various societies should also engage in a cross-cultural dialogue to exchange insights and strategies of internal discourse and promote the global acceptance of their shared objectives. Cross-cultural dialogue can also seek to promote the universality of shared values at a theoretical or conceptual level by highlighting moral and philosophical commonalities of human cultures and experiences.

Ultimately, the key to all this is that the human agency of social change proponents should be able to motivate the human agency of the population at large in favor of the proposed change. The methodology of cultural legitimacy therefore emphasizes the central role of human agency by firmly locating the impetus for change within the social and cultural lives of communities and individuals, rather than viewing persons and communities as passive subjects of change. At the same time, human agency operates in the context of networks of social action and interaction, which emphasizes the need for collaboration and cooperation. It is clear that nothing happens in human relationships, whether good or bad, except through the agency of some person or groups acting or failing to act. But it is also clear that this conception of the role of human agency must be inclusive of all human beings, especially in today's globalized world, and cannot be limited to Muslims alone. Consequently, the outcome of human agency in any society is contingent on what else is happening in the world around us and not only on what happens within our societies or communities.

The history of Islamic thought also shows that human agency has been central to the development of Sharia. As emphasized earlier, the inherent nature of Sharia is that it is necessarily the product of human interpretations of the Quran and Sunna of the Prophet. This process was conducted by scholars and jurists, who developed and applied the sources or methodology (*usul al-fiqh*) completely independently of the state but with due regard to the circumstances and concerns of their communities and political institutions. These scholars also accepted diversity of opinion as a healthy and creative feature of their work, while seeking to enhance consensus among themselves and their communities. Thus, every single principle of Sharia became established through consensus (*ijma'*) and voluntary compliance by Muslims at large, and never through an institutional authority, whether official or nonofficial. In other words, the validity and binding authority of any Sharia principle was always the product of the human agency of scholars and communities of Muslims, operating through many generations.

Concluding Reflections

The purpose of the theory of the relationship among Islam, state, and society I am proposing is to ensure the institutional separation of Islam and the state, despite the organic and unavoidable connection between Islam and politics.[3] The relationship among Islam, state, and society is always the product of a constant contextual negotiation, rather than the subject of a fixed formula of either total separation or complete fusion of religion and the state. In this tripartite relationship, various understandings of Sharia will remain in the realm of individual and collective practice as a matter of freedom of religion and belief, subject to established constitutional safeguards to ensure the institutional separation of Islam and the state. As explained above, Sharia principles *as such* cannot be enforced as the law of the state by virtue of their being decreed by Sharia. The outcome of any attempt to enforce Sharia as law of the state is the product of the political will of the state and not the religious values of Islam. Religious norms shall continue to influence the behavior of believers, but this relationship must remain outside the institutions and services of the state.

In the final analysis, however, major transformations of public consciousness and personal practice cannot be achieved and sustained by theoretical articulation alone. They must also be reflected in cultural expression and sociological orientation, as well as in the general popular worldview and everyday practice. It is as if transformative change is realized on all levels of human experience and practice at once, in which theoretical articulation is merely one aspect of social experience trying to catch up with transformative change that is already in progress.

References

An-Na'im, Abdullahi A. 1984. "A Modern Approach to Human Rights in Islam: Foundations and Implications for Africa." In *Human Rights and Development*

---

[3] For elaboration and documentation of this proposition, see my articles and book chapters: An-Na'im (2009, 2010, 2011, 2013, 2015, 2016).

in Africa, edited by Claude E Welch Jr and Ronald I Meltzer, 75–89. New York: State of New York Press.

An-Na'im, Abdullahi A. 1990. *Toward an Islamic Reformation: Civil Liberties, Human Rights and International Law*. Syracuse, NY: Syracuse University Press.

An-Na'im, Abdullahi A. 1993. *Human Rights in Cross-Cultural Perspective: Quest for Consensus*. Philadelphia: University of Pennsylvania Press.

An-Na'im, Abdullahi A. 2008. *Islam and the Secular State: Negotiating the Future of Shar'ia*. Cambridge, MA: Harvard University Press.

An-Na'im, Abdullahi A. 2009. "Religion, the State and Constitutionalism in Islamic and Comparative Perspectives." *Drake Law Review*, 57, no. 4: 829–50.

An-Na'im, Abdullahi A. 2010. "The Compatibility Dialectic: Mediating the Legitimate Coexistence of Islamic Law and State Law." *Modern Law Review*, 73, no. 1: 1–29.

An-Na'im, Abdullahi A. 2011a. "Religious Norms and Family Law: Is it Legal or Normative Pluralism?" *Emory International Law Review*, 25, no. 2: 785–809.

An-Na'im, Abdullahi A. 2011b. *Muslims and Global Justice.* Philadelphia: University of Pennsylvania Press.

An-Na'im, Abdullahi A. 2013. "Complementary, Not Competing, Claims of Law and Religion: An Islamic Perspective." *Pepperdine Law Review*, 39, no. 5: 1231–55.

Bechor, Guy. 2007. *The Sanhuri Code, and the Emergence of Modern Arab Civil Law (1932–1949)*. Leiden Netherlands: Brill.

Coulson, N. J. 1964. *A History of Islamic Law*. Edinburgh: Edinburgh University Press.

Hallaq, Wael B. 2009. *Sharia: Theory, Practice, Transformations*. Cambridge: Cambridge University Press.

Said, Edward W. 1978. *Orientalism*. New York: Pantheon Books.

Said, Edward W. 1993. *Imperialism and Culture*. New York: A.A. Knopf.

Vikør, Knut S. 2005. *Between God and the Sultan: A History of Islamic Law*. New York: Oxford University Press.

Weiss, Bernard G. 1998. *The Spirit of Islamic Law*. Athens: University of Georgia Press.

https://doi.org/10.1142/9781800611689_0002

Chapter 2

Between Separation and Unity: The Interplay of Law and Morality in Islamic Jurisprudence

Mohammad Hashim Kamali

International Institute of Advanced Islamic Studies,
Jalam Ilmu off Jalan Universiti,
59800 Kuala Lumpur, Malaysia
hkamali19@gmail.com; ceo@iais.org.my

Introduction

The development of a moral precept into a legal norm represents moral progress in the sense that the moral precept in question gains the critical mass of public support for it to become the subject of a binding law. In essence, a great deal of the law in any society consists of the concretization into binding rules of their underlying moral precepts. On the negative side too, when violation of a moral precept becomes widespread to the extent of representing a social mischief, it becomes the responsibility of the government and the justice system to take appropriate measures to protect society against its menace. This is often done through legislation. A manifest neglect or legislative inaction would risk leaving society vulnerable to abuse, since appeals only to conscience without positive inducement may well put those who respond with self-restraint at a disadvantage with respect to those who are bent on transgression. This has unfortunately become a problem not just of individuals and communities but also of the international community of sovereign states, in which might and right are often conflated and ethical norms are violated in the pursuit of self-interest and the quest to dominate. Thus, it becomes necessary to develop substantive ethical principles into international conventions and binding instruments. A substantive harmony between morality and law enhances the prospects of enforcement, and a disconnect between them weakens it.

Ethical norms are often rooted in religious beliefs. However, unlike religious beliefs, which could be exclusive of other religions, ethical norms tend to be shared between followers of different faiths across territorial boundaries. It is advisable therefore to identify commonalities in ethical norms of wider humanitarian concern that could, in turn, be transformed into legal principles and instruments of international human rights law.

Morality seeks to impose limits on people's freedom, often through integrating responsibility and obligation into the fabric of freedom. Yet "moral limits" need to be broadly understood, because ethical, religious, and legal limits often tend to converge and overlap in almost all major religions and legal traditions. That said, traditional ethics and religions are nearly all questioned by secularist modernity and science. Religious beliefs are also too well entrenched to readily surrender to the claims of modernity and science. Hence the controversy continues. Adaptation and change, inevitable as they are, are also the Achilles' heels of older traditions and ethics.

The globalized world in which we live should aspire to a globalized ethics that transcends political and cultural boundaries, just as the demands of globalization aim at penetrating borders and removing barriers to the outside world. Yet it is often said that weaker countries can ill afford to yield to the demands of opening their doors wide to the more powerful ones without subjecting the latter to a common code of ethics. Postmodernism, in turn, has questioned traditional norms, as has post-Islamism. Whereas ethical limits advocate restraint, scientific modernity and liberal capitalism are pushing humanity in the opposite direction. This raises a question that is perhaps more worrying: is there a crisis of values, and is the clash of civilizations real?

Morality and Law: Separation or Unity?

A quick response to the question posed in this heading is that law and ethics need to be unified in some ways and separated in others. When one speaks of integrity within the fabric of the applied law, one is naturally concerned with integrating a moral dimension into the law. Law is by definition the command of the sovereign that demands compliance, but it must maintain a substantive grounding in ethics for it to ensure public acceptance and support. Otherwise, a law that the public does not accept and considers to be unethical would be difficult for law enforcement agencies to enforce. When the nexus between law and ethics is disturbed, law is likely to become a dead letter. This is not what the sovereign authority, nor indeed the general public, want to see. Hence, the concern of conformity to ethical norms is a shared concern of the people and their governments. The coherence of law and ethics enriches social coherence. Law needs to have a grounding in ethics and ethics need, in turn, to have a grounding in religion. According to a global attitudes survey in 2007, conducted by the Pew Research Center in 47 countries around the world, large majorities agree that faith in God is a necessary foundation for morality and good values.

Law and morality in Sharia tend to meet and penetrate one another, as it is the moral rectitude of conduct that often provides the basis of its legality. Sharia is divided into three parts: dogmatic theology (*'aqida*), morality (*akhlaq*), and positive law (*fiqh*). This division also reflects the relative significance of each. In this order of values, *fiqh* essentially serves and implements, in practical legal terms, the dogma and ethical norms of Islam. In commercial transactions and contracts, for instance, morality and law tend to be either united or stand in close proximity to one another (Zarqa 1998, 1:46). Sharia law subscribes to the basic freedom of contract and permits stipulations in contracts that do not violate public order and morality. This is the purport of the *hadith* that "Muslims are bound by their stipulations, except for that which renders permissible what is unlawful or prohibits that which is permissible" (Abu Dawud, Tirmidhi, cited in Zarqa 1998, 1:57).

Islamic law also requires all contracts to be clear of fraud, cheating, and deception, failing which the law entitles the aggrieved party to the option of whether to ratify the contract. This is also the purport of the *hadith* that "harm may neither be inflicted nor reciprocated in [the name of] Islam" (Ibn Majah 1987, *hadith* 234). Yet another *hadith* states: "Acts are judged by their underlying intentions." In the event where the nondisclosure of material facts leads to the imposition of exorbitant harm in a contract, the contract is susceptible to revocation. Contracts are also to be interpreted, especially in terms of what they do not specify, in light of the prevailing custom. Thus, it may be concluded that the Islamic law of contracts is tempered by positivist considerations and the common mores and customs of society.

A substantive coherence between law and morality is maintained in the Sharia, as in many other legal traditions, although they may differ regarding how this coherence is articulated in applied law.[1] Important as it is, morality is not legally enforceable, because that is likely to impinge on the moral autonomy of the individual. As will be noted, three of the five value points in the Sharia scheme of values—namely the reprehensible, the recommendable, and the permissible—consist mainly of moral advice. Committing a *makruh*, omitting a *mandub*, and omitting or committing a *mubah*, when clear of abusive practices, is not justiciable before the courts. Even the obligatory (*wajib*) under Sharia is subject to certain limitations, as in the case of devotional performances (*'ibadat*), which normally do not admit of court litigation. Morality is not legally enforced for yet another reason, which is that people's perceptions of the philosophy or ideology they may subscribe to often differ on moral values. What is considered just and morally correct, whose need or benefit should be given priority, what is the extent of the required observance, and so forth are questions that may receive different responses from different philosophies, individuals, and societies. Whereas utilitarian philosophy considers the greatest benefit to the largest number as the criterion of a good law, natural law and natural justice theories emphasize the essential harmony of law with natural reason and natural needs of people. Pro-liberty philosophers such as Bentham, Austin, and Mill, on the other hand, maintained that granting maximum liberty to the individual, limited only by the liberty of others, should be the basic guideline of lawmaking. The religious traditions are on the whole strongly informed by morality but also by a variety of other considerations, as they do not subscribe to a particular philosophy as such (Kamali 2002, 133–4).

This also explains the need for a set of authoritative commands, or a constitution for that matter, that establishes the perimeters of enforceability.

[1]This may be illustrated by comparing the Sharia law concept of option of defect (*khiyar al-'ayb*) and the common law concept of *caveat emptor*. The former entitles the buyer in a sales contract to revoke the contract in the event of nondisclosure by the vendor of a material defect in the object of sale. Caveat emptor (buyer beware) entitles the vendor instead to nondisclosure of defects in the object of sale. See for details Kamali (2009, 243–63, at 251).

When this becomes the case, and when the public throws its support behind a moral precept, the latter is often adopted into law. Much of this can also be said of the Sharia concept of general consensus (*ijma‘*), which is a mechanism for elevating a moral or customary precept into a legal rule, or *hukm*, of Sharia. Whether one speaks of *ijma‘* or of a modern constitution and act of parliament, they all establish legal norms. From that point onwards, compliance becomes necessary, and a mere moral argument is not enough to overrule it. Yet from an essentialist perspective, it may be said that morality exists fairly independently of the law and does not need the formal approval of authorities for it to exist, whereas law can only come about when it is formally ratified. Thus, it may be concluded that law shows greater dependency on morality than vice versa.

Proponents of the positivist theory of morality emphasize the importance of pragmatism. The ethical value of a subject is thus to be determined by juxtaposing it with the living conscience of contemporary man, who is surrounded by a particular set of socioeconomic and geographic conditions (Masoodi and Dhar 1995–96). The common beliefs of society thus have a role to play in the ethical evaluation of conduct. Therefore, it would be less than advisable to apply medieval ethical perspectives to contemporary reality in total disregard of societal changes. It would also be a mistake to turn a blind eye to the lines of division between law and morality and extend the law to matters of individual conscience.

Sharia law is intrinsically duty-oriented: the notion of obligation or concern for the rights of others plays a more prominent role compared to one's own right over others. The textual sources of Islam emphasize duty, which has a deeper grounding in morality. Hence, Sharia's rulings on *halal* and *haram* (permissible and forbidden) and its perception of the public good (*maslaha*) or what it considers corruption and harm (*mafsada*) are strongly influenced by ethical considerations. In one of his renowned statements, the Prophet Muhammad declared that "I am sent in order to accomplish [or take to perfection] the virtues of morality" (al-Tabrizi 1979, *hadith* 5096). The Prophet interestingly saw his mission as taking to perfection the moral legacy of his time and not, as it were, to start with a clean slate. This is, in turn, reminiscent of many affirmative references in the Quran to the ethical norms of Christianity and Judaism (Quran 5:44, 6:90, 42:13; Kamali 2003, 306*ff*). Hence, I conclude that Islam endorses the ethical values of Christianity and therefore, to a large extent, of the essence of morality in common law. If there are lines of distinction between the two religious traditions, one may assume that these largely reflect the differences in cultural attributes, geographical settings, and customs of their respective societies. The basic code of ethics may, in other words, be said to be shared between the two traditions, but their positivist morality may have dictated a different course. In the sphere of substantive law too, many principles of Sharia and common law relating to the formation, types, termination, and dissolution of contracts and to profit and loss, negligence and trust, legal personality and partnership, et cetera tend to be identical or bear close similarity to one another.

Common law rules are generally associated with the concept of "private law," emphasizing its concern with the interests of private persons. In this respect, it is also similar to Islamic law, or *fiqh*, which has focused not so much on the relationship of the individual with the state but on relations among individuals. Thus, common law and Sharia both tend to be concerned more with private ordering rather than a top down system of regulations of a centralized government.[2]

Islamic Ethics: *Akhlaq*, *Falsafa*, and *Kalam*

The contemporary understanding of ethics is mainly concerned with judgments people make about right and wrong or good and evil, especially in relation to human conduct, attitudes, and beliefs. In the Islamic tradition, one finds several genres of discourse offering differential understandings of ethics. The term nearest to ethics in relation to personal conduct is *akhlaq*, or *'ilm al-akhlaq*, "the science of virtues," which speaks mainly of wisdom, courage, resistance to provocation (*hilm*), purity (*'iffah*), moderation (*tawassut, i'tidal*), and cultivation of desirable traits in speech and manner that characterize a good person. The related term *adab*—meaning letter but also courteous behavior—is concerned mainly with the literary aspect of ethics in the practice of for instance statecraft, business, *fatwa* issuance, and judgment. Good examples are Abu'l-Hasan al-Mawardi's (d.450/1058) *Adab al-qadi* (etiquette of judges), the Seljuk vizier Nizam al-Mulk's *Siyasat namah* (epistle on

[2] *Fiqh* leaned toward private law for much of its history, and it was only in the twentieth century that Muslim scholars extended *fiqh* to the public law of concern to regulate relations between the individual and the state (for details, see Masud 2005, 3*ff*). This characterization of *fiqh* does not include *siyasa shar'iyya*, which is an allied yet separate discipline that also has an older history.

politics), and a late nineteenth-century text by Ishaq b. Ali al-Ruhawi (d.c. AD 1200) titled *Adab al-tabib* (etiquette of physicians).

The more philosophical dimension of a quest for personal and intellectual excellence is explored in works of *falsafa* by writers like al-Farabi (d.338/950), Ibn Sina (d.428/1037), and Ibn Rushd (d.520/1198). These works bear the influences of Greek philosophy, that is then developed in relation to Islamic themes. Al-Farabi understands philosophy as a quest for personal excellence, particularly in terms of intellect and moral character. For al-Farabi, prophecy and *falsafa* are essentially one. The main difference is that prophets perceive truth suddenly by inspiration, while philosophers gain wisdom through long and arduous efforts. Further, prophets have a special ability to put the truth sought by philosophers in terms that the masses can comprehend. Thus, revelation is philosophy for the masses, and prophets become popular examples of moral excellence (Kelsay 1995, 1:442–3).

Kalam theology exhibits a different set of concerns, such as the nature of ethical judgment, free will and predestination, and the places of rationality and justice in dogmatic theology. *Kalam* is primarily concerned with the correct understanding of divine oneness (*tawhid*), the attributes of God, prophethood, and the hereafter, and the necessity of belief in them (al-Salimi 2017, 127). According to the Mu'tazili articulations of *kalam* theology, moral judgment is closely associated with reason. Thus, it is stated that God made the world to be governed by moral laws that have objective meanings, and endowed human beings with the intellectual capacity to grasp them. Reason was thus capable of making empirical observations and drawing ethical conclusions independent of revelation. Since humans have the capacity to make moral judgments and choose which acts to perform, prophetic revelation refers to these principles, and confirms, extends, and strengthens them (Nanji 1991, 112).

The Ash'ariyya maintained different theological/*kalam* positions. Its founder Abu'l-Hasan al-Ash'ari (d. 324/935) subscribed to total predestination. When humans perform praiseworthy or blameworthy acts, they do so by God's will. The only way for humans to distinguish good from evil is through reading and interpreting the revealed text. This textualist tendency underpinning the Ash'ariyya position prevailed and is generally followed by Sunni Muslims and mainstream *fiqh* scholars. Sunni juristic discourse assumes that judgments about human activity are a matter of discerning God's commands by employing certain modes of reasoning developed in *fiqh* and *usul al-fiqh* (Kelsay 1995, 444; Nanji 1991, 115).

From Morality to Law: *Usul al-Fiqh*, *Fatwa*, and *Maqasid*

The Quranic language is diverse and does not label or specify its value contents into categories such as *mandub*, *makruh*, or *mubah*, or *wajib* and *haram*, although these last two are often indicated in the text with varying degrees of clarity. It is the interpreter and jurist who extract specific rules from the text and place them into one or the other of the said five categories.

Usul al-fiqh establishes a hierarchy of revealed texts and expounds the rules of interpretation and suitable methods of reasoning therein. In his famed *Risala*, al-Shafi'i (d.205/820) indicated that *fiqh* provides guidance so that one who adheres to it will not go astray. *Fiqh* and *usul al-fiqh* also expound modes of reasoning on how and when moral precepts, rational concepts, juristic opinion, and customary practices can be elevated into the legal rules, or *ahkam*, of Sharia.

The Quran and Sunna are the most authoritative bases of moral obligation and are, in turn, interpreted, selected, and applied as God's commands and prohibitions by the respective juridical schools and scholars of Sharia. Makdisi maintains that Muslim books of law mostly express such formulations in ethical terms, using five categories known as *al-ahkam al-khamsa*. Jurists further set these categories in a dual framework of obligations toward God and toward society. In each instance, transgression was perceived in both legal and theological terms as constituting crime as well as sin. The jurists attempted to specify the conditions under which these could duly materialize (Makdisi 1985; Nanji 1991, 113).

Quran commentators and jurists—who obviously cannot claim a monopoly on truth—have nevertheless given the most faithful interpretation of the Quranic text, as Fakhry observed, grounded in grammatical, literary, and linguistic usage. This is however not the case for other ethical and philosophical writers. The theologians have relied, in varying degrees, on extra-textual evidence in their attempt to elicit the meaning of the text: Greek logic, Christian theology, and natural reason. The ethical and philosophical premises of al-Farabi, Ibn Rushd, and al-Razi (d.313/925) are often embellished by syllogistic reasoning that determines the conclusions they arrive at. Put differently, for the theologians, and even more so for the jurists, the sacred text is the ultimate arbiter of truth; for the philosophers, it is reason (Fakhry 1991, 2).

The five values of Sharia mentioned above are also not monolithic categories, as each have subdivisions, some of which may be more emphatic than others. Further elaboration of these is beyond our scope here, however (for details, see Kamali 2003, 410–55). *Wajib* and *haram* combine moral, legal, and theological contents, which may be the reason for the recognition in *usul al-fiqh* of the two corresponding categories of commands and prohibitions (*al-amr wa'l-nahy*) that can subsume both religious and civilian subject matter and are not always coterminous with *wajib* and *haram* (for details, see Kamali 2003, 187–202). The latter two, on the other hand, are often determined by the clear text of Quran or *hadith*, which secular authorities and governments are not authorized to originate or delete. Government authorities may, however, regulate how *wajib* and *haram* can best be implemented, through for example regulating the mosque and Hajj affairs (for details, see Kamali 2003).[3]

Under the Sharia-oriented policy (*siyasa shar'iyya*), lawful authorities (*uli al-amr*) are also vested with the power to issue commands and prohibitions for the best management of community affairs.[4] Thus, even within the said scale of five values, the ruling powers are authorized in the sphere of civil transactions (*mu'amalat*) to raise the recommendable (*mandub*) or that which is merely optional (*mubah*) to the level of a command, or to turn what is reprehensible (*makruh*) into a prohibition when public interest (*maslaha*) or morality dictate this. For instance, the second caliph, 'Umar b. al-Khattab (d.644 C.E.), restricted meat consumption, which is basically *mubah*, to three days a week during the year of the drought in Medina. The rules of *mu'amalat* are applied based on their identifiable causes, and collapse when their effective causes become absent. When a moral case is created for adjusting the law, then the law may be adjusted. For instance, 'Umar b. al-Khattab suppressed a ruling of the Quran on one of the eight categories entitled to receive the *zakat* religious tax, namely the *mu'allafat al-qulub* (influential people, not necessarily poor, nor Muslim, who had helped Islam). The Quran entitled them to a portion of *zakat*, but the caliph suspended it, saying that God Most High had strengthened Islam and that it was no longer dependent on their

---

[3] The timing of Friday prayers can be fixed at any time from mid-morning to late afternoon. See for details al-Qaradawi 2005, 73–6.

[4] *Siyāsah Shar'iyyah* authorizes legitimate leaders to make discretionary decisions in cases and situations where strict legality may fail to deliver equitable solutions. It also authorizes legitimate rulers to introduce new measures, procedures, and policies in the interest of good governance and justice. For details, see Kamali (2008, Chapter 11).

help. The effective cause of the Quranic entitlement had, in other words, ceased to obtain in the case of *mu'allafat al-qulub* during 'Umar's time.[5]

Some adjustment to the conditions and subsidiary details of Sharia rules may similarly be made based on *maslaha* and ethics. For instance, *zakat* was initially not levied on perishable goods, such as vegetables, or on horses that were used for jihad. Due to subsequent changes, however, these items became commercial commodities and therefore "zakatable." The moral of this was that wealthy individuals who owned expensive horses and rich merchants who engaged in the import and export of fresh supplies between countries should not be exempt from *zakat* while a person of average means who barely fulfills the quorum of *zakat* is liable to pay it.

In a similar vein, the Quran strongly encourages care for and cleanliness of residential quarters and the natural environment, censuring those who corrupt and pollute the earthly habitat of humans and animals. But the culprits get away with their wrongdoing partly because the Quranic dispensations on the subject have hitherto remained in the realm of moral advice. Now that issues of sustainability and environmental damage have acquired fresh urgency, the Quranic dicta on them may also be elevated to the level of binding commands: manifest harm to the environment that threatens human safety and survival on the planet may similarly be made the subject of prohibitions.

With reference to the permissible (*mubah*), as already mentioned, governments may impose restrictions based on *maslaha* or *siyasa*. Examples of this may include a ban on imports of certain commercial items, including staple food, in order to protect domestic industry and low-earning producers at home. The *hadith* quoted earlier that "Muslims are bound by their stipulations" means that Muslim rulers may initiate policy measures and legislation on environmental safety and the sustainability of natural resources. Another *hadith*-cum-legal maxim that was already mentioned, "Harm may neither be inflicted nor reciprocated," can also be used to turn moral advice into law when this is deemed necessary to curb corruption and harm. For example, one of the sultans in Malaysia declared in March 2018 that he will no longer accept token souvenirs

[5]Notwithstanding caliph 'Umar's ruling on this matter, it is generally seen as a temporary suspension not affecting the continued validity of the Quranic entitlement. In contemporary Malaysia, for instance, *mu'allafat al-qulub* assistance from *zakat* funds is now usually given to new converts to Islam.

when opening public events and conferences. It is customary in Malaysia to present tokens of appreciation to dignitaries on such occasions. The trend had, however, grown into giving pricey gifts as tokens. So, the sultan (of Perak, Dr. Nazrin Muizzuddin Shah) put a stop to a *mubah* activity for fear of indulgence in corruption. Next, in August 2018, then Minister of Transport in Dr. Mahathir's administration, Anthony Loke, also politely refused to accept two mobile telephones presented to him as a token souvenir by a local e-hailing company. He said he must abide by the government rule that "no minister or higher officer should accept gifts presented by organizers at any event."[6] In this way, an ethical aspect of conduct in an originally permissible matter seems to have quickly developed into a policy ban that may well lead to legislation.

Notwithstanding the difficult conditions that need to be fulfilled under the *usul al-fiqh*, general consensus (*ijma'*) was the principal instrument for elevating a moral precept into a binding rule of Sharia. Yet *ijma'* was too slow to accommodate society's ongoing need for new laws. That role has, for all intents and purposes, been overtaken in the modern period by parliamentary legislation. In his renowned book *The Reconstruction of Religious Thought in Islam*, Muhammad Iqbal (d.1938) acknowledged that under the Western nation-state model, there was little choice but to vest the authority of *ijtihad* and *ijma'* in an elected legislative assembly of Muslims, which includes Sharia experts in its ranks.[7] The traditional *siyasa* powers of the head of state in a Muslim polity have also been largely restricted and regulated by modern constitutions and elected parliaments, although the head of state remains the original locus of that authority.[8]

An instance of change in Sharia that took place due to a moral build-up against it was child marriage, which was permissible (*mubah*) but was either banned or circumvented through the statutory marriageable age, fixed by many Muslim countries at 16 for girls and 18 for boys. This was due to abusive practices of greedy parents and relatives, who often married off young girls for money and other questionable motives. Some countries later raised the age to 18 for both sexes but allowed the marriage

---

[6] *New Straits Times* report of August 22, 2018, at https://www.nst.com.my/news/nation/2018/08/403660/anthony-loke-declines-gift-event-organiser-stands-govts-no-gift-policy.

[7] See for details on Iqbal's views, see Kamali (2003, 256–7).

[8] See n. 4 above on siyasa shar'iyya.

of a person of 15 years old with permission of the court (Kamali 1985, 106–7). Similarly, the modern reform of Islamic family law in Jordan and Morocco restricted the husband's ability to enter a polygamous marriage, whereas Tunisia banned it altogether. Under conventional *fiqh*, the husband was only morally responsible to be fair in his decision when taking a second wife. Modern law thus elevated a hitherto ethical position into a rule of law.

An aspect of Islamic jurisprudence that has attracted renewed interest is the *fatwa* issuance function of *muftis*, which was not bureaucratized under the *fiqh* provisions. Any qualified Sharia scholar could issue a *fatwa* in a private case or an issue of public concern. However, the *fatwa* issuance authority is now mainly entrusted to official *muftis*, *fatwa* committees, and councils, although individual scholars are still able to give *fatwas*.[9] It is possible that moral advice is elevated into a legal ruling by virtue of such *fatwas*. An example of this is the number of *fatwas* on smoking in recent years. Whereas some *muftis* in Malaysia declared smoking to be reprehensible (*makruh*), others declared it as prohibited (*haram*) mainly on the ground of harm (*darar*) to life and health.

Historically, the *fatwa* has been one of the principal means of elaborating, expanding, and modifying the law to meet the exigencies of changing times. A *fatwa*'s efficiency is due partly to the fact that it consists of a brief response to a question posed by a real or hypothetical practitioner. Modern technology and the internet made that role even more efficient. *Fatwa* also acquired renewed significance because of new issues arising from the interface of religion and science, political upheavals, and the ever-accelerating pace of modernity. Conflicting *fatwas* are sometimes issued, as can be seen in countries impacted by the Arab Spring. Although the youth demonstrations in various parts of the Middle East were not connected to religion from the outset, religion acquired a prominent role later on and proved to be a "potent and influential source of legitimation" (Zulfiqar 2017). A religious value that presented a central challenge was that demonstrations caused social disorder (*fitna*) and were therefore forbidden. Other Sharia scholars maintained that in order to pursue freedom, justice, and human rights, the incumbent autocratic system had to be overturned. How could these conflicting positions be reconciled?

---

[9]Collections of *fatwa*s are often published in large volumes by al-Azhar jurists like Muhammad 'Abduh (d.1905), Muhammad Rashid Rida (d.1935), Yusuf al-Qaradawi, etc., on legal and religious, and medical questions and even state policy matters.

Egypt's official *fatwa*-issuing body, the Dar al-Ifta', issued a prohibitive *fatwa* on demonstrations and sit-ins to say that it was a legal obligation under Islamic law to obey the *wali al-amr*, a reference to the head of state (Raysuni 2013, 7*ff*). The Jordanian Muslim Brotherhood followed suit, although later adjusted its position to say that demonstrations were permissible. The demonstrators asked for Ahmad al-Raysuni's *fatwa*, and he wrote one entitled "The legal obligation to remove the Egyptian President and try him in court." Renowned Egyptian jurist Yusuf al-Qaradawi suggested, as was carried by Al-Jazeera Arabic (February 18, 2011), that the label of *khawarij* (lit. outsiders—referring to an early rebel movement) cannot be applied to protesters, because their rebellion is not with weapons but with their tongues. Therefore, nonviolence cannot be labeled rebellion (cited by Zulfiqar 2017, 472).

Moaz al-Khatib, former Imam of the Umayyad Mosque in Damascus, stated at the start of the Syrian uprising that "freedom is God's greatest blessing to humanity," and that "faith cannot be true without freedom."[10] Raysuni made the even more categorical statement that "the will of the people is an extension of the will of God" (cited by Zulfiqar 2017, 473). As can be seen, divergent *fatwas* were issued. They are persuasive opinions but fail to establish definitive Sharia positions, unless general consensus (*ijma'*) throws its support behind one or one is adopted into applied law.

Another principle of Islamic jurisprudence that became the focus of renewed attention in recent decades is the *maqasid* (higher purposes) of Sharia, which were traditionally overshadowed by the *usul al-fiqh* methodology. Now that the *maqasid* have been revived, they are also used as a source of reference for rulemaking and *ijtihad* in order to protect a certain set of values, namely of life, religion, intellect, family, and property. Thus, the *maqasid* can be used to justify elevating an ethical precept of Islam into a legal rule. For instance, education (protection of the intellect and religion) has been made compulsory in many Muslim countries for basic literacy and essential teachings of Islam to Muslim children. Child marriage has also been banned in many Muslim countries in order to protect the family against corruption and abuse.

In his book *Risalat al-tawhid* (*Theology of Unity*), Muhammad 'Abduh attempted to find a middle way between the Mu'tazila and the

[10] Al-Khatib's *fatwa* can be found at http//www.youtube.com/watch?v=nQJfz1DtSpk (accessed February 1, 2019).

Ash'ariyya on the place of moral intuition and revealed text in matters of ethics. For 'Abduh, moral intuition is sufficient to establish the first principles of morality that play an important role in the social and political life of the community. Morality is grounded, in turn, in true religion, since most human beings require the encouragement provided by "the promise and threat" associated with the Day of Judgment as an incentive to adhere to moral principles (Kelsay 1995, 444).

In Shi'i jurisprudence, *fiqh* also assumed first position among the classical genres associated with ethics. Shi'i *fiqh* considers reason (*'aql*) as a source by which human beings comprehend divine guidance, a position that distinguished the Shi'i approach to ethics. The Shi'i tradition is also distinct in regard to its understanding of the relationship between *fiqh, kalam,* and *falsafa*. In particular, its position on justice is akin to that of the Mu'tazili *kalam* theology in its recognition of rationality as a basis of moral judgment. When under Safavid rule in Persia, some Shi'i scholars (the minority Akhbariyya) advocated that the emphasis on *'aql* be reduced in favor of the textual evidence, the larger Usuliyya group maintained otherwise and prevailed in upholding the Shi'i position on the validity of reason as an independent source of judgment. In sum, somewhat like the early theological and philosophical schools, Shi'ism affirmed the distinctive role of reason in ethical judgment and law (Kelsay 1995, 445; Nanji 1991, 115).

Is There a Crisis of Values?

British historian Isaiah Berlin valorized the twentieth century in these words: "No other century can be compared to the twentieth century in its savagery, for the merciless slaughter people inflicted on each other time and again. That is the disheartening realization we must live with now" (quoted in Daisaku and Tehranian 2005, 143). Whereas the eighteenth century had a casualty rate of 50 per million per year, compared to 60 per million during the nineteenth century, this went up to over 460 per million for the twentieth century. Judging by the hit/kill ratio of weapons and military conflicts, "the new century might even be bloodier" (143). We have improved our technologies and engineering of death by design well beyond our moral imagination. It is time for humankind to make a whole new start: a deep spiritual transformation that can only come about by rekindling the vital role of basic morality that has been so severely marginalized.

The excesses of aggressive twentieth-century capitalism are visited most harshly on the weakest people and economies. Poverty, the arms race, environmental degradation, and other such issues are taking their tolls on an unprecedentedly large scale in a world where exploitation and aggressive profit maximization are seen as the "natural" workings of the market. The manufacture and sale of arms, sometimes to both sides of a conflict, become the mainstay of an economy that thrives on the death and devastation of conflict-ridden people, record numbers of refugees and displaced populations, and unprecedented terrorism. Two prominent economists argued that "economic crisis can trigger WW3," due mainly to an overreliance on monetary policies, fiscal intervention, and liquidity management (Sundaram and Popov 2019):

> Economic recovery efforts since the 2008–2009 global financial crisis have mainly depended on unconventional monetary policies. As fears rise of yet another international financial crisis, there are growing concerns about the increased possibility of large-scale military conflict. "Protracted economic distress, economic conflicts or another financial crisis could lead to military confrontation by the protagonists, even if unintended" (Sundaram and Popov 2019).

With reference to religion and science, modernists and secular humanists argue that modern science provides a sufficient basis for a global ethics of human rights and democratic participation. From this viewpoint, religion is at best inconsequential and at worst an obstacle to human progress; the free flow of ideas and free expression at all levels is imperative for unhindered human progress.

One can readily add here that there is more freedom now but also more social conflict and a clash of values within and among societies and cultures. It is impossible to feel calm in a society that only demands freedom of expression but is oblivious to its limitations. Is it not true then that a sense of restraint is good for social harmony?

Postmodernists negate the validity of any metanarrative, be it religious or secular. From their perspective, all metanarratives or teleological philosophies of history are actually or potentially hegemonic, aiming at domination and exploitation. A complex variety of other religious and secular worldviews present their own views of civility in order to develop an ethics commensurate with the increasing complexities of our world. Among them, one finds fundamentalists as well as mystics, totalitarians and liberals, Islamic communitarians and Western individualists, idealists as well as pragmatists.

One of the challenges facing religious leaders is to clarify how aware they are of the new currents, drug addiction, horrifying criminality, aids, and official corruption—should these not be the focus of their attention? Do they still want to be devoted to a ritualist Islam so confined, in Friday sermons and elsewhere, to endless reminders about prayer and fasting? How much attention are religious leaders giving to the issue of isolation, to youth and women issues? Our religious leaders have to decide for themselves how much of the male domination practiced in their communities is based on divine orders and how much has to do with outmoded culture and custom.

Salient Moral Teachings of Islam

Morality in Islam mainly originates in the religion and has developed within its eschatological framework, which makes the destiny of the individual dependent on what he or she does in the present world and on whether his or her conduct furthers or hinders Islam's guidance. With regard to the Quran's outlook on the "good" and "bad," Izutsu and Fakhry maintain that moral goodness in Islam is greatly manifested in *salihat* (sing. *salih*—righteous conduct), which signify ethico-religious excellence (Izutsu 2002, 236; Fakhry 1991, 13). *Salihat* consist of "beliefs" expressed in outward conduct. And so it is that the expression *alladhina amanu wa 'amilu al-salihat* (those who believe and do good deeds) occurs over 50 times in the Quran, stressing that religion—"believe"—and morality, "do good," should go together, as in the following passage: "Those who believe and do good deeds, such shall be the inhabitants of Paradise, to dwell therein forever" (Quran 2:82).

What this means is that "those who believe are not [true] believers unless they manifest their inner faith in deeds that deserve the appellation of *salih*" (Izutsu 2002, 237). This is, in fact, how the *khawarij* constructed their principal theological doctrine to say that faith does not materialize without "good deeds" and that one who commits a major sin also exits the fold of Islam.

On the other hand, however, the fact that in its typical phrase *alladhina amanu wa 'amilu al-salihat* the Quran uses two different concepts, *iman* and *salihat*, may be taken as evidence that these are in fact two different aspects of the religion. According to this view, which is that of the Murji'a (proponents of hope for salvation), faith is a state of mind that does not need any other element to exist, and that means that one remains hopeful even if one falls into a major sin.

But what are these "good deeds"? A basic answer to this appears to be given in verse 83, which immediately follows the passage just quoted and specifies five elements: to worship none save God; to be good (kind and benevolent—*ihsan*) to parents, near relatives, orphans, and the needy; to speak kindly to everyone; to perform prayer; and to pay alms.

For Quran commentator al-Razi, doing good (*ihsan*) refers to the kindness and benevolence that marks the conduct of good people toward their fellow men. Al-Razi then quotes several Muslim mystics who declared that "the perfection of the path to (spiritual progress) lies in one's devotion to truth and kindness to God's creatures" (al-Razi 1862, 392). In the language of Sufism, *ihsan* seeks a closer alignment between the inner dimension of the human person and his or her external conduct (Chittick 2000, 2–12). *Muru'a* is another overarching concept and summation of a personal trait that combines generosity, bravery, courage, patience, trustworthiness, and truthfulness, and describes a person with highly ethical characteristics (Farooqui 2005, 400).

Islam also commits its followers to compassion, uprightness of character, and justice. Islam's ethical code is rooted in Abrahamic ethics, which is the shared heritage of all monotheistic religions (Quran 2:130; 22:78). Humankind's capacity for wrongdoing is never to be underestimated; yet the Quranic outlook on human nature is that its inclination to good is greater. This essential optimism is sustained by God's expression of trust (*amana*) in humankind and his designation of a vicegerent (*khalifa*) on earth to establish justice among people. Other salient ethical concepts in the Quran are *ma'ruf* (good and approved, as in *qawl ma'ruf*—approved speech), *al-khayr* (beneficial, good), *al-birr* (right conduct), *al-haqq* (truth), and *al-qist* (fairness), which mean acts that earn God's pleasure and benefits humanity.

The Quranic principles of the promotion of good and prevention of evil (also known as *hisba*), cooperation in good works (*ta'awun*) among believers and wider humanity, and resistance against provocation (*hilm*) are salient moral concepts. *Hilm* is a composite concept that may briefly be defined as "the act of reigning one's soul and holding back one's nature from the violent emotion of anger."[11]

[11] For this definition and further details on *hilm*, see Izutsu (2004, 31*ff*). Izutsu has taken the definition of *hilm* from *Taj al-'arus* by al-Zabidi.

Human nature is endowed with ethical insight, as in the Quranic verse:

> And by the soul that We fashioned, and then inspired into it the awareness of wrongdoing and righteousness. Truly one who purifies it attains success, and one who corrupts it brings failure unto himself (Quran 91:8).

All humans are equal in the eyes of the Creator, and there is no recognition in Sharia either of the superiority of one over the other, just as everyone is accountable and will be questioned about what they do without distinction or privilege (Quran 15:92; 37:21).

Islam, Renewal, and Reform

The Quran proclaims that "God will not change the condition of a people unless they change what is within themselves" (Quran 13:11). This affirms the moral autonomy of the individual and group of individuals, who must take responsibility and initiative for a needed change. For Islam subscribes to the notions of *islah* (reform) and *tajdid* (renewal), especially on occasions when history and time detach Muslims from its essential values (Kamali 2013). In his book titled *Ayn al-khalal* (Where is the fault-line?), al-Qaradawi singled out the moral dimension of renewal when he wrote: "The most important aspect of Islam is inner purification (*tazkiyat al-anfus*)," in that "when the inner self of people changes, society changes with it, and so does the course of history" (al-Qaradawi 2004, 19). Then he added that yes, Muslims do celebrate religious occasions and festivals, fill sermons, books, and media with religious narratives, and decorate their places with verses from the Quran, yet "all of this does not seem to have penetrated below the surface" (19).

Islah, *salah*, and *salih* (pl. *salihat*) come from the same root. *Islah* in the Quran often refers to the general good of the people. The believers are thus called on to engage themselves in righteous conduct—*'amal salih*, which may consist of that which is good and recommendable (*ma'ruf*) or that which seeks to bring peace and reconciliation among people (*islah bayn al-nas*) (Quran 4:114). *Islah* may also consist of the eradication of corruption (*fasad)*, which is the opposite of *salah* (Quran 7:56). People's intention, and not only their actions, to achieve peace and *salah* also earns them a reward, for "God certainly knows the *mufsid* [agent of corruption] from the *muslih* [agent of good]" (Quran 2:220) and shall reward the *muslihin* and all those engaged in God-ordained work of benefit to humankind (cf. Quran 7:170).

Literally meaning renewal, *tajdid* applies to something that is known to have existed in an original state and then became overwhelmed by factors that changed it. When it is restored to its state prior to that change, this is *tajdid*. Jalaluddin al-Suyuti (d.911/1505) wrote that "*tajdid* in religion means renewal of its guidance, explanation of its truth, as well as eradication of pernicious innovation (*bid'ah*), of extremism (*ghuluw*) or laxity in religion." He then added that *tajdid* also means observance of "people's benefits, societal traditions, and the norms of civilization and Sharia" (al-Jazari 1983, 321). *Tajdid* originates in the authority of a renowned *hadith*, which states that "God will raise for this *umma*, at the head of each century, someone who will rejuvenate for them their religion" (al-Tabrizi 1979, I, *hadith* no. 247).[12]

A fuller discussion of this *hadith* can be found in the present writer's previous works (Kamali 2009, 488). Suffice it to say here that *tajdid* is intimately related to *islah*, based on the analysis that *tajdid* for its own sake would mean little unless it is ultimately aimed at *islah*. It is further acknowledged that *islah* often involves a challenge to the predominant religious, moral, and intellectual *status quo*.

General custom (*'urf*) is also a recognized source of law and judgment. Custom tends to interact with ethics and may moderate it in line with the evolving educational and cultural attainments of the community (Kamali 2003). Sharia may thus be said to uphold a positivist morality that aspires to people's consensus and support.

Changing Trajectories: Postmodernism, Post-Islamism, and Sharia

Diversity in ethical viewpoints and prevailing realities often leads to uncertainties. Whose ethics are normative, and is it justified to establish a context for ethical limits? Which culture, religion, or civilization does one choose as a basic framework for ethical limits? If one does make a choice, the question arises whether the boundaries should be wider and more

[12] Tabrizi's *Mishkat al-masabih* is a collection of verified *hadith*s from the six major books of *hadith*, known as *Al-kutub al-sittah*. For an analysis of this *hadith* and its significance to civilizational renewal, see also Kamali (2009, 51*ff*).

inclusive, such that they include followers of other faiths. Inclusivity is important simply because the network of relations among people cannot be limited by the boundaries of a particular religion. There is exceeding diversity, not only among the various traditions and philosophies but also within them.

Even within the Islamic world, Muslim countries vary widely with respect to their living realities, such that an observer is led to conclude that no response coming from one or more of them can be regarded as normative for all. The contentious course of events since the closing decades of twentieth century point to the same conclusion. Ethical questions can hardly be reflected in unified and monolithic responses. They must take into account the diversity of views and interpretations that has marked the Muslims of the past and those of the present. The postcolonial era has also witnessed reforms of Sharia law (Nanji 1991, 118).

International human rights law is in basic harmony with Sharia, as both subscribe to a moral vision designed to protect and promote human dignity. There may be differences in orientation in so far as Sharia stresses both rights and obligations and seeks to limit aspects of personal freedom. That said, areas of commonality and convergence between Sharia and human rights are predominant. Most of the applied constitutions of Muslim countries also affirm women's equality before the law, and the mid-twentieth century Sharia law reforms in many Muslim countries adopted important changes in support of women's rights. Yet, this is still a work in progress, but it is one that now enjoys greater public support (Kamali 2008, 267–78; 2017, 131–60).

In the contemporary neoliberal era, the Muslim world has begun to take a post-Islamist turn. "Post-Islamism," which is a subset of postmodernism in reference to Islam, has begun to question many of the prevailing Sharia narratives and has sought to replace them with alternative readings of the tradition. Post-Islamism is described as a new sociopolitical trend that entails a retreat from the idea of creating an Islamic state. Instead, it seeks greater accommodation for the rights of women, youth, and non-Muslims. It maintains that the only recommendable *jihad* is the one waged against injustice and religious persecution. For post-Islamists, capital punishment for apostasy was only for those who disdainfully rejected the prophetic message after receiving conclusive evidence from the Prophet himself. The freedom to convert to other religions is premised on the idea of exercising one's religious freedom without any coercion (Ghamidi 2009, 138*ff*; Amin 2016, 117). The scope of post-Islamist ideas and influence varies across the Muslim world and depends on numerous contextual conditions. Post-Islamism was initially observed in Iran, Egypt, and Turkey, and has now spread to much of the Middle East. New modes of electronic and social media also facilitated its information flow. In Husnul Amin's assessment,

> Pakistani society is now experiencing a larger trend of post-Islamism … enjoying institutional support and popular sentiment in some cases. Elsewhere it exists only in intellectual discourses and discursive communities (Amin 2012, 171).

The proponents of post-Islamism argue that Islamists' failure to establish an Islamic state has given birth to an emergent intellectual and social trend. Yet, post-Islamism, as Asef Bayat wrote, is neither anti-Islamic nor un-Islamic or secular. Rather, it represents an endeavor to fuse religiosity and rights, faith and freedom, Islam and liberty. It tends to emphasize rights instead of duties, plurality instead of a single authoritative voice, historicity rather than fixed scripture, the future instead of the past. It also tends to harmonize Islam with democracy and modernity. Bayat argues that the doctrinal text is subject to multiple interpretations, and thus the content of questions on Islam, democracy, and pluralism depend on how individuals find them and the social movements erecting institutions for them. Specific approaches to interpretation thus identified the Quran and Sunna as the only valid authentic sources of Islamic injunctions. Sunna and *hadith* have also been distinguished from one another. Unlike *hadith*, Sunna refers to the religious traditions of the Abrahamic faith, which Prophet Muhammad reaffirmed, after their adjustment and reform, for the community of his followers. The Sunna was transferred to us from generation to generation through perpetual adherence.

Post-Islamism emerged in many ways as a response to the static and anachronistic interpretations of "essentialist" readings of Islam, typified by Orientalists like Bernard Lewis, Bassam Tibi, Daniel Pipes, and Emmanuel Sivan, who assumed Islam was monolithic, immutable, and unchanging, with little attention for Islam as a living tradition. The Orientalists have been accused of essentialism and insensitivity to the change, negotiation, development, and diversity that characterizes lived Islam. Anthropologist Clifford Geertz's pioneering study *Islam Observed* broke away from the Orientalists in that it studied a "contextualist" Islam as it was actually lived and not as a single religion in scripture and text (Amin 2012, 172–5).[13]

Conclusion and Recommendations

The evidence reviewed in this chapter shows that there is a crisis of values on various fronts and also that there is awareness of it on the part of especially major actors, politicians, industrialists, and multinationals. The vagaries of liberal capitalism and its unconscionable exploitations, the incessant arms race, and the production of vastly destructive weapons of all kinds are not abating or showing signs of any impending changes. The environmental crisis, though widely known and publicized, has yet to find consensus-based solutions. America's unilateral withdrawal under President Trump from the Paris climate accord and the nuclear treatises with Russia and Iran point in the same direction, notwithstanding President Biden's corrective action on some of them. It is also too early to say whether actual policy changes are being made by national governments to actualize the outcomes of the December 2018 climate change conference in Katowice, Poland, on capping the temperature rise at 1.5°C. Oil-producing countries and companies are not even considering the adoption of environmentally protectionist decisions in their production plans. The moral inertia behind these hard-set attitudes is at once self-evident and alarming.

On a positive note, one may mention perhaps the selective post-Islamist responses, reviewed above, that speak of changing long-standing religious-cum-Sharia positions of great moral import. Important as they are though, these are not likely to have an immediate impact, and their adherents are also not major world actors of the kind who can curb the crises just mentioned.

Economic planners would need to center people in their agenda and make the eradication of poverty, rather than economic growth, the focus of economic planning. If one accepts that economic growth is necessary to combat poverty, one must also ask about its consequences, who benefits from it, and whether there is a limit to the costs that it brings with it. This will also require a reordering of the present power structures in governments, businesses, media, and education sectors such that peaceful coexistence and harmony as well as the common good of all become the driving forces of planning. The market economy is like a storm whose

[13] Cf. Husnul Amin, quoting Ovamir Anjum's (2007) paper.

intensity keeps right in step with the frenzy of consumption and acquisition. A certain reordering of priorities within family, community, and civil society units may also be recommended to achieve a fresh focus on social harmony and the common good.

The market should not be allowed to be the arbiter of its own behavior. The root causes of terrorism are fairly well known but generally ignored. The hotbeds of conflict in Palestine, Iraq, Afghanistan, Syria, Libya, Yemen, and elsewhere and their ensuing human tragedies continue to shock our conscience; yet, these conflicts are not finding solutions. Political and hegemonic agendas, a geopolitics of domination, power rivalries, and greed for material gain must give way to humanitarian causes, conflict resolution, and the restoring of peace to war-torn countries and communities.

There were suggestions in recent decades for a tax on international currency transactions and a world poverty tax. None has been taken up, however, because of the enormous power of multinational corporations and a general lack of political will on the part of governments to make any real changes.

A comprehensive moral transformation is called for to turn the tide of moral indifference and decay. Yet moral transformation is not expected to occur overnight, nor indeed in a big leap. It can only occur when there is widespread awareness, participation, and support from individuals, civil society organizations, and governments. Collective mobilization by the education system, media, government institutions, and religious and political leaders is indispensable.

Our schools and universities have a vital role to play in the creation of a new ethical basis for our common future. Skills and professional training are, however, not by themselves the makers of change. Educational targets should also include locally set targets for teaching the importance of ethical values, both through curricula and through encouraging youth to acquire virtues such as generosity, honesty, compassion, and a sense of justice.

The media is instrumental in the promotion of moral values to counteract cheap and aggressive individualism, admiration of wealth and status, and the lack of a long-term vision to curb irresponsible behavior. Excessive consumerism is a problem that needs to be addressed at the level of industrial planning, production, and marketing channels to identify practices that inflict harm on the living environment and negatively impact youth, family, and society.

Religious leaders need to pay attention to moral degradation, official corruption, environmental issues, and so on, provide practical guidance that engages youth, parents, and others, each in their own context, and make suggestions for how they can be active partners in achieving the moral transformation we all urgently need. In addition to mosque sermons, they could also deliver public lectures and participate in discussion groups and seminars at schools and universities, government centers, and civil society gatherings. It is also hoped that these institutions help provide suitable opportunities to engage with religious leaders and educators and then publish and disseminate the best possible outcomes.

References

Amin, Husnul. 2012. "Post-Islamist Intellectual Trends in Pakistan: Javed Ahmad Ghamidi and His Discourse on Islam and Democracy." *Islamic Studies*, 51, no. 2: 169–92.

Amin, Husnul. 2016. *Post-Islamism: Pakistan in the Era of Neoliberal Globalisation*. Islamabad, Pakistan: Iqbal International Institute for Research and Dialogue.

Anjum, Ovamir. 2007. "Islam as a Discursive Tradition: Talal Asad and His Interlocutors." *Comparative Studies of South Asia, Africa and the Middle East*, 27, no. 3 (January): 656–72.

Bayat, Asef. 2007. *Making Islam Democratic: Social Movements and the Post-Islamist Turn*. Stanford, CA: Stanford University Press.

Chittick, William C. 2000. *Faith and Practice of Islam: Three Thirteenth Century Sufi Texts*. Lahore, Pakistan: Suhail Academy.

Fakhry, Majid. 1991. *Ethical Theories in Islam*. Leiden, Netherlands: E.J. Brill.

Farooqui, Jamil. 2005. "Islamisation of Traditional Values." *Islamic Studies*, 44, no. 3: 391–409.

Ghamidi, Javed A. 2009. *Burhan*. Lahore, Pakistan: al-Mawrid.

Ikeda, Daisaku, and Majid Tehranian. 2005. *Global Civilisation, A Buddhists-Islamic Dialogue*. London: British Academic Press.

Ibn Majah, Sunan, ed. 1407/1987. *Fu'ād 'Abd al-Baqī*. Beirut: Dar al-Kutub al-Islāmiyya.

Izutsu, Toshiko. 2002. *Ethico-Religious Concepts in the Qur'an*. Kuala Lumpur: Islamic Book Trust.

Izutsu, Toshiko. 2004. *Ethico-Religious Concepts in the Qur'an*. First published 2002 by Islamic Book Trust. Reprinted Kuala Lumpur: Islamic Book Trust.

Jazari, Mubarak bin Muhammad Ibn al-Athir al-. 1983. *Jāmi' al-uṣūl fī aḥādīth al-rasūl* [The collected fundamentals in the hadiths of the Prophet], edited by Abd al-Qadir al-Arnaut, 3rd ed. Beirut, Lebanon: Dar al-Fikr.

Kamali, Mohammad H. 1985. *Law in Afghanistan: A Study of the Constitutions, Matrimonial Law and the Judiciary*. Leiden, Netherlands: E.J. Brill.

Kamali, Mohammad H. 2002. *Freedom, Equality and Justice in Islam*. Cambridge: Islamic Texts Society.

Kamali, Mohammad H. 2003. *Principles of Islamic Jurisprudence*. 3rd ed. Cambridge: Islamic Texts Society.

Kamali, Mohammad H. 2008. *Shariah Law: An Introduction*. Oxford: Oneworld Publications.

Kamali, Mohammad H. 2009. *Civilisational Renewal: Revisiting the Islam Hadhari Approach*. 2nd ed. Kuala Lumpur: International Institute of Advanced Islamic Studies.

Kamali, Mohammad H. 2013. "Tajdīd, Iṣlaḥ and Civilisational Renewal in Islam." *Islam and Civilisational Renewal*, 4, no. 4: 484–512.

Kamali, Mohammad H. 2017. *Sharia Law: Questions and Answers*. Oxford: Oneworld Publications.

Kelsay, John. 1995. "Ethics." In *The Oxford Encyclopedia of the Modern Islamic World*, edited by John L. Esposito, 442–3. Oxford: Oxford University Press.

Makdisi, George. 1985. "Ethics in Islamic Traditionalist Doctrine." In *Ethics in Islam*, edited by R. Hovannisian. Malibu, CA: Undena Publications.

Masoodi, G. Saqlain and Lalita Dhar. 1995–96. "Euthanasia at Western and Islamic Legal Systems: Trends and Developments," *Islamic and Comparative Law Review*. XV & XVI, 7.

Masud, Muhammad Kh. 2005. "Teaching of Islamic Law and Shariah: A Critical Evaluation of the Present Prospects for the Future." *Islamic Studies*, 44, no. 2: 165–88.

Nanji, Azim. 1991. "Islamic Ethics." In *A Compendium of Ethics*, edited by Peter Singer, 106–18. Oxford: Blackwells.

Qaradawi, Yusuf al-. 1425/2004. *Ayna al-khalal?* [Where is the faultline?]. 8th ed. Cairo: Maktabah Wahbah.

Qaradawi, Yusuf al-. 1426/2005. *Fī fiqh al-aqaliyyāt al-muslima: Ḥayat al-muslimīn wasaṭ al-mujtama'āt al-ukhra* [Fiqh for Muslim minorities: The life of Muslims in other societies]. 2nd ed. Cairo: Dar al-Shurouq.

Raysuni, Ahmad. 2013. *Fiqh al-Thawra: murāja'āt fi'l-fiqh al-siyāsī al-islāmī* (Law of Revolution: A Review of the Islamic Law of Governance)(Cairo: Dār al-Kalima, 2013).

Razi, Muhammad ibn 'Umar Fakhr al-Din al-. 1862. *Mafātīḥ al-ghayb* [Unseen keys]. Cairo: Matba'ah al-Misriyah al-Amiriyah.

Salimi, Yasin al-. 1438/2017. "Ḍaruratu taḥdīth 'ilm al-kalām wa mustawiyyātuh" [The need for renewal of Islamic theology and its levels]. *Islamiyyāt al-M'rifah* 90: 113–37.

Sundaram, Jomo Kwame and Vladimir Popov. 2019. "Economic Crisis Can Trigger WW3." Kuala Lumpur: *New Straits Times*, February 14, 2019, p. 15.

Tabrizi, Muhammad ibn 'Abd Allah Khatib al-. 1399/1979. *Mishkāt al-maṣābīḥ* [The niche of lanterns]. 2nd ed., edited by Muhammad Nasir al-Din al-Albani. Beirut: Al-Maktab al-Islami.

Zarqa, Mustafa al-. 1418/1998. *Al-fiqh al-Islāmī fi thawbihi al-jadīd* [Islamic fiqh in its new dress]. Damascus: Dar al-Qur'ān.

Zulfiqar, Adnan A. 2017. "Revolutionary Islamic Jurisprudence: A Restatement of the Arab Spring." *University Journal of International Law and Politics*, 49, no. 2 (winter): 443–97.

https://doi.org/10.1142/9781800611689_0003

Chapter 3

Sharia and the Capabilities of the Soul in Mulla Sadra's Early Thought

Rula Jurdi Abisaab

Institute of Islamic Studies, McGill University,
Morrice Hall, 3485 McTavish Street,
Montreal, Quebec H3A 0E1, Canada
rula.abisaab@mcgill.ca

Introduction

The discursive connections and tensions between worship (*'ibada*) as delineated by Sharia and piety (*wara'*) as delineated by Sufism have been at the center of long and intense discussions in Islamic society since the medieval period. Sufis have associated *'ibada* with the normative legal-moral obligations and prohibitions articulated by Sharia. They have depicted faith (*din*) as the true Islamic piety of the Sufis, the select (*al-khawas*) (al-Qushayri 1989, 300; al-Sha'rani 1993, 24–5).[1] Nonetheless, Sufi scholars have placed increasing emphasis on outward conformity to Sharia, especially in public spaces where they are surrounded by

[1] Sufi scholars also included a third category of believers, namely the select of the select (*khawas al-khawas*), that is, the Sufi masters. Abu 'Ali Daqqaq (d.405/1015) of Nishapur, the teacher of al-Qushayri (d.1072/465), noted that non-Sufis express reliance on God (*tawakkul*) and Sufis express surrender to God (*taslim*), while Sufi masters express relegating all power to God (*tafwid*). On the "commoners, laity" (*'awam*), see al-Qushayri (1989, 157, 190).

non-Sufis. By the late medieval period, it was unlikely for a Sufi master to validate the start of the Sufi path for his disciples before they acquired knowledge of the Quran and *hadith* and expressed adherence to Sharia (Bashir 2003, 77, 136; Hussaini 2011, 249–50; Karamustafa 2007, 38, 74; al-Sulami 1990, 52–3).[2] To be sure, the processes of empire-building under the Safavids, the impetus for religious homogenization (Matthee 2010; Streusand 2011, 143–45; see also Dale 2009),[3] and the integral role that normative Sharia patterns played in helping this premodern state achieve sociolegal standardization changed the Sufi scene from the thirteenth to the fifteenth century. Sociolegal standardization was conducive to greater administrative control and centralization. All these changes brought an increasing suppression of controversial Sufi practices, such as audition (*sama'*), whose nature and conditions have been debated by Sufi scholars. The outcome was not an elimination of Sufism, but decreasing patronage and socioeconomic support for the Sufi orders, the suppression of overt heterodox-messianic features, and the elimination of those orders viewed by the Safavid sovereigns as politically threatening, either through their mobilization abilities or political ambitions and alliances, as was the case with the Ni'matullahi Sufi Shia order (Pourjavady and Wilson 1978). The overall outcome was to push many Sufis outside formal public spaces of worship, hence increasingly privatizing their practice.

This chapter examines the relationship between Sharia, mystical wayfaring, and the attainment of Sufi *'irfani* (gnosis) wisdom, articulated by one of the most luminous Islamic thinkers of the seventeenth century: Sadr al-Din Muhammad b. Ibrahim b. Yahya Qawami Shirazi, known as Mulla Sadra (d.1640; on his life and works, see Rizvi 2019, 1–4). Born in Safavid Shiraz, he emerged as a major Iranian philosopher and theologian. He lived during the reign of Shah Abbas I (r.996–1038/1588–1629), which saw intense polemics—defense and rebuttals—of various types of Sufi orders (*tariqa*s) and doctrine. I delineate Mulla Sadra's views on Sharia and Sufi practice through one of his earliest

[2] The pattern depicted by Ahmet Karamustafa with respect to an early Islamic Sufi figure, Sahl al-Tustari (d.283/896), shows that before embarking on the Sufi path, he engaged in "severe fasting, and training in the Qur'ān and the *ḥadīth*." See Ahmet Karamustafa (2007, 38, 74).

[3] Dale's view that "Islam" was an organizing force in the Safavid Empire unlike in the Ottoman Empire is inadequate. His emphasis on Safavid "religious zeal" overlooks the many ways in which the Ottoman sultans and leaders of legal movements weeded out what they considered to be "unorthodox" Sufi Sunni practices. On the nature of the early modern Ottoman state and the ruling social class, see the crucial work of Abou-El-Haj (2005, 6–8).

works, titled *Kasr asnam al-jahiliyya fi al-radd 'ala al-mutasawwifa* (Shattering pre-Islamic idols: A refutation of Sufi claimants), subsequently referred to as *Kasr* (Mulla Sadra 2005).

Mulla Sadra praises the sages (*hukama'*) and the "authentic" Sufis against the corrupt or "false" ones (*mutasawwifa*). He considers the journey on the Sufi *'irfani* path essential for the cultivated philosopher who possesses special spiritual gifts and is hence required, morally and intellectually, to seek wisdom beyond the framework offered by Sharia (Mulla Sadra 2005, 76). Sufism (*tasawwuf*) and gnosis (*'irfan*) are interwoven, paired, or used interchangeably throughout *Kasr* as necessary mediums for attaining wisdom (Mulla Sadra 2005, 85, 121). Mulla Sadra attacks common believers who start the Sufi *'irfani* path without a knowledge of the demonstrative sciences or who engage in erroneous physical and spiritual exercises.

In *Kasr*, Mulla Sadra strongly recommends a strict adherence to Sharia for those who have not cultivated philosophical knowledge or been endowed with special capabilities that would open up the possibility of mystical wayfaring. The person embarking on this journey must also possess a taste for divine gnosis and mystical unveiling, which does not derive from applying the legal obligations and prohibitions of Sharia but rather from a profound attachment to the hidden knowledge about God and the intellectual-moral pleasure this generates (Mulla Sadra 2005, 123). As such, the Sufi *'irfani* path is a culmination of the philosophical path as it comes together with ratiocinative reasoning, resulting in human perfection. Wisdom leads not only to knowledge of God but also to self-knowledge. Ultimately, Mulla Sadra supports selective and private applications of Sufi exercises and rituals. He turns away from many of the public rituals and communal patterns of Sufism, which have been integral to Iranian piety in the last few centuries. Because he considers the aim of Sufi practice to be nothing short of attaining wisdom and perfection, he overlooks the diverse spiritual-social functions of Sufi rituals for believers from various walks of life.

Sharia: Good Health and Cure for the Heart

Mulla Sadra draws new boundaries between prevalent Sufi practice and Sufi-*'irfani* wayfaring. He separates the corrupt, "false" Sufis from the "true" ones.[4] As such, necessary to "cleanse" Sufism from many of the

---

[4]Even though some of the Sufi practices attacked in *Kasr* apply to the Qalandars, others do not, and thus show that he is not concerned with specific Sufi orders but rather with practices that cut across diverse Sufi circles. On the Qalandars, see Ridgeon (2010, Chapter 4).

ideas and practices that gave it a bad name. This approach, one must say, is aimed at saving and validating important features of the Sufi tradition. Only then can Sufism become the basis for "practicing" wisdom. It is the culmination of philosophical pursuits and the stage where one attains final truths.

Wisdom (*ma'rifa*), Mulla Sadra notes, has to be based on knowledge (*'ilm*), which is derived from Sharia. Like many Sufi masters of the late medieval period, he declares that a person who starts the spiritual struggle (*mujahada*) and physical-psychological exercises (*riyada*) before having achieved the knowledge of the primary acts of worship—that is, what is enjoined and what is prohibited by Sharia—has gone astray and is leading others astray (Mulla Sadra 2005, 62–3). He is beguiled into joining false Sufis and starts to beguile others (*ghawin mughwin*). When one engages in these exercises without having acquired the knowledge of the divine commands and laws (*nawamis*), one would achieve opposite results. Ignorance of these laws is not merely harmful to the disciple (*murid*) but has, in Mulla Sadra's view, a far-reaching destructive effect on friends, associates, and anyone attending the council of a false Sufi sheikh. It would ultimately extinguish piety in the heart.[5]

Mulla Sadra endorses emulation (*taqlid*) as the basis for protecting and preserving faith in Islamic society. Worship, he noted, is based on the emulation of the Prophet and the implementation of his commands as well as the commands of the Imams, his legatees. It is a safe path to salvation. *Nomos* encompasses the rules and regulations imparted to common believers through the scriptures (Quran and *hadith*) and through the jurists' delineations of the foundations of religion (*usul al-din*), acts of worship (*'ibadat*), and transactions (*mu'amalat*) (Mulla Sadra 2005, 62–3). All these rules and regulations furnish normative modes of knowing God as well as expressing obedience to Him. They are a protective shield against erosion of faith. Common believers who have not cultivated the demonstrative sciences or enjoyed God-given spiritual gifts, would cause their own perdition if they were to undermine *nomos*. They would be prone to follow false Sufis, gaining nothing of the knowledge of a true sage (*'arif*) while losing salvation (Mulla Sadra 2005, 45). As such, common believers must not rely on their own judgments or the opinions

[5]Mulla Sadra's audience appears to be largely male. Sufi *tariqa*s integrated and developed Sufi settings for women, some of whom appeared in biographical and literary sources. On Sufi women, see Silvers (2014) and Sultanova (2011).

of false Sufis in arriving at answers to legal-doctrinal and metaphysical questions. Rather, they must rely on emulation, that is, follow exemplary righteous men who implement what they were commanded to do by the Prophet and the Imams (divinely guided successors). They should not risk exposing themselves to punishment and hellfire (Mulla Sadra 2005, 45). There is a tendency among the weak-minded, he adds, to become dazzled by false Sufis and gullibly attribute miracles (*karamat*) and superior qualities to anyone who resides in the inner secluded niche (*khalwa*) of a Sufi order. Some also become impressed by those who utter Sufi statements while in a state of intoxication.

Mulla Sadra elucidates the idea of a safe path to salvation. He argues that a believer who, through emulation of pious men, repeats what s/he has learned without reflection would attain salvation, whereas fake philosophers and Sufis, who rely on their own logical reasoning or independent intuition, may act in disobedience to God. The Quran, he notes, encourages adherence to Sharia. He refers to Sura 21: al-Anbiya, Verse 23,[6] "He cannot be questioned for His acts but they will be questioned (for theirs)."

Mulla Sadra also invokes a rare *hadith* that had circulated since at least the time of the Shafi'i scholar Imam al-Haramayn al-Juwayni (d.478/1085), namely "*'alaykum bi-din al-'aja'iz*" (follow the faith of the elderly [women]).[7] Al-Juwayni appears to have made the following statement: "I declare that I will die following the belief of the elderly women of Nishapur [a city in northeastern Iran]."[8] The statement also appears in the infamous work, *Ihya' 'ulum al-din* (The revival of the religious sciences) by al-Juwayni's student, the prominent scholar Abu Hamid al-Ghazali (d.505/1111). He includes it in a section dealing with the prerequisites of Sufi self-discipline and spiritual struggle

[6] All quotes from the Quran are based on *The Holy Qur'an*, translated by A. Yusuf Ali, available through https://quranyusufali.com/2/, accessed March 10, April 15, 2019.

[7] Al-Munawi (1391/1972, 424). One scholar also traced it to the Prophet, where he had allegedly advised Muslims to turn to the faith of "the people of the steppes and women" if great divergence in belief emerges. Al-Munawi includes a statement that points to its being fabricated. Muhammad Baqir Majlisi (d.1111/1699), a prominent jurist of late Safavid Iran, included it among the weak *hadith* in his compendium, *Bihar al-anwar*, vol. 66, 135.

[8] On the notion of "the faith of elderly women," see also al-'Asqalani (1423/2002, 318–9); al-Jabrin (1419/1998, 65).

(Al-Ghazali 1426/2005, 961 and footnote 1. See also Griffel 2008 for more on al-Ghazali). The wording is as follows: "You must adhere to the faith of elderly women." It is a faith based not on thorough knowledge or reason but rather on oral transmission, which is how the elderly's piety is formed. It is also a type of faith nurtured through emulation and rituals.

The idea of a nonargumentative faith passed on without investigation, that is, "the elderly's faith," is seen as guaranteeing salvation. It is the faith of the naively moral who is not concerned or capable of knowing how or why an act is good. Mulla Sadra notes that the faith held by the elderly is described as suitable and sufficient for those who are debilitated by old age or handicapped to the extent of being incapable of walking. Symbolically, these physical impediments point to believers who are weak in intellect and personal capability, and whose comprehension is thus limited. They are unable to walk on the path of God or "seek knowledge about His angelic world (*malakut*) and the secrets of His power and the world of Dominion" (Mulla Sadra 2005, 107). Those who are blind like bats cannot take off the veil of the Sun either, because it will be the source of their punishment and ruin. They are advised to acquire and express their faith through emulation of upright persons in their communities, who impart and carry out the commands of Sharia.[9]

Mulla Sadra distinguishes between those who carry out their religious obligations methodically and those who, in addition to that, possess ethical values (*akhlaq*) and moral-spiritual capabilities (*mulkaat*) (Mulla Sadra 2005, 100). The "noble Sharia" urges believers to perform certain acts, which have been commanded by the Quran. Some examples of these legal commands are found in Sura 2: al-Baqara, Verse 245:

> Who is he that will loan to God a beautiful loan which God will double unto his credit and multiply many times? It is God that giveth (you) want or plenty and to Him shall be your return.

It enjoins believers to offer alms (*zakat*) and charity (*sadaqa*), but those who carry them out for the sake of conforming to Sharia would apply them merely when the conditions tied to them are present. However, the souls of those who go beyond these commands and feel morally inclined to perform them carry spiritual aptitudes (*mulkaat nafsiyya*), and

[9]For more on the aims of acts of worship and Sharia-based obligations, see Mulla Sadra (2005, 147–51).

their hearts experience spiritual-mystical states (*ahwal qalbiyya*) that are gifts from God (Mulla Sadra 2005, 101). These capabilities and states are embedded; they emanate from God, the Highest Principle. The believer has no choice or say in them, for her/his role is only indirect. For those who possess these capabilities and states, the promise of heavenly reward (*targhib*) and the threat of punishment (*tarhib*) in hell would be extinguished in the heart. Reward and punishment would cease to be the basis for performing these obligations.

Mulla Sadra evokes a long-standing symbolism of *shar'* (law) as a cure for the ailments of "the heart." The majority of believers cannot detect these ailments nor are they aware that they could occur when their ties to Sharia are cut, he notes. Those who declare licit what God has forbidden through the law are arrogant and will not obtain salvation. They say that "God does not need our worship. Therefore, it holds no benefit for us or for Him to pray or perform pilgrimage or give alms. God is too rich to borrow anything from us!" (Mulla Sadra 2005, 101). Based on this reasoning, they ignore how the infidels were depicted in the Quran, as in Sura 36: Ya Sin, Verse 47:

> And when they are told "Spend ye of (the bounties) with which God has provided you." You Unbelievers say to those who believe: "Shall we then feed those whom if God had so willed He would have fed (himself)? Ye are in nothing but manifest error."

Mulla Sadra argues that this verse and others show that among the infidels are those who utter the truth, for indeed God does not need or depend on the believer's worship (Mulla Sadra 2005, 101–2). Yet, the verse also shows that they were demolished eternally due to their truthfulness, which nullified God's commands transmitted through the Quran. The false philosopher (*mutafalsif*) who takes up spiritual struggle and mystical wayfaring without acquiring true philosophical knowledge will have the same fate. In this section, we see Mulla Sadra directing his criticism toward the more learned scholars, who offer rational arguments in support of discarding Sharia or ignoring Quranic commands.

Meanwhile, Mulla Sadra legitimizes individualized and selective paths toward wisdom. He argues that Sharia is like a medicine, a cure for heart ailments. God has provided clear proofs about the effectiveness of this medicine, but actual recovery rests in His hands. God is "the Principle of Truth," which is like a stream that flows and touches every living being in as much as it deserves (Mulla Sadra 2005, 102). Prophets and pious followers are likened to the doctors of the soul, and they hold the cure for "illness" caused by ignorance (66).

The path of mystical wayfaring is open to only the choicest. It is not, however, accessible or suitable to legal scholars, who can only derive the legal ruling (*hukm*) on a particular act, relying on linguistic analysis and the apparent literal proofs (*zawahir*) of the sacred texts (Mulla Sadra 2005, 107–8). Despite their profound knowledge of Sharia, such scholars cannot reach universal truths. The true learned ones, those "rooted in knowledge" (*rasikhuna fi al-'ilm*) who also follow the ideal pious conduct revealed by God and expressed by His Prophet should not discuss their inner revelations with these legal scholars, and anyone "muted by the muzzle of prohibition" (*uljimu bi-lijam al-man'*). It is for this reason that the keepers of Sharia have ordered everyone who is not fit to pursue wisdom to remain silent about that which they are incapable of understanding.

Between the Apparent and the Hidden

Mulla Sadra discusses the pitfalls of some of the major philosophical and Sufi groups who have, in his view, violated Sharia and/or reason. The Sufis, he notes, are similar to the esotericists (Batinis), in that they seek the hidden meaning of the scriptures (Mulla Sadra 2005, 70–1). They both rely on interpreting (*ta'wil*) the literal statements of Sharia to go beyond their apparent meanings (71). The extreme literalists (Hashwis), on the other hand, much like the members of the ascetic legal movement of the Karramiyya,[10] look at the legal rulings with their one blind eye, and thus see only their direct literal meaning (71). The esotericists, from the opposite side, ignore the applied acts of worship and mannerism entailed by Sharia and their literal significance. Both these groups are blind, in the right eye and the left eye, respectively. The true sage (*'arif*) has two sound eyes and can see clearly without the blindness found in the literalists and the esotericists (72). He adds that they do not suffer from the "eye puss" of the Ash'aris or the Mu'tazilis, two Islamic theological groups that emerged during the early medieval period (Madelung 1970; Robinson 1998; Schmidtke 2008). The sage is also free from the innate blindness of

[10] See Zysow (2011). This group declares that a literal articulation of faith confirms one's belief.

the ignorant, pre-Islamic pagans, and does not suffer from "itchiness" in the eyes like those who assign deterministic power to time (*dahr*) or insist on the preeternity of the world, namely, that it has no beginning in time (Mulla Sadra 2005, 73).

Through their complete reinterpretation of the apparent meaning of Sharia, the esotericists have destroyed it, Mulla Sadra notes (2005, 74). He explains that the mode of existence of the rulings, acts, and attributes found in the revealed laws (*shara'i'*) and divine commands (*nawamis*) are not an abstraction and thus they exist in and of themselves (*fi nafs al-amr*) (141). In another place, he thanks the jurists for delineating the five legal states of human action, namely: acts that are licit or obligatory or forbidden or recommended or abhorrent. These legal categories fall into the realm of the apparent Sharia (*al-shari'a al-'amaliyya*). These states, however, correspond to five others in the realm of the hidden Sharia (*al-shari'a al-batiniyya al-'ilmiyya*), which is of a theoretical nature (142–3). For this reason, committing what has been forbidden by Sharia is not merely a legal violation but also causes the essence of the self or soul (*jawhar al-nafs*) to become dark (142). As such, those who are in possession of their rational faculties and are at the same time legally bound to observe Sharia should not substitute its rules with anything else without a legal reason, and this is what is meant by legal "obligation" (*fard*) (142).

Mulla Sadra, as such, reformulates the conflicts that would arise between the apparent and the hidden Sharia by presenting them as parallel and not conflicting realms. Sufi rituals and embodied acts—which have, in the eyes of the jurists, violated Sharia-delineated purity—would have to be discarded. At the same time, he endorses Sufi states such as passion (*shawq*) and ecstasy (*wajd*), which have been at the center of controversy among legal scholars and theologians alike. He considers them essential features of mystical wayfaring.

Sufi *Dhikr* (Recollection of God) and Audition (*Sama'*)

Mulla Sadra attacks the commoners who, in his view, form the wider base of Sufi claimants (*'ammat al-mutasawwifa*) and includes preachers (*'awam al-wu'aaz*) and storytellers. He objects to their loud, melodious enunciation of Quranic verses and Sufi poetry, intertwined with a host of other rituals. He directs his criticism against a loosely-defined group of Sufis and public practitioners calling them "charlatans," using "ornate poetic phrases" to depict carnal love, the physical beauty of lovers, the bliss of their communion, and the pain of separation (Mulla Sadra 2005, 68). The poets, he adds, are enticers who have gone astray. He refers to Quran 26:224–25:

> And the Poets, it is those straying in Evil, who follow them: Seest thou not that they wander distracted in every valley? And that they say what they practice not?

The circles and councils (*majalis*) where poetry is recited, Mulla Sadra writes, are filled with the riff-raff (*ajlaf al-'awam*) and the gullible (*sufaha'*), whose hearts are stuffed with desire. He objects to the use of musical instruments in these pietistic activities and to the listening to voices of beautiful singers reciting the Quran or reading "love poetry." Mainstream Sufi orders have treated "carnal" or "love poetry" as metaphorical, functioning on a nonliteral level and standing for divine love but Mulla Sadra makes no distinction between various types of poetry and their symbolisms. He recommends that all kinds of poetry be extracted from the exercises leading to Sufi *'irfani* wisdom. Undoubtedly, poetry has been a dynamic medium, not only for mediating Sufi sensibilities but also for reformulating them. It has defied control and confinement due to its very nature, encompassing the symbolic, nonliteral, and also esoteric experiences. It has taken a life of its own within several pietistic activities and literary-social arenas, where mixed forms of social entertainment and worship are present. Mulla Sadra denigrates the value of poetic recitals in achieving mystical-intellectual knowledge, let alone a state of nearness to God.

The vocalized ritualistic Sufi *dhikr* is also a target of his criticism. He shows that it has appeared in the circles of "false" Sufis, especially commoners (Mulla Sadra 2005, 66, 68). Vocal *dhikr* is performed through a stream of repeated recitations of the name of God or phrases exalting Him, with the aim of concentrating on His presence within the soul.[11] Mulla Sadra writes that *dhikr* aims at knowing God and His attributes as well as the deformities and deficiencies of one's soul (67). *Dhikr* must evoke introspection, turning one's attention to one's imperfections and wrongdoing. It allows believers to realize their need to express gratitude to God and accept His divine decree (*qada'*) and destiny (*qadar*) (67). Ignorant Sufi claimants try to validate their habitual vocalized *dhikr* council on the basis

[11] On *dhikr*, see Böwering and Momen (1994) and Ohlander (2008, 222–5).

of *hadith* reports (67). *Dhikr* is not the vocalization of words glorifying God, repeated without reflection, for this is only a literal monotheism. He invalidates the embodied acts involving special enunciations and the eliciting of certain sounds and bodily movements during *dhikr*. He insists that such intellect-numbing *dhikr* is not salvific (66). *Dhikr* must be preceded by an advanced level of knowledge of the demonstrative sciences and a level of intellectual discipline. In many ways, Mulla Sadra's view of *dhikr* departs from most Sufi pedagogies of the period, where the repetitive ritualistic act of *dhikr* was seen as enabling the disciple to reach another level of consciousness and displacing habits routinized by normative patterns of worship. *Dhikr* is in fact the numbing of the intellect in Sufi tradition, because the intellect and logical reasoning are not in the realm of revelatory experiences. Mulla Sadra, to the contrary, emphasizes the wakeful and willful features of *dhikr*. It is useful here to note that his views come close to those of the Naqshbandi Sufis, who started to denigrate vocal *dhikr* and moved away from it without prohibiting it.[12]

The most severe attacks are reserved, however, for audition (*sama'*) and the integration of musical instruments, like the lute and oud, into Sufi councils.[13] In its basic Sufi form, audition is a melodious recital of Quranic verses and/or the singing of Sufi poetry with the accompaniment of the reed flute or other musical instruments, including those that elicit rhythmic beats. Audition may prompt vivid bodily expressions and movements and enhance the onset of spiritual states, such as enchantment (*tarab*), fear (*khawf*), and ecstasy (*wajd*) (al-Sulami, 1990, 373). Sufi masters and scholars went to great pains to delineate the specific conditions, attitudes, activities, and states that would result in an "authentic" audition (66).[14] As such, they specified the nature of the poetry and music

---

[12] On the Naqshbandis, see Le Gall (2005, 116) and Bilgrami (2005, 293–4). The example of the Sufi scholar Baqibillah Naqshbandi, who questioned ecstatic mystical states and expressed adherence to Sharia, is only one of many examples of this trend. See Ter Haar (1998).

[13] Mulla Sadra in comparison invalidated the rituals of these practitioners on the basis that they turned the exercises into occasions for seeking sexual pleasure and seeking outward beauty, turning to those persons who have attractive appearances (Mulla Sadrā 2005, 68).

[14] See also Hujwiri (1980, 237–9, 382–3) (d. circa 465/1072); Bakharzi (2004, 181–2, 185, 191) (d.736/1335–36). On spiritual exercises, audition, and *wajd* (passion, rapture), see also al-Ghazali (1426/2005), 739–80. On *dhikr*, see 348–60. On Sufi *riyadat al-nafs* and *mujahada*, see 929–4.

delivered and ways of preserving chastity, warning against turning audition into entertainment (*lahu*) or a mundane activity. Clearly, the debate over music and ecstasy did not emerge solely among legal scholars but Sufis and as such, the `ulama in general. In the medieval period, the term "'ulama" applied to a diverse group of scholars with a range of legal, Sufi, theological-philosophical, and scientific expertise, among others.

Mulla Sadra declared that audition, unlike *dhikr*, is prohibited categorically due to its enhancement of sexual desire. He noted that the Sufis themselves have likened audition to "burning coal" or a match that puts "the body" on fire. Audition, he argued, does not enhance spiritual qualities, because it excites unchaste emotions of commoners (*'awam*), and "the debased" (*ardhal*) and awakens their dormant desires (Mulla Sadra 2005, 68–9). These types of false Sufis "screech and experience rapture" (*yaz'aquna wa-yatawajaduna*) in a state of ecstatic love, claiming that they are expressing their love for the divine. He curses them openly, asking that God "[b]lacken their faces in both abodes" (the world and the hereafter) (68–9). It is important to note that the debate on the delivery of various Sufi rituals, particularly audition and its amelioration, seems to have unfolded in Sufi orders and among Sufi scholars themselves since the eleventh century (Abisaab, forthcoming).

Yet, the debates over audition and ecstatic utterances (among others)—which took place between supporters of Sufi practice, on the one hand, and the clerics empowered by the state, on the other—became more accentuated during the age of empires. Sufi orders that expressed little interest in social-political mobilization and that had, at the same time, maintained strong ties with the textual tradition and Sufi scholarship, appear to have fared better in Safavid Iran. In comparison, messianic-heterodox groups were suppressed, and the Sufi *futuwwat* were absorbed in Twelver Shia devotional spaces. The sovereigns considered the Twelver Shia Sufi orders capable of mobilizing large communities for religious-political action a threat (Arjomand 1981; Babayan 2003, 226; Algar n.d.; Gevorkian 2013, 8–10; Ridgeon 2010, Chapter 3). The departure of several Sunni orders from Iran during the sixteenth century and the displacement of their communal socioeconomic settings at the hands of the Safavid state did not mean that Twelver Shia orders would fare well. From the sovereigns' viewpoint, any order that had the potential of extending worldly dominion to the Sufi master, and hence become militant (like the Safavids themselves), would be a direct threat to their authority.

Finally, Mulla Sadra denounces ecstatic utterances (*shathiyyat*) such as declaring: "I am God," which some practitioners express when they experience Sufi intoxication and rapture. Through these utterances, he adds, they claim to experience a state of union with God (*ittihad*) and note that the "veil has been lifted" and God has revealed Himself (Mulla Sadra 2005, 69–70). He stressed the harm done to believers in listening to or repeating them. He discusses, however, the dilemma of articulating Sufi *'irfani* revelations in speech, concluding that it is not possible to communicate such revelations to common believers. One is only permitted to repeat the ecstatic statements of major Sufi figures such as al-Husayn b. Mansur al-Hallaj (d.309/922) and Abu Yazid al-Bistami (d.261/874–5 or 234/848–9)—for example "I am God, there is no God but He, so worship me!"—as part of an account (69–70). Al-Hallaj and al-Bistami preceded the rise of formalized mass-based Sufi practice during the sixth/twelfth century (Böwering 1989; Mojaddedi 2003).

Obedience to God through the Hidden Sharia

Mulla Sadra distinguishes between obedience to God (*al-ta'a al-malakutiyya*) through an *'irfani* form of worship and obedience to God through Sharia (Mulla Sadra 2005, 63–4). The former is founded on a particular type of knowledge, that of the First Truth (God), the Prophets, the revelations, and the soul. Certain types of spiritual and physical exercises are needed to cultivate this form of knowledge. They encompass the practice of true asceticism as well as listening to the words of sages being recited in the form of a great oration with eloquent style, especially with the accompaniment of suitable melodies (64). He does not provide any details about these melodies, and vaguely notes that the melodies operate through the forces of the self in their noble state. This prepares the soul to receive knowledge of the Divine (*al-haqq*).

Those who have not acquired the type of knowledge imparted by demonstrative disciplines/sciences (such as arithmetic and logic) cannot achieve Sufi *'irfani* knowledge (Mulla Sadra 2005, 65). These sciences are doors that open to heaven. Spiritual intuition derived from Sufi states must be anchored in logical reasoning (65).[15] Mulla Sadra evokes the words of al-Hallaj to assert that demonstrative reasoning is essential for

[15] Sajjad Rizvi argued that, in terms of method, Mulla Sadra emphasized the complementarity of demonstration and spiritual intuition. See Rizvi (2019). See also Ernst (2001).

the Sufis. He notes that, when asked about proof (*burhan*), al-Hallaj answered that proofs are received through the heart, so the soul cannot refute them" (45). Here and elsewhere, Mulla Sadra does not mention contemporary Sufi masters or founders of Sufi orders of the last two centuries. Most of his Sufi models and quotations are associated with the earlier period, when Sufism was not yet formally organized and spread out into orders.

The genuine wayfarer on the path of *'irfan* discards emulation as an assertion of his worthiness (Mulla Sadra 2005, 189–93). He engages in activities that nurture disdain for money and worldly power. But in order to implement and maintain attitudes of austerity and selflessness, the wayfarer needs a mentor to instruct him and guide him through the path. As such, Mulla Sadra builds on models of mentoring and spiritual molding based on the disciple-master (*murid-pir*) bond and student-teacher relationship present in the Sufi and philosophical traditions, respectively. A disciple, he notes, offers no resistance to his sheikh, spiritually or physically, much like "a corpse" between the hands of its washer (189–90). The sheikh would train the disciple to regularize habits of silence, hunger (*ju'*), and sleep deprivation. The latter wears down the body, that is, its desires, and clears the heart. Seclusion in a dark place causes further transformation. Mulla Sadra, as such, sees the importance of hunger in developing Sufi *'irfani* sensibilities and intuitions. Historically, forms of food deprivation practiced by Sufis have differed in frequency, quality, and intensity from the type of fasting enjoined by Sharia during Ramadan. Mulla Sadra considers them essential for enabling intellectual and spiritual unraveling.

These four features—silence, seclusion, hunger, and sleep deprivation—encompass the main embodied acts recommended by Mulla Sadra. They tend to emphasize an emotional energy directed inward, for the body seems to be stripped down to minimal expressiveness (191–3). He places major weight on seclusion and separation from others. It is in the *khalwa*, the inner secluded place within or outside the *khanaqah*, that the genuine seeker can find Truth (193). Neither *dhikr* nor *fikr*, that is, occupying one's mind with ideas of self-importance, would lead the wayfarer to Truth, because feelings of happiness, deceit, and self-admiration are antithetical to the pursuit of wisdom (193).

Conclusion

Mulla Sadra argues that a profound knowledge of the Quran and *hadith* as well as adherence to Sharia precede the journey on the Sufi *'irfani* path.

The worthy seeker who cultivates the demonstrative sciences and is also endowed with special moral and spiritual aptitudes turns to forms of worship that fall outside the normative framework of Sharia, and can therefore strive to attain wisdom. Common believers, however, who have intellectual limitations and none of the gifts—those capabilities of the soul—embedded in them by God must not rely on their own judgment. To achieve salvation, they must apply the commands of the Quran and emulate exemplary pious Muslims. As he delineates the physical-spiritual exercises that prepare the body and soul for mystical wayfaring, Mulla Sadra adapts significant elements of Sufi theory and practice. He emphasizes the centrality of the pedagogic-spiritual bond between disciple and master. What he rejects and what he accepts from traditional Sufi practice is equally significant, and thus, the picture that emerges from *Kasr asnam al-jahiliyya* is one of appraisal of the diverse Sufi teachings and activities with the aim of carving out the one deemed adequate for attaining wisdom.

References

Abisaab, Rula J. Forthcoming. "Sufi Habitus and *Shari'a* Practitioners in Late Safavid Iran." In *The Safavid World*, edited by Rudi Matthee. New York: Routledge.

Abou-El-Haj, Rifa'at 'Ali. 2005. *Formation of the Modern State, Sixteenth to Eighteenth Centuries*. New York: Syracuse University Press.

Algar, Hamid. 1993. "Dhahabiyya." *Encyclopedia Iranica*, vol. 6, fasc. 6: 578–81.

Arjomand, Said A. 1981. "Religious Extremism, Ghuluww, Ṣūfism and Sunnism in Safavid Iran: 1501–1722." *Journal of Asian History*, 15, no. 1: 1–35.

'Asqalani, Ibn Hajar al-. 1423/2002. *Lisān al-mīzān* [Scale's Beam], vol. 6, edited by Salman 'Abd al-Fattah Abu Ghudda. Beirut: Maktab al-Maṭbū'āt al-Islāmiyya.

Babayan, Kathryn. 2003. *Mystics, Monarchs, Messiahs: Cultural Landscapes of Early Modern Iran*. Cambridge, MA: Harvard University Press.

Bakharzi, Abu al-Mafakhir Yahya. 2004. *Awrād al-aḥbāb wa-fuṣūṣ al-ādāb*, vol. 2, edited by Iraj Afshar. Tehran: Dānishgāh-i Tehran.

Bashir, Shahzad. 2003. *Messianic Hopes and Mystical Visions: The Nūrbakhshiya Between Medieval and Modern Islam*. Columbia: University of South Carolina Press.

Bilgrami, Fatima Z. 2005. *History of the Qadiri Order in India: 16th–18th Century*. Delhi: Idārah-i Adabiyyāt-i Delli.

Böwering, Gerhard. 1989. "Bāyazīd Besṭāmī." *Encyclopedia Iranica*, vol. 4, fasc. 2: 183–6.

Böwering, Gerhard, and Moojan Momen. 1994. "Ḏekr." *Encyclopedia Iranica*, vol. 7, fasc. 3: 229–33.

Dale, Stephen F. 2009. *The Muslim Empires of the Ottomans, Safavids, and Mughals*. Cambridge: Cambridge University Press.

Ernst, Carl W. 2001. "Sufism and Philosophy in Mulla Sadra." In *Islam-West Philosophical Dialogue: The Papers presented at the World Congress on Mulla Sadra (May, 1999, Tehran)*, vol. 1, 173–92. Tehran: Ṣadrā Islamic Philosophy Research Institute.

Gevorkian, Khashik. 2013. "*Futuwwa* Varieties and the *Futuwwat-nāma* Literature: An Attempt to Classify *Futuwwa* and Persian *Futuwwat-nāmas*." *British Journal of Middle Eastern Studies*, 40, no. 1: 2–13.

Ghazali, Abu Hamid al-. 1426/2005. *Iḥyā' 'ulūm al-dīn* [Revival of the religious sciences]. Beirut: Dār Ibn Ḥazm.

Griffel, Frank. 2008. "Al-Ghazali." *The Stanford Encyclopedia of Philosophy*, Fall 2008. https://plato.stanford.edu/entries/al-ghazali/.

Hujwiri, 'Ali b. 'Uthman. 1980. *Kashf al-maḥjūb* [Revealing the Hidden], translated by Is'ad 'Abd al-Hadi Qandil. Cairo.

Hussaini, Sh. Kh. 2011. "Abū ʿAbd-al-Raḥmān Solamī." *Encyclopædia Iranica*, I/3, 249–50. http://www.iranicaonline.org/articles/abu-abd-al-rahman-solami-mohammad-b.

Jabrin, 'Abdullah b. 'Abd al-Rahman al-. 1419/1998. *al-Ta'liqāt al-zakiyya 'alā al-'aqīda al-wāsiṭiyya* [The Pure Commentaries on Ibn Taymiyya's treatise, "Illuminating the Creed for Radiyy al-Dīn al-Wāsiṭī"], vol. 1. Riyāḍ: Dār al-Waṭan.

Karamustafa, Ahmet T. 2007. *Sufism: The Formative Period*. Berkeley: University of California Press.

Le Gall, Dina. 2005. *A Culture of Sufism: Naqshbandīs in the Ottoman World, 1450–1700*. New York: SUNY Press.

Madelung, Wilferd. 1970. "Imamism and Muʿtazilite Theology." In *Le Shîʿisme imâmite*, edited by Toufic Fahd, 13–30. Paris: Press Universitaires de France.

Majlisi, Muhammad Baqir. 1403/1983. *Biḥār al-anwār al-jāmi'a li-durar akhbār al-a'immat al-aṭhār* [Seas of Lights: Collection of Pearls from the Reports of the Pure Imams], edited by Ibrahim al-Mayaniji and Muhammad al-Baqir al-Bahbudi, vol. 66. Beirut: Iḥyā' al-Turāth al- 'Arabī.

Matthee, Rudi. 2010. "Was Safavid Iran an Empire?" *Journal of the Economic and Social History of the Orient*, 53, nos. 1–2: 233–65.

Mojaddedi, Jawid. 2003. "Abu'l-Mogīt Ḥosayn al-Ḥallāj." *Encyclopedia Iranica*, vol. 11, fasc. 6: 589–92.

Mulla Sadra. 2005. *Kasr aṣnām al-jāhiliyya fī al-radd 'alā al-mutaṣawwifa* [Shattering the Idols of Ignorance: A Refutation of Sufi Claimants], edited by H. al-Ṭaqsh. Beirut: Ma`had al-Ma`ārif al-Ḥikamiyya.

Munawi, ʻAbd al-Ra'uf Muhammad al-. 1391/1972. *Fayḍ al-qadīr: Sharḥ al-jāmi' al-ṣaghīr min aḥādīth al-bashīr al-nadhīr* [Abundance of the Almighty: Commentary on the Small Collection of the Prophet's Hadith], vol. 1. Beirut: Dār al-Maʻrifa.

Ohlander, Erik S. 2008. *Sufism in an Age of Transition: 'Umar al-Suhrawardī and the Rise of the Islamic Mystical Brotherhoods*. Leiden: Brill.

Pourjavady, Nasrollah, and Peter L. Wilson. 1978. *King of Love: The Poetry and History of the Niʻmatullāhī Sufi Order*. Tehran: Imperial Iranian Academy of Philosophy.

Qushayri, Abū al-Qāsim al-. 1989. *Al-Risāla al-Qushayriyya* [Al-Qushayri's epistle], edited by Maḥmūd b. al-Sharīf. Cairo.

Ridgeon, Lloyd. 2010. *Morals and Mysticism in Persian Sufism: A History of Sufi-Futuwwat in Iran*. London: Routledge.

Rizvi, Sajjad. 2019. "Mulla Sadra." *Stanford Encyclopedia of Philosophy*, 1–42. https://plato.stanford.edu/entries/mulla-sadra/. First published Tuesday, June 9, 2009; substantive revision February 5, 2019.

Robinson, Neal. 1998. "Ash'ariyya and Mu'tazila." In *Islamic Philosophy: From the Routledge Encyclopedia of Philosophy*, general editor Edward Craig, subject editor, Oliver Leaman. Cambridge: Routledge. http://www.muslimphilosophy.com/ip/rep/H052.

Schmidtke, Sabine. 2008. "Jobbā'i." *Encyclopedia Iranica*, vol. 14, fasc. 6: 666–72.

Sha'rani, ʿAbd al-Wahhāb al-. 1993. *Lawāqiḥ al-anwār al-qudsiyya fī bayān al-ʿuhūd al-muḥammadiyya [Winds of Sacred Lights: Revealing Muhammadan Pledges]*, edited by M. A. al-Idlibī. Aleppo, Syria.

Silvers, Laury. 2014. "Early Pious, Mystic Sufi Women." In *The Cambridge Companion to Sufism*, edited by Llyod Ridgeon, 24–52. Cambridge: Cambridge University Press.

Streusand, Douglas E. 2011. *Islamic Gunpowder Empires: Ottomans, Safavids, and Mughals*. Boulder: Westview Press.

Sulami, Abu ʿAbd al-Rahmān al-. 1990. *Ādāb al-ṣuḥba* [The proper ways of companionship], edited by M. F. al-Sayyid. Egypt: Tanta.

Sultanova, Razia. 2011. *From Shamanism to Sufism: Women, Islam, and Culture in Central Asia*. London: IB Tauris.

Ter Haar, J. G. J. 1998. "Bāqībellāh Naqšbandī." *Encyclopedia Iranica*, vol. 3, fasc. 7: 728–9.

Zysow, Aaron. 2011. "Karrāmiyya." *Encyclopedia Iranica*, vol. 15, fasc. 6: 590–601.

https://doi.org/10.1142/9781800611689_0004

Chapter 4

Islamic and Christian Theology in Legal Hermeneutics: In Search of a Theology of Law

Julio César Muñiz Pérez

UNED, Faculty of Law, Calle del Obispo Trejo, 2, 28040 Madrid, Spain
juliocesar.muniz@der.uned.es

Introduction

This chapter strives to articulate the importance of religious categories in legal hermeneutics. Over time, the close connection between theology and law, which constitutes a historical phenomenon, has mutated. The many schools of law, particularly Islamic schools, coupled with the unique development of the various sources in different territories have complicated this connection even more. Researching comparative law establishes as many multiple artists as it does historic, economic, social, and cultural constraints. A detailed review exceeds our proposal; thus, this work has been limited to abstractly considering those institutions based on Quranic and Biblical sources, notwithstanding more specific examples expressing the importance of the connection between both categories.

Our starting point is the importance of the religious element and how dogma[1] affects society. Generally, this is studied from the scope of other social sciences such as history or sociology and then applied to the legal field. However, it is precisely in the current legal framework of Western society where this statement is least frequently encountered. The fundamental purpose of our work lies in reclaiming the importance of theological elements when facing comparative law studies and the serious interpretive difficulties encountered by judiciary officials (for example, judges and courts) as they fail to take this factor into consideration. This factor is especially important for relationships between Christian-based legal systems and those of Islamic origin, all of which derive from the theological roots of their institutions. A number of noteworthy examples are presented herein to show the religious roots of certain legal systems and identify the nexus between both realms, as well as their implications.

Theology and Law

The interconnection between theology and law is, in many cases, not only unknown to most Western-style legal systems but also underestimated and even denied. Today's jurists are usually overly concerned with the most recent jurisprudence and the latest legislative mandates. Undoubtedly, this phenomenon is motivated by modern judicial dynamics and the general secularization of Western society. On the other hand, expressing this connection also involves the risk of being biased or indoctrinating. In all truth, most authors who study the "theology of law" are, to a greater or lesser degree, linked to the field of "believers." However, it is equally true that religious rules and major religious texts repeatedly tend to discuss the legal reality. This treatment is what leads to sacred texts being considered "standard rules of faith and life" (Artola and Sánchez Caro 1989, 64).

Western civilization faces a progressive loss of contact between the legal order and its theological source. Berman (1997) provides an "extravagant example" that shows to what extent these orders maintain categories of a religious origin despite having lost all contact with their theological sources. He states:

> If a sane man is convicted of murder and sentenced to death, but prior to serving his sentence he becomes insane, his execution shall be

[1] Dogma is understood as a set of undisputed beliefs that are mandatory for the followers of a given religion.

> delayed until he recovers his sanity. In general, this is established law in Western countries as it is in many other nations. Why? The historic response in Western society is that if you execute a man while he is insane, he will be denied the opportunity to freely confess his sins to then receive the Holy Sacrament of Communion. The prisoner should be allowed to recuperate his sanity before he dies so that his soul is not condemned to eternal flame; thus, he may atone for his sins in Purgatory and finally, on Judgment Day, he may enter the Kingdom of Heaven. However, in a place where this line of thought is not standard belief, then why keep an insane man alive until he recovers to then execute him? (Berman 1997, 177–8)

Clearly, this interconnection has a historical origin. All sacred book-based religions express strong legal content. The Torah is configured as people's consultation with God (Isaiah 8:20; Jeremiah 2:8; 18:18); normatively, Deuteronomy—regarding *mishpatim* or custom law (Deuteronomy 8:11)—is equivalent to the Torah (Isaiah 51:4), the Decalogue (Deuteronomy 5), the *piqqudim* (Samos 118:4.15.27), and the *miswot* or commandments (Exodus 15:26) together with the *huqqim* or written precepts (Exodus 12:24).[2] This legal aspect leads to the tendency toward these foundation texts being written, thus linking them to the belief of faithful communities in the triple value of the Word being true, revelation, and the norm (Artola and Sánchez Caro 1989, 44). That is precisely why the Bible and the Quran were drafted in writing. In the case of the Bible, the various versions, with the correlative effort to unify texts, has a hermeneutic reasoning, among other aspects. In the case of the Quran, there have been no variations since it was originally compiled under the rule of Caliph Osman.

From the perspective of the phenomenology of religion, prior oral tradition is a constant, even when the timeline is reduced, as in the case of Islam. Thus, Zoroastrianism constitutes its Avesta under the Persian Sassanian Kings in the sixth and seventh centuries AD. Buddhists have the texts of Ashoka, all of which have staunch legal implications. Christianity quickly faced the systematic study of sacred texts, which generated theology as a discipline.

It is from this connection with the legal phenomenon that the expression "theology of law" arises, as pointed out by authors such as Rouco

[2] Cf. McKenzie (1960, 202–5).

Varela (1967). The revelatory nature of the religious text shows an unchangeable and static tendency, one that is dogmatically free of historical events. This is why authors such as Coulson (1998, 11) point out the traditional vision (overcome today) that "the notion of the historic process in law was fully alien to classic Islamic jurisprudence." This notion comes from a Christian conception, while Islam expresses greater dynamics in the derivation of legal regulations from religious texts by means of methods known as *ijtihad*.[3] Both the legislation established by the Prophet, and after his death by his companions, known as *Sahaba*, was recognized by the legal schools by means of *Fiqh* (jurisprudence or doctrine). However, this "ideal law" has to be interpreted and applied in and for changing categories. This interpretation and adaptation is expressed both in Christian history—for example in the Reformation and the corresponding Counter-Reformation[4]—and in the modern-day Islamic legal schools of thought, which understand the will of God expressed in the Quran as general principles that allow for interpretations and applications according to the historical circumstances of the moment.

The problem with these religious notions is that independently of subjects' lack of knowledge, they influence them in a more or less conscious manner. In fact, we can track the ties with legal hermeneutics using theology itself, as well as the endeavors to establish the text. Traditionally, historical epistemology is usually demoted to a subsidiary or subordinate role and with that, the role of legal epistemology is mediated by the prevailing theological, religious and historical categories in society. As Gadamer (1999, 599) pointed out, hermeneutics, as a discipline, was specifically taken into consideration in biblical studies to ponder legal hermeneutics as the primary typology through which the rules would be obtained to cover gaps in enacted law, with enacted law. Hermeneutics has a legislative nature because of its creative applicability to updating law.

Thanks to hermeneutics, it is not at all surprising to see the link between dogma and law, given that hermeneutics has played an

---

[3]According to al-Alwani (1994, 3), it is a rational interpretation system of Islamic legal (*fiqh*) sources (*usul*) to establish jurisprudence that provides solutions for the application of the Sharia.

[4]Readers should note that the term Reformation implies the return to the original form; in other words, the desire to return to the original message of Christ, which was understood to have been historically undermined.

extremely relevant role in theology and jurisprudence (together with historical-philosophical science). Berman (1997) states that there are similarities between jurisprudence and theology stemming from the connection between legal institutions and theological doctrines. Thus, theology creates the basis for legal institutions. In fact, the fundamental objective of this work lies in associating the respective theological fundaments of certain legal institutions with secular legal systems by comparing the differences and similarities between Islamic and Christian traditions.

In terms of methodology, hermeneutics gains momentum with the work of such authors as Larenz and Engisch (1953). It all develops from the assessment of historical objectivism so that the theological categories may be approached from a global perspective, without any theological purposes. In methodological terms, I seek to position myself in a more balanced position between the objective and the subjective element of all understanding (as did Betti 1955, even if in the end he fell into subjectivism), while at the same time being aware of its difficulties. When analyzing law (as with all other hermeneutics), the person analyzing extrapolates his/her own bias, social environment, historical tradition, etc. This problem is especially dangerous when trying to apply or analyze the standards of other states, chiefly those arising from different religious cultures and traditions. Each of these traditions implies the configuration of a series of values that have obtained an increasingly greater status throughout biblical/Quranic tradition, to then filter down into society as its own values and characteristics.

Legal Institutions

Let us now analyze some of the influential manifestations of religious dogma in legal institutions. In general, it is much easier to identify the influence of the religious categories in civil law categories, where persisting categories of religious sets of law are frequently seen, whether due to their historical integration into the source system or due to the expansion of the principle of autonomous free will. The influence of dogma also extends to other aspects of public law, such as the reasoning behind sentencing or the political system. This influence is best understood by delving into religious sources and analyzing their more or less perfect transposition into the governmental legal sphere. With this in mind, I focus on the Bible and the patristic exegesis for the Christian perspective and on the Quran and the legal institutions[5] typically found in Muslim law for the Islamic perspective.

Theology and sovereignty

One of the spheres of civil law with greatest relevance to dogma refers to the conception and function that the religious body grants the state. At this point, we must consider that the methodology places us within the scope of conceptual history, or *Begriffsgeschichte* (Koselleck 1983). I must therefore count on a traditional critique: the difficult task of aligning modern notions with historical realities and very diverse concepts. Thus, I use the word sovereignty and even state, although this latter concept appeared in the sixteenth century with Machiavelli; as such it was inexistent when biblical and Quranic texts were written.

In Christianity, there are various constructions regarding the concept of sovereignty and the progressive and necessary relationship between church and state. This aspect is conditioned by the initial development of Christianity coexisting with the Roman Empire, which led to the formulation of various doctrines—ranging from the identification of the church and the Empire through the doctrine of Augustinian *Civitas Dei* through the doctrine of the two swords (*utrumque gladium*) in medieval times.

Islam did not develop in a context of being submitted to sovereignties outside of it, which determined its configuration: without a general separation of religious and civil spheres. The four Sunni legal schools coincide on the nature and characteristics of political sovereignty. With the doctrine of the caliphate (based essentially on authority and charismatic nature), two minority groups failed to support this transfer of power. On the one hand, Shia Islam came to accept the divine nature of sovereignty,[6] while the Khawarij, on the other extreme, maintained the election of rulers. In this regard, the notion of sovereignty would coincide with the concept of *wilaya* as "sovereign power" or "power delegated by the sovereign." Nevertheless, it does contain certain features that could identify it with the concept of *imperium* (in addition to its civil use in the sense of "guardianship" of a minor). "Sovereignty" appears early on with an ecumenical

---

[5]Legal institution as defined by the historic School of Law and by Friedrich Carl von Savigny (1878).

[6]In Twelver Shia Islam, *wilaya* is the authority invested in the Prophet and the Prophet's family (*ahl al-bayt*) as the representatives of God on Earth.

power. I need not forsake the similarities of this configuration during the caliphate with the ecumenical notion that appears in the Roman Empire with Constantine and the Council of Nicea, from which similar political categories (Roman and Islamic) arose to assimilate political power with the religious factor, with the first of these being configured as universal (or ecumenical). In fact, this conclusion is shared by Milliot and Blanc (1987, 60–1). These authors indicated how the universal caliphate, which more than a reality was a speculation of theologians-jurists, was accepted by European diplomacy, which used it to find a way to centralize relationships with the Muslim world "comparable to the Roman Pontificate and recognizing it as a jurisdiction and spiritual supremacy in Islam." Admittedly, as Hana Jalloul Muro (2016, 300) pointed out, classic Sunni Islamic doctrine granted the caliphate both spiritual and political authority. However, this was only the case with the first four Caliphs, with thought-provoking, self-appointed *Julafa Rasul Alla*[7] as the vicars of God's Prophet. Successive rulers would have executive and religious, but not spiritual power. The only exception was the *mihna* or inquisition, which lasted fifteen years under the Abbasid caliphate.

To exemplify this comparative process (between theological structure and secular law), the Treaty of Kuchuk-Kainarji, signed in 1774 between the Russian and Ottoman Empires, has been used. Said treaty differentiates between two types of authority in the sultan: one religious (it protects Muslims living in the territories granted to Russia) and another more temporal, in evident concomitance with medieval Christian development and the theory of two swords. Is this evolution specific to Islam, analogous to Christianity, or an interpretation imported from Christian theological categories (in the case of Russia) and foreign to the authentic Islamic tradition? Whatever is the case, these categories seem to be merged, given that at a later date, Sultan Abd Al-Hamid adopted the title of the official "protector of the Islamic world" in the 1876 Ottoman Constitution. Equally linked to the Ottoman Empire was the Khilafat Movement in India. This movement could be considered the confirmation of this ecumenical idea of the caliphate once the Ottoman Empire had fallen and as a restoration movement in itself. Obviously, and as with the ecumenical conception of the Western church, this universal sovereignty of an ecumenical empire is more theological hope than a reality.

[7] *Julafa* here means *khulafa* (Caliphs).

Given the complexity of this sphere, a detailed study of proper Islamic aspects is essential, together with the necessary pinpointing of possible external influences to adequately assess what this parallelism is within evolution and what stems from a reciprocal influence. Finally, it is noteworthy to point out how in both Western and Eastern civilizations, monarchs rule with absolute powers. It was not until the eighteenth century, when the doctrine separating powers was announced by Montesquieu, that such powers were questioned. Clearly, this doctrine is rooted in Aristotle, with noticeable Greek influence, but the conception also shows similarities with categories that are religious in nature. God the Father bequeaths the Ten Commandments (Exodus 20), thus identifying with legislative powers; Jesus Christ is yet to come to judge the living and the dead (II Timothy 4:1), while the Holy Spirit could be identified with the executive branch of power, as he is the instrument of the Father (for example, Luke 1:35). This resemblance between the Trinity and the division of powers was already pointed out by Leon Duguit (1928, 669–70 and 886–7), who outlined the spontaneous link between the theory of the political trinity and the divine Trinity. This same conception and line of reasoning are the foundation for both: divinity is one and indivisible. Its attributes form different *personas* who are equally divine, but the divinity remains to be one and indivisible in substance, despite the existence of three divine *personae*. Likewise, sovereignty is one and indivisible. Its attributes form three different people who are equally sovereign. Each of them is a sovereign power, but sovereignty remains indivisible. So, the theological theory of the Trinity works as a model for the legal theory of three powers as attributes for the personification of sovereignty.

Kafala

The *kafala*, as a legal institution, constitutes one of the clearest cases of dogmatic influence in the constitution of legal institutions, especially when undertaking a comparative analysis with the mutation that the legal institution for adoption suffers when Christianity appears during the late Roman Empire. Throughout late antiquity, the Roman institution of adoption expressed the mutual power of the *pater familias* within a new family configuration and the institution of *patria potestas*. Bonfante (1925, 26) points to the transformation of the classic Roman point of view in favor of the Helleno-Christian view. With this, the focus changes from the father's parental authority to the need for the adoptive father to concentrate on the adopted child. It all mutates from an institution that regulated power within the family to one that protects the minor; it shifted from focusing on the interests of the adoptive parent to safeguarding the interests of the adopted child. The pagan model invigorated the family group; on the contrary, Christian adoption places the accent on the protective function and brotherhood. The ties to the dogmatic aspect can clearly be seen in Saint Augustine's comments referring to the Gospel of John or in his sermons where Christians are seen as adopted children of God, while the Jews are considered direct descendants of God. The scatological heritage of Christianity is that of an adopted child, to which the observations of Biondi (1952, 532*ff*) may be added. This author states that in general, "the essence of evangelical preaching lies in the precept of charity, [sic] if one accepts the literalism of the text, it would translate into the distribution of a legal system rather than its adaptation."

The Christian identification of adoption as a category making up part of the dogma differs from Islam, which excludes it, as indicated in Sura 33: al-Ahzab, of the Quran:

> 4. Allah has not placed two hearts in the bosom of any man … nor has he allowed your adopted sons to be your own sons. That is what your lips say. Allah, however, tells the truth, and guides you along the pathway. 5. Call them by their father's name. That is more righteous before Allah. And if you know not who his father is, then may he be your brothers in the faith and under your protection. You are not guilty if you make a mistake, unless you do it deliberately.

This is contrary to the pre-Islamic period, when adoption was standard practice (Milliot and Blanc 1987, 415). The aforementioned text clearly prohibits adoption; however, the institution of the *kafala* is underlying the aforementioned text as it fulfills the same sociological function seeking to protect minors as in the case of adoption, but without any paternity ties between the subjects. Consequently, we must understand this legal institution as being similar to "fostering," although it incorporates both the child's education and his/her protection.

This divergence appears in the practice of law and even in international relationships between the kingdoms of Spain and Morocco when it comes to describing an institution that is foreign to one's own legal tradition. Morocco—as other Muslim countries—accepts the *kafala*; Article 149 of Morocco's family code states that "adoption is considered null and shall not produce any legitimate relationship." In Spain, there is ample jurisprudence that shows attempts to transform the *kafala* into adoption, even when Article 19.4 of the International Adoption Law states that adoption is not possible if it is prohibited or not contemplated in the national legislation of the adopted child. However, there is jurisprudence accepting this conversion. This situation generated a formal complaint lodged by the Moroccan government, which also considered fraud perpetrated by certain couples who were unable to adopt in Spain and turned to Morocco to obtain a *kafala* (which includes converting to Islam). At a later date in Spain, this *kafala* was transformed into an adoption. The case has been studied in depth (see, for example, Calvo Caravaca and Carrascosa González 2012, 360*ff*).

Inheritance and legitimacy

Civil and, more specifically, family law traditionally constitute one of the most fruitful fields for the development of consuetudinary and religious regulations. In fact, part of civil legislation is social by nature and protects the family. That is why a common point between biblical and Quranic texts covers the matter of inheritance; more precisely its tendency toward the figure of legitimacy. In this case, both the Bible and the Quran—being similar—find divergent legal traditions that enter into conflict with each other.

In the case of the Bible, Numbers 27:8–11 states:

> And you shall say unto the people of Israel: If a man dies, and has no son, then you shall cause his inheritance to pass to his daughter. And if he has no daughter, then you shall give his inheritance to his brothers. And if he has no brothers, then you shall give his inheritance to his father's brothers. And if his father has no brothers, then give his inheritance to his kinsman that is next to him of his family, and he shall possess it. And it shall be for the people of Israel a statue and ordinance, as the Lord commanded Moses.

This text clearly expresses the denial of freedom to leave a will, but this tradition was neutralized to a greater extent by the freedom to write a will, as established by Roman law. Once again, we see the Christianization of the Empire, and the patristic influence in Roman legislation, with the appearance of legitimacy limiting freedom to bequeath in the Roman law.

Let us use a single example, as in the case of Sermon 355:4 by Saint Augustine, in which he renounces inheritances left to the church, which ends up appearing in certain medieval texts that accept the legitimate part of the inheritance as ecclesiastical influence. Augustine stated:

> Do as I have exhorted you to do so many times, knowing that if you have only one son, think of Christ as another son; if you have two, consider Christ as a third; if you have ten, consider Christ as the eleventh; in that case I will accept. Being I have behaved this way in certain matters, they want to shatter my goodness or my reputation, accusing me of not wanting to accept offerings from devotees. Consider those I have accepted; what need is there to innumerate them? Just as an example: I accepted the inheritance of the son of Julian. Why? Because he died without heirs.

Sura 2: al-Baqara, Verse 180 states: "It is prescribed for you, when death approaches any of you, if he leaves wealth, that he make a bequest to parents and next of kin, according to reasonable manners. This is the duty of those who fear Allah." Or Sura 4:7: "There is a share for men and a share for women from what is left by parents and those nearest related, whether the property be small or large—a rightful/legal share." Although the standard regarding this topic is established in the text, there are differences between Sunni and Shia Muslims in terms of its application, especially with regard to women. These are but a few fragments from among many others that explain how the settlement of inheritance is imperative by nature, and we must attribute these to maintaining law and order. Disinheritance is forbidden—whether directly in a will or indirectly by disposing of worldly assets free of charge while alive—as no one may fully disinherit his/her heirs, especially legal heirs (established in Sura 4:33). Thus, as Milliot and Blanc (1987, 483) pointed out, one's status as an heir depends on one's family status. The Islamic inheritance law, or *al-fara'id*, is an inheritance system with mandatory quotas, the complexity of which derives from the exclusive treatment of the topic in the Quran, which leads to the "science of the *al-fara'id*."

With regard to inheritance, traditional Roman law essentially follows the will of the testator, with Christianity mitigating free use, but the Islamic tradition is based on the will of God. Succession is involuntary and offers descendants more guarantees, as confusion of wealth is not possible because debts of the departed are always liquidated. With this, the mandatory Quranic heirs (*dhawu al-fard*) receive a fixed amount and are assigned the legitimate heirs, guaranteeing the protection of the family further than in the case of Christian rights. The Quran is very clear about many points, and this has been directly incorporated into legislation. For other, more obscure points, one must consult the science of *fiqh* or jurisprudence and the methodology of *usul al-fiqh* to clarify contents.

To conclude this subject, it is noteworthy that in recent times, there is a tendency in Europe to promote one's freedom to dispose of one's assets in detriment to the legitimate heir. This coincides with the tendencies in the latest legislative changes in Islamic countries to reinforce the rights of nuclear family heirs (Maíllo Salgado 2005, 76), without the excesses of the former law.

Marriage

As an inevitable institution, a complete review of marriage is difficult. Therefore, the focus will be on one of its most eye-catching elements: the inclusion of reasons to dissolve a marriage for religious reasons.

Within the sphere of Christian law, it has already been stated (Muñiz Pérez 2015, 183) that the configuration of the institution of marriage stems from Christian symbolism and ecclesiology. The connection and arguments are once again found in the patristicism era and explained by Ratzinger (1992). By identifying the church as the wife and Christ as the husband, theological categories are incorporated into the Catholic institution. This, in turn, leads to indissolubility or monogamy with it becoming an essential element of Christian marriage.

Another similarity between the Bible and the Quran is mutual dissolution in the case of mixed marriages. In the case of Christianity, there is the Petrine and Pauline privilege. The Pauline privilege, granted by Saint Paul in I Corinthians 7:12–15, states:

> [T]o the rest I say, not the Lord, that if any brother has a wife who is an unbeliever, and she consents to live with him, he should not divorce her. If any woman has a husband who is an unbeliever, and he consents to live with her, she should not divorce him. For the unbelieving husband is consecrated through his wife and the unbelieving wife is consecrated through her husband. Otherwise, your children would be unclean, but as it is, they are holy. But if the unbelieving partner desires to separate, let it be so; in such a case, the brother or sister is not bound.

At the canonic level, four conditioning factors have been established to apply this reason to dissolve the matrimony: a valid marriage between two people who are not baptized, the conversion and baptism of one of the spouses, the physical separation or the morals of the unbaptized spouse, and the appeal on behalf of the unbaptized party for his/her baptism, or at least to live in peace with the baptized person. A negative response leads to separation.

The Petrine privilege on the other hand grants the pope the power to dissolve a marriage for the benefit of the faith (the Petrine privilege on the other). Canon laws 1148 and 1149 establish two circumstances: polygamy, considering later marriages null, and a situation where it is impossible to reestablish cohabitation due to captivity or persecution. The legal solution adopted is the putative marriage.

In contrast, the *talaq* (repudiation) rule as a reason to dissolve a marriage is specifically regulated in Sura 65. This institution contemplates several ways to dissolve a marriage, including repudiation as such, declared unilaterally by the husband, dissolution by mutual agreement, or dissolution based on a sentence from the *qadi* (judge) or at the request of one of the spouses. Dissolution of the marriage is also considered following the death of a spouse. This institution has been included because it is the solution in the case of apostasy of a spouse (more difficult in the case of a mixed marriage), which leads to the immediate dissolution of the marriage because it is seen as almost a type of civil death. It even leads to the commencement of succession (in part sustained in Sura 9:74). In fact, divorce as described in the Quran works as a legal Islamic institution (nonexistent in Christianity, which resorts to annulment to attain the same objective). Therefore, in most Islamic-Arabic countries, divorce falls under the authority of the judge and his dictates, which are in most cases based on the *fatwas* of the *ulama*. These mandates are determined by Quranic texts for religious-legal resolutions. Indeed, with the influence of Western codes throughout the nineteenth century, the authority of the judges has diminished, as has the competence of the courts regarding personal rights.

Taxes

Returning to public law and the scope of taxation, this is regulated in both fundamental texts. Civil taxes, ordered by public powers, are differentiated from contributions for religious purposes.

Sura 2:43 of the Quran states: “And establish prayer and give the fixed amount of alms and bow with those who bow!” Among many other aspects, the word *zakat* is mentioned among the obligations for all Muslims, as indicated in Sura 9:71: “The believing men and believing women are allies of one another. They enjoy what is right and forbid what is wrong and establish prayer and give zakat [fixed amount of alms] and obey Allah and His Messenger. Allah will have mercy upon them; Allah is Exalted in Might and Wise.” Or Sura 23:1–4, “Blessed are the believers ... who are observant of *zakat*.” In Islam, there is an obligation to give alms, which is clearly indicated in Sura 9:18: “The mosques of Allah are only to be maintained by those who believe in Allah and the Last Day and establish prayer and give zakat and do not fear except Allah, for it is expected that those will be of the rightly guided.” Jesus Riosalido (1993, 177) considers this tribute as an honor and contrasts it with the taxation of non-Muslims subject to *dhimmi.*[8]

Then there are the *mukus,* or civil taxes levied by the sultan (as the *zakat* cannot be used to sustain ordinary government needs). At this point, an interesting similarity appears between the Muslim and the Roman taxation system, in which, for example, the *dhimmi* is comparable to the *capitatio* (capitation or poll tax). The underlying principle is the same in both cases: paying taxes is an expression of citizenship (in Rome) or belonging to Islam. With this model, which establishes the *zakat* as a low tax burden (compared to the *mukus*, which is much higher tax burden), a fiscal incentive is created for conversion while at the same time the expansion of the Islamic Empire is financed with taxes that nonbelievers pay in exchange for being allowed to maintain their customs and beliefs. In this regard, Riosalido (1993) contemplates the Islamicization of the Roman or Assyrian tax system, but it is noteworthy that the tax on wealth (*zakat*) is less demanding in comparison with those subject to the Roman obligation of *capitatio* (for example, the Code of Justinian 11, title 47:10). Here, we

---

[8] *Dhimmi* constitutes a category worthy of study, as it covers a wide range of meanings and is used for its legal capacity while being linked to *vinculum iuris* [legal tie] between creditor and debtor. However, our concern now is the notion of *dhimmi* as a contract by which the Muslim community agrees to provide hospitality and protection for members of other revealed religions, as found in the Quran, Sura 22:17. Thus, the *dhimmi* is a protection contract that includes a poll tax or *jizya* and an additional real estate contribution, *kharaj*. It also incorporates other obligations for these non-Islamic communities living in Muslim territories, such as not expressing their faith publicly and certain personal limitations.

will avoid delving into the many differences in taxation models, as well as into the various taxes on precious metals, animals, or post-fasting festivities.

Likewise, the Bible also states the obligation to sustain the expenses of the Christian Empire by means of taxes. There is a renowned phrase in Matthew 22:15–21: "Render therefore to Caesar the things that are Caesar's and to God the things that are God's." It is even more complex to find precise points for comparison in Christianity, as there is no preestablished amount of alms or a legal almsgiving. People are encouraged to give alms, but without establishing a mandatory amount in the form of a tax. There is a specific duty in a given point, which is the obligation of the faithful to contribute to the upkeep of the church. It appears as a right of the priests, who are free to demand it. The biblical cornerstone is found in I Corinthians 9:7–11:

> Who serves as a soldier at his own expense? Who plants a vineyard without eating any of its fruit? Who tends a flock without getting some of the milk? Does not the law say the same? For it is written in the law of Moses, "You shall not muzzle an ox when it is treading out the grain." Is it for oxen that God is concerned? Does he not speak entirely for our sake? It was written for our sake, because the plowman should plow in hope and the thresher thresh in hope of a share in the crop. If we have sown spiritual good among you, is it too much if we reap your material benefits?

Then there is Philippians 4:17, which is precisely the version used by Saint Augustine (Sermon 46:4), which states: "Not that I seek the gift; but I seek the fruit which increases to your credit." The Saint continues in that same sermon, verse 5 regarding priests: "They shall receive from the people what is necessary for their maintenance, and the Lord shall reward their service." With the expression *stipendaria multitudo* (community taxation) found in Sermon 351:5, he refers to laymen.

Nevertheless, we must consider the differences. Saint Paul established the obligation to provide funds for the priest, while in Islam, this falls within almsgiving, which also appears in the Christian Bible but not as a legally established amount. Moreover, giving alms is the third pillar of Islam, following prayer and religious practice, while in the Christian system, giving alms as a religious commitment enjoys a different position. Sura 9:60 points out the benefit of this: "Giving alms is not only for the poor and for the needy and for those employed to collect it, but for bringing hearts together and for freeing captives, and for those in debt and for the cause of Allah and for the traveler—an obligation by Allah." Originally, the theological function of this mandate within Islam is comparable to its Christian counterpart, which would be the tithe given to the church. This amount could be distributed accordingly to the needy (including priests, who were maintained by it). The difference lies in the fact that the topic of alms is well established in Islam, while in Christendom it appears in a more indirect manner.

The implementation of both categories is suffering a crisis. Christianity has lost all tributary power, except possible collaboration agreements with certain governments. In Islam, giving alms is an obligation. Although some authors point out its tendency toward oblivion, it is common practice, especially in those countries that remain committed to tradition.

Others

Undoubtedly, there are many other similarities that are worthy of study. These include the category of *ijma'*, or Muslim consensus, as both a direct source of law and a criterion that regulates the authority of human reasoning. A similar figure known as *traditio* (tradition) appears time and again in the Bible and in Catholic patristics as a direct revelation of God to his people. This constitutes the basis of Christian tradition, which is also found in Islam; Goldziher (1981, 50) mentions *dalala* and *ajarakum*,[9] which states that "my community will never agree on error." *Consensus ecclesiae* and papal infallibility work in a similar manner. In fact, in jurisprudence among the main sources of the methodology, we have what is known as *usul al-fiqh*; Jalloul Muro (2016, 298) highlights the Quran, the Sunna, *ijma'* (consensus), and the analogy. I see this consensus, which today is accepted by jurists, as similar to *consensus ecclesiae*.[10]

The role played by the courts and their relationship with power is noteworthy. Due to the development of the caliphate in Islam—at least during the Abbasid period (Coulson 1998, 130)—the Sharia courts failed

[9]The mistake lies in dalala (error): a lack of dalala shows the guidance of God, while ajarakum expresses divine protection in three areas, among which God does not abanodon the community of believers (Goldziher 1981, 50).

[10]Ecclesia is, in the real sense of the word, the community of believers.

to attain a position of supreme judicial authority independent of political control. However, the independence of judicial authority was noted in the reaction of the *fuqaha'*, or experts in Islamic jurisprudence and law, whose protests were directed against the vulnerability of the decisions made by the judges. A similar process is seen in the late Roman Empire period, in which a growing independence of ecclesiastic courts from civil Roman courts was seen. This arose from the patristicism for the exclusion of governmental jurisdiction in favor of a religious court in the case of believers, as expressed by Saint Augustine: "he [Saint Paul] stated that it was equally a crime to be litigating in courts regarding temporal matters; this would be bearable, he warns, if such litigations were sentenced by Church tribunals" (Sermon 351:5) in an effort to exclude Roman Imperial jurisdiction in favor of judicial functions carried out by the bishops. The basis for this is found in I de Corinthians 6:1–7.

Other legal institutions (such as punishment, basic principles of criminal law, confession…), which fall outside the scope of this chapter's analysis due to space constraints, reiterate the importance of the dogma as an influential element of law. This is despite the strong acculturation (transculturation, in the words of Jalloul Muro) seen in colonial times that, following Western positivist models, transformed the legal tradition in Muslim countries in a process equally concomitant with the Roman Empire, with rights for the conquered peoples.

Conclusions

I have sought to summarize some of examples that I consider demonstrate the close connection between law and dogma. The usage of philosophical terms, and predominantly the concept of justice as the object of law, leads to this connection of law with dogma. Said connection shows the concomitance of institutions such as the *consensu ecclesia* and the *ijma*, but also the divergence in terms of the configuration of institutions such as the *kafala*. I consider these comparative studies to be especially necessary when considering laws rooted in a variety of theological sources.

The usefulness of recognizing the theological connection with legal institutions unfolds in a variety of spheres. First, it is a legal-social research method, from the perspective of both the history of law and the philosophy of law. Second, there are practical applications in this analysis, that allow criteria to be adopted when seeking to solve controversies more effectively, thus avoiding conflicts such as those pointed to by the institution of the *kafala*. Third, these studies identify differences that express possible points of dysfunction, especially when Western society seeks to impose legal conceptions that are totally foreign to other societies.

Continuing with this third reasoning and revealing the origin in Christian theology of the division of power, I must explain the importance of the topic within the scope of international relationships. It is worth questioning the appropriateness of the extrapolation of Western society's legal model to the Islamic world in detriment to its own tradition and legal institutions. The Western world's governance is based on the division of powers and rooted in a dogmatic basis. I have mentioned the dysfunction caused by the incorporation of Western models into Islamic legal traditions. However, is the encouragement of the Western model a new form of proselytism with hidden theological categories that appear in Western legal influence since the nineteenth century? This is a question which, once the role of dogma and theology is recognized in the general categories of law, appears on its own accord, and once again, exhibits the close connection between legal and theological hermeneutics.

References

Alwani, Taha J. al-. 1994. *Source Methodology in Islamic Jurisprudence* (*usul al-fiqh al Islami*). Herndon, VA: International Institute of Islamic Thought.

Artola, Antonio M., Sánchez Caro, José M. 1989. *Biblia y palabra de Dios. Introducción al estudio de la Biblia*. Estalla, Spain: Verbo Divino.

Berman, Harold J. 1997. *La formación de la tradición jurídica de Occidente*. Madrid: Fondo de Cultura Económica.

Betti, Emilio. 1955. *Theoria generale della interpretazione*. Milano: Giuffré.

Biondi, Biondo. 1952. *Il diritto romano Cristiano*, vol. 3, edited by Giuffré. Milan: Giuffré.

Bonfante, Pietro. 1925. *Corsi di diritto romano, 1° Diritto di famigli*. Rome: Ed. Sampaolesi.

Calvo Caravaca, Alfonso L., and Carrascosa González, Javier (eds.). 2012. *Derecho internacional privado*, vol. 2, 13th ed. Granada, Spain: Editorial Comares.

Coulson, Noel J. 1998. *Historia del derecho islámico. Biblioteca del Islam contemporáneo*. Barcelona: Ediciones Bellaterra.

Duguit, Leon. 1928. *Traité de droit constitutionnel*. vol. 2, 3rd ed. Paris: Boccard.

Engisch, Karl. 1953. *Die Idee der Konkretisierun in Recht und Rechtswissenschaft unserer Zeit, Abhandlungen der Keidelberger Akademie der Wissenschaften*. Heidelberg: C. Winter.

Gadamer, Hans G. 1999. *Verdad y método*. Salamanca, Spain: Ediciones Sígueme.

Goldziher, Ignac. 1981. *Introduction to Islamic Theology*. Princeton, NJ: Princeton University Press.

Jalloul Muro, Hana. 2016. "La charía y el fiqh: Su significado como corpus legal." *Anuario da Facultade de Dereito da Universidade da Coruña* 20: 292–320.

Koselleck, Reinhard. 1983. *Gegenstand und Begriffe der Verfassungsgeschichtsschreibung*. Berlin: Duncker & Humblot.

Maíllo Salgado, Felipe. 2005. *Diccionario de derecho islámico*. Gijón, Spain: Ed. Trea.

McKenzie, John L. 1960. "The Word of God in the Old Testament." *Theological Studies*, 21: 183–206.

Milliot, Louis and Blanc François P. 1987. *Introduction à l'étude du droit musulman* [Introduction to the study of Islamic law]. Paris: Dallot.

Muñiz Pérez, Julio C. 2015. "Civitas y cives en San Agustín. La construcción de la iglesia como estado: Fundamentos de orden constitucional. *Antigüedad y Cristianismo* 31–32: 4764.

Qayrawani, Ibn A. Z. al-. 1993. *Risāla fi-l-fiqh. Compendio de derecho Islámico*, edited by Jesús Riosalido. Editorial Trotta: Madrid.

Ratzinger, Joseph. 1992. *Volk und Haus Gottes in Augustins Lehre von der Kirche*. München: EOS Verlag St. Ottilien.

Rouco Varela, Antonio M. 1967. "Filosofía o teología del derecho? Ensayo de una respuesta desde el derecho canónico." In *Wahrheit und Verkündigung, Michael Schamaus zum 70. Geburtstag*, vol. 2, edited by L. Scheffczyk and R. Dettloff, 1967–1741. München: Heinzmann.

Savigny, Friedrich C. 1878. *Sistema del derecho romano actual*. Madrid: Góngora.

Part II

Historical Perspectives

https://doi.org/10.1142/9781800611689_0005

Chapter 5

Legal Authority and Interpretation in Islamic Law

Knut S. Vikør

Department of AHKR / History, University of Bergen, Bergen, Norway
knut.vikor@uib.no

Introduction

As the legal scholars of early Islam rejected, and were able to resist, any attempts from the caliph to influence the formation of Islamic law, the issue of legal authority became unavoidable. The law was to be based on God's revelation, in the form of the Quran and the Prophet Muhammad's acts and statements, but these sources could be and were interpreted in a myriad of different ways.

In order to become a practicable law, the sources of revelation would have to go through a process where they were formulated into legal rules, through methods known collectively as *ijtihad* (Kamali 1991, 86–123; Vikør 2005, 53–72). Then, following the often conflicting rules that were the result of such *ijtihad*, a choice had to be made about which rule or interpretation was to become the law to be followed. Someone had to make that selection and give it such an authority and legitimacy that the Muslims would follow it and the courts could apply it.

As the state was denied the authority to establish what God's laws were, and since there was no recognized hierarchy or assembly of scholars that could decide in the name of the scholarly community, the only way to achieve such an authoritative selection was through the principle of consensus (Hallaq 2001; Hasan 1984; Turki 1984, 56–7). A rule that legal scholars jointly agreed on became the positive rule that should be applied in society. This consensus was known as *ijma'*. Ideally, all scholars in the world should reach such a consensus around a positive rule. This turned out to be possible, but for only a few fundamental issues.

Instead, there appeared after some generations a number of loose groupings of scholars who came to share opinions on various legal issues. From about the tenth century AD, these groupings solidified into more or less organized bodies of scholars, often with a recognized leadership, that became known as "schools of law," or *madhhabs* (Bearman, Peters, and Vogel 2005; Melchert 1997). Initially, there were more than a dozen such informal groups, but from about the eleventh or twelfth century, they coalesced into four schools of law among the Sunni majority, while the Shi'i and other theological minorities each formed one or more schools of their own.[1]

These *madhhabs* can then best be seen as four parallel bodies of law, or four independent varieties of Sharia. Since they shared a basis in the same divine revelation, they agreed on many issues; however, each of the four developed their own methodologies for how the rules had been elaborated from the revelation. As time passed, each legal scholar was required to attach himself to one such *madhhab* and follow that exclusively in his decisions. The jurisprudence of each school was expressed in a body of literature, starting with the foundational books ascribed to the eponymous founders of the four schools, Abu Hanifa (d.767), Malik ibn Anas (d.795), Muhammad al-Shafi'i (d.820), and Ahmad ibn Hanbal (d.855) (Brockopp 2000; Dutton 1999; Halm 1974; Hurvitz 2002; Tsafrir 2004). From these grew a large body of commentaries and glosses that elaborated and discussed individual rules, often with remarkable disunity. However, the authority of the four founders (and their closest companions in each school) became the bedrock that the legal literature was based on. Any development that hoped to win recognition had to demonstrate that it was based on a view held explicitly or implicitly by these founders, in the various types of legal elaborations (*ahkam, fatawa,* etc.) that over the centuries expanded the scope of *madhhab* rulings.

---

[1]For the sake of simplicity, I will focus only on the Sunni majority of Islam in this chapter. Unlike those of the minority groupings' different schools, the distinctions between the four Sunni *madhhabs* were not theological.

From the thirteenth century on, a set of simplified works, the *mukhtasars* or compendia of law, were produced (Fadel 1996). They set out the preferred rule for each case, summing up what the author saw as the consensus of the school. These became standard works for judges and later legal scholars but were only based on the authority of their authors. Any later judge or scholar was free to disagree, as long as he could attach his view to another recognized authority in the legal literature of his *madhhab*. In addition, recognized legal experts wrote legal opinions, *fatwas*, on individual cases brought to them. Collections of *fatwas* made by famous scholars were edited and reproduced and could also be used as a literature of reference and authority (Hallaq 1994).

The autonomous nature of this scholarly authority over the law could clearly lead to two opposite approaches: On the one hand, there theoretically was an openness to legal discussion and development, as no outside political authority could censor the debate. On the other hand, it led to a conservative impulse against changes, since many scholars held that a consensus, once established, was to be respected by future generations. This was formulated in the phrase that "the gates to *ijtihad* are closed" (Schacht 1964, 72–5). To some, this meant that independent law formation in the manner of the original four founders could no longer be done, since no one now had their outstanding competence. No further schools of law could be founded beyond the four. To others, no more legal development at all was possible. The established rules—be it in the commentaries, the *mukhtasars*, or the early *fatwa* collections—were exhaustive of all issues, and could not be changed or reformed.

Premodern Calls for *Ijtihad*

While historians have shown that legal development did in fact continue unabated within the schools, the conservative understanding of consensus prevailed, at least in the official discourse. Real changes could be introduced but had to be presented as if they were "actually" the views of the founders or other early legal authorities (Jackson 1996). One principle that came into discussion was the restriction of legal debate to one's own *madhhab*. The four schools recognized each other, and a verdict passed by a judge belonging to one *madhhab* was respected as final by judges and scholars of the other *madhhabs*, even when they would have given a different verdict following their school's rules. In regions where several *madhhabs* were present (which was the case in most of the Arab world, from Algeria to Iraq), each *madhhab* could have its own court for litigants to choose. Scholars from different *madhhab*s could even work together in a joint courthouse, each working according to his own rules, or participate in joint councils with the sultan or governor of the town (Brunschvig 1965; Tucker 1998, 84–5). These practices varied with time and place.

Thus, the schools related to each other. Nevertheless, the doctrine was that, while a Shafi'i judge, for example, was allowed to read a Maliki text, he was not allowed to use the other's opinions or arguments in his own works; only those of his own school. Many scholars found this too restrictive and demanded the right to consider the authoritative views of other schools in their legal discussion, and even possibly to prefer the discussion of that other school in specific cases if they found the argumentation compelling and not in contradiction with the foundational methodology of their own school. This "borrowing" across *madhhab* boundaries was known as *talfiq* and became more acceptable in legal discussion from at least the eighteenth century (Ibrahim 2015, 105–25; Krawietz 2002). Many conservative scholars, however, rejected this blurring of the lines.

At the same time, more radical views appeared that rejected the idea of the "closing of the gates" altogether, and claimed the continuous right to *ijtihad*: "no era can exist without *ijtihad*." Such views typically grew in strength, not in the main scholarly centers of the Muslim world such as Cairo or Istanbul but in peripheral centers such as India and Fez in Morocco, or in the desert regions of Libya or the Arabian Peninsula where scholars had settled (Peters 1980). The extent to which scholars wanted to go varied. Most reacted against what they called "*madhhab* fanaticism," that is, to always put the rules of one's own school above all others. This was even called *shirk*, unbelief, because, it was claimed, if such a bad scholar was shown a *hadith* that contradicted the views of his school, he would prefer his school over the revelation of the *hadith* and thus over God (Radtke *et al.* 2000, 95–130). Such radical criticism of the *madhhab* system could lead to rejecting it altogether, with claims that each scholar should read and interpret the revealed sources independently from any established scholarly tradition.

More common, and a more practical interpretation of the demands for *ijtihad*, was a loosening of the restrictions of the *madhhab* without rejecting them altogether. A mild version of this was to emphasize *talfiq*: legal scholars must be able to take the development of all four schools into account and to prefer the established views of other schools over one's own. This position can be found in the premodern period (as far back as the Mamluks) but became more widespread in the nineteenth century. A more principled view stated that the touchstone of any discussion must be the Prophet's example in *hadith*, not the views of the later legal scholars. Many legal discussions in the early periods dealt with the evidentiary value of individual *hadith* narratives, structuring them into categories from "sound" (clearly a true representation of something the Prophet had said or done) through various levels of "probably true" to "weak" (the Prophet may or may not have said it). This kind of evaluation must also be open to later generations, the *ijtihad* proponents argued, establishing different levels of *ijtihad* competence according to the scholar's level of knowledge (Vikør 2000). A modern scholar should not accept the traditional categorization of any particular *hadith* as sound or unsound at face value, but must be able to arrive at his own conclusion. He might, for example, be aware of evidence that was not available in earlier times. In other words, later legal scholars must be able to do *the same kind of legal development* as was done in the formative periods—the early centuries after the Prophet's death cannot be seen as sacrosanct.

This kind of *ijtihad* was not in any way an open door to a personal interpretation of legal rules in light of modern conditions, or to individual whims. The methodology of the *mujtahid* (the person exercising *ijtihad*) was the same as in the classical period, and in principle the resulting rules were just as universally valid over time and space as those originally arrived at—but they could be different.

The Arrival of the State

In the nineteenth century, a series of profound changes came to the Muslim world, which can be seen as effects of inevitable modernization or of a Western and colonial impact. In the field of law, the most essential change probably occurred in the relationship between the law and the state, or religious authority and political power, in favor of state authority. This was however not completely unprecedented. The application of Sharia in the courtroom had always been the domain of the state. The caliph, sultan, or emir appointed the judge who presided over the court, and it was state officials who implemented the verdict of the court (Tyan 1960). But the laws and rules that the judge applied in his verdict fell outside the sultan's competence. That power belonged only to the independent scholars, who had warded off the few attempts by the early rulers at establishing a "caliphal" law on their own authority.

However, the pressure from the state to gain some authority over the content of the law did not abate, and the Ottoman Empire (which existed from the mid-fourteenth century in Anatolia and the Balkans and from the early sixteenth century in the Arab Middle East) changed the balance in its favor with two major moves.

One was to promote one *madhhab* over the other three, namely the Hanafi school that they favored (Gerber 1994). This became the "state-sponsored" school, and the only one recognized by the authorities in matters that they were concerned with. That did not mean that the other schools or their scholars were banned in any way—they could continue to practice or even have their own courts—but the Hanafi school and court were favored in matters that required official sanction, such as the condemnation of criminals. In ritual matters, however, Muslims were allowed to follow whichever *madhhab*'s system they preferred. Thus, many areas under Ottoman control that had previously been dominated by another *madhhab*, such as Tunisia and Algeria (both Maliki), now acquired a pluralism of *madhhabs*, with Hanafis entering the stage.

The other move was the formulation of a legal code that based its authority not on the views of the legal scholars but on the sultan: the *qanun* (Repp 1988). These were edicts published by each sultan, collected in "*qanun* books" (*qanunname*), which regulated primarily issues of administration but also economic matters and penal law. They were not meant to supplant Sharia, which remained the paramount law of the empire, but to "fill the gaps" where Sharia did not provide details, or to clarify how Sharia was to be understood. However, in spite of its apparent subjugation to the classical Sharia rules, the *qanun* soon became the prominent law in the areas under Ottoman rule. The courts were instructed that they should, when they made a judgment, first check the *qanun* for a rule to follow. Only if they could not find the answer in the *qanunname* could they look to established Sharia for their judgment. The legal scholars (*muftis*) were required to include the *qanun* in addition to or over the classical legal literature when producing their *fatwa*s (Imber 1997; Repp 1986). Thus, the *qanun* became a form of early codification of the law in those areas of law that it covered. It was a step beyond the summaries of the medieval *mukhtasars* in that, unlike the earlier works, the *qanun* was an emanation of the power of the Ottoman sultans and gave them their legitimacy and authority.

It must however be emphasized that the intention behind the *qanun* was always to implement the principles of Sharia and God's divine rulings and that, in most matters, the *qanun* did not contradict the contents of existing Sharia rules (in their Hanafi version). However, it was still a major shift in principle that the state, and not the religious scholars, provided authority to the *qanun* law.

The Nineteenth Century

As the European powers began to gain political and economic influence in the Muslim world and the Middle East, there was also an effect on the legal field. Not surprisingly, the need for change was felt first in the areas of economic law, as the European traders did not easily accept that contracts and other economic relations with Muslim partners should be handled according to Sharia, and not their European laws. As European traders and others settled in Muslim cities for longer or shorter periods, they were also increasingly reluctant to be treated as *dhimmis* or subject to Sharia (Van den Boogert 2005). Thus, they demanded concessions, "capitulations," that ensured that Europeans would be subject to European laws, even in Muslim countries. European laws were of course based on the authority of Europeans' respective states, which was thus transferred to the embassies, consuls, or other local representative of each major European state in the Middle Eastern country in question.

In effect, these consuls became lawmakers not only for relations between Europeans but also for relations between Europeans and local Muslims, as the influence and power of the Europeans grew in many Muslim countries. To counteract this development, Egypt instituted a system of "mixed courts" for relations between Europeans and local Muslim residents; courts that should rule by recognized (mostly French-inspired) rules of law, and be staffed by a mixture of Egyptian and European judges (Roberson 1993). Rather than a balanced framework that reined in the uncodified authority of the consuls, however, these mixed courts largely became instances where European judges ruled over those local Muslims who had contacts with Europeans, according to European or European-inspired laws.

At the same time, fundamental changes also began to impact the laws of the Muslim states themselves, both those that came under direct European control as protectorates or colonies and those that were independent but went through a process of modernization under European influence. The Ottoman Empire was itself one of the early actors in this process, through the process known as the "reorganization" (*tanzimat*) from 1839 to 1876. In many ways, the legal changes introduced by the *tanzimat* can be seen as a continuation of the tipping of the balance away from scholars and toward the state, starting in the *qanun* period (Vikør 2005, 222–53). But there were basic differences that changed both the methodology and content of law formulation and their application in the courts. The most important ones can be summed up under the headings of codification, modification, and application of the laws in the courts.

Codification

Both the medieval *mukhtasars* and the Ottoman *qanun* can be seen as steps on the way from the uncodified nature of classical Sharia toward the establishment of structured law codes in the late nineteenth and twentieth centuries. However, the *mukhtasars* did not have any formal authority beyond being practical tools used by judges when formulating their verdicts—they could freely deviate from them, even though most were satisfied with applying the "established opinion" of the *mukhtasar*. The *qanun* did have a firm political authority behind them but were methodologically separate from Sharia and limited in their areas of application—the Sharia rules still existed in their classical form for scholars to refer to if the *qanun* did not apply to the case. And, of course, only a small part of the Muslim world was actually under Ottoman jurisdiction, and even in the empire, the *qanun* were more meticulously applied in the central than in the more peripheral regions, where the direct power of Istanbul was lighter.

The fully codified laws were different in form, formulated in a hierarchical structure from principles to details, like European laws, while classical Sharia law was more "casuistic," dealing sequentially with case by case without necessarily specifying the unifying principles that connected the cases. As the authority behind the codified law was the state alone, the legislator could also formulate it according to his own logic, while even the *qanun* always had Sharia, and thus God, as their ultimate authority (Peters 2002). Thus, the codified law severed the link between the law and religion.

This dramatic change was however mitigated in that the legislator could choose to base the contents of the codes on existing Sharia. This was particularly the case for the family laws and laws of personal status, where the dominant opinions of one or more *madhhab* were structured and sanctioned by the legislator as positive family law codes. However, this was still at the discretion of the legislator, and most countries used the occasion to modify the family laws in line of the social and political aims of the political powers. To stay within a "Sharia-based" discourse, they availed themselves of the classical principle of *talfiq*, to borrow across *madhhab* borders. The laws appeared to be based on the dominant *madhhab* in the country, and thus the Hanafi school in many cases, but quite eclectically imported Maliki, Shafi'i, or Hanbali rules so that they could be changed in the desired direction. The rules for marriage are a typical example: Hanafi law accords the bride a much stronger position than the other schools (she can, for example, marry herself off without a male guardian, which is not acceptable in the other schools). In divorce, however, Hanafi law is extremely restrictive: the wife is basically not given any opportunity to seek divorce through the courts, while the Malikis in particular give the courts broad options to dissolve a marriage at the wife's request. So, as the modern states wished to improve the position of women, they freely picked the Hanafi rules for marriage and the Maliki rules for divorce (Tucker 2008).

Many scholars also see codification as a restriction or freezing of laws (Tucker 1998). The diversity of views in the classical system and the possibility to refer to minority views within the legal literature gave judges and *muftis* the possibility to seek the result that was seen as most just in any particular case. Some went so far as to see the court of law almost as an arena for negotiations, where the parties together with the judge seek the solution most acceptable to all, which could then be justified either by referring to a *fatwa* or by linking it to a statement found in the expansive body of legal literature. With codification, these possibilities to find an answer that fit the case were severely restricted: now, only one answer to a case was fixed by the legislator, and it was much harder to use the variation of legal opinion to seek out alternate solutions.

Outside the field of personal law, the changes following codification were more substantial. Sharia is a law for Muslims, not for the religious minorities living in the Muslim state. In their internal affairs, they were ruled by the laws of their religion (with their rabbis and patriarchs as legal authority) (Emon 2012). This is still the case in family law in many countries of the Middle East, both in Muslim Egypt and Syria and nondenominational Lebanon: Muslim men can freely divorce their wives, Christians (men or women) most often cannot. In most other fields, however, this link between legal and religious status was abolished together with the *millet* system of organizing minorities: penal law, tax law, and laws on economic relations were now general for all, irrespective of religion.

Muslim penal law is a fairly complicated matter, divided into three systems that are structured totally differently from each other: the Quranic punishments (the *hudud* rules against theft, rebellion, fornication, false accusations of fornication, and drunkenness); the "eye for an eye" penalties for murder and bodily harm; and everything else (*ta'zir*) (Peters 2005). European authorities found the first two barbaric and unacceptable, and quickly introduced new penal laws based on European models. (In the Arab world, the model was often French codified law, while Muslim countries in Africa under British control could apply the common law of England.) In economic and administrative affairs, Sharia-based rules were eventually also replaced with laws based on European models. Similar changes were put into effect in the Ottoman Empire and other countries independent of Europe (Starr 1992).

The courts

The legal field was therefore marked by a form of legal pluralism, in that some parts of the law were still founded on principles found in Sharia, while others took their inspiration from a fundamentally different, European conception of law. In many countries, an even clearer pluralism was found in the application of the law in the courts. During much of the nineteenth century, many countries had two parallel court systems that could deal with the same cases, but with different laws and procedures and hence different outcomes (Peters 1997). They maintained a system of Sharia courts, which by and large dealt with cases using the classical methods of these courts. Alongside them were "civil courts" that ruled according to the codified state laws.

An example could be a murder case. Under the Sharia system, which does not know the concept of public prosecution, it would always be the injured party (for murder, the heirs of the deceased) who took the case to court, making a claim against a suspected killer. The judge would then hear the case, taking testimony and any other evidence into account, to see if the case could be proved. If he found that to be true, he would present the successful plaintiffs with the choice according to Sharia law: either have the identical injury applied to the perpetrator, thus the death penalty for murder (revenge); or receive a compensation meted out according to specific, set rules. This compensation could be substantial: the set figure for the murder of a free male was one thousand dinars (equivalent of some four kilograms of gold) (Peters 2005, 51).[2] This was meant to compensate for the economic loss of a family provider for a lifetime. However, the plaintiffs had to choose: either revenge or compensation. They could not have both. But the rules of procedure in the Sharia courts were very strict. Intention to kill had to be proven beyond any doubt and, in some *madhhabs*, on purely formalistic or technical grounds, e.g., two witnesses had to be in full agreement on what they had observed, or only particular types of weapons (swords, not clubs) proved intentionality. It could often be quite difficult to gain conviction in penal cases in Sharia courts, even when the suspicion of guilt was overwhelming.

The civil courts, on the other hand, often manned by judges trained in Western-inspired law colleges, used a modern type of procedure. Here, conviction could be easier if, for example, circumstantial evidence indicated the guilt of the accused beyond reasonable doubt. On the other hand, the penalties could be more graduated, including prison, forced labor, or similar, which Sharia courts hardly applied in such cases. These courts also had public prosecution and could take cases of their own accord or could accept a charge made by the victim or injured party. Thus, the relatives of a murdered person had a choice: if they took the issue to a Sharia court, making a claim against a known suspect, they could gain considerable compensation (or the satisfaction of revenge), but they could well lose if they did not have the type of evidence the Sharia court required. If they went to a civil court, the chances of conviction were higher, but they received nothing except for the satisfaction of seeing the killer behind bars.

Such a pluralism of forums was strictly speaking not a novelty; it was also reflected in premodern times in a system of "sultanic" or *mazalim* courts presided over by the sultan, governor, or other representative of state authority (often, however, a dedicated judge) (Tyan 1960, 433–526). These courts were also meant to work on the basis of Sharia rules but were freed from the procedural limitations of actual Sharia courts, since they were based on the authority of the sultan and not of religious scholars. They were thus meant to "fill the gaps" or, as the term *mazalim* indicates, "right wrongs" that for one reason or another the Sharia courts were unable to address.

Nevertheless, the distinction between civil and Sharia courts in the nineteenth century was much sharper, since the actual laws were different.

---

[2] The set figure could also be negotiated between the parties.

Also, the procedural differences between the two were more profound than those between the medieval Sharia and *mazalim* courts, where individual judges often went from one to the other or could both rely on *fatwas* to resolve legal unclarities. Such a commonality would be impossible for the later civil and Sharia courts. These features were thus rather clear signs of the transition from a legal system based on Sharia authority to one based on state authority.

Incompatibilities between the two court systems

The absence of a public prosecution system, which stems from the fact that Sharia does not fully distinguish between "public law" and "private law"—every case is seen as a resolution to a conflict between a plaintiff and a defendant—was one of the main features that Western law found alien and unacceptable in the Sharia system. There were elements of public prosecution in Sharia, both through the *mazalim* courts and the concept of *hisba*, which here can be translated as public order. A representative of the public could be a plaintiff on behalf of the community in certain cases that violated the public interest (Müller 1999; Omer 1981). But these functions were not sufficient for a modern court system.

Another, equally alien feature was the absence of legal representation for the parties. The courts were based on the two parties presenting themselves in person to plead their case, while it was up to the judge to transform their cases into a legal language and thus fairly represent the interests of both parties before passing judgment. Parties who were not present (such as women, particularly those from the upper class) could let themselves be represented by a spokesman, *wakil*, but this representative had roughly the same position and prerogatives as the party him- or herself. The modern legal system found this detrimental to legal justice, since the parties clearly did not always have the competence to present their case to the court in the best way (Jennings 1975; Tyan 1960, 262–74). Therefore, all modern court systems began training professional lawyers to advise and represent the parties. At first, such legal training was done at Western academies, but institutions for legal education were soon established in the Muslim countries as well. They were however aimed at the state, or civil courts, and their training was based on Western conceptions of law and legal procedure. They usually included basic training in Sharia law and procedure, but far from the level of sophistication of the traditional specialists of Islamic law. In parallel, Islamic universities instituted departments of Sharia studies, eventually with modern teaching methods, but directed at practitioners of Sharia courts.

The third feature of the Sharia court system that the modern legal theorists found unacceptable was the absence of an appeals system (Powers 1992). In the Sharia courts, the verdict given by the judge in any case was final and to be applied immediately. There was no option to appeal a case. Again, there were marginal or peripheral ways to get around this. It was not possible to take a case from one *madhhab*'s court to another—a judge would, as mentioned, not hear a case already decided by a different *madhhab* court. But if a judge had been deposed by the sultan or another authority, there was a window of opportunity to approach the new judge and claim the original verdict was wrong due to the corruption or incompetence of the departing judge. The new judge could hear the case again, but was not bound to. It was also possible, in some circumstances, to take a case heard in a Sharia court to the *mazalim* court for a second opinion. But, as has been noted, the Sharia court judges were often present at the *mazalim* sessions, and the *mazalim* magistrate might refuse to take the case if it was simply rehashing the arguments presented to the Sharia court.

This absence of a formal appeal was considered arbitrary by modern authorities, and they quickly set up multilevel systems. These were not really antithetical to the Sharia way of thinking, and many Sharia court systems similarly adopted a multilevel system. Even Saudi Arabia, which prides itself on applying pure Sharia law in its Sharia courts (even free of *madhhab* restrictions), has introduced a multilevel system, with a High Court where several Sharia judges sit in a panel (while the classical Sharia court always had one unique judge in each setting) (Vogel 2000, 83–117).

Demise of the *Madhhabs*?

In the twentieth century, most remaining Sharia courts were integrated into state-based court systems. Nevertheless, Sharia is very much present in modern legal systems in the Muslim world, but in ways that are fundamentally different from those of the classical, or premodern period. Saudi Arabia is unique in its support of an uncodified legal system based as much as possible on the traditional model of scholarly, rather than state, authority. Other countries, both in the Gulf and elsewhere, also keep larger or smaller elements of their family law uncodified, or insert classical jurisprudence (*fiqh*) as a “source” that can be used in courts alongside codified law, for example if the answer to a question is not found in the state law codes (Ballantyne 1990, 149–60).

Sharia is however mostly present through the codified laws, in particular personal and family laws, implemented and authorized by state authorities. This is also true for states that claim to have reintroduced Sharia, like Iran, Sudan, states in Northern Nigeria, and others. They have enacted family law codes with content taken from Sharia, with modifications according to the political will of the legislator. However, some countries following an Islamist ideology have given a special place to the *hudud* penal rules, and stated that as these are prescribed by God, they should be implemented directly (Schirazi 1997). In practice, they often do this through the elaborations of classical *fiqh*, and the degree to which these states actually apply the *hudud* systematically, rather than as occasional convictions or executions to make a political point, varies.

Do the classical *madhhabs* thus have any relevance in the legal field today? Many claim that they do not. The *madhhabs* arose because there was no other way to establish an operational authority to legitimize the classical rules of law. Lacking state authority and a universally accepted religious authority like a pope or *imam*, or even a universal body of scholars, the law could only be based on the consensus of scholars, which among Sunnis turned out to be the four *madhhabs*. However, that is no longer the case: the state now provides such an operational authority for the law, be it Sharia law or civil law. Therefore, the state and its legislative bodies can substitute themselves for the *madhhabs*. That is in effect what is happening in the widespread use of *talfiq*. In this manner, each nation-state also defines its own Sharia, so that the law loses its global nature. The *madhhabs* were not limited by political borders, but modern Sharia state law is, like any other state law: it only applies within the confines of the state that issued it.

There are moreover various ideological attempts to break down the traditional borders between *madhhabs* for idealistic reasons. God did not institute the four *madhhabs*; they only came about because of the failings of fallible humans to achieve a global consensus, critics would argue. God did not have four different rules for any situation; He only has one, and Muslims should not be divided in this way. One current making such claims is Salafism in its various strands, which discards (more in theory than in practice, as it happens) the “ossification” of later legal scholarship and instead wants to apply radical *ijtihad*: the answer to all questions lies in the Prophet's example and his time, and the sources of that example are the Quran and the *hadith* traditions from the Prophet, not later legal scholarship. Thus, today's Muslims must go directly to the *hadith* and study them critically to establish what was the true *hadith* for each case (Hamdeh 2017). This is of course what Muslim legal scholars did for centuries, but their answers cannot be any more authoritative than those we reach today.

A more moderate effort in the same direction is what is known as "the Sharia according to the four *madhhabs*." Rather than discarding the legal traditions, these are attempts to unify them. A number of works map their viewpoints in various domains of law and seek a solution that can be accepted as common between them as far as possible, in a way applying systematic *talfiq*, where the result should be one single *madhhab* to replace the four (al-Jaziri 2009). This also works on the basis that Muslims must seek unity, and that the *madhhabs* of classical law, while necessary in their time, are no longer needed. Unlike the opportunistic *talfiq* of state law, however, the aim here is to institute a global, but practicable, Sharia law based on the systematic scholarship of classically trained legal scholars.

All these efforts have modified the impact of *madhhab* boundaries in the last two centuries. However, there is no doubt that the weight of Islamic legal scholarship is found within the four *madhhab*s. Even the Salafist attempts to remove the contaminations of centuries of human scholarship most often result in a discourse that is fairly similar to classical legal debates, and indeed often cite traditional authors. It may be argued that in order to understand the revealed sources, or at least transform them into any form of legal structure, a process parallel to that carried out by the early legal scholars is inevitable (Vikør 2003). Discarding that tradition may only lead to repeating the same processes, and it then falls onto the modern remakers of the law to convince believers that the new process of *ijtihad* is fundamentally different and less humanly fallible than the one that has existed for more than a millennium.

In practice, therefore, when modern lawmakers do turn to Sharia, codified or uncodified, they either look to the existing legal tradition of the *madhhabs* or they make modern laws, based on the legal logic that the legislator wishes to apply, and then reference a verse in the Quran or a *hadith* that seems to justify, in some form or another, the law they wish to apply.

In this way, the Sharia can be said to exist and be applied today primarily in a more or less hybrid form, ranging from classical *madhhab* rules moulded into a modern, codified form and applied by courts and judges who may or may not have training in classical *fiqh*, to modern civil laws that refer only tangentially to Sharia (in the form that the nation's laws "should not oppose the undisputed rules of Sharia," for example) (Lombardi 2006), and many variants in between. How this is implemented and applied is often a political and social issue and is determined by what the community of believers in each country is willing to accept and abide by.

References

Ballantyne, Wiliam. 1990. "A Reassertion of the Sharī'ah: The Jurisprudence in Gulf States." In *Islamic Law and Jurisprudence*, edited by Nicholas Heer, 149–60. Seattle: University of Washington Press.

Bearman, Peri, Rudolph Peters, and Frank E. Vogel (eds.). 2005. *The Islamic School of Law: Evolution, Devolution and Progress.* Cambridge, MA: Harvard University Press.

Brockopp, Jonathan E. 2000. *Early Mālikī Law: Ibn ʿAbd al-Ḥakam and His Major Compendium of Jurisprudence.* Leiden, Netherlands: Brill.

Brunschvig, Robert. 1965. "Justice religieuse et justice laïque dans la Tunisie des Deys et des Beys jusq'au milieu du xixe siècle" [Religious justice and secular justice in the Tunisia of the Deys and Beys until the mid-nineteenth century]. *Studia Islamica*, 23: 27–70.

Dutton, Yasin. 1999. *The Origins of Islamic Law: The Qurʾan, the Muwaṭṭaʾ and Madinan ʿamal*. London: Curzon Press.

Emon, Anver M. 2012. *Religious Pluralism and Islamic Law: Dhimmis and Others in the Empire of Law*. Oxford: Oxford University Press.

Fadel, Mohammad. 1996. "The Social Logic of *taqlīd* and the Rise of *mukhataṣar*." *Islamic Law and Society*, 3, no. 2: 193–233.

Gerber, Haim. 1994. *State, Society and Law in Islam: Ottoman Law in Comparative Perspective*. Albany: State University of New York Press.

Hallaq, Wael. 1994. "From *fatwās* to *furūʿ*: Growth and Change in Islamic Substantive Law." *Islamic Law and Society*, 1, no. 1: 29–65.

Hallaq, Wael. 2001. *Authority, Continuity, and Change in Islamic Law*. Cambridge: Cambridge University Press.

Halm, Heinz. 1974. *Die Ausbreitung der šāfiʿitischen Rechtsschule von den Anfängen bis zum 8./14. Jahrhundert* [The expansion of the Shāfiʿī school of law from its earliest time to the eighth/fourteenth century]. Wiesbaden, Germany: Ludwig Reichert.

Hamdeh, Emad. 2017. "Qurʾān and Sunna or the Madhhabs? A Salafi Polemic Against Islamic Legal Tradition." *Islamic Law and Society*, 24, no. 3: 1–43.

Hasan, Ahmad. 1984. *The Doctrine of ijmāʿ in Islam: A Study of the Juridical Principle of Consensus*. Islamabad: Kitab Bhavan.

Hurvitz, Nimrod. 2002. *The Formation of Ḥanbalism: Piety into Power*. London: Routledge Curzon.

Ibrahim, Ahmed F. 2015. *Pragmatism in Islamic Law: A Social and Intellectual History*. Syracuse, NY: Syracuse University Press.

Imber, Colin. 1997. *Ebu's-Su'ud: The Islamic Legal Tradition*. Edinburgh: Edinburgh University Press.

Jackson, Sherman. 1996. "Taqlid, Legal Scaffolding and the Scope of Legal Injunctions in Post-Formative Theory: *muṭlaq* and *ʿāmm* in Jurisprudence of Shihāb al-Dīn al-Qarāfī." *Islamic Law and Society*, 3, no. 2: 165–92.

Jaziri, Abd al-Rahman al-. 2009. *Islamic Jurisprudence according to the Four Sunni Schools*. Louisville, KY: Fons Vitae.

Jennings, Ronald C. 1975. "The Office of Vekil (wakil) in the 17th Century Ottoman Sharia Courts." *Studia Islamica*, 42: 147–69.

Kamali, Mohammed H. 1991. *Principles of Islamic Jurisprudence*. London: Islamic Texts Society.

Krawietz, Birgit. 2002. "Cut and Paste in Legal Rules: Designing Islamic Norms with *talfīq*." *Die Welt des Islams*, 42, no. 1: 3–40.

Lombardi, Clark B. 2006. *State Law as Islamic Law in Modern Egypt: The Incorporation of the Sharīʿa into Egyptian Constitutional Law*. Leiden, Netherlands: Brill.

Melchert, Christopher. 1997. *The Formation of the Sunni Schools of Law: 9th-10th Centuries C.E.* Leiden, Netherlands: Brill.

Müller, Christian. 1999. *Gerichtspraxis im Stadtstaat Córdoba: Zum Recht der Gesellschaft in einer mālikitisch-islamischen Rechtstradition des 5./11. Jahrhunderts* [Judicial Praxis in the City State of Córdoba: On the Society's Justice in a Mālikī Islamic Legal Tradition in the Fifth/Eleventh Century]. Leiden, Netherlands: Brill.

Omer, Ahmed I. 1981. "The Institution of al-hisba in the Islamic Legal System." *Journal of Islamic and Comparative Law*, 10: 63–76.

Peters, Rudolph. 1980. "Idjtihād and taqlīd in 18th and 19th Century Islam." *Die Welt des Islams*, 20, nos. 3–4: 131–45.

Peters, Rudolph. 1997. "Islamic and Secular Criminal Law in Nineteenth Century Egypt: The Role and Function of the Qadi." *Islamic Law and Society*, 4, no. 1: 70–90.

Peters, Rudolph. 2002. "From Jurists' Law to Statute Law or What Happens when the Sharia is Codified." *Mediterranean Politics*, 7, no. 4: 82–95.

Peters, Rudolph. 2005. *Crime and Punishment in Islamic Law: Theory and Practice from the Sixteenth to the Twenty-First Century.* Cambridge: Cambridge University Press.

Powers, David S. 1992. "On Judicial Review in Islamic Law." *Law & Society Review*, 26, no. 2: 315–41.

Radtke, Bernd, John O'Kane, Knut S. Vikør, and R. S. O'Fahey. 2000. *The Exoteric Aḥmad Ibn Idrīs: A Sufi's Critique of the Madhāhib and the Wahhābīs: Four Arabic texts with Translation and Commentary*. Leiden, Netherlands: Brill.

Repp, Richard. 1986. *The Müfti of Istanbul: A Study in the Development of the Ottoman Learned Hierarchy*. London: Ithaca.

Repp, Richard. 1988. "Qānūn and sharīʿa in the Ottoman Context." In *Islamic Law*, edited by Aziz Azmeh, 124–45. London: Routledge.

Roberson, Barbara A. (1993). "The Emergence of the Modern Judiciary in the Middle East: Negotiating the Mixed Courts of Egypt. In *Islam and Public Law*, edited by Chibli Mallat, 107–39. London: Graham & Trotman.

Schacht, Joseph. 1964. *An Introduction to Islamic Law*. Oxford: Clarendon.

Schirazi, Asghar. 1997. *The Constitution of Iran: Politics and State in the Islamic Republic*. London: I.B. Tauris.

Starr, June. 1992. *Law as Metaphor, From Islamic Courts to the Palace of Justice.* Albany: State University of New York Press.

Tsafrir, Nurit. 2004. *The History of an Islamic School of Law: The Early Spread of Hanafism*. Cambridge, MA: Harvard University Press.

Tucker, Judith. 1998. *In the House of the Law: Gender and Islamic Law in Ottoman Syria and Palestine*. Berkeley: University of California Press.

Tucker, Judith E. 2008. *Women, Family, and Gender in Islamic Law*. Cambridge University Press, Cambridge.

Turki, Abdel-Magid. 1984. "L'ijmāʿ ummat al-mu'minīn entre la doctrine et l'histoire" [The ijmāʿ ummat between doctrine and history]. *Studia Islamica*, 59: 49–78.

Tyan, Émile. 1960. *Histoire de l'organisation judiciaire en pays d'islam* [A History of Judicial Organization in Islamic Countries]. Leiden, Netherlands: Brill.

Van den Boogert, Maurits H. 2005. *The Capitulations and the Ottoman Legal System: Qadis, Consuls and Beratlıs in the 18th Century*. Leiden, Netherlands: Brill.

Vikør, Knut S. 2000. "Opening the Maliki School: Muhammad b. ʻAli al-Sanusi's Views on the *madhhab*." *Journal of Libyan Studies*, 1, no. 1: 5–17.

Vikør, Knut S. 2003. "The Sharīʿa and the Nation State: Who Can Codify the Divine Law?" *al-Mashriq*, 1, no. 4: 47–68.

Vikør, Knut S. 2005. *Between God and the Sultan: A History of Islamic Law.* London: Hurst.

Vogel, Frank E. 2000. *Islamic Law and Legal Systems: Studies of Saudi Arabia.* Leiden, Netherlands: Brill.

https://doi.org/10.1142/9781800611689_0006

Chapter 6

Fiqh and Legislation in the Middle East and Africa*

Delfina Serrano-Ruano

Instituto de Lenguas y Culturas del Mediterráneo y Oriente Próximo, National High Council for Scientific Research, Spain
delfina.serrano@cchs.csic.es

Introduction

Much has been written about the transformations experienced by Islamic law in the contemporary period. This chapter uses a selection of outstanding references to produce a personal synthesis that moves away from the religious/secular divide focus and provides some updates that confirm or nuance previously outlined tendencies. The ideas presented in this chapter are borrowed from the sources listed in the references section and selected from the perspective of a student of the relationship between law and society in the premodern Islamic West. A number of continuities are

*In what follows, Sharia and *fiqh* are sometimes used interchangeably to refer to Islamic divine law. Other times, a distinction is made between, (1) Sharia—in the sense of divine law contained within the Quran and Prophetic tradition; (2) *fiqh*—meaning human intellectual activity to derive legal principles and practical rules from these sources as well as the corpus of jurisprudence resulting from this activity; and (3) *qanun*—legislation enacted by modern nation-states. My understanding of classical *fiqh* includes court decisions; my use of the expression Islamic law, without quotation marks, encompasses *fiqh* and governmental law (*qanun*; *siyasa shar'iyya*) as distinct from modern state legislation.

emphasized that challenge the view of Islamic law in the contemporary period as the result of a drastic break with the past. The transformations experienced by Islamic law are treated mainly as the result of a dynamic and, for the most, endogenous process determined by modern states' enhanced capacity to control their citizens by means of technological advance, to levels unknown to premodern Islamic polities.

Distortions and misconceptions

Sharia is subject to essentialist misconceptions about its alleged unchangeable and general, binding nature. Islamists in first instance often hold isolated and decontextualized legal opinions and rules mentioned in authoritative texts to represent the entire Islamic legal system or the entire Islamic civilization and culture. Western scholarship sometimes ignores historical and political contexts and presents an image of Sharia in which religious teachings and traditions are confused with the legal and political agendas of country elites or else, the extent to which religion shapes institutions is underestimated. In turn, essentialist perspectives going against actual social practice and historical experience feed Islamophobia in the West (Kalanges 2014, 285; Masud 2019, 81–88). In addition, media reports do not always distinguish Islamic court rulings from primitive mob justice and the abuse of authority by local policemen or other officials, in flagrant violation of Sharia's basic procedural and evidence rules (Otto 2010, 648).

Recent studies provide historical examples of what contemporary Western lawyers would call "legality," "due process," and "justice" and of a conciliatory legal methodology that led to a moderate tradition capable of accommodating the needs of each time and age (Feldman 2008; Otto 2010, 650–51; Peters and Bearman 2014, 9; Serrano-Ruano 2017). Sharia is not opposed or alien to modernity, as long as the meaning of modernity is not restricted to the influential European modes of social life or organization. Understood as the capacity to reinterpret historical origins, modernity can adopt different forms and is present in all societies (An-Na‘im 2014, 307–9, 318; Masud 2013, 177–208; Masud, Salvatore, and van Bruinessen 2009).

General chronological overview

The transformations experienced by Islamic law from 1800 onwards did not represent a radical departure from a religious toward a secular legal system (Otto 2010, 617). The significance of the process relies primarily on the new centrality achieved by the state in defining the contents of the law and its scope. Thus far, this role had been played by the religious scholars.[1] The ruler was entitled to make new laws, but his legislative powers were derived from the principle of *siyasa* (Sharia-compliant governance). The religious scholars retained the capacity to determine whether and to which extent the *siyasa* implemented by the ruler deserved to be labeled as Sharia-compliant (*siyasa shar'iyya*) (Masud 2013, 248–79; Otto 2010, 625).

It would be misleading to understand the far-reaching and unprecedented reforms that affected Islamic law in the nineteenth and twentieth only as the result of external influences and to ignore the complexity of the process of exchange and dialectics in which European and local stakeholders got involved in this period, combining orientalist and reformist views of the Sharia with political aspirations (Buskens 2014, 218). Changes imposed by new social, economic, and administrative internal demands were already implemented by the Ottoman authorities in Anatolia and the semiautonomous province of Egypt. Legal reforms implemented in the Middle East often radiated eastward and southward, whereas reforms originating elsewhere had few repercussions in the Middle East (Fahmy 2018; Mayer 2019, 26).

Reforms targeted both legal methodology and substantive law. In the Ottoman Empire, Egypt, and Persia, local elites deliberately introduced European legal concepts. In Asia and Africa, local rulers, chiefs, and religious personnel were incorporated in colonial structures led by Europeans and moved to a secondary position (Otto 2010, 623–4).

During the colonial period, new legislation completely distinct from Sharia was systematically enacted. Also, some singular forms of mixing took place, like "Anglo-Muhammadan" law or "Le droit musulman *algérien*." Meanwhile, modernist religious scholars like al-Afghani and Muhammad Abduh proclaimed the reopening of the gate of *ijtihad* and paved the way for the further codification and modernization of Islamic legal doctrine on marriage (Masud 2009; Otto 2010, 624).

Today, most Muslim states have replaced the classical Sharia structures and practices with new legal institutions and rules. Given the weight of Sharia's intellectual heritage and most citizens' sensitivities, national legislation has preserved important elements of *fiqh*. Although the

[1] Henceforward also referred to as ulama or *fiqh* experts (*fuqaha'*).

resulting laws are often referred to as Sharia, they do not look like classical *fiqh*, and their import no longer depends on the authority of the religious scholars (Berger 2014, 231; Otto 2010, 617). The modern period is also marked by the dissolution of the classical legal schools, though legal interpretive communities have remained in place (Messick 2005).

In the 1970s, an antiwesternization wave moved a number of states to enact laws that selectively revived elements of traditional Islamic law. Other Muslim governments thought it prudent to amend their constitutions to introduce Sharia as a source of legislation. Also, legislative and judicial authority was reclaimed by lay Muslims. Sharia, which had evolved from a corpus of norms ruling private relations to legal codes enacted by the government, has now become an argument to enforce morality in the public domain, opening up a Pandora's box of at times mutually contradictory interpretations (Berger 2014, 223, 226, 231; Mayer 2019, 26–7). This process—treated in the fifth section, on re-Islamization, below—is referred to as "legal re-Islamization."

The legislatures of modern Muslim nation-states have either adopted Sharia in family and, especially after re-Islamization, criminal law, or adapted their constitutional and finance law to Sharia, or declared their readiness to comply with Sharia. The latter method is applied by most Muslim-majority countries to their civil, state, criminal, international, financial, and commercial laws, which were already subject to modern and international legal standards and concepts. Both constitutional and finance law are underdeveloped in Sharia. As happened with *qanun*, which went from designating governmental law or codified *fiqh* to meaning national legislation, certain concepts like *shura* (consultation) or *ijma'* (consensus) have been given a new sense in combination with modern notions of "republic" and "democracy" (Berger 2014, 228–9; Fahmy 2018, 226–70; Masud 2019, 97).

The dissociation between law and religion in the legal systems of Muslim-majority countries has emphasized the association between Sharia and identity, be it individual, collective, or national (Cammack 2005). National identities in postcolonial societies have been also built by locating "an authentic past" in women's bodies and women's position in the family opposed to the norms associated with colonialism (Emon 2012, 67).

Sharia remains an authoritative legal, ethical, and theological worldview strongly determined by the state and sociocultural norms. Conversely, legislators tend to base laws on norms that enjoy widespread social acceptance. Those who feel that contemporary Muslim societies are losing Sharia, and with it their identity, appear to disregard the fact that law is the product of the society that is subject to its rules. The relationship between Sharia, state, and society is complex; it is the product of a constant negotiation that varies according to context, rather than the subject of a fixed formula of either total separation or complete fusion (An-Naʿim 2014, 315; Masud 2019, 97–8; Peters and Bearman 2014, 9; Vikør 2006, 227).

Codification and Secularization of Islamic Law Under the Late Ottomans

By the late nineteenth century, the idea that the state is the sole legislator and that legislation should take the form of enacted codes was adopted throughout much of the Muslim world. This idea, inspired by the European civil law tradition, meant that only the state determines what law is, that state-enacted law is the highest form of law, and that law can be changed through legislation.[2] The validity of the legal rules passed depends on the constitutional rules of the state and no longer on their Quranic or Prophetic roots or the criteria of the religious scholars. Secularization of the legal system in this way did not mean the disappearance of Sharia but rather that Sharia became part of a legal system of territorial reach, whose jurisdiction was decided by the state according to partial codifications of its rules or the accustomed *fiqh* manuals. The transition toward a secular legal system was facilitated by the prevalence of the abovementioned *siyasa shar'iyya* principle, which gives rulers more leeway to determine punishments and admits less complicated procedural and evidentiary rules (Peters and Bearman 2014, 8; Vikør 2006, 207–9, 346, 347).

---

[2]The civil law tradition emerged in Continental Europe and heavily influenced modern legal reforms in North African countries, Mali, and Mauritania. The civil law tradition is characterized by written legal codes and a unique set of judicial procedures. By contrast, the common law tradition, which heavily influenced legal reforms in Sudan and Gambia, developed in England from the local corpus of judgments, doctrines implicit in those decisions, and customary practices. Judicial precedents are sources for authoritative law alongside written legislation, and the judicial procedures differ significantly from those of civil law systems. Some countries, like Somalia, mixed common and civil law traditions with Islamic and customary ones (Rabb 2018, 38).

The Ottomans did not stand out from their predecessors because of the promulgation of governmental laws running parallel to those found in *fiqh* manuals, but rather because of their systematic compilation of these rules in special collections called *qanun*. Here we have the forerunners of the modern legal codes, but with a fundamental difference. The governmental laws enacted by the Ottoman sultans from the fifteenth century onward aimed at supplementing rather than replacing Sharia there where the latter was silent or imprecise, like in land, fiscal, and criminal regulations. However, those *qanun* collections did not yet imply the state's monopoly on lawmaking, and their regulations were not superior to other types of law (Peters and Bearman 2014, 8).

Codification proper began with the legal reforms undertaken by the Ottoman sultans between 1839 and 1876. This is known as the *tanzimat* (reorganization) period. The old legal, educational, and military institutions were deemed insufficient to meet the changing internal and external demands of the empire (Rabb 2018, 38). Among the former, recent scholarship has underlined the need to bolster the Islamic legitimacy of the regime in face of domestic challenges to its authority (Emon 2012, 65; Fahmy 2018, 35–8; Mayer 2019, 27).

Codified Sharia excluded moral injunctions (e.g., opinions expressing disapproval of a certain practice) or rulings about Islamic rituals. Codification also involved a piecemeal selection of the variant and at times mutually contradictory opinions transmitted by *fiqh* manuals. For the sake of clarity, fairness, and homogeneity, codification ended with the plurality of legal opinions (*ikhtilaf*), which may foster arbitrariness, yes, but also allowed judges to accommodate customs and a flexible judicial practice. Codification also involved the risk of crystallizing rigid rules (Buskens 2014, 212; Emon 2012, 67; Peters and Bearman 2014, 8; Rabb 2018, 40). Moreover, the interpretation and application of Sharia was taken from the hands of the religious scholars, and the approach to Sharia as religious legal scholarship shifted to that of modern law (Berger 2012, 225).

Both governmental and *fiqhi* laws were revised and codified. The most significant result of this reform was the Mecelle (Majalla in Arabic), a codification of relevant Hanafi *fiqh* rules concerning trade and contracts promulgated between 1869 and 1877. It was organized following the French Civil Code of 1804 and included rules concerning property, torts, and procedure to guide judges in the still running Sharia courts. Rules were selected "that best furthered social welfare," regardless of their ranking within Hanafi School doctrine. In addition, European commercial law was given jurisdiction over European merchants operating in the Ottoman realm (Mayer 2019, 27; Rabb 2018, 38, 40).

Qadis and *muftis* became civil service officials organized according to a hierarchy headed by the *Shaykh al-Islam*, or official *mufti* of the empire (Vikør 2006, 212–3). Other institutions emerged, like the Council of Judicial Ordinances in 1839. Mixed civil and criminal courts staffed by both European and Ottoman judges were created in 1847, as was a Council of State after the model of the French *Conseil d'État* in 1868. Their operation resulted in a new curriculum for the training of judges, following European lines, and in the establishment of secular courts. Competence in the Islamic religious sciences lost relevance for the actual operation of the courts, and the jurisdiction of religious courts was restricted to family matters or eliminated. The religious scholars were replaced by new legal professionals in the newly established legal institutions. This led to tensions, as individuals who combined competence in both Western law and *fiqh* were very exceptional (Mayer 2019, 26–7). The Mecelle restricted the discretion of judges, already undermined by their lack of *fiqh* training; over time, it proved unworkable (Rabb 2018, 45–6).

In 1917, a Law of Family Rights was enacted. It combined rules from the four Sunni schools but also from minority and ancient schools of law with the aim to accommodate new social needs, but it was short-lived. In 1924, with the end of the Ottoman Empire and the birth of the Turkish state, the government abolished Sharia courts. Two years later, the Mecelle was replaced with the Swiss Civil Code. In 1928, Islam ceased to be the state religion in Turkey, and in 1937, the Turkish Republic was declared to be a secular state (Mayer 2019, 28; Rabb 2018, 45–6).

In other regions under Ottoman rule, such as Egypt, the jurisdiction of the Sharia courts was also curtailed as a result of the *tanzimat* reforms and of legal codification. In the first decades of the nineteenth century, new civil tribunals were introduced alongside the Sharia courts. The new tribunals applied both classical Islamic law and laws promulgated by the Egyptian government. In 1874, mixed courts with jurisdiction over civil and commercial cases between Egyptians and foreigners, between foreigners of different nationalities, or where a foreign interest was involved were established utilizing a civil code inspired by the French Civil Code. Following the British occupation in 1882, national courts were established for Egyptians based on a code similarly drawn from the French model, which also included Islamic commercial rules borrowed from the Mecelle. Personal-status matters remained under the jurisdiction of Sharia courts, but these were reorganized and new regulations regarding judges' qualifications were introduced. A new school for their training was set up in 1907. Various so-called *milli* courts survived to address non-Muslims' personal-status disputes outside state regulation. In 1956, the jurisdiction of Sharia and *milli* courts was transferred to the national courts by Nasser, though the applicable law remained dictated by the parties' religious affiliations. Many Arab countries used Egypt's experience as a guide to their own legal reforms (Mayer 2019, 31; Rabb 2018, 39).

The legal reforms undertaken under the Ottomans and, subsequently, under colonial rule were accompanied by internal proposals to accommodate Islamic traditions to the challenges of the new times. Muhammad Abduh (1849–1905) is a significant example of this trend. Educated at al-Azhar, he engaged with the Egyptian nationalist cause and became Grand Mufti of Egypt in 1899. His reformist ideas and his commentary on the Quran, *Tafsir al-manar* (The beacon exegesis) were disseminated by his disciple Muhammad Rashid Rida (1865–1935). Like Ibn Taymiyya—and al-Shatibi—Abduh held that *fiqh* areas other than rituals could be adjusted to changing circumstances in accordance with the criterion of social well-being (*maslaha*). This approach led him to criticize polygamy. Abduh's influence on reformist thought was far-reaching, but his actual impact on Egyptian law was limited (Masud 1995; Mayer 2019, 30–1).

The Colonial Period

Codification took place both in areas still under Ottoman rule and others that, by the end of the nineteenth century, passed into the hands of European colonial powers. With the latter's arrival in the Middle East and Africa, Sharia became almost exclusively restricted to family, inheritance, and the administration of pious endowments, and was codified (Vikør 2006, 250–1).

The impact of colonialism on the legal systems of the Middle East and Africa was more pronounced in property and commercial law and less so in penal matters that, since well before, had been under the jurisdiction of *siyasa* courts (Vikør 2006, 228; 278–9). Within the domain of family law, the *fiqhi* rules to enter the codes were selected in a great variety of ways. In Algeria, for example, the colonial administrator integrated the Sharia courts into a national court system dominated by French judges, controlling all judicial decisions in the colony. A hybrid system known as "Le droit musulman algérien" emerged, combining *fiqh* with French law according to French legal categories and concepts (Berger 2014, 224; Mayer 2019, 30). In Ethiopia, however, the Sharia courts established at the beginning of the twentieth century for the local Muslim population received even wider recognition during the Italian occupation (Kebede 2019).

The reduction of Sharia's jurisdiction during the colonial period is a fact but also a topos involving the relationship between power, law, the formation of political nationalist identities in Europe, and the legitimization of colonial enterprises on the grounds of efficient administration. European scholars and colonial administrators viewed Sharia as rigid, static, ambiguous, and unfit to operate in a modern state alongside other legal traditions. Looking through the lens of their own legal traditions, they equated Sharia with "Islamic law" and custom with customary law. "Islamic law" was conceived as a set of unequivocal binding rules to be imposed by the state. In addition, some colonial rulers privileged either *fiqh* or custom, like the British in Northern Nigeria, who in their bid to favor Sharia over custom imposed a legal system that had never existed before. The French, on the contrary, considered that the Berbers in Morocco should live according to their customary law. The conceptualization of Sharia as "Islamic law" translated into legislation—with all the above-described consequences—new institutional and archival practices, teaching programs, and printed handbooks and studies that represented European interests but also those of Muslim reformists and protonationalists (Buskens 2014, 211–3, 218; Emon 2012, 67, note 54; Masud 2013, 98–107; Masud 2019, 85–6).

The unrest generated by the colonial experience provided the breeding ground for the emergence of two influential faith-based movements: the Muslim Brotherhood, founded in Egypt in 1928 by Hasan al-Banna (d. 1949), and Jamaat-e-Islami of Pakistan, established in 1941 by Abu l-A'la Mawdudi (d. 1979) (Mayer 2019, 35–6).

Modernist Legislative Reform in the Postcolonial Nation-States of the Middle East and Africa

The codes that began to be promulgated in Egypt from the middle of the nineteenth century onward had no lasting effect until Abd al-Razzaq al-Sanhuri's code of civil law, combining elements of French and Islamic law, was adopted in 1949. Al-Sanhuri (1895–1971) combined expertise in both Western and Islamic law and thought that applying the principles of modern comparative law was the best means of breathing new life into the Islamic legal heritage. Relying on his code, Egypt made the above-mentioned transition from the mixed to the national courts system. The code was adopted as a model by Syria already in 1949, by Iraq in 1951, was imported verbatim by Jordan in 1976, replacing the Ottoman Mecelle, and by some Arab countries in the Gulf (Mayer 2019, 31; Rabb 2018, 39–40, 45–6).

By the mid-twentieth century, the codification, reform, and nationalization process undergone by Sharia law in the preceding decades was accelerated with the predominance of hybrid legal systems in which family issues and inheritance remained governed by Sharia. The constitutions enacted after those countries achieved independence provided that Islam was the state religion and commonly required that the head of state should be Muslim. However, Lebanon, whose 1946 Constitution was reconfirmed in the 1989 Taif Accord, designated a Maronite Catholic as the head of state, whereas the 1973 Syrian Constitution did not establish Islam as the religion of the state. A differentiation can be made between constitutions that mention Sharia either as one among other sources of legislation or as "a" source of legislation, or as "the only" source of legislation. Further, there is a distinction between legislation that should "draw" on Sharia and legislation that should "comply" with Sharia. The constitutions of Lebanon, Gambia, and Senegal do not mention Islamic law, but some courts in these countries apply Islamic law in personal-status cases. In Ethiopia, Ghana, Israel, Kenya, and Tanzania, Sharia is applied to Muslims by specific courts or by the national secular courts in personal-status matters (Berger 2014, 226; Lau 2014, 236; Mayer 2019, 28; Otto 2010, 631, 635; Peters and Bearman 2014, 8; Rabb 2018, 45–6). "Islamic law" is the only religious source of law expressly mentioned by the Ethiopian Constitution, whose Article 34 permits the adjudication of personal and family law disputes according to religious or customary laws (Kebede 2019).

Modernization, development, nation-building, and socioeconomic progress became major goals for almost all newly independent states. The adoption of a modern, unified national legal system with a division of power and the reform of personal-status legal matters were considered essential prerequisites for social transformation. All citizens of the new nation-state became subjects to a single legal system run by a new legal profession. A blend of Arab nationalism, socialism—with its emphasis on equality, also between men and women—and authoritarianism shaped the new regimes of the Middle East, especially under the leadership of Egypt's president Nasser (Berger 2014, 223–4; Mayer 2019, 31; Otto 2010, 622–3).

The codified versions of Islamic family law enacted by most governments deviated considerably from classical *fiqh*. In addition, some legislators attached equal value to all legal schools, including the Shi'i ones, and considered themselves free to choose from among their different rules those that best fit their aims (Otto 2010, 632; see subsection "Consequences" of the fifth section on re-Islamization below). To minimize objections from conservatives, reforms were often made via procedural expedients or by decree, imposing requirements such as the registration of marriages, a minimum age for marriage—thereby deterring child and forced marriages—or compliance with certain bureaucratic formalities and conditions to discourage polygamy and the husband's use of discretionary divorce (Berger 2014, 224–5; Mayer 2019, 31–2). In Egypt, a reforming personal-status law promulgated by decree by President Anwar Sadat in 1979 eliminated a husband's right to compel his disobedient wife to return to the marital home, required that the husband register a divorce and inform the wife he was divorcing her, and provided that a husband's taking of a second wife constituted grounds for divorce by the first wife. Also, the law enhanced the wife's rights in matters of maintenance, child custody, and post-divorce division of property (Mayer 2019, 32). Yet in Sudan, Mali, and Nigeria, the man can still cast off his wife on his own authority, with no or hardly any restriction (Otto 2010, 631).

In Algeria, a High Islamic Court was created in 1976 whose competence extended to the promotion of *ijtihad* as long as the result of its application did not overlap with or contradict a secular regulation (Mayer 2019, 30). Morocco's family law (the *Mudawwana*) drew from a selection of rules from the four Sunni schools of law, with an emphasis on Malikism—which is dominant in the area—plus the Imami Shi'i legal school. Until the promulgation of the new *Mudawwana* in 2004 (see "Consequences" section in the section on re-Islamization below), the 1956 Tunisian family code was considered the most "revolutionary" reform attempt ever carried out in a Muslim-majority country. Polygamy was abolished and men and women were given equal rights in divorce. Furthermore, adoption was legalized in 1958 (Berger 2014, 226; Mayer 2019, 32).

Codified *fiqh* on inheritance has been less subject to reform than marriage regulations. In practice, people have always managed to find ways to leave to their daughters shares equal to those corresponding to their sons, but formally, women receive one-half of the share corresponding to a man in an equal position (Otto 2010, 632). In Iraq, a law adopting German inheritance law promulgated in 1959 was canceled in 1963. An earlier reform plan was then brought back, combining relevant Sunni and Shi‘i *fiqh* (Mayer 2019, 32).

The authority of the religious scholars was further relegated to the fields of worship and morality, or to legitimating reforms of Sharia, where the ultimate power of selection and interpretation was exclusively assigned to the national legislatures. The monopoly on determining the applicable Sharia rule was transferred to the judiciary, whose work relies on codified sets of rules. Issuing judgments on the basis of modern legal codes required professional skills, imparted at newly established faculties of law where the study of Sharia was limited to an introduction of its basic principles and to family law. Tribal and community leaders, who had been in charge of customary law for so long, were also marginalized (Berger 2014, 225; Otto 2010, 623; Peters and Bearman 2014, 8).

Conversely, from the 1960s onward, the implications of the sacred sources for areas not covered by *fiqh* thus far, or where earlier doctrines were deemed inadequate, were developed. A new literature was produced by Muslims from different educational backgrounds and outlooks, like the Iraqi Shi‘i scholar Muhammad Baqir al-Sadr (d.1980). Their writings are more oriented toward ideology than toward jurisprudence, and focus on public-law issues such as government, penal law, and macroeconomic principles. Their theories did not fit into the traditional categories, thus contributing to making the barriers formerly separating the schools of law and Islam's major divisions more permeable. Some, like the Sudanese Hassan al-Turabi (d. 2016), supported the idea of states constituted according to Islamic criteria. Theoretical debates went on about the degree to which Islam was compatible with the post–World War II system of international law and the degree to which an Islamic system was susceptible to incorporating democratic principles (Masud 2013, 143–76; Mayer 2019, 35–6).

Legal Re-Islamization or Traditionalist Legislative Reform

Motivations

The independent Muslim countries faced huge challenges. Many states succeeded in stabilizing society and in using their oil revenues to develop agriculture, industry, education, and public health, but much went wrong too. Attempts at bringing family and property law closer to rule-of-law standards caused considerable resistance, whereas the implementation of these laws proved disappointing for many people. Individual rights were systematically subordinated to the general goods of "stability" and "development." Policies were made in the name of the people without giving them a political voice. Moreover, most countries were unable to maintain effective courts to control illegal practices and provide remedies. Bureaucracies blocked and frustrated private business initiatives. The cases of politicians, civil servants, and army officers who used their public positions for their own private interests undermined their reputation. Ethnic conflicts, separatist movements, military coups, and other conflicts threatened the stability of many young states. In addition, people's attachment to tradition was underestimated. By the mid-1960s, the centralist, authoritarian, mostly socialist ideology of the times started to crack. People's dissatisfaction with their governments gave religious scholars and tribal chiefs new opportunities to regain lost powers. The ulama reacted by calling for religious and cultural authenticity, but at the same time, other domestic and transnational actors began to promote democratization, privatization, human rights, anti-corruption measures, and rule-of-law policies (Otto 2010, 621, 623, 626).

The ideology of Islamization—whose emergence was sketched at the end of the previous section—intensified and resulted in an open call for the rejection of Western laws because of the West's political, military, and economic dominance and its "moral decadence." Law has always played a central role in Islam, and contemporary political Islam is no exception in that regard. Islamist standpoints are based on the belief that economic development, justice, and prosperity will follow automatically from the establishment of an Islamic legal order and social system. The resulting movements summon Muslims to replace governments in power with genuinely Islamic governance systems that, apart from law, should extend to education, politics, economics, and finance. The necessary inspiration should be drawn from the important contributions to learning and civilization made by their forerunners (Lau 2014, 243; Masud 2013, 125–33; Mayer 2019, 34; Otto 2010, 621; Saeed 2014, 248–9).

Today's most famous puritan movements claim to be Sunni and are, in some cases, sponsored by Saudi Arabia. They call for a better society and government and present themselves as true and pious Muslims. Only a few are individual models of selflessness. Groups like the Muslim

Brotherhood provide social services where the government is absent, an activity that understandably earns them a large number of followers. In doing so, they become catalysts of popular discontent. Some puritans are militant and are ready to die as martyrs. Their international impact has been tremendous, with the political successes we are going to see next, but also triggered a variety of negative reactions that have undermined their credibility (Otto 2010, 621, 645–7).

Facts

From the 1970s onward, a number of initiatives were launched to reinstate Islamic law. Punishments considered typical of classical Sharia, *zakat* taxation, and bans on interest on loans were integrated into legal systems that remained strongly shaped by their Western models; innovations were not introduced by referring the judiciary to the classical *fiqh* books but by referring them to codifications of the relevant rules promulgated at the state's initiative. Legal re-Islamization also affected constitutional and family law. However, the legitimacy of Islamization has been measured by the degree to which Islamic penal law has been reinstated and enforced, particularly the *hudud* punishments (i.e., amputation of the limbs, stoning to death, flogging, and the death penalty), retaliation in kind (*qisas*) and blood money for intentional and unintentional corporal damage and killing respectively. Islamic criminal law has thus become the hallmark of political Islamization, with an emphasis on sexual offenses, the consumption of alcohol, the free mixing of unrelated members of the opposite sex, apostasy, and blasphemy. Modern reconstructions of Islamic criminal law and the way its punishments are implemented today have often overlooked important substantive and procedural requirements developed by premodern jurists to verify that they are applicable and, if so, avoid their implementation as much as possible. However, lack of historical precedent does not make this trend less relevant to the shaping of contemporary understandings of the nature and applicability of Islamic law, and does not render Islamist political forces less capable of exerting pressure on Muslim governments and oppressing people (Berger 2014, 226–7; Lau 2014, 236, 243; Mayer 2019, 34; Peters and Bearman 2014, 8–9; Saeed 2014, 249; Shabana 2017, 290–1).

Legal re-Islamization varied according to the specific contexts in which it took place. Islamic criminal law was reintroduced in a codified form in Libya in 1972 (Berger 2014, 227). Sudan followed suit in 1983 and 1989, raising strong opposition among Animist and Christian Southern Sudanese, and violence in the Darfur region after 2003 (Köndgen 2017; Mayer 2019, 34–5; Otto 2010, 621, 637–38).

Elsewhere, governments were forced to respond to the pressure exerted by Islamists by either introducing isolated Islamic laws or making constitutional amendments regarding Sharia's relevance to national legislation. In Egypt in the 1970s and 1980s, proposals like making apostasy from Islam a capital crime were put forward, raising objections from the Coptic community and leading to confessional tensions. Most proposals came to nothing, but a law prohibiting alcohol was passed and came into force in 1976 (Mayer 2019, 35). A new clause was introduced in the Egyptian Constitution that declared Sharia as the principal source of legislation (Rabb 2018, 39–40). The abovementioned personal-status law of 1979 was nullified in 1985 by Egypt's High Constitutional Court. However, to placate the feminists, several changes were subsequently reintroduced into the amended 1979 law, giving women more options for divorce (Mayer 2019, 32). In Algeria, the conservative reaction came in 1984 in the form of a new family law that, presented as a return to Maliki legal doctrine, brought back male guardianship of women, gave husbands the right to divorce at will while requiring the wife to establish grounds, and reasserted polygamy (Mayer 2019, 32).

The 2012 Provisional Constitution of Somalia provided that "[n]o law which is not compliant with the general principles of Shariah can be enacted." Equally, the 2005 Constitution of Iraq provides that "[n]o law may be enacted that contradicts the established provisions of Islam" (Lau 2014, 236). In none of these cases, Sharia was reintroduced as a specific law—leaving the door open for multiple interpretations—nor were its contents defined. The same lack of definition applies to the reservations that many Muslim states have about international human rights treaties in the name of "Islam," "Sharia," or "Islamic law" (Berger 2014, 227–9).

In the 1990s, waves of democratic decentralization led to the empowerment of the 12 Muslim-majority states to the north of the Nigerian Federation. Between 2000 and 2001, their parliaments used the legislative powers accorded to them by the secular constitution to pass some Sharia-inspired criminal provisions, a dress code for women and men, and compulsory lessons in religion. Some prohibited the consumption of food and drinks during Ramadan, the consumption of alcohol, or "indecent behavior," in particular extramarital sex. Also, the jurisdiction of Sharia courts, thus far limited to family issues, was extended at the cost of general courts (Lau 2014, 239; Otto 2010, 628, 640–1; Peters 2003, 2004).

Consequences

Since the mid-1980s, a sense of moderation about some of the early legal reforms is discernible: countries are either moving to constitutionalism (Sudan), or continuing the liberalization of marriage laws (Egypt), or exercising restraint in the execution of cruel corporal punishments (Nigeria). Judicial executions of cruel corporal punishments such as stoning and amputation in the countries where such punishments are legally in force are reportedly very rare—with the exception of Iran and Saudi Arabia. The expansion of Sharia criminal law has lost much of its practical application. Muslim scholars have criticized these criminal laws for not adhering to the conditions set by *fiqh,* for being "repugnant to the teachings of the Qur'an and the Sunna," or for incumbent judges' lack of training to act according to those teachings. Occasionally, such criticisms have had legislative consequences. Politicians in the Muslim world seem to have lost interest in pursuing a policy of Islamization, due to its association with the violent attacks for which Islamists claimed responsibility (Berger 2014, 227; Masud 2019, 80; Otto 2010, 633, 649).

Islamists tend to consider local custom, music and dancing, Sufism, and the veneration of saints as un-Islamic, for which reason they are sometimes accused of "cultural genocide" (Otto 2010, 647). The puritans' believed that Sharia was curtailed and that its incorporation into national law was a corrupt and failed process, contaminated by Western values. For them, the only viable alternative to this was the complete replacement of national law by "true Sharia" and the establishment of an Islamic state. This view is simplistic and essentialist (Otto 2010, 616–617). The legislators and Islamist activists who advocate for the Islamic state do not seem to be aware that their approach to Sharia is rooted in the above-described colonial concept of "Islamic law" (Buskens 2014, 218). Islamists' reenactment of an imaginary historical conception of Sharia as law of the state is conceptually incoherent, historically unprecedented, and practically unworkable today; actually, most Muslim-majority countries are secular (An-Na'im 2014, 307). The idea that Islam requires the establishment of a so-called Islamic state is a myth, and enforcement of Sharia norms as state law goes against the rationale of those very same norms (An-Na'im 2014, 307–9, 318; Emon 2012, 68).

Recent studies on Sudan have shown the adverse impact of cruel, inhuman, and degrading punishments, the application of which has adopted a political and class bias, particularly against women from marginalized groups (Köndgen 2017). Moreover, though the severe *hudud* punishments have largely remained symbolic, they have kept a repressive and social control function that may foster the abuse of power and use of violence outside the courts (Oette 2018, 290–1).

Re-Islamization in Nigeria has been accompanied by similar controversy. The introduction of corporal punishments like amputation and stoning to death has damaged the country's reputation, internally and externally. The constitutionality of the new criminal rules and the extension of the jurisdiction of the Sharia courts have been also questioned (Lau 2014, 239–40, 244). Be that as it may, almost two decades since its inception, the introduction of Sharia has already become a nonissue in the country. The judiciary has not allowed any stoning so far. Hundreds of sentences ordering the amputation of hands have been issued, of which three were implemented. Since 2002, however, no more amputations have been carried out. Moreover, the federal government has decided to allow Islamization only as long as judgments do not violate the constitution. Despite this evidence of moderation, there are some signs of reverse trends, and there is no reason to expect that political pressure to incorporate Sharia in national law will disappear (Lau 2014, 239–40; Otto 2010, 620–1, 632–3, 641, 645; Peters 2005). The latter remark has been confirmed by Brunei's recent reinstatement of stoning to death as a punishment for gay sex and adultery ("Brunei says controversial Sharia law aimed at 'prevention'").

The suggestion of supremacy produced by the presence of Sharia in the constitutions of Muslim-majority countries must be questioned since, as we have seen, many provisions in those very same constitutions testify to the supremacy of the constitution itself and to the rule-of-law standards laid down therein (Otto 2010, 629–30, notes 3 and 4). The legitimacy of the legislative, judicial, and executive structures adopted by Muslim-majority countries upon independence—with their parliaments, elections, legislation, codifications, constitutions, and courts—have rarely been questioned by the Islamists. They have been more interested in discussing contents. In fact, the call for Islamization of the national laws was issued within the framework of a westernized legislative and judicial system and, with the exception of Sudan, most legal areas have not been pervaded by Sharia (Berger 2014, 224, 228; Otto 2010, 627).

The secular orientation of Mali's legal system and constitution explains, at least in part, why the activities of the influential local Islamists did not translate into legal re-Islamization. Rooted in its French colonial heritage, Mali's legal system allows only limited space to Sharia in family and inheritance law, with marriage subject to a secular code promulgated in 1962 and elaborated further in 1975. Another reason is the growing influence of the Western organizations that provided financial assistance to former president Moussa Traoré in the 1980s. However, in most rural and urban zones of contemporary Mali, physical punishment, practices reaffirming women's inferior status, and even polygamy are widespread, but they are not identified as Islamic. Efforts to amend family law have been frustrated for many years due to the conflicting views of Islamists and moderates, and of Western and Islamic donors (Otto 2010, 641–3; Schultz 2010, 545–7).

Since they are in charge of interpreting and implementing constitutional law and codified Sharia, judges play a crucial role in determining the outcome of the re-Islamization process (Berger 2014, 228; Lau 2014, 239). Following the 2005 Comprehensive Peace Agreement, the pluralistic Sudanese Constitution of 1998 was reconfirmed and put under the safeguard of a Constitutional Court (Köndgen 2017, 38–65). In Egypt, the scope of the Sharia referent has been kept within narrow limits by the Supreme Constitutional Court, which is the only court allowed to decide whether Egyptian legislation is compatible with Sharia. Moreover, only legislation implemented after 1980 must conform to the principles of Sharia. The constitutional courts have demonstrated a remarkable knowledge of Islamic jurisprudence and independence in determining (*ijtihad*) what Sharia is to be codified, with the exception of areas considered immutable, like Islamic rituals. In the issue of apostasy, however, the Egyptian Court of Cassation has been heavily criticized for giving in to fundamentalist views (Berger and Sonneveld 2010, 65–74; Lau 2014, 237; Otto 2010, 628). Elsewhere, the constitution has assigned the task of ensuring conformity of existing laws with the injunctions of Islam to a special advisory council, which is also tasked with recommending the necessary reforms (Masud 2019, 92–4).

Islamist interpretations of the law have spread, especially among judges of lower courts. This fact has been attributed to the poor quality of the Islamic legal training they receive in the secular law faculties.

An example is the use that lower Nigerian courts make of Islamic criminal laws regarding pregnancy out of wedlock (Berger 2014, 228, 231–2; Masud 2013, 288–90; Peters 2003).

Codification and legal nationalization also meant the disappearance of the state's enforcement of Islamic public morals through the *muhtasib*. Khaled Fahmy (2018) has convincingly argued that some recent studies advocating for the continued validity of the *hisba* institution to keep Islamic societies ethically virtuous ignore that *muhtasibs* used to be closely attached to rulers. They also ignore the high degree of violence that was inherent to the performance of their functions. Be that as it may, from the 1970s onward, the enforcement of Islamic morals was gradually taken over by social groups wishing to impose their understanding of Islamic piety to all. Apart from the already mentioned norms of decency, piety, and dress regulated by law in several countries, Islam-compliant behavior is further enforced by means of laws on blasphemy and violation of public order or state security. Activities such as publishing books, airing films allegedly critical of Islam, but also cases of homosexuality have been labeled as un-Islamic by groups who tend to identify the state with Islam and their actions as safeguarding the integrity of Islam (Berger 2014, 229–32).

Islamic public morals can also be enforced indirectly, as illustrated by apostasy from Islam in those countries where it is not legally forbidden. The identity card in most Muslim countries contains the religion of its holder; conversion from Islam is often not accepted by officials, contrary to conversion to Islam, which is readily recorded on the identity card. Moreover, most national Muslim family laws prohibit marriage between a Muslim woman and a non-Muslim man (Berger 2014, 230).

The emergence of "Muslim laypeople" has been central to realizing the demand to be Islam-compliant, which was brought about by the re-Islamization wave, and to enforce Islamic public morals. Relevant research identifies them with modern-day intellectuals, "alternative elites," or new authorities with credentials inferior to those of *fiqh* experts, combining self-esteem gained through education with an acute awareness of their Muslim identity. They may have studied the religious sources, but independently from the ulama, whose authority they challenge; actually, the line between them all has become blurred (Berger 2014, 230). They are no longer content with only asking for *fatwas*, but have themselves started to turn into semi-educated or grassroots "prosumers" who use the new research possibilities offered by the internet to navigate Islamic legal scholarship and come to their own conclusions (Krawietz 2014, 302; Yilmaz 2005, 198–200). The relationship between the religious scholars and the Islamists is ambivalent: many scholars feel criticized by the Islamists and see them as overzealous and lacking a sound knowledge of *fiqh*, but also as the forefront capable of bringing about an Islamic state in which the scholars would play a leading role (Otto 2010, 646).

There was a certain degree of consensus between the ulama and the state on determining what Sharia is or is not. Yet, the Muslim laypeople have become an important third voice, which they make heard through political activism or proselytism or by forming isolated communities where they live in accordance with their interpretation of Sharia. Some do resort to violence. Others have keenly used the national laws and the judiciary system to impose their moral code and worldview, especially since the 1990s, by filing court cases against other individuals for allegedly un-Islamic behavior or even apostasy (Berger 2014, 230–1).

Such accusations usually fall under the umbrella of criminal law—in which the state, rather than individual citizens, acts as accusing party—but even when they do not, some radical elements among lay Muslims have, in collaboration with judges of lower courts, taken it upon themselves to act against persons with a public profile whom they deem to be un-Islamic. The most infamous action of this kind was the court case filed against Egyptian university professor Nasr Hamid Abu Zayd (d.2010), but similar cases have occurred in other Muslim countries. Most were found to be lacking sufficient legal basis and dismissed by the court or overturned by higher courts. However, until that happens, mostly after a lengthy process, the accused remains in prison. The prospect of being brought before a court is sufficiently terrifying to force the accused to give in to the claims of the accusers, retracting certain statements, withdrawing a book or film, or merely reasserting the sincerity of his or her religious beliefs (Berger 2014, 228, 231–2; Peters 2003).

Legal re-Islamization has occurred without reference to a *madhhab*. Rather, there has been a preference to go directly to the Quran and the Sunna (Berger 2014, 228–9). The call for a new *ijtihad* by Muslim modernists at the end of the nineteenth century and the much more recent emergence of Muslim laypeople have deeply affected the structure of the established legal schools as institutionalized manifestations of the principle of consensus, to the point of dissolution (Cammack 2005; Masud 2013, 87–97; Ziadeh 2018, 19). The Hanafi School continues to be the most widespread. It is still the official school for issuing *fatwas*, for personal-status matters, and for religious rituals of Sunni Muslims in the successor states of the Ottoman Empire, including Egypt, Syria, Lebanon, Iraq, Jordan, and Israel-Palestine, as well as in the Balkans. Its adherents are estimated to make up more than one-third of the world's Muslims. Malikism is the official legal school in Morocco and continues to be predominant among the people of Algeria, Tunisia, and Libya. It has also spread to Upper Egypt and Sudan. Today, although the Hanafi School is officially enforced by the courts in matters of personal status, many Muslims in Egypt—particularly in the rural areas, Palestine, Jordan, Syria, Lebanon, and Iraq—follow the Shafiʿi School in ritual matters. The Hanbali School has many adherents in Palestine, Syria, Iraq, and elsewhere (Ziadeh 2018, 14–8).

A key modern development, already hinted at above, consists in crossing the boundaries of the various schools in order to find juristic opinions in support of reform. *Takhayyur* (selecting the best) and *talfiq* (combining parts of the doctrines of different schools or jurists—including the Shia—into a new doctrine) have been applied several times in the past, as in the abovementioned Ottoman Family Law of 1917. The Egyptian Law of Testamentary Dispositions of 1946 allowed a bequest to an heir within the "bequeathable third" without the consent of the other heirs, contradicting the Sunni position on the matter (Ziadeh 2018, 19; see above, Section 4). The Jaʿfari School (also known as the "fifth *madhhab*") was accredited by Mahmud Shaltut, the rector of al-Azhar University in Cairo, along with the four Sunni schools, in 1959 (Sachedina 2018, 22.) Crossing *madhhab* boundaries became particularly instrumental to improving women's family rights during the 1950s and 1960s; for instance, the Maliki School allowed women certain grounds for divorce without the consent of their husbands, the Hanafi School allowed a woman to marry without a guardian's consent, and the Hanbali and Maliki Schools allowed for stipulations and conditions in the marriage contract (Ibrahim 2017; Masud 2019, 76–7; Otto 2010, 632; Ziadeh 2018, 19). *Talfiq* and *takhayyur* are also practiced by individual Muslims and by collective national and transnational *fiqh* organizations. They all engage in "inter-*madhhab* surfing" to bridge the gap between social and cultural change and self-perceptions of Muslim identity (Masud *et al.* 2019; Yilmaz 2005).

Two examples of emerging jurisprudential fields are *fiqh al-aqalliyyat*, or jurisprudence on Muslim minorities, and "Islamic bioethics." *Fiqh al-aqalliyyat* is devoted to the concerns of Muslims living as religious minorities in majority non-Muslim countries. The European Council for Fatwa and Research (ECFR), founded in London in 1997, is the most prominent organization engaged in the theory and practice of this matter, which is also subject to individual contributions by Muslim jurists. Many critics argue that the methodology of the ECFR is too eclectic and leads to unacceptable exceptions. Critics are also concerned that these exceptions become the norm in the majority-Muslim world (Caeiro 2011; Hassan 2019; Hendrickson 2018, 24–5; Masud 2013, 117–4).

The introduction of the modern natural sciences, medical education, and general healthcare into the Islamic world by the end of the eighteenth century led to normative assessments and reactions to them in the form of *fatwas*, studies, reports, conference discussions among experts (including physicians), and debates in mass media, in Arabic as well as in other languages relevant to Muslims. From the mid-twentieth century, knowledge on specific medico-jurisprudential questions began to circulate widely among the general public. Today, a number of states consult with the religious scholars about their biomedical policies and regulations. These are also present as ethical advisors in medical institutions and as representatives of their nations in international forums (Ghaly 2015; Krawietz 2014, 291, 301; Shabana 2019).

Most national and transnational Sunni *fiqh* organizations refuse to acknowledge the capacity of the advancements of medicine and biology to change Islamic jurisprudence, especially as far as the family is concerned. They oppose surrogate motherhood, third-party reproduction, and paternity establishment out of wedlock through genetic testing, while they are open toward some innovations such as organ transplantation (Krawietz 2014, 301–2; Shabana 2013, 2019). Feminist bioethics in the sense of liberation jurisprudence (Abou El Fadl 2001) is rare, especially in Muslim "core" countries. Nevertheless, contemporary Islamic bioethics provides many examples of creative readings of classical Islamic jurisprudence triggered by modernity and technological development, especially at the level of individual contributions (Krawietz 2014, 302; Serrano-Ruano 2018, 300–3).

If criminal law has been used as a marker of the authenticity of legal re-Islamization programs, civil law—particularly the laws of personal status—has provided a testing ground to observe the interplay between gender and family relations and the requirement to preserve the state and society's "Islamic identity." This is no surprise, given the relevance of civil law to people's everyday lives and the widespread awareness of the rights and obligations of marriage and divorce. All this helps explain the frequent recourse to courts in many Muslim countries to mediate family law disputes and is one reason that reform of Islamic family law codes is so central in the agenda of governments and civil society organizations (Rabb 2018, 40).

Actually, the emergence of "Islamic feminism" can in a certain way be viewed as an unexpected side effect of the re-Islamization wave. Muslim feminists fight for equal rights and the improvement of women's legal status with Islamic reasoning and rules. Though still grossly misunderstood—especially in the West, where no distinction is made between arguing on the grounds of the Islamic tradition and the gender predeterminism of Islamist women's movements—this strategy has been rather successful, in particular regarding women's autonomous right to divorce and the legal position of unmarried mothers (Berger 2014, 227; Serrano-Ruano 2018). Islamic gender activism has been intertwined with "human rights" (*huquq al-insan*) claims. The latter concept has become a very important political argument to both legitimize and criticize the government (Masud 2013, 209–47; Otto 2010, 639–40, 649; Rabb 2018, 40).

In 2003, the Moroccan *Mudawwana* was amended at King Mohammed VI's initiative. The reform was undertaken after massive protests against the existing family laws between 1992 and 2000, avowedly with the aim to reconcile universal human rights, justice, equality, and amicable social relations with the country's Islamic traditions by means of *ijtihad* (Mayer 2019, 33; Rabb 2018, 41). The parties involved in the debate on family law articulated their positions almost entirely in Islamic terms (Buskens 2003; Otto 2010, 639–40). With the amendment, the family was placed under the joint responsibility of husband and wife. The minimum age for marriage was raised from fifteen to eighteen years (for both genders), women and men were given the right to contract their own marriages without the legal approval of a tutor, a man's right to unilateral divorce was restricted, verbal repudiation by the husband was invalidated, "discord" (*shiqaq*) was established as a reason for divorce, and important limits were put to polygamy—for example, women were given the right to make the marriage contract contingent on husbands' compromise not to take other wives. The amendments were praised by local women's groups and international human rights NGOs as an example of "progressive" personal-status laws from within an Islamic framework (Berger 2014, 227; Mayer 2019, 33; Rabb 2018, 41).

The need to strike similar balances between different political and social forces has translated into amendments of the family law, or of issues impacting family relations, in Tunisia (1998 and 2003) and Algeria (2005). Already in 1981, a new provision gave divorced Tunisian wives the right to claim a payment or an allowance to maintain the same standards they enjoyed when married (Mayer 2019, 32). Law no. 75 of October 1998, known as "Patronymic Name Law," gave unmarried mothers and other concerned persons the right to demand registration of a child under the biological father's family name and to claim or establish paternity by acknowledgment, testimony, and genetic testing. All these legislative moves have earned the Maghreb a special reputation for advancing gender equality and respecting children's rights (Serrano-Ruano 2018, 296–97). Other bold steps from the Maghreb include the revocation of the law banning Tunisian Muslim women from marrying non-Muslims in September 2017 ("Tunisian women free to marry non-Muslims"). On November 2018, a law stipulating gender equality in inheritance was approved by the Tunisian cabinet (Sadek 2018). However, the law, "seems to have vanished into the limbo of parliamentary debate" (Belkaïd 2019).

In Egypt, a new marriage law promulgated in 2000 gave women the right to unilaterally divorce their husbands through *khul'*. *Khul'* is a well-known *fiqhi* procedure for women to obtain divorce from their husbands in exchange for their dower (*mahr*). This time, however, the prerequisite consent by the husband was removed. Given the strongly opposing forces that mark the relation between Sharia and national law in the country, the provision's compliance with Sharia had to be stressed (Berger 2014, 227; Masud 2019, 94–5; Otto 2010, 640; Sonneveld 2012).

No aspect of modern life can escape the economy; thus, re-Islamization also had a visible impact on how Muslims, individually or corporately, view their earning, spending, borrowing, saving, and investing activities (Saeed 2014, 248–9). Since the 1960s, Sharia-based finance has evolved into a thriving business, present in Muslim and non-Muslim-majority countries on all continents. In both, Sharia-based and conventional financial systems coexist; Sharia-based finance attracts many customers, including non-Muslims ("Why non-Muslims are converting to sharia finance"). Though it is uncertain whether all so-called Islamic financial products would stand an authenticity test, many Muslims believe that by dealing with them, they are in compliance with the Quranic prohibition on *riba*, and that the future prospects of Islamic finance seem rather good (Saeed 2014, 258).

Islamist economists regard the *zakat* income tax that individual Muslims must pay in fulfillment of one of the five pillars of Islam as a very powerful instrument for bringing about a more egalitarian economic system. *Zakat* was easier to introduce than a public Islamic finance system. In 1983, Sudan made a move toward an interest-free banking system but, as elsewhere, enough loopholes were left so that banks and financial institutions remained functioning within the international financial markets (Berger 2014, 227–8).

Sharia Today and Future Prospects

In the modern world, lawmaking and the legitimate use of force are often considered to be the exclusive prerogatives of a centralized sovereign state that defines the operation of individual rights and public institutions within delineated geopolitical boundaries. Externally, the modern state operates within an international system in which all states are considered equal sovereigns and engage each other through trade negotiations, diplomatic relations, or international organizations. The state system in which Islamic law is immersed today extends to the arenas of government, civil, political, and economic society, bureaucracy, and judiciary. The legal systems of the contemporary Muslim-majority nation-states are primarily based on European models of civil law and governance, and incorporate Islamic law only partially (Emon 2012, 63, 67–8; Otto 2010, 644).

After the above-described adaptation to different forms of national law, Sharia is now subject to democratization and constitutionalization. This process strongly depends on domestic politics; it is also increasingly shaped by contemporary understandings of justice. As in most developing regions, political culture in the Middle East and Africa is still marked by authoritarianism, but new market forces have created an entrepreneurial middle class whose success has come to depend on that of the rule of law. Corrupt behavior is pervasive but openly discussed and tolerated less and less. The relevance of Sharia to Muslims' social and private lives is one of the most debated issues in contemporary Islamic thought. However, Sharia's relevance in contemporary Islamic societies should not be exaggerated. Other issues—like security and stability, economic growth, public finance, poverty reduction, education, public health, housing, decentralization, elections, and foreign relations—are considered far more pressing. Sharia comes into the spotlight occasionally with regard to politically sensitive issues such as gender segregation, reform of family law, religiously motivated violence, and interreligious conflict (Otto 2010, 630–7, 644, 651; Saeed 2014, 249).

On the international level, the activity of transnational organizations like the Organization of the Islamic Conference has had a visible impact on discourses about Sharia and the rule of law, especially as far as respect of human rights and the promotion of gender equality are concerned. Since the 1990s, governments of Muslim countries—including those with re-Islamized legal systems—have become signatories to international treaties and have adopted human rights in national constitutional law (Mayer 2019, 36; Otto 2010, 634). At the grassroots level, Islamic laws affecting women are, as we have seen, increasingly evaluated in terms of their conformity with the modern norm of male-female equality (Mayer 2019, 36). However, certain human rights violations regarding gender, religion, and sexual orientation and cruel corporal punishments continue to be justified on the grounds of Islamic legal traditions or even Sharia-based legislation (Otto 2010, 618–9).

Sociocultural norms have traditionally informed the state's definition of the public interest or are subordinate to local custom. Customary norms were, and continue to be, deeply rooted in kinship, power, and economy (Otto 2010, 647). Conversely, many Muslims identify with Sharia or with Islamic traditions, values, and practices that are alien to the prescriptions of *fiqh*, such as honor killings and female genital mutilation (Peters and Bearman 2014, 9; Vikør 2006, 227, 244–55). For this reason, women's rights movements in Nigeria, Tanzania, and other countries view Sharia as the desired antidote against arbitrary tribal justice and repressive customs. Yet, it must be taken into account that the only available alternative in many places is not an effective and fair state justice system, but a semi-functional customary one. In the case of Libya and Somalia, the legal and justice systems have been destroyed by violent conflict. Meanwhile, tribal and community leaders are essential to peace and national political stability because of the power they still hold in many areas of the Muslim world. However problematic the kind of justice they impart, governments take care to keep these leaders satisfied and include them in the delicate balances they have to strike between opposed social groups when deciding on Sharia-related matters (Otto 2010, 618, 647–9).

In spite of the setback experienced by the ulama as a consequence of the nationalization and codification of the law in the Middle East and Africa, they retain important religious-legal functions and hence, much capacity to exert social and political influence. As judges in family courts, many of them have earned a reputation of fairness and the ability to find reasonable solutions to problematic cases. As preachers, they lead the Friday prayer and are called to attend to the important "rites de passage" of birth, marriage, and death. As *muftis*, they provide legal advice and moral guidance to the people and do not hesitate to use new technologies, the mass media, and the internet to reach their audience. In addition, they oversee educational institutions, the management of *waqf* land, the pilgrimage to Mecca, and the collection of Islamic alms (*zakat*). Last but not least, their opinions have preserved the capacity to enhance the legitimacy of the state (Otto 2010, 646).

Future ways of incorporating Sharia—or rather, of reconstructing it in the framework of *ijtihad*—will depend on politicians, legislators, judges, *fiqh* experts, and bureaucrats in interaction with civil society. As elsewhere, Muslim governments aim for stability, prosperity, and social justice. These goals require a modicum of democracy, sound administration, an effective legal system, and the ability to convince opposing and complex ideological forces to reach compromises (Masud 2019, 95–7; Otto 2010, 643–7).

One of the most convincing proposals for defining the future role of Sharia has been put forward by Sudanese scholar Abdullahi an-Na'im. He relies on the premise of a separation between Sharia and the state for, in his view, the integrity and validity of religious experience itself requires the religious neutrality of the state. Yet, the premise that Sharia should not be enforced by the state does not necessarily entail its suppression or the denial of its cultural and political role or its capacity to order Islamic societies (An-Na'im 2014, 307–9, 318).

An-Na'im emphasizes the efficiency of practice over theoretical analysis or legal stipulation to mediate the paradox of the separation between Islam and the state on the one hand and the connection between Islam and politics on the other. According to An-Na'im, the main premises of mediation are as follows: First, the modern territorial state should neither seek to enforce Sharia as positive law or public policy nor claim to interpret its doctrine and general principles for Muslim citizens. Second, Sharia principles can be a source of public policy and legislation if they are submitted to the constitutional and human rights of all citizens equally and without discrimination (An-Na'im 2014, 315).

Well-informed debates about Sharia's role in contemporary societies and the relevant regulations and policies require the insights of many disciplines and the consideration of the complex interplay of law, politics, and the demands of daily life. Yet, a solid knowledge base to make the theory compatible with actual practice is not enough to produce workable institutions. Winning over public opinion requires political sophistication. Arguments may come from a variety of perspectives, but it is clear that those made from within Islam will remain essential. This is an important reality to those seeking to promote democracy, development, and human rights in Muslim-majority states, which experts recommend not to disregard (Buskens 2010, 130–4; Emon 2012, 68; Kalanges 2014, 285; Otto 2010, 639–40, 650).

It might be argued that the prerogative of defining the contents of Muslims' religion, and hence, those of Sharia, belongs to Muslims, and that Sharia might be defined as an understanding of Islamic law shared by Muslims of a given time and place. Yet, as Knut Vikør has observed, such common understandings are seldom reached, let alone become universal among adherents of a single religion. A rule's consistency with Sharia may be decided by reference to the sources of authority rather than by a given form of religious expression or belief. *Fiqh* is part of Islamic legal history and as such, an objective point of reference in Muslims' debates (Vikør 2006, 227, 244–55, 347). Authority on the grounds of competence is thus a key question in defining and accommodating Sharia to present-day living conditions. The challenge is not reduced to arguing that a given interpretation of the Quran is not convincing; discerning how the sacred sources were used to justify certain positions will probably be more helpful. Classical Islamic legal scholarship makes clear that the interpretation of the revealed sources was based on reason and logic, and considered valid and applicable not because of any inherent quality but in as much as it was accepted as just and beneficial by the community of authoritative interpreters (Cammack 2005; Emon 2012, 61; Masud 2019, 78–9, 95).

According to Muhammad Khalid Masud, there is an epistemological crisis in the modern interpretation of Sharia. The methods of formal logic and syllogistic reasoning typical of classical Islamic legal interpretation have been challenged by modern notions of justice, judiciary, rights, and equality, giving way to new methods like deontic logic (Masud 2013, 73–4). Abdullahi an-Na'im proposes to rely on "civic reason." Based on this, Muslims and others should be able to propose policy and legislative initiatives emanating from their beliefs, provided they can support their proposals in a public, free, and open debate with reasons that are accessible and convincing to the generality of citizens, with all the basic constitutional and human rights safeguards against the tyranny of the majority. Private voluntary compliance with Sharia should not affect the rights of others, since coercion is incompatible with the piety guiding religious practice that, in turn, must be voluntary and deliberate. Muslims would also definitely not be entitled to wield Sharia to justify the violation of state law. Modern states should guarantee that Muslims are able to exercise their right to religious/cultural self-determination within the framework of state law and its constitutional safeguards, like any other religious/cultural community (An-Na'im 2014, 315–8).

Religious scholars, leaders of civil religious movements, and judges have the task of making constructive use of the intellectual heritage of *fiqh*, acting as "cultural brokers" to facilitate the compatibility between Sharia, modernity, the rule of law, and human rights, and to raise awareness of existing Islamic law and rule-of-law-based rights among the common people (Otto 2010, 651–2; Von Carlowitz and Kirschweng 2012, 5–6; Yilmaz 2005). In doing so, the key point is to treat all such references as the product of human interpretations of the Quran and the Sunna and hence, as subject to accommodation and change, not as the binding word of God. This does not mean that Sharia is essentially incompatible with the principles of international law and the rule of law. The key question is, who has the authority to define Sharia and its scope? And since this is not a question of logic but one that depends on the power relations among the relevant actors and stakeholders, no human institution should be considered capable of "declaring or amending Islamic doctrine" on behalf of the bulk of the world's Muslims (An-Na'im 2014, 317–8; Masud 2019, 78–9, 95; Vikør 2005, 256–7).

An-Na'im's proposal to consider Sharia through "civic reason" and democratic process is meant to enable Muslims to press for legislation consistent with their religious beliefs, without asserting that belief as the rationale of state enforcement or their own religious conviction or cultural affiliation as a categorical justification. The secular legislative organs of the modern territorial state must have the exclusive monopoly on enacting state law, which is however shaped by Islamic norms and values, and secular judicial administrative organs must have the exclusive authority to interpret and apply it (An-Na'im 2014, 317–8).

As long as the state's legal systems keep suffering from serious shortcomings, Islamists will have to be taken into account as a necessary social and political interlocutor and Sharia will fuel new legal, moral, and political aspirations (Otto 2010, 652). As Jean Michel Otto remarks, the legal systems of most Muslim-majority countries are oppressive and restrictive in several aspects: Islamic fundamentalist ideas have been able to take root in the mind of judges and lawyers, and efforts to remove discriminatory provisions in national laws are met with resistance from conservative forces, even when based on a reinterpretation of the Quran and the Sunna (e.g., Masud 2019, 94–5). Since significant groups among Muslims do not seem to be satisfied with this situation, a new phase is foreseeable in the interaction between Sharia and the nation-state that corrects abuse and manipulation of the law, for example to get rid of political opponents, and reviews the training of legal professionals. Infringement of human rights in the name of Sharia is due to avoidable domestic governmental failures. This is demonstrated by the considerable progress made in the last decades by legislatures, bureaucracies, and courts in the Muslim world, despite political controversies and intellectual confusion. Legislators, administrators, and judges have displayed impressive balancing capacities, keenly combining norms of *fiqhi* and Western origin and making use of legal ambiguity. Judges in particular have shown that codified *fiqh* does not prevent them from finding creative solutions to acute social problems like the discrimination of unmarried mothers and their children. There is hope that domestic and international programs to strengthen judiciaries and the mechanisms of modern law will contribute to soften contradictions between Sharia and the rule of law (Berger 2014, 232; Masud 2013 4, 301–5; Otto 2010, 635, 647, 651; Serrano-Ruano 2018).

Haste in bringing about democratization, especially when imposed from outside, has proved detrimental in many cases. Longer periods should be considered for civic institutions, courts, political parties, and the economy to begin to function before organizing elections. Be that as it may, the quality of legal process and human rights protection could benefit much from international cooperation and from technical and financial assistance (Otto 2010, 649–50).

Investment in the rule of law and the protection of human rights is essential, in Muslim-majority countries but elsewhere too. The use of the rule of law in the international arena remains undertheorized. The fact that international law has religious and theological underpinnings needs to be recognized and discussed more systematically.[3] Care must also be taken

---

[3] This point has been made recently by Muhammad Khalid Masud in connection with his research in progress on al-Shatibi's contribution to the emergence of international law.

that the invocation of the rule of law in the international realm does not undermine the values that are supposed to be safeguarded by this ideal within each country. To complicate things even more, international institutions themselves are not totally bound by the rule of law. This is surprising, because the UN and its agencies, for example, vehemently advocate for the rule of law within individual countries. However, they maintain diplomatic immunity with various—unconvincing—arguments (Waldron 2016, 13–4). The legitimacy of Western nations and international organisms to impose respect for human rights and the rule of law in Muslim-majority countries is further undermined by the exceptions and double standards applied when geostrategic, energy, and economic interests are involved, such as the torture and mistreatment of prisoners in extraterritorial prisons in the name of security.

Nevertheless, convergence toward rule-of-law standards is incompatible with interpretations of Sharia that exert a powerful influence on Muslims' social relations and political behavior, such as those supporting male authority over women (*qiwama*), legal superiority of Muslims over non-Muslims (*dhimma*), aggressive *jihad* (An-Na'im 2014, 316), discrimination of children on the basis of lineage, etc. The emancipation of women, the democratization of politics, and the increase in respect for human rights are inescapable developments that can be hindered but not halted (Otto 2010, 635).

References

Abou El Fadl, Khaled. 2001. *Speaking in God's name: Islamic Law, Authority and Women*. Oxford: Oneworld Publications.

Belkaîd, Akram. 2019. "Tunisia Balks at Inheritance Changes." *Middle East Online MEO*, August 5, 2019. https://peoplepill.com/people/akram-belkaid/news.

An-Na'im, Abdullahi A. 2014. "Epilogue: The Normative Relevance of Sharia in the Modern Context." In *The Ashgate Companion to Islamic Law*, edited by Ruud Peters and Peri Bearman, 307–19. Burlington, VT: Ashgate.

Berger, Maurits S. 2014. "Sharia and the Nation State." In *The Ashgate Companion to Islamic Law*, edited by Ruud Peters and Peri Bearman, 223–34. Burlington, VT: Ashgate.

Berger, Maurits S. and Nadia Sonneveld. 2010. "Sharia and National Law in Egypt." In *Sharia Incorporated. A Comparative Overview of the Legal Systems of Twelve Muslim Countries in Past and Present*, edited by Jan M. Otto, 51–88. Leiden, Netherlands: Leiden University Press.

"Brunei says controversial Sharia law aimed at 'prevention.'" *BBC News*, April 12, 2019. https://www.bbc.com/news/world-asia-47906070. Buskens, Leon. 2003. "Public Debates on Family Law Reform. Participants, Positions, and Styles of Argumentation in the 1990s." *Islamic Law and Society*, 10, no. 1: 70–131.

Buskens, Leon. 2010. "Sharia and National Law in Morocco." In *Sharia Incorporated. A Comparative Overview of the Legal Systems of Twelve Muslim Countries in Past and Present*, edited by Jan M. Otto, 89–138. Leiden, Netherlands: Leiden University Press.

Buskens, Leon. 2014. "Sharia and the Colonial State." In *The Ashgate Companion to Islamic Law*, edited by Ruud Peters and Peri Bearman, 209–21. Burlington, VT: Ashgate.

Caeiro, Alexandre V. 2011. *Fatwas for European Muslims: The Minority Fiqh Project and the Integration of Islam in Europe*. PhD diss., University of Utrecht.

Cammack, Mark E. 2005. "Islam and Nationalism in Indonesia: Forging an Indonesian Madhhab." In *The Islamic School of Law. Evolution, Devolution, and Progress,* edited by Peri Bearman, Ruud Peters, and Frank E. Vogel, 175–90. Cambridge, MA: Harvard University Press.

Emon, Anver M. 2012. "Shari'a and the Modern State." In *Islamic Law and International Human Rights Law*, edited by Anver M. Emon, Mark Elis, and Benjamin Glahn, 26–39. Oxford: Oxford University Press.

Fahmy, Khaled. 2018. *In Quest of Justice. Islamic Law and Forensic Medicine in Modern Egypt*. Oakland: University of California Press.

Feldman, Noah. 2008. "Does Shariah Mean the Rule of Law?" *New York Times*, March 16, 2008. http://www.nytimes.com/2008/03/16/news/16iht-16shariaht.11119704.html.

Ghaly, Mohammed. 2015. "Biomedical Scientists as Co-Muftis: Their Contribution to Contemporary Islamic Bioethics." *Die Welt des Islams*, 55: 286–311.

Hassan, Said F. 2019. "*Fiqh al-aqalliyyāt* and Muslim Minorities in the West." In *Routledge Handbook of Islamic Law*, edited by Khaled Abou El Fadl, Atif A. Ahmad, and Said F. Hassan, 313–23. London: Routledge.

Hendrickson, Jocelyn. 2018. "Minority Jurisprudence." In *The Oxford Encyclopedia of the Islamic World, Oxford Islamic Studies Online*, 23–26. http://www.oxfordislamicstudies.com/article/opr/t236/e0473.

Ibrahim, Ahmad F. 2017. "Talfīq/Takhayyur." In *The [Oxford] Encyclopedia of Islam and Law, Oxford Islamic Studies Online*. http://www.oxfordislamicstudies.com/article/opr/t349/e0082.

Kalanges, Kristine. 2014. "Sharia and Modernity." In *The Ashgate Companion to Islamic Law*, edited by Ruud Peters and Peri Bearman, 277–89. Burlington, VT: Ashgate.

Kebede, Michael. 2019. "Commentary: Ethiopia's 1999 Federal Courts of Sharia Consolidation Proclamation: The Function of the Sharī'a Courts." *Islamic Law Blog*, August 29, 2019. https://islamiclaw.blog/category/shari%CA%BFa-courts/.

Köndgen, Olaf. 2017. *The Codification of Islamic Criminal Law in the Sudan. Penal Codes and Supreme Court Case Law under Numayrī and al-Bashīr*. Leiden, Netherlands: Brill.

Krawietz, Birgit. 2014. "Sharia and Medical Ethics." In *The Ashgate Companion to Islamic Law*, edited by Ruud Peters and Peri Bearman, 293–305. Burlington, VT: Ashgate.

Lau, Martin. 2014. "The Re-Islamization of Legal Systems." In *The Ashgate Companion to Islamic Law*, edited by Ruud Peters and Peri Bearman, 235–46. Burlington, VT: Ashgate.

Masud, Muhammad Kh. 1995. *Shāṭibī's Philosophy of Islamic Law*. Islamabad: Islamic Research Institute Pakistan.

Masud, Muhammad Kh. 2009. "Anglo-Muhammadan Law." In *Encyclopaedia of Islam*, vol. 3, edited by Kate Fleet, Gudrun Krämer, D. Matringe, John Nawas, and Everett Rowson. Leiden, Netherlands: Brill.

Masud, Muhammad Kh. 2013. *Shari'a Today. Essays on Contemporary Issues and Debates in Muslim Societies*. Islamabad: Iqbal International Institute for Research and Dialogue.

Masud, Muhammad Kh. 2019. "Modernizing Islamic Law in Pakistan: Reform or Reconstruction?" *Journal of South Asian and Middle Eastern Studies*, 42, no. 2: 73–97.

Masud, Muhammad Kh., Armando Salvatore, and Martin van Bruinessen (eds.). 2009. *Islam and Modernity, Key Issues and Debates*. Edinburgh: Edinburgh University Press.

Masud, Muhammad Kh., Joseph A. M. Kéchichian, Brinckley Messick, Ahmad S. Dallal, and Jocelyn Hendrickson. 2019. "Fatwā." In *The Oxford Encyclopedia of the Islamic World, Oxford Islamic Studies Online*. http://www.oxfordislamicstudies.com/article/opr/t236/e0243.

Mayer, Ann E. 2019. "Modern Legal Reform" (updated by Joseph A. Kéchichian). In *The Oxford Encyclopedia of the Islamic World, Oxford Islamic Studies online*, 26–39. http://www.oxfordislamicstudies.com/article/opr/t236/e0473.

Messick, Brinkley. 2005. "Madhhabs and Modernities." In *The Islamic School of Law Evolution, Devolution, and Progress*, edited by Peri Bearman, Ruud Peters, and Frank E. Vogel, 175–90. Cambridge, MA: Harvard University Press.

Oette, Lutz. 2018. "Buchbesprechungen/Book Reviews: Olaf Köndgen, *The Codification of Islamic Criminal Law in Sudan*, Leiden: Brill, 2018, *Verfassung und Recht in Übersee*." *Law and Politics in Africa Asia Latin America*, 51, no. 2: 288–92.

Otto, Jan M. 2010. "Towards Comparative Conclusions on the Role of Sharia in National Law." In *Sharia Incorporated. A Comparative Overview of the Legal Systems of Twelve Muslim Countries in Past and Present*, edited by Jan M. Otto, 613–54. Leiden, Netherlands: Leiden University Press.

Peters, Ruud. 2003. *Islamic Criminal Law in Nigeria*. Ibadan, Nigeria: Spectrum Books.

Peters, Ruud. 2004. "The Reintroduction of Sharia Criminal Law in Nigeria: New Challenges to the Muslims of the North." In *Beiträge zum Islamischen Recht*, vol. 4, edited by Silvia Tellenbach and Thoralf Hanstein, 9–23. Frankfurt A. M., Germany: Peter Lang.

Peters, Ruud. 2005. *Crime and Punishment in Islamic Law, Theory and Practice from the Sixteenth to the Twenty-First Century*. Cambridge, MA: Cambridge University Press.

Peters, Ruud and Peri Bearman. 2014. "Introduction: The Nature of Sharia." In *The Ashgate Companion to Islamic law*, edited by Ruud Peters and Peri Bearman, 1–10. Burlington, VT: Ashgate.

Rabb, Intisar A. 2018. "Civil Law"; "Courts." In *The Oxford Encyclopedia of the Islamic World, Oxford Islamic Studies Online*, 38–41; 42–47. http://www.oxfordislamicstudies.com/article/opr/t236/e0473.

Sachedina, Abdulaziz. 2018. "Shīʻī Schools of Law," *The Oxford Encyclopedia of the Islamic World, Oxford Islamic Studies Online*, 21–23. http://www.oxfordislamicstudies.com/article/opr/t236/e0473.

Saeed, Abdullah. 2014. "Sharia and Finance." In *The Ashgate Companion to Islamic Law*, edited by Ruud Peters and Peri Bearman, 249–59. Dorchester, UK: Ashgate.

Sadek, George. 2018. "Tunisia: Cabinet Approves Bill Requiring Equal Inheritance Shares for Men and Women." *Global Legal Monitor*, December 4, 2018. http://www.loc.gov/law/foreign-news/article/tunisia-cabinet-approves-bill-requiring-equal-inheritance-shares-for-men-and-women/.

Schultz, Dorothea. 2010. "Sharia and National Law in Mali." In *Sharia Incorporated. A Comparative Overview of the Legal Systems of Twelve Muslim Countries in Past and Present*, edited by Jan M. Otto, 529–52. Leiden: Leiden University Press.

Serrano-Ruano, Delfina. 2017. "Judicial Procedure and Legal Practice on *Liʿān* (Imprecatory Oath) in Andalus: The Evidence from Model *Shurūṭ* Collections, 11th-12th Centuries." In *Justice and Leadership in Early Islamic Courts*, edited by Intisar A. Rabb and Abigail B. Krasner, 149–70. Cambridge, MA: Harvard University Press.

Serrano-Ruano, Delfina. 2018. "Redefining Paternal Filiation through DNA Testing: Law and the Children of Unmarried Mothers in the Maghreb." *Journal of Middle East Women's Studies*, 14, no. 3: 292–313.

Shabana, Ayman. 2013. "Negation of Paternity in Islamic Law between *Liʿān* and DNA Fingerprinting." *Islamic Law and Society*, 20, no. 3: 157–201.

Shabana, Ayman. 2017. "Empowerment of Women between Law and Science. Role of Biomedical Technology in Enhancing Equitable Gender Relations in the Muslim World." *Hawwa*, 15: 193–218.

Shabana, Ayman. 2019. "Islamic law and Bioethics." In *Routledge Handbook of Islamic Law*, edited by Khaled Abou El Fadl, Atif A. Ahmad, and Saeed F. Hassan, 112–24. London: Routledge.

Sonneveld, Nadia. 2012. *Khulʿ Divorce in Egypt: Public Debates, Judicial Practices, and Everyday Life*. Cairo: American University in Cairo Press.

"Tunisian women free to marry non-Muslims." *BBC News*, September 15, 2019. https://www.bbc.com/news/world-africa-41278610.

Vikør, Knut S. 2006. *Between God and the Sultan: A History of Islamic Law*. London: Hurst Publishers.

Von Carlowitz, Leopold, and Stefanie Kirschweng. 2012. "Islamic Law, the Rule of Law, and International Peace Operations." *ZIF Conference Report*, March 2012. https://www.un.org/ruleoflaw/blog/document/islamic-law-the-rule-of-law-and-international-peace-operations/.

Waldron, Jeremy. 2016. "The Rule of Law." In *The Stanford Encyclopedia of Philosophy* (Summer 2020 Edition), edited by Edward Zalta, 1–18. https://plato.stanford.edu/archives/fall2016/entries/rule-of-law/.

"Why non-Muslims are converting to sharia finance." *The Economist Britain*, October 20, 2018. https://www.economist.com/britain/2018/10/20/why-non-muslims-are-converting-to-sharia-finance.

Yilmaz, Ihsan. 2005. "Inter-Madhhab Surfing, Neo-Ijtihad, and Faith-Based Movement Leaders." In *The Islamic School of Law Evolution, Devolution, and Progress*, edited by Peri Bearman, Ruud Peters, and Frank E. Vogel, 191–206. Cambridge, MA: Harvard University Press.

Ziadeh, Farhat J. 2018. "Sunni Schools of Law." *The Oxford Encyclopedia of the Islamic World, Oxford Islamic Studies online*, 12–21. http://www.oxfordislamicstudies.com/article/opr/t236/e0473.

https://doi.org/10.1142/9781800611689_0007

Chapter 7

The Politics of Torture

Kathleen A. Cavanaugh

Pozen Center for Human Rights,
University of Chicago, Chicago, USA
kac1@uchicago.edu

Introduction

In contrast to the notion that international law is a "stable set of normative demands opposed to international politics," Martti Koskenniemi argues that it "is better understood as an aspect of hegemonic contestation, a technique of articulating political claims in terms of legal rights and duties" (Koskenniemi 2004, 197). As a hegemonic technique, law is a surface over which political struggles are waged (198–200), reflecting the political uncertainties of the time. That international law is situated within, not apart from political realities is not in question. Therefore, before we can begin to explain universal international law, we must first clarify "what or whose view of international law is meant" (199). This *Weltanschauung* unpacks the traditional reading of international law and pries open a space within which we can (re)conceptualize law against the backdrop of the hegemonic contestation over its narration.

Such a view of international law—as shaped by interests as opposed to universally shared values and norms—is hardly new. As Samuel Moyn (2010, 7) argues in his deconstruction of historiography of the international human rights law, "rights have long existed, but they were from the beginning a part of the authority of the state, not invoked to transcend it." That said, the normative developments that have occurred within the state of emergency "maximally deployed" post 9/11 have brought this particular reading of law into sharp focus, and it is in the legal narrative of the "war on terror" that the political resurfacing of international law is so clearly illuminated. The "war on terror" discourse has shifted the boundaries of permissible state action, including the use of torture. Where the debate now lies is whether the current state of exception has a relation to law or now exists entirely outside of it.

Challenges (old and new) to the notion of international law as prepolitical, fixed, and stable can also be found in the writings of Islamic legal scholars and thinkers. As Islam is not an actor, the various readings of Islam both depart and arrive at different interpretations of Prophetic revelations. The struggle between what I will call the "textualist" and "contextualist" readings is a struggle between a reading of Islam that is fixed and immutable and one that endeavors to read the text within a specific historical context. Although the various tendencies within Islam spring from the same normative criteria, these differentiated readings yield differentiated approaches to the interpretation and applicability of the norms and principles of Islamic law particularly in the ways in which these discourses intersect with the various international legal norms and prescriptives. Recalibrating our understanding of the force of law in this way brings us nearer to understanding how legal rules can shift and change, allowing the language of "emergency" and "security" to legitimize systematic and routinized violence (including torture), repression, and discrimination.

Against this backdrop, this chapter examines how the politics of law has played out within the fields of international and Islamic law, specifically focusing the prohibition on torture. When we turn to how the prohibition on torture is read within the Muslim world or, as I will detail, at the international level, I suggest symmetry in the ways in which differentiated approaches to the interpretation of law (and related doctrines) have endeavored to capture and shape how law is applied. The chapter is divided into two main sections. The first section begins by looking at how differentiated approaches to interpreting international law are captured before turning to the legal ban on torture and other forms of ill-treatment at the international and regional levels. Although the legal prohibition on torture itself is quite clear and without exception, many courts and institutions tasked with its interpretation have yet to produce a consistent approach to the understanding of torture and other forms of ill-treatment. This has, in turn, allowed states to press against the prohibition, endeavoring to re-narrate how the practice is understood.

The different trends of analysis that are evident in public international law are also present in Islamic legal discourse and give rise to competing narrations whenever Islam enters the public square.[1] The second section examines how these various readings and interpretations of Islamic law challenge the notion that its content, scope, and application is fixed and stable. The section then turns to how the variation with which Muslim legal scholars deal with criminality and punishable offenses maps out onto the question as to whether torture is prohibited or allowed under Islamic law. This examination reveals that states (Muslim or non-Muslim) apply similar techniques—keeping law untouched by practice and practice untouched by the ban.

Performing Law

The deeply performative nature of how legal rules operate in international law reveals a constructive ambiguity that opens a space in which the contestation over the "what" and the "whose" reading of the law plays out. Although the primary sources of international law identified under the Statute of the International Court of Justice (ICJ), Article 38 (treaty, custom, general principles, and judicial decisions) are not contested, much like Islamic law, its norms and principles are subject to interpretation and different trends of analysis. The differentiated approaches to interpreting international law are captured in three ways. The first is a textualist approach, in which a restrictive interpretation based on an "ordinary meaning" of the text is applied. Similar to a textualist reading of Islamic law, this approach places a great deal of weight on the literal meanings of the texts. The second "subjective" approach factors the underpinning of a treaty and the intent of its drafters and reads a treaty "in its context" when

[1] There is a significant difference among Muslim scholars and jurists as to whether torture is permissible under certain conditions (investigative, for example). For a more in-depth discussion on these points, see Masud (2007).

interpreting respective principles. A third approach is interpretative (sometimes called effective interpretation). Here, a text is read "in the light of its object and purpose" (similar to what I describe as a contextualist approach within Islam).

The legal ban on torture

While provisions of international law are constructively ambiguous, the prohibition on torture and other ill-treatment under international law is seemingly rather straightforward. The constitutive elements of torture and other forms of ill-treatment are found in international and regional instruments and institutions and provide some uniformity in the way that provisions on torture and other ill-treatment are codified. The prohibition is absolute—there is no qualifying exception (not even in cases of self-defense); the prohibition is non-derogable—it cannot be suspended in any circumstance whatsoever (for example, to stop a ticking bomb or in a state of emergency).[2] In addition, the ban on torture and on other forms of ill-treatment is recognized as customary international law, and the prohibition on torture is recognized as a norm of *jus cogens*.[3] A norm of *jus cogens* is a peremptory norm "accepted and recognized by the international community of States as a whole as a norm from which no derogation is permitted."[4] Accordingly, all states are bound to observance of the norm, regardless of their participation in the respective torture treaties. This reflects the fact that the prohibition on torture has become "one of the most fundamental standards of the international community."[5] All of

---

[2] See, for example, the Convention for the Protection of Human Rights and Fundamental Freedoms (adopted November 4, 1950, entered into force September 3, 1953), 213 UNTS 221 (European Convention on Human Rights), Article 15.

[3] Restatement (Third) of Foreign Relations Law of the United States ss. 702 (*American Law Institute* 2, 1987) describes torture as an act the commission of which by a state constitutes a violation of international law. While not all acts under ss. 702 constitute *jus cogens*, the commentary adjoining ss. 702 indicates that torture is one of the peremptory norms (ss.702, Comment n.). This was later reiterated by the International Court of Justice in *Questions relating to the Obligation to prosecute or Extradite (Belgium v. Senegal)* [2012] ICJ Rep 422, §99.

[4] The peremptory status of other forms of ill-treatment is still debated. Vienna Convention on the Law of Treaties (adopted May 23, 1969, entered into force January 27, 1980), 1155 UNTS 331, Article 53.

[5] *Prosecutor v. Furundzija* (Judgement) IT-95-17/1-T (December 10, 1998) paras 153–4.

this means that torture, inhuman treatment, degrading treatment, inhuman punishment, and degrading punishment are all out of bounds everywhere as a matter of law (Moyn 2013).

Article 5 of the Universal Declaration of Human Rights (UDHR) represents the foundation and the basis for all subsequent international agreements on torture (Addicott 2003, 849, 858). It provides that, "[n]o one shall be subjected to torture or to cruel, inhuman or degrading treatment or punishment."[6] This wording is mirrored in the International Covenant on Civil and Political Rights, with the addition of "[i]n particular, no one shall be subjected without his free consent to medical or scientific experimentation." Last, the UN system includes a specialized treaty, the Convention against Torture and Other Cruel, Inhuman or Degrading Treatment or Punishment (CAT), which came into force in 1987 (Article 1). Article 1 of CAT provides the first definition of torture to be included in an international treaty. It states:

> [...] the term torture means any act by which severe pain or suffering, whether physical or mental, is intentionally inflicted on a person for such purposes as obtaining from him or a third person information or a confession, punishing him for an act he or a third person has committed or is suspected of having committed, or intimidating or coercing him or a third person, or for any reason based on discrimination of any kind, when such pain or suffering is inflicted by or at the instigation of or with the consent or acquiescence of a public official or other person acting in an official capacity (CAT Article 1).[7]

[6] Universal Declaration of Human Rights (adopted December 10, 1948), UNGA Res 217 A(III) (UDHR), Article 5. This norm is replicated in the International Covenant on Civil and Political Rights (adopted December 16, 1966, entered into force March 23, 1976), 999 UNTS 171, Article 7; European Convention on Human Rights (n 12) Article 3; African Charter on Human and Peoples' Rights (adopted June 27, 1981, entered into force October 21, 1986), 1520 UNTS 217, Article 5; Arab Charter on Human Rights, reprinted in 12 *International Human Rights Reports* 893 (2005), entered into force March 15, 2008, Article 8(1); and the American Convention on Human Rights (adopted November 22, 1969, entered into force July 18, 1978) 1144 UNTS 123, Article 5.

[7] Article 16 of the Convention also contains a state obligation "to prevent ... other acts of cruel, inhuman and degrading treatment or punishment which do not amount to torture" (Article 16[1]). It does not contain any explicit prohibition on torture or other forms of il-treatment as it recognizes "that [torture, cruel, inhuman and degrading treatment or punishment] are already outlawed under international law" (Nowak and

This definition suggests a number of constitutive elements of torture: (1) the infliction of severe pain to the body or mind, as distinguishable from other offenses (Cullen 2003, 32); (2) the act must be inflicted intentionally, either by act or omission (Cullen 2003, 33); (3) the treatment must be inflicted in order to achieve a specific purpose, such as to punish or obtain information (Addicott 2003; Cullen 2003, 33); and (4) only state actors may be guilty of torture (Addicott 2003, 857; Cullen 2003, 34).[8]

CAT places an obligation on the state parties to take "effective legislative, administrative, judicial or other measures to prevent acts of torture in any territory under [their] jurisdiction."[9] States are also obliged to incorporate the crime of torture into their national criminal justice systems (CAT, Article 4). Torture is condemned in all circumstances: "[no] exceptional circumstances whatsoever, whether a state of war or a threat of war, internal political instability or any other public emergency, may be invoked as a justification for torture" (Article 2 [2]). The Convention follows the principle of compulsory universal application, applicable to all countries and not only to contracting states. Additionally, CAT prohibits the state parties from extradition, expulsion, or *refoulement* of a person to another state where there are substantial grounds to believe that the person will be subjected to torture (Article 3).

McArthur 2008, 23, 51, 61). Despite this, the Committee against Torture, when dealing with individual complaints, does treat Article 1 as though it contained a prohibition or offense that can be violated. For a recent example, see *Bendib v. Algeria* (November 8, 2013), UN Doc CAT/C/51/D/376/2009, paras 6.2–6.3: "In the absence of any substantive refutation by the State party, the Committee concludes that due weight must be given to the author's allegations and that the facts, as submitted by the complainant, constitute acts of torture, within the meaning of Article 1 of the Convention. In the light of the above finding of *a violation of article 1…*" (emphasis added). Overall, however, "[t]he principal aim of the Convention is to strengthen the existing prohibitions of such practices by a number of supportive measures" (Burgers and Danelius 1988, 1).

[8] Cullen does suggest that, in some cases, private individuals may also be held accountable: "Under the definition, torture is only recognized if it is committed 'at the instigation of or with the consent or acquiescence of a public official or other person acting in an official capacity.' Although the Convention is directed primarily against actions of state officials, the wording of the definition is broad enough to effectively include some actions by private individuals" (Cullen 2003, 34).

[9] Convention against Torture and Other Cruel, Inhuman or Degrading Treatment or Punishment (adopted December 10, 1984, entered into force June 26, 1987), 1465 UNTS 112, Article 2(1).

At the regional level, the prohibition is located under Article 5 of the American Convention on Human Rights, which adopts the language of the Universal Declaration with an additional sentence that states, "[a]ll persons deprived of their liberty shall be treated with respect for the inherent dignity of the human person." The Inter-American system also contains a specialized treaty, the Inter-American Convention to Prevent and Punish Torture, which entered into force in 1987. The prohibition is located in Article 5 of the African Charter on Human and Peoples Rights, although it is expressed in language that departs from other human rights instruments:

> Every individual shall have the right to the respect of the dignity inherent in a human being and to the recognition of his legal status. All forms of exploitation and degradation of man, particularly slavery, slave trade, torture, cruel, inhuman or degrading punishment and treatment shall be prohibited.

Under Article 3 of the European Convention on Human Rights (ECHR), "[n]o one shall be subjected to torture or to inhuman or degrading treatment or punishment." This, again, appropriates the wording of Article 5 of the UDHR, save for the omission of the word "cruel," which William Schabas argues was an apparent "inadvertent change" (Schabas 2015, 164). The European Court of Human Rights (ECtHR) has held that Article 3 "enshrines one of the most fundamental values of democratic societies."[10] The formulation of Article 3 leaves no room for exceptions; indeed, the Court has stated that "even in the most difficult of circumstances, such as the fight against organized terrorism or crime, the Convention prohibits in absolute terms torture or inhuman or degrading treatment or punishment."[11]

Despite these international and regional prohibitions, the very meaning of torture and of other forms of ill-treatment and the ontological rationale for the absolute prohibition remain contested and uncertain. There is disagreement about the contents of the various terms (with states employing linguistic and definitional creativity to evade the ban), about how they should be distinguished from each other, and about which level of severity of violence is required to meet the minimum threshold of the prohibition.

---

[10] *A v. United Kingdom* (2009) 49 EHRR 29, §126.

[11] *Aksoy v. Turkey* (1997) 23 EHRR 553, §62.

Just how this contestation manifests is evident when reviewing the jurisprudence of the ECtHR, the oldest human rights instrument that has generated the largest body of case law.

Examining the jurisprudence to flow from the ECHR reveals the politics in law debate quite clearly. While the ban in the Convention is unambiguous, the Court has not been immune from the wider political context of its decision. This was evident in the way in which the Court approached its first interstate case—Ireland v. United Kingdom—where claims of torture were made by one state against agents of another (see Schabas and O' Sullivan 2007, 3; Donahue 1980, 377). Ireland argued that the United Kingdom had subjected fourteen detainees, known as the "hooded men," to five "disorientation" or "sensory deprivation" techniques—wall standing, hooding, sleep deprivation, reduced diet, and white noise—and that these techniques reached the threshold of torture. While the ECHR agreed, the case was then referred to the Grand Chamber of the ECtHR. In its decision, the ECtHR shifted its focus from an examination of the perpetrator's intentional infliction of the acts (key to the earlier European Commission decision) to the impact of the acts on the victims and the experience of suffering. In doing so, the Court found that the techniques "did not occasion suffering of the particular intensity and cruelty implied by the word torture."[12] Fionnuala Ní Aoláin argued that in the face of a leading liberal democracy and influential member state, the Court felt the "political weight" of the case (Aoláin 2004, 216).

While the international legal machinery continues to perform—embedding and restating the absoluteness of the prohibition against torture in treaty law—states increasingly endeavor to situate torture within a state security discourse, slowly dripping exceptions into the rule. That torture is now thinkable[13] is evident in the so-called "ticking bomb" scenario.[14] This construct has made its way into the public domain and

[12] *Ireland v. United Kingdom* (n 12) §167.

[13] Sanford Kadish (1989, 345) warned, "When torture is no longer unthinkable, it will be thought about."

[14] The scenario takes a number of forms but, in general, torture proponents use the hypothetical as a technique to argue that in the case of an imminent attack on innocents, coercive tactics (e.g., torture) might not just be permissible but morally necessary. While there are a number of versions of this scenario, broadly speaking the ticking-bomb scenario is as follows: a person, detained by a state authority, has information regarding where a bomb has been planted. The state has good reason to believe that the bomb is set to go off

has made the question as to whether "inquisitorial" torture should be allowed speakable. Ironically, the scenario presented by the construct is often framed as a moral imperative—the absolute duty on the part of a state to torture for the common good. This need to defend the state and political community against the "other"—the ticking-bomb terrorist—has increasingly placed the law (in its exceptional self) firmly within, rather than outside, the push and pull of that security discourse. As judges are part of and not separate from this securitized political landscape, judicial pronouncements on torture are often thick with culture and, "once we create a torture culture, only the naive would suppose that judges will provide a safeguard. Judges don't fight their culture. They reflect it" (Luban 2005, 1452).

"Islamic" Law

The question posed earlier—the "what" or "whose" version of law—adopted within international legal discourses can also be applied to how we engage with the various readings and interpretations drawn from Islamic law. As Emon, Ellis, and Glahn (2012, 7) rightly argue, to negate the "effect of the state on the content, scope and application of Islamic law today" is to "address abstract ideas in a vacuum and to turn the risk of pursuing 'red herrings'"(6). Disrupting the idea that these legal regimes are fixed, stable, and pre-political moves us beyond the reproduction of rather worn arguments on Islam and human rights and requires that we emancipate some of the concepts seen as inextricably linked to each.

Distilling the "ideals" expressed within the different readings of Islam from "the actual laws, legal institutions and policies in Muslim countries" (Mayer 2007, xiii) reveals that the legal practices specific to an individual country—including the rhetorical use of human rights as well as the adoption of formal rights-based language in constitutions, etc.—draw on a variety of sources that can shift over time in ways that are not identical to Western experiences and may not be consistent across Muslim cases. At a regional level, the three main Islamic declarations of human rights—the

immediately. Under these conditions, and allowing for the costs/benefits, the state has a duty to use extreme methods to gain information necessary to prevent the explosion. Despite the fact that there is substantial critique on this argument, including the implausibility of the scenario, it has continued to be argued in the public domain.

General (Universal) Islamic Declaration of Human Rights (1981),[15] the Cairo Declaration of Human Rights,[16] and the Arab Human Rights Charter[17]—approach rights-based discourse in a variety of ways. For example, while all three include a prohibition on torture, the General Islamic Declaration of Human Rights is clear in that the torture it prohibits is confessional, while the prohibition in the Cairo Declaration of Human Rights and the Arab Human Rights Charter bans any form of physical or psychological torture.[18] Studies have also shown that there is a multiplicity of views on human rights among Muslims living in the Middle East, suggesting—as Ann Mayer has argued—that we should not "speak of 'Islam' and human rights as if Islam were a monolith or as if there existed one established Islamic human rights philosophy that caused all Muslims to look at rights in a particular way" (Mayer 2007, xi). Although purportedly drawing from the same sources, these shifting constructions and "plural readings" of Islam are critical to understanding why Muslim voices are complex and varied when engaging with questions of human rights.

The plurality of discourses also explains why Muslim state practice with regard to public law (implementation and interpretation) varies. This is, in fact, the contradiction inherent in this debate—a plurality of readings of Islam, with each argued to be fixed and stable. This may also well explain why some scholars assert that "the sources and methods of Islamic law contain common principles of good government and human welfare that validate modern international human rights ideals" (Baderin 2003, 13) while public law injunctions of, ostensibly, Islamic legal principles are used to restrict or define women's legal status or, in criminal procedure, to select penal laws and procedures or to restrict the freedom of religion of religious minorities.

[15]Universal Islamic Declaration of Human Rights (September 19, 1981), http://www.alhewar.com/ISLAMDECL.html (hereinafter "1981 Universal Declaration").

[16]Cairo Declaration on Human Rights in Islam (August 5, 1990) (translator unknown), http://www.alhewar.com/ISLAMDECL.html Universal Islamic Declaration of Human Rights (alhewar.com).

[17]Arab Charter on Human Rights (May 23, 2004), Article 8(a), http://hrlibrary.umn.edu/instree/loas2005.html?msource=UNWDEC19001&tr=y&auid=3337655.

[18] Article 20(2) Cairo Declaration and Article 13(a) of the Arab Charter. For a discussion on this point, see Rabbi and Badshah (2018, 4–5) and Masud (2015, 9–15).

It is not possible or necessary to discuss the doctrines (or minor techniques) that inform these legal rules and principles in any detail, as there are other contributors in this volume who will undertake this task. What is important to note, however, is that much like public international law, asking just "what" or "whose" view of Islamic law we engage is critical when turning to "Islamic" restrictions with regard to human rights. To be clear, this is not to attempt to satisfy (or even engage) in such a debate. It is, however, to argue that in each domain, there is mediation between the text and the interpretation—an exercise of hegemonic control by sites of power. Against this, there are a few points related to the development of Sharia and its intervention in the public space that merit some review.

The Quran has a small number of verses that deal directly with legal subject matters.[19] It sets out the legal consequences of a particular action in only a few specified cases (*hudud*[20] and *qisas*[21]). This has led one scholar to note that "the primary purpose of the Qur'an is to regulate not the relationship of the man with his fellows but his relationship with his Creator" (Coulson 1994, 12). What legal content the Quran has provided has been drawn to exact the most from the rather limited measures but, even in these instances, and "with very rare exceptions, [Islamic principles are] general, and give guidance in a certain direction, rather than fixing a restricting framework" (Ramadan 2005, 145). As well, some nonlegal verses have also been constructed so as to provide legal guidance. Therefore, what we refer to as Islamic law is not defined (primarily) by the Quran or Sunna but rather has emerged as the jurisprudential guidance of jurists over a long and historical process, with the final authority in the domain of the *madhhab*.

The contributions to Sharia by the Sunna open up greater avenues of contention. Putting aside the legal implications for the moment, the

---

[19] Only a small number of Quranic verses have a legal element. A majority of the verses relate to worship rituals, leaving only about 80 verses that, in strict terms, deal with legal subject matter.

[20] *Hudud* are fixed punishments generally prescribed for six offenses: for theft (*sariqa*), amputation of a hand; for armed robbery or rebellion (*hiraba*), amputation of the hand and foot, banishment, crucifixion, or death; for adultery, stoning to death; for fornication (*zina*), 100 lashes; for apostasy (*ridda*), death; for intoxication (*sharb al-khamr*), 40 or 80 lashes.

[21] *Qisas* are offenses for which the punishment is discretionary and rests with the victim of the offense (or his/her heirs) and the judge (or state).

authenticity of the Sunna has led to questions of possible fabrication. For Sunnis, the criterion for authenticity was continuous acceptance (*tawatur*), which signals that a historical report or a Prophetic tradition is supported by a large number of *isnad* strands. For the Shia, the criterion is continuity of acceptance in the family of the Prophet. These questions have been raised to suggest possible mediation by those who may have believed to have known the Prophet's thinking on certain matters and recorded *their* beliefs, as opposed to the actual recorded sayings or actions of the Prophet himself. This human construct leaves open the possibility of fabrication and questions as to the genuineness of a particular report. Since most of the authentication of the Sunna was undertaken during the second century (Islamic calendar), returning to this task today would prove impossible. Nonetheless, there are some scholars who query the authentication process, even when referencing the compilations by the six scholars accepted by Sunni Muslims.

The legal methods of *ijma'* and *qiyas* are considered secondary sources of Islamic law, as these are the "products of human reasoning" (Baderin 2003, 37) rather than (solely) divine revelation and are limited to specific situations, unlike the primary sources of the Quran and Sunna. *Ijma'* is best understood as "consensus" and "constitutes a strong 'source' of law in the absence of a direct text of the Quran or the Sunna on any issue" (Baderin 2003, 87). That said, the source of this consensus has raised additional questions; e.g., is it the consensus of *mujtahidun* (Islamic legists[22]), the Companions, and their community in Medina, or is it the consensus of the community of Muslims?[23] Baderin suggests that *ijma'* may, contemporaneously, source its consensus from the practice of Muslim states (much like customary law).[24] The second subsidiary source of Sharia is *qiyas*, or analogy. As this process is based on human reason (and, as noted, *ijtihad* was to have closed at the end of the ninth century

[22] *Mujtahid* (singular). Scholars note that there are two types of Islamic legists: one who extracts legal rulings from scriptural sources without reference to a particular juridical school (*al-mujtahid al-mutlaq*), and one for whom the extractions are tied to a particular juridical school (*mujtahid al-muqayyad*).

[23] The Prophet was to have said, "My people shall never be unanimous in error."

[24] Baderin was writing this with regard to the practice of slavery and arguing that by understanding *ijma'* as consensus among Muslim states, one can conclude that "the doctrine of the overall objective of Sharia strongly supports the consensus on the total abolition of slavery under Islamic law" (Baderin 2003, 88).

ad), there is some controversy when using *qiyas* as a source for Sharia. However, the process of *qiyas* is confined to those cases where "none of the other sources is applicable and the outcome is seen to be fully consistent with the totality of Sharia as well as with any of its established principles and rules" (An-Na'im 1992, 25).

As already noted, the Quran is mostly preoccupied with questions regarding the relationship between the individual and the Creator, with less attention for the question of an individual's relationship with others. Yet, it is precisely in this latter category that the lacuna between existing jurisprudence (*fiqh*) and the needs and challenges presented by an ever-changing political and social landscape is greatest. Within the different Islamic tendencies, there is a struggle between those who believe that all has been revealed through existing sources from either primary, secondary, or minor sources, methods, and techniques, and those who believe that we must revisit either the process that gave rise to current Islamic law or reopen the gate of *ijtihad*, which will allow for the renewal of the sources. The differentiation in approach among Muslim legal (and other) scholars maps out onto how civil and political rights, as defined within international law, relate to what are "Islamic" restrictions (or punishments) that ostensibly conflict with human rights (including the prohibition against torture). Revisiting the public interventions of Islamic law—including the application of Sharia in domestic law—and their interface with international human rights law is not to suggest that the various readings of Islam have no consequences for how the right to have rights plays out within Muslim states. The crafting of Islam as the gatekeeper, which limits access to a "universalist" reading of human rights is, of course, unique to Muslim states. As Mayer reminds us, factoring culture and context into the interpretation and application of international law requires some consideration, as Asian or Islamic "culture-bound" values and norms have "political usefulness" for "foes of human rights" (Mayer 2007, 10) and there are challenges in wresting this concept from political agendas.

That said, two points must be stressed when examining these public interventions of "Islamic" law. First, as I have detailed, the development of what comprises crime and punishment in Islam is not found in *fiqh* alone. Historically unpacking its evolution reveals

> a history of competing interests between those who theorized and wrote about, those who implemented, and those who suffered legal

> punishment. In consequence, more attention deserves to be given to the social actors involved in this history, whether they be the institutions of the repressive state apparatus, the different types of legal experts or indeed the victims of legal violence, that is, those who were punished as criminals (Lange 2010, 694–5).

A second point follows: both value (and indeed interests) systems are challenged by the social realities they confront. Indeed, it is only when we examine what is unfolding in the broader political space that we come closer to understanding the legal landscape of any particular state or regional system. Any engagement of so-called "Islamic" legal interventions in the public sphere, then, must be understood against this backdrop.[25]

Crime and Punishment in Islamic Law

The gap in textual (and guidance) authority is most acute when we turn to Islamic criminal law and procedure. As the Quran and Sunna, from which Islamic law is extracted, are religious and not legal texts,

> early Muslim scholars and jurists did not distinguish between the religious, ethical, and legal aspects of Sharî'ah let alone identify specific legal fields. Consequently, those principles and rules of Sharî'ah relevant to what is known in modern terminology as criminal law, evidence and procedure can be extracted only from general and extensive treatises of Islamic jurisprudence (An-Na'im 1992, 104).

While this area of Islamic law receives much attention, particularly by Western scholars, it is also its most underdeveloped.[26] Uriel Heyd has noted that it was not until the fifteenth century that the first Islamic

---

[25]This goes some way to explaining the necessity to clarify, define, omit, and constantly restate the unsettled part of Islamic law so often seen in texts on the subject matter.

[26]That said, Muslim legal scholars routinely engaged with questions dealing with criminal responsibility and the punishability of offenses with considerable variation (and contestation). There are a number of baseline distinctions that are made by the *fuqaha'* (or doctors of law) between offenses that require as retribution a "divinely ordained punishment" (*hadd* or *hudud*); offenses that call for talionic punishment (*qisas*); and offenses that are to receive discretionary punishment (*ta'zir*) by the judge (*qadi*) or temporal ruler. While *hadd*

criminal codes appeared. During the Ottoman period, sultans promulgated *qanuns* (or rule books) of criminal law. The relationship between these rules and Islamic religious law (or Sharia) was not explicit. Rather, these rules were based on two primary concepts—political expediency (or *siyasa*) and the common good (*al-maslaha al-'amma*) (Heyd 1973). It was not until later that, in what Sadiq Reza argues was the final concession of Islamic jurists' power, the doctrine of *siyasa shar'iyya* was developed, which provided a legal pathway for practices under *siyasa* to be consistent with Sharia law. Under the doctrine of *siyasa shar'iyya*, a ruler's action is considered to be consistent as long as it advances public welfare and does not violate clear commands of the sacred texts.

Contemporary (post–World War II) systems of Islamic criminal law are enforced using procedural rules and principles that did not originate to govern Islamic criminal law (Reza 2013, 3), and reflect the grafting together of

> criminal prohibitions and punishments originating from Islamic doctrines that are up to fourteen hundred years old but operate mostly under codes and practices of procedure that were adopted from European nations in the twentieth century (Reza 2013, 2).

The result has been, Mayer (1983, 363) argues, "anachronistic projections of modern principles of criminal justice back into a legal order in which they were unknown." As well, while the last two decades have seen a number of writings from Western scholars (and others) concerning crime and punishment in Muslim states, the first, "systematic attempt in the English language to survey *fiqh* doctrines of crime and punishment" (Lange 2010, 694) did not occur until 2006 with the publication of Rudolph Peters's *Crime and Punishment in Islamic Law* (Peters 2006). This is important to note, as it is necessary to distinguish between what is actually prescribed under *fiqh* and how it has been narrated by sites of power, including but not exclusively the state.

Against this, the "what" and "whose" view of Islamic law becomes dependent on the reading (and therefore, mediation) of the "doctrines of Muslim jurists and practices of Muslim rulers and other state actors that

---

punishments are claimed by the *fuqhaha'* as "rights of God" and talionic punishments as "rights of men," *ta'zir* is a category that combines elements of both (Johansen 1979).

are ostensibly sanctioned by those doctrines."[27] Much of the enforcement of criminal prohibitions and punishments is derived through the authority of the state and subject to varying interpretations by Muslim jurists.[28] This provides some understanding as to why Muslim state practice differs in the public law injunctions of "Islamic" legal principles, especially as it interfaces (and ostensibly conflicts) with human rights.

Torture under Islamic Law

Such differing approaches to what is required (or permitted) under Islamic law are evident when we turn to the question of whether torture is prohibited or allowed (and under what conditions) in Islamic law. The answer may well be found in the push and pull between the two realms of Islamic law related to crime and punishment—*fiqh* and *siyasa*, the text and the narrator. Endeavoring to unpack the prohibition on torture under Islamic law reveals a plurality of views, ranging from scholars who argue that torture under Islamic law is prohibited[29] to those who argue that punishments (that would reach the threshold of torture) are allowed if the suspect has been convicted of a prior wrongdoing[30] and, finally, to scholars who endeavor to balance between the two realms by suggesting that while torture is forbidden to *qadis*, it is allowed for Muslim authorities.[31]

When Muslim jurists and scholars engage with the question of torture, the focus is on its intent or purpose, which is divided into two categories—punitive torture, defined as torture inflicted as a punishment for a crime, and investigative torture, defined as "physical or mental coercion by state officers to obtain confessions or other information from individuals in their custody" (Reza 2013, 22). The first category relates to criminal punishments (or *hadd*; pl. *hudud*). The discussions around the doctrinal

[27] Sadiq Reza (2007). "Torture and Islamic Law," *Chicago Journal of International Law* Vol. 8: No. 1, Article 4, 24.

[28] As Rabbi and Badshah (2018, 5) argue, "how individual rules are interpreted, or facts judged by law are sometimes unpredictable and highly dependent on the views of respective judges."

[29] This view is attributed to Ibn Hazm (d.1064) and al-Ghazali (d.1111) of the Shafi'i School of law and the Zahiri school of law.

[30] This view is often attributed to Ibn Taymiyya (d.1328), Ibn Qayyim (d.1351), Ibn Farhun (d.1396), Maliki jurist, and al-Tarabulusi (d.1440), the Hanafi jurist.

[31] Mawardi (d.1058) of the Shafi'i School of law.

imperatives of *hadd* crimes are many, but the punishments are notoriously harsh, rise to the threshold of torture, and are, therefore, irreconcilable with contemporary human rights norms and principles. I will not dwell on these here, save to note that most scholars of Islamic law argue that punitive torture is permissible when a person has been found guilty of a prior wrongdoing. The second category—torture as an investigative method—is not settled, with some scholars arguing that confessional torture is prohibited, but investigative torture for security purposes is permitted. In their *Review of the Jurisprudential Arguments for the Permissibility of Torture in Islam*, Mohsen Razmi and Morteza Enferadi Kolarkatteh argue this point by suggesting that the justification for security torture is found through an "indirect" rule of "avoidance of the more corrupt by the corrupt one" (Razmi and Kolarkatteh 2018, 1931). They suggest that where there is a situation similar to the "ticking bomb" scenario (1932), torture is permitted.

Of note, however, is that while "Islamic law does not forbid torture in practice—*siyasa*—any more than it does in theory—*fiqh*" (Reza 2013, 34) the prohibition is enshrined in the Universal Islamic Declaration of Human Rights, the Cairo Declaration on Human Rights in Islam, and the Arab Charter on Human Rights, albeit with some differences. Article VII of the General Islamic Declaration of Human Rights contains an explicit prohibition on torture:

> No person shall be subjected to torture in mind or body, or degraded, or threatened with injury either to himself or to anyone related to or held dear by him, or forcibly made to confess to the commission of a crime, or forced to consent to an act, which is injurious to his interests.

Article 20 (2) of the Cairo Declaration on Human Rights states:

> It is not permitted without legitimate reason to arrest an individual, or restrict his freedom, to exile or to punish him. It is not permitted to subject him to physical or psychological torture or to any form of maltreatment, cruelty or indignity. Nor is it permitted to subject an individual to medical or scientific experiments without his consent or at the risk of his health or of his life. Nor is it permitted to promulgate emergency laws that would provide executive authority for such actions.

Finally, Article 8 of the Arab Charter on Human Rights states:

> 1. No one shall be subjected to physical or psychological torture or to cruel, degrading, humiliating or inhuman treatment.
>
> 2. Each State party shall protect every individual subject to its jurisdiction from such practices and shall take effective measures to prevent them. The commission of, or participation in, such acts shall be regarded as crimes that are punishable by law and not subject to any statute of limitations. Each State party shall guarantee in its legal system redress for any victim of torture and the right to rehabilitation and compensation.

Finally, nearly all Muslim-majority countries have signed up to the CAT, and "notwithstanding Qatar's Islamic-law reservation, there is no obvious correlation between a commitment to the law or religion of Islam and the decision of a Muslim country to join or abstain from the 1984 Convention Against Torture" (Reza 2007, 36). This performative aspect of public pronouncements (including treaty ratification), which often contrasts with state practices, is not unique to the Muslim world. In fact, this section reveals that the use of Islamic law as a way of framing whether torture is permitted in a state and a Muslim state's engagement with the international human rights machinery is notable only in how unremarkable it is. As Reza has rightly observed,

> there may be sufficient authority to say that Islamic law forbids torture—but that authority has clearly not proven sufficient to eradicate torture in modern Muslim practice. In that respect, the relationship between Islamic law and Muslim practice resembles the relationship between international law and state practice generally: even a state's commitment to an international norm as unambiguous as a ban on torture does not necessarily reflect or result in state compliance with that norm (Reza 2007, 40).

Conclusion

I have chosen to focus this "comparative" analysis on the prohibition (and practice) of torture. I have done so deliberately. Within the international legal machinery, the prohibition on torture has no qualifying exception. Yes, as the first section of this chapter has detailed, the interests (moral, political) of states sometimes overlap, but are often in conflict with the international rights machinery; a machinery that is also in conflict with itself. This contestation is evident even where the norm in question—like torture—is *jus cogens*. The reality is that despite the absolute ban on torture under international law, practice—both inside and outside the Muslim world—has never been touched by the prohibition. Understanding why brings us back to the start of this piece: law is situated within, not apart from sites of power. Against this, when examining "whether Islam law forbids torture is the same as the answer to so many ultimate questions of Islamic law (and of 'American' [and international] law too for that matter): it depends on who you ask" (Reza 2007, 22).

References

Addicott, Jeffrey F. 2003. "Into the Star Chamber: Does the United States Engage in the Use of Torture or Similar Illegal Practices in the War on Terror?" *Kentucky Law Journal*, 92: 849–912.

An-Na'im, Abdullahi A. 1992. *Toward an Islamic Reformation: Civil Liberties, Human Rights and International Law*. Cairo: The American University in Cairo Press.

Baderin, Mashood. 2003. *International Human Rights & Islamic Law*. Oxford: Oxford University Press.

Burgers, J. Herman, and Hans Danelius, (eds.). 1988. *The United Nations Convention against Torture: A Handbook on the Convention against Torture and Other Cruel, Inhuman and Degrading Treatment or Punishment*. Dordrecht, Netherlands: Martinus Nijhoff Publishers.

Coulson, Noel. 1994. *History of Islamic Law*. Edinburgh: Edinburgh University Press.

Cullen, Anthony. 2003. "Defining Torture in International Law: A Critique of the Concept Employed by the European Court of Human Rights." *California Western International Law Journal*, 34, no. 3: 29–46.

Donahue, Deirdre E. 1980. "Human Rights in Northern Ireland: Ireland v. United Kingdom." *Boston College International and Comparative Law Review*, 3, no. 2: 377–432.

Emon, Anver M., Mark S. Ellis, and Benjamin Glahn. 2012. "Editors' Introduction: From 'Common Ground' to 'Clearing Ground': A Model for Engagement in the 21st Century." In *Islamic Law and International Human Rights Law: Searching for Common Ground?* edited by Anver M. Emon, Mark S. Ellis, and Benjamin Glahn, 1–16. London: Oxford University Press.

Heyd, Uriel. 1973. *Studies in Old Ottoman Criminal Law*. Oxford: Oxford University Press.

Johansen, Baber. 1999. *Contingency in a Sacred Law: Legal and Ethical Norms in the Muslim Fiqh*. Leiden, Netherlands: Brill.

Kadish, H. 1989. "Torture, the State and the Individual." *Israel Law Review*, 23 (2–3): 345–56.

Koskenniemi, Martti. 2004. "International Law and Hegemony: A Reconfiguration." *Cambridge Review of International Affairs*, 17, no. 2 (July): 197–218.

Lange, Christian. 2010. "Crime and Punishment in Pre-Modern Islamic History: A Framework for Analysis." *Religion Compass*, 4, no. 11 (November): 694–706.

Luban, David. 2005. "Liberalism, Torture, and the Ticking Bomb." *Virginia Law Review*, 91: 1425–61.

Masud, Muhammad Kh. 2007. "Muslim Perspectives on Global Ethics." In *The Globalization of Ethics: Religious and Secular Perspectives*, edited by William M. Sullivan and Will Kymlicka, 93–116. New York: Cambridge University Press.

Masud, Muhammad Kh. 2015. "Islamic Jurisprudence of Human Rights." In *Fundamental Rights, The Promise of a Just Society*, 9–15. Islamabad: Law and Justice Commission of Pakistan.

Mayer, Ann E. 2007. *Islam and Human Rights: Tradition and Politics*. Boulder, CO: Westview Press.

Mayer, Ann E. 1983. "Book Review: *The Islamic Criminal Justice System*, by Cherif Bassiouni." *The American Journal of Comparative Law*, 31, no. 2 (Spring): 361–8.

Moyn, Samuel. 2010. *The Last Utopia: Human Rights in History*. Cambridge, MA: Harvard University Press.

Moyn, Samuel. 2013. "Torture and Taboo: On Elaine Scarry." *The Nation*, February 5, 2013. https://www.thenation.com/article/archive/torture-and-taboo-elaine-scarry/.

Ní Aoláin, Fionnuala. 2004. "The European Convention on Human Rights and its Prohibition on Torture." In *Torture: A Collection*, edited by Sanford Levinson, 213–28. Oxford: Oxford University Press.

Nowak, Manfred, and Elizabeth McArthur. 2008. *The United Nations Convention against Torture: A Commentary*. Oxford: Oxford University Press.

Peters, Rudolph. 2006. *Crime and Punishment in Islamic Law: Theory and Practice from the Sixteenth to the Twenty-First Century* (Themes in Islamic Law). Cambridge: Cambridge University Press.

Rabbi, Fazal, and Syed Naeem Badshah. 2018. "Islam, Sharia, and the Constitutional Prohibition of Torture in Pakistan. *Al-Azhār* 4, no. 2 (July/ December): 1–9.

Ramadan, Tariq. 2006. *Western Muslims and the Future of Islam*. Oxford: Oxford University Press.

Razmi, Mohsen, and Morteza Enferadi Kolarkatteh. 2018. "A Review of Jurisprudential Arguments for the Permissibility of Torture in Islam." *Quaestio Iuris*, 11, no. 3: 1924–45.

Reza, Sadiq. 2013. "Due Process in Islamic Criminal Law." *George Washington Journal of International Law*, 46: 1–27.

Reza, Sadiq. 2007. "Torture and Islamic Law." *Chicago Journal of International Law*, 8, no. 1: 21–41.

Schabas, William A. 2015. *The European Convention on Human Rights: A Commentary*. Oxford: Oxford University Press.

Schabas, William A., and Aisling O' Sullivan. 2007. "Politics and Poor Weather: How Ireland Sued the United Kingdom under the European Convention on Human Rights." *Irish Yearbook of International Law*, 2: 3–30.

https://doi.org/10.1142/9781800611689_0008

Chapter 8

The Islamic Institutions: Role and Application

Hana Jalloul Muro

Madrid Parliament, Spain
hana.jalloul@uc3m.es

Introduction

This chapter seeks to explain how Islamic religious institutions and the body of Muslim jurists throughout Islamic history have developed since the time of the Prophet Muhammad till modern times; mainly educational centers for religious-legal studies, religious institutions for the issuing of fatwa and religious courts.

Prophet Muhammad, the first Islamic jurist, was dealing with the events of a society undergoing change and a revelation that would transform social, economic, religious, and political customs for approximately 23 years. His successors, the first four caliphs, proclaimed themselves *khulafa' rasul Allah* (Caliphs of the Messenger of God). They were considered the spiritual and political heads of the Islamic community, deriving norms from the Quran and Sunna and practicing *ijtihad*. In the time of the Umayyad and Abbasid caliphates, and during the Ottoman Empire (with some differences), the *ulama* were the depositaries of religious interpretation, with the caliph as guarantor of the observance and implementation of Sharia.

This was the case in certain times, or whenever there would be a subsistence and cohabitation relationship between the political and the religious classes. Thus, for example, there were *ulama* that supported the military state, as long as it would protect the lands of Islam (An-Na'im 2008, 65). The fact that the *ulama* and other intellectuals (such as Mawardi, see Mawardi 1996)[1] supported political power on many occasions does not imply that for them, the unity of the *umma* and consequently the Islamic spiritual sphere should not be a priority to the political order. But it was the caliph who could maintain the unity of the Islamic world, at least in the military field, and in that sense the unity of the rule of law. Therefore, theories that justify political authority will emerge in times of political upheaval, such as would be the case with the Mongol invasion, which would imply at times the use of jurisprudence to provide the ruler with the necessary legitimacy. On the other hand, the leaders had to respect the autonomy of the *ulama* to achieve the necessary credibility that conferred religious legitimacy on the state,[2] without thereby allowing this religious elite to participate in political power. In short, relations between the two were not always friendly.[3] There were exceptions, like the *mihna* or Great Inquisition, whose end marked the end of the caliphal claim to religious authority.[4]

---

[1]Mawardi lived in a turbulent time that included the decline of the Abbasid caliphate, the dismemberment of the Umayyad caliphate of Cordoba, the rise of the Fatimid caliphate of Egypt, and the entry into Baghdad of the Seljuk Turks two years before his death. This is reflected in the need the author felt for a strong and unifying authority. At the same time, there is the case of many *ulama* who showed loyalty even to the invaders in order to maintain the established order. When Tamerlane invaded Syria, a part of the *ulama* were prepared to repel the conflict, while others—such as the Hanbali jurist Ibn Muflih—suggested surrendering.

[2]A *hadith* quoted by Ghazali says: "In hell there is a valley only reserved for the *ulama* who visit the kings." For that reason, virtuous *'alim* should not visit unjust princes or officials (Hourani 1992, 145).

[3]One thing to highlight is that in almost all the cases in which an *ijma'* is pronounced, and they are recorded in textbooks, reference is made to the consensus of the *ulama* and private jurists, a space in which the government never played any role. Meanwhile, the government authorities always encouraged the use of *taqlid* (Kamali 2003, 503).

[4]This began with the Abbasid caliph al-Ma'mun and continued with al-Mu'tasim, al-Wathiq, and al-Mutawakkil. The latter closed the *mihna* in the second year of his caliphate. It lasted about fifteen years. Its origin lies in the "doctrine of the created Quran" and not in the uncreated word of God; it was supported also by the rationalist Mu'tazila movement,

In the twentieth and twenty-first centuries, the *ulama* no longer had the past relevance in the religious field, and Islamic courts were reduced to personal status codes separated from civil courts under the competence of the state. The body of Muslim jurists lost its past influence in a moment of history in which many actors and movements arose as new interpreters of Sharia and Islamic jurisprudence, such those sheikhs not part of a legal official institution but of an Islamist religious movement.

This chapter includes an interview with the director of Dar al-Ifta's *kulliyat shar'ia* in Lebanon, as an example of the election of the body of jurists within legal religious institutions and legal studies in a Lebanese context.

Evolution of Islamic Institutions and the Role of Its Personnel

The social, political, and religious changes in Islamic countries from the late eighteenth and nineteenth centuries onward entailed the decrepitude of institutions and the relevance of religious personalities. Nevertheless, neither ever stopped having influence in the Islamic world. The *fatwas* pronounced and transmitted by religious institutions and their personnel did not cease to be a necessity in the life of every Muslim who was facing unknown situations. Some institutions—such as the *kulliya*[5] and *madrasas* or centers of teaching of religious doctrine—remain in operation, especially for the instruction of *hadith*,[6] *tafsir*,[7] Quran, the hermeneutics of sacred texts, etc. Usually, they are close to mosques or institutions such as the house of the *fatwa* or Dar al-Ifta'/Dar al-Fatwa, also called Islamic

---

which many *ulama* were forced to adopt. Thus, the caliph entered the terrain that belonged to the field of jurists, in which he never had any prerogative. This showed the conflict between the *ulama* and the caliphs in relation to religious authority.

[5] Luz Gómez García mentions the *kulliya* as an architectural complex attached to the main mosques of the Ottoman period. It housed the activities associated with religion, but which were not especially liturgical, such as teaching, healing, or lodging (Gómez García 2009, 188). In general, the *kulliya* to which I refer can have the same origin, but its objective is religious education; they are centers with associated libraries. The *licentia docendi* or *ijaza* of the most prestigious Muslim field, taught by reference centers such as the Islamic Universities of Azhar in Egypt, Mecca, Jedda, and Medina in Saudi Arabia and some in Pakistan.

[6] A *hadith* is a narration of the conduct of the Prophet, whereas *sunna* is the example or the law that is deduced from it. *Hadith* in this sense is the vehicle or the carrier of *sunna*. *Sunna* thus referred not only to the *hadith* of the Prophet but also to the established practice of the community (Kamali 2003, 61).

[7] Quranic exegesis.

Councils. And although they have lost relevance in favor of Islamic universities, they still exist.

Educational and legal institutions such as the *madrasas* became important teaching centers for the study of subjects including the *fiqh*, the principles of the religious creed, and the *usul al-fiqh*. These *madrasas* were established as pious foundations, with the same status as the *waqf*, around the eleventh century.[8]

In the madrasa one could teach the legal theory of a *madhab* of the four schools of law, or all of them. The legal-religious schools are the *Hanafi, Maliki, Shafii*' and *Hanbali.* Weiss clarifies that (Weiss and Bernard 2005, 1–2):

> "*Madhab* which literally means 'way' becomes in Muslim juristic usage the designation for a body of doctrine, or principles, or methods, propounded by a scholar who has the rank of *muytahid.* Doctrine is, of course, entailed in the meaning of 'school'" although the primary reference of this term is to a group of 'persons who hold a common doctrine or accept the same teachings or follow the same intellectual methods' or 'who are the disciples or followers of a teacher'. Schools, we must say, exist at the level of people, whereas *madhhabs* exist at the level of doctrine" … "A *madhhab* is always fundamentally the doctrine or method of an individual scholar."

Muftis and *qadis* were formed in these centers, but on a higher level, and even prepared to perform *ijtihad*. When a student finished a book, his teacher could give him a certification or *ijaza* that authorized him to transmit that work. The *madrasa* worked based on the pedagogical phenomenon of the *halaqa*: a circle of students learned around a private teacher, a phenomenon predating the creation of the *madrasas*.[9] The *ulama*, according to Makdisi (1970, 259), would be "the heirs of the Prophets"

---

[8] Other authors establish the creation of the first *madrasas* in the tenth century (Armstrong 2001, 141).

[9] Under the teaching of the jurist and theologian Imam al-Haramayn al-Juwayni, Abu Hamid al-Ghazali wrote his thesis or ta'liqa, the Mankhul. See Hallaq (2009, 135–46). It is important to bear in mind that toward the end of the fifteenth century, it was the *madrasa* and not the professor who determined the rank of the student and his professional gifts. While the *halaqa* are students who freely gather around a teacher without any political interference, the *madrasa* for its part was a more political phenomenon.

(*al-ulama warathatu l-anbiy'ah*). While in the Christian religious hierarchy, the popes are the last guardians of orthodoxy, the *ulama*, lacking this hierarchy, are the ones preserving and propagating orthodoxy.[10]

During the time of the Ottoman Empire, Islamic law was imposed under the guidance of the Hanafi School, which was the official *madhhab* in all territories. The Empire also created the figure of *Shaykh al-Islam*, a title attributed to the Grand Mufti of Istanbul.[11] As head of the new professional hierarchy created by the Ottomans, he was responsible for supervising the provinces from Istanbul, especially the schools and their teachers. The office of the *qadi* was also the object of this hierarchically organized system, designated by the sultan. One of the great *muftis*, Abul-Su'ud, achieved reconciliation between the *qanun*, the administrative law of the Ottoman Empire, and the Sharia, before being named Grand Mufti. Under the sultan's orders, he reviewed the land laws of the European provinces and applied the principles of Sharia to them (Schacht 1966, 90).

Both Islamic law and jurisprudence operated according to the same scheme they had used from the beginning: the sultan was responsible for ensuring the legal-political administration (*siyasa shar'iyya*) of the community, while the experts in law took responsibility for deducing norms from the sacred texts and watching over Sharia, either by means of *taqlid*[12] or *ijtihad* (more restricted). The *qadi* also administrated in the courts the law that the *ulama* had been charged with formulating. This was

---

[10]The author also refers to the fact that while in medieval Europe, there was a Christian based institutional system which was hierarchical and organized, in medieval Muslim times, this educational system was individualistic and personalized.

[11]He had to oversee the observance of the sacred law in the state and supervise the activity of the *qadis*. The institution also had the benefit of confirming the new sultans, who once invested as sultan had an authority superior to that of the *Shaykh al-Islam*. He also had religious dispensations, such as the issuance of *fatwas*. Throughout the history of Islam, other Islamic scholars would be named *Shaykh al-Islam*, but their role would be neither hierarchical nor the same as that performed during the Ottoman Empire. Thus, Islamic law scholars who held this designation were Imam Ahmad ibn Hanbal, Imam Malik ibn Anas, Imam al-Shafi'i, Ibn Taymiyyah, or Muhammad bin Abd al-Wahhab.

[12]*Taqlid* as strict following of any established doctrine, and *ittiba'*, which involves a more reasoned monitoring, in which the choice of certain interpretations is studied and analyzed. It is important to note that nearly all instances of *ijma'* that are cited in the textbooks refer to the consensus of *ulama* and private jurists, there being hardly a single record of a government-sponsored assembly of the learned to have acted as a vehicle of *ijma'* or even *ijma'* in which the government played a visible role. For their part, government authorities seem

a balanced scheme that conferred the necessary legitimacy to the religious establishment.

The Ottoman policy of centralization was one of the main characteristics of the Empire, which also entailed the creation of sultanic *madrasas*. The goal was to integrate the legal profession into the state apparatus by using it within the administration of the Empire. Within this new scheme and, I could say, emanating from *siyasa shar'iyya*, *qanun* arose, which reflects not only the provisions of religious law but also certain legislative activity on the part of the sultan that is more focused on public order. The *qanun* and the Hanafi School texts complemented each other: the first with sultanic decrees, where the *qadi* was the administrator and interpreter of the *qanun*, and the second with the legal doctrines of the Hanafi School. Both, in turn, adapted to the historical circumstances of the moment. In this relationship, Sharia and Islamic legal doctrine always were the highest authority of reference for the government, although as we have seen, they were also mixed with provisions of the *qanun*.

Throughout the nineteenth century, European law, especially criminal and commercial law, was introduced into the Ottoman Empire through the system of capitulations, which guaranteed Western citizens who lived in the geographical area of the Empire to be governed by their own laws. This European law ended up influencing Ottoman law through the *tanzimat* or reforms, which began in 1839 and ended in 1876. At that time, this was considered "the need to reconcile Islamic principles with secularizing recipes based on the concept of citizenship advocated from Europe" (Gutierrez de Teran Gómez-Benita 2003, 15). The aim was to modernize the Empire, protecting its territorial integrity, especially due to the new scenario in which nationalist movements developed and in which the maintenance of the *millet* legal system for minority religious communities became unsustainable, largely as a consequence of the influence of European powers.

The system persisted by promulgating new codes of laws based on European examples, such as criminal or mercantile laws of French origin. These were applied by a new system of secular courts called *nizamiya*, which gave rise to the Majalla or Mecelle, the civil code in force in the Ottoman Empire since 1869, which also represented a first attempt to codify part of Islamic legislation. With time, and due to the influence of

---

to have condoned and encouraged *taqlid*, as this meant the leadership and initiative in both political and legal spheres rested with the government in power (Kamali 2003, 503).

colonial powers, different European codes were applied in the different provinces of the Empire. These ended up confining, from the end of the nineteenth until the beginning of the twentieth century, the Sharia and the *fiqh* to the scope of the personal status codes. This was the culmination of the journey of the Muslim world's history,[13] which was dominated by Islamic law and its jurisprudence and entailed a political-social and religious life model.

The obsession of attempting to understand the East through Western models ended up relegating the law to foreign codes and to the establishment of a state with civil administrative control over legal areas, with the objective of nationalizing institutions. The traditional Islamic legal system was outside the authority of the state, as constituted in the nation-state. In the past, Muslim society had another concept, established by the practice of their community, related to the system of government. These governments never created Sharia nor the *fiqh*, although they guarded its correct implementation. The opposite happened in modern legislations, where the law was now the product of the state.

As Ernest Gellner comments, I could allude to the fact that the Muslim world in its internal organization and life possesses a Durkheimian religion, in which the sacred is embodied in periodic rituals, sacred objects, sacred practices, and sacred individuals. Islam existed in a permanent oscillation between failed reforms and reversals of old cultural habits (Gellner 1996).[14] This would be reminiscent of a past that is wished to be built in the present, where Islamic law would prevail as the operational center of the community. That individual and social desideratum was achieved through coexistence in the community of God.

Religious personnel have always been fundamental in the history of legal trajectory. I will mention the role of *qadis*, *mujtahids*, *muftis*, and the *fuqaha'*.[15] All of them belong to the religious sphere of Islamic legal

---

[13] Saudi Arabia, Yemen, the protectorate of Aden, Hadramaut and the principalities of the Persian Gulf would remain outside European influence. See Coulson (1998, 163 and 159–71).

[14] The author talks about rural Muslims, the upper classes, urban classes, and individualists, among others.

[15] There have been books on the education and procedures of the *qadi* and the *mufti* since ancient times, which are called the *adab al-qadi* and *adab al-mufti*. One of the most comprehensive manuals on the *muftis* is by Ibn al-Salah, entitled *a*dab al-mufti wal-mustafti (Al-Qader 1986). The *mufti* must be highly qualified to carry out his office under

history and have specific roles. While the *qadi* is understood as a judge whose decisions are binding, the *mujtahid* is the one who exercises the independent reasoning of *ijtihad*, the *mufti* is the jurist trained to issue, upon request, a legal opinion that is not binding in relation to the Islamic norm and that is called a *fatwa*, and, finally, the *fuqaha'* are specialized in *fiqh*.

The mission of the *mujtahid* would be to apply the principles of *usul* to establish a corpus juris, based on the knowledge of the primordial textual sources. This gave him the capacity to exercise his legal and interpretative qualities. The derived norms, or *ahkam*,[16] will be those applicable to specific cases that the jurist-*mujtahid* deals with.[17]

These figures play a role today that is no longer the same as the role they once played in the past, because their profession has been greatly impaired. Several criticisms are aimed at the personality of the *mufti*, whose education and training are reflected in the *fatwa* that he promulgates. In many cases, his education takes place in educational centers that promote the knowledge of a single legal school. His interpretive work

---

examination of the caliph, and the position of the judge is subject to the caliphate. See the discussion of their offices in Ibn Khaldun (2005, 172–3). On the appointment of judges, see al-Mawardi (1996, 72–86).

[16]The deduction of norms is achieved by three methods: first, through reason (*'aql*), whose norms are known as *ahkam al-'aqliyya*; second, based on natural feelings and senses, known as *ahkam hissiyya*; and third, through the accepted texts, which is known as *ahkam shar'iyya*. The principles of the *usul al-fiqh* belong to the third area, in addition to being concerned with all norms concerning human actions and activities they belong to, what is called *ahkam 'amaliyya* (Ramic 2003, x and xv). One must also consider the importance of the principles of linguistics in the *usul al-fiqh* (Ramic 2003, xiv; al-Alwani 1994, 6). Ramic mentions that *usul* scholars must be versed in logic and its predictions, linguistics, orders and prohibitions, complete (*'amm*) and particular (*khass*) terms, inconclusive (*mujmal*) and determinate (*mubayyan*) concepts, abrogation (*nasj*), works—in particular those of the Prophet—and their meaning, the consensus, narrations of the Sunna, *qiyas*, the preference in case of contractions, the *ijtihad*, *taqlid*, and knowledge of the sources.

[17]It is said of the person who interprets the sources of Islamic law (usul al-fiqh) to create jurisprudence/doctrine, a specialist who is dedicated to *ijtihad*. There were the *ahl al-taqlid* (traditionalists) or *ahl alra'i* (rationalists). Since the eleventh century, it has been used as a legal-historiographical technicality (Gomez Garcia 2009, 222). The word has its root in the verb *ijtahada*, which in turn comes from the word *jahada*, which means to make an effort, in this case an intellectual effort in relation to a legal matter on which there was no previous regulation.

follows the *adilla* or indications of sacred sources such as the Quran and the *hadith*. In addition, his knowledge should, in my view, be versed in the legal matters of other religions, such as Christianity and Judaism. *Muqallids* can also issue legal opinions. Legal opinions in general are usually private, when the *mufti* responds to a question of a person in relation to *'ibadat* or ritual questions.

Although the Prophet was the visible head of the community, this did not prevent his companions from issuing *fatwas*[18] as well as using mechanisms such as *ijtihad*. Terms such as Sharia and *fiqh* are often confused. It must be understood that the first is the compendium of the original sources—the texts from which the norm will be derived: the Quran and the Sunnah—while the second includes the norms derived through the hermeneutics of Sharia.[19]

In relation to the *qadis*, they issue judgments with binding legal value, always based on the *fatwa* dictated by a *mufti* that they believe they must apply. For this, they can resort to a house of *fatwa* or consult the court's manual that serves as a precedent, always applied to the sphere of family law. When this happens, the *fatwa* becomes a *hukm* or judgment.[20] There is also the legal *fatwa*, as requested by a *mustafti* (a lay person who makes the request) and answered by a *mufti*, whose resolution will be accepted or rejected by the *qadi*. The interpretive work of the *qadi* follows the evidence or *hijaj*, which includes testimony, confession, and oath. The courts in which the latter functions are often referred to as *mahakim shara'i*. The prerogatives that these courts had are extinct at present and limited to personal status laws. The scope of work of the *qadi*, who is appointed by the government, is limited to that of a judge and public notary, both in relation to Sharia and the positive (*qanun*) law.

---

[18] Plural of this word is *fatawa*: a legal opinion pronounced by a *faqih* and *'alim*, a *mufti* or *mujtahid*, in any matter pertaining to Islamic law or also to *fiqh*.

[19] To Ibn Khaldun, jurisprudence is the knowledge of the classification of the laws of God, concerning the actions of all responsible Muslims, as mandatory, prohibited, recommendable, neutral, or permissible. They are derived from the Quran and Sunna and from the evidence established by Muhammad. The laws derived from this evidence are called jurisprudence (Ibn Khaldun 2005, 344–5).

[20] It is interesting to see how al-Qarafi clarifies the distinction between *fatwa* and *hukm* by identifying *fatwa* with *khabar* (assertion or report) and *hukm* with an *insha'* (origin), in Jackson (1996, 170–84).

Masud, Messick, and Powers (1996) indicate "as represented in the Quran the activity of the consultation involves a three-way relationship between God, Muhammad, and the Muslim community, with Muhammad serving as the medium through which community members Know God´s ñaws and ordinances" (Masud, Messick, and Powers 1996, 5). In addition, the Quran contains the linguistic forms that characterize the activity of the legal consultation (*futya*) in its classical manifestation. In two verses of Sura 4 (Women), the verb *yas'alunaka* is replaced by *yastaftunaka*. In addition, in Verse 176, Muhammad receives the instruction: "When they ask for you for a pronouncement (*wa-yastaftunaka*) say: 'God pronounce to you (*yuftikum*) concerning *al-Kalala*'. From the Quranic use of the verbs *afta* and *istafta*, the terminology associated with the classical activity of legal consultation is derived: *mufti*, *mustafti* (questioner), *futya* (legal consultation), *ifta'* (*fatwa*-giving), and *istifta'* (request for a *fatwa*) (Masụd, Messick, and Powers 1996, 5–6).[21] These days, this last word refers to the popular referendum or plebiscite.

It is important to mention that authority in Shi'ism, is different than is sunnism, refers to the *marja'* or religious authority that is followed. The *marja'* issues fatwas that include practical treatises (*risala-yi amaliyya*) and works that attempt to clarify problems of daily life (*tawdih al-masail*). Tabatabai lists more than fifty fatwas collections from the *Ja'afari* school. In Shi'ism generally the term *mujtahid* (practicing *ijtihad*) and faqih (legal specialist) are somehow synonymous with mufti. In Masud, Messick, and Powers (1996, 13–4). It should not be forgotten that the Shi'ite *ulama* (called mullah) belongs to the clerical hierarchy, he can be *marja'*, ayatollah, mullah ... the mujtahid must have the quality of justice or adalat.

The Change of Legal Paradigm, from Sharia and Legal Hybridization to Family Status Code

Islamic institutions and schools of law have been considered the references that preserved jurisprudence[22] and the entities that transmitted its knowledge, always related to the implementation of *fiqh*.

---

[21] According to the authors, traditional sources identify approximately 130 Companions who are said to have functioned as *muftis* during the first century A.H./seventh century A.D. (al-Qasimi 1986, 35, 7).

[22] It seems more appropriate to call Sharia "Islamic law," while I should refer to *fiqh* as Islamic doctrine or legal doctrine. The word *fiqh* is used, in Spanish, as Islamic

Over time, the importance of these institutions was reduced to the scope of personal status codes. This encompassed laws related to marriage, divorce, inheritance, and custody of children. The civil sphere would be in charge of the domains that did not belong to personal status; areas in which the legal codes of other countries would be imposed.

The Islamic world suffered a shock when colonial entities began their domination project through "the discourse" and incursion into its territory. At the legal level, this authority involved the extrapolation of new foreign legal codes, which caused the disappearance of Sharia as a legal system in most Islamic countries (Ruiz-Almodóvar 2005, 497–529). The Islamic tradition that conceived the juridical sphere as an integral and elementary part of a system of life, which was also combined with political and social life, was marginalized to the field of family status or personal status code within the model of nation-states.

One of the essential differences between Islamic law and the nation-state, as Hallaq mentions, is that "hierarchy within Islamic law was largely universal and self-sufficient, unlike the hierarchy existing in the judicial system of the nation-state, which ultimately reports to a higher political order. The referential authorities of the *qadi* are other *qadis* and muftis" (Hallaq 2009, 362).

---

jurisprudence, while the term jurisprudence is used more broadly and carries one of the descriptions exposed by the dictionary of the RAE (Royal Spanish Academy) as a set of doctrinal sentences and the doctrines that they contain. This is why, sometimes, we will find throughout our work the term "jurisprudence" in a broader sense that includes the doctrine. I think it is important to differentiate concepts such as Sharia and *fiqh*. If Sharia is understood as a whole that encompasses the *fiqh*, in the same way, one can confuse what pertains to the immutable in Islamic legal matter and what refers to the field of interpretation by the professionals of the law (which belongs to the science of *fiqh*). That is, confuse as immutable that which does not have to be but has to necessarily be applied to specific social contexts, the essential role of *fiqh*.

Therefore, the current assertion about the creation of an Islamic State and the application of Sharia as a mandate of God, in a specific way, is a very controversial subject that is easily questionable. This is especially so because the law reflected in Sharia cannot be applied to many cases that occur in current societies, unless the norm is previously derived. Due to the confusion and terminological identification that this entails, I think that it would be more practical to identify sacred/Islamic/Sharia law strictly with what the terms Quran and Sunna encompass and to refer to *fiqh* with the expression "Islamic doctrine" (Jalloul Muro 2016, 292–320).

The rigidity of the system meant that the civil and religious fields were completely separated. Personal status fell under Islamic courts, while the rest of subjects that were previously treated by Sharia became a state prerogative under civil courts. This hybrid system had not been accommodated until then in the Islamic world. The religious establishment, including the *ulama*, was deeply affected. This was especially so for the *fiqh* and its methodology, which would no longer have a voice in the derivation of norms from sacred texts to be adapted to a modern society, except for rulings related to the laws of the personal status code.[23] The Islamic legal dynamism was lost, leaving Islamic law closed in the mold of *entexting*, which entailed the fossilization of Sharia within the framework of the colonial codification of laws. In the words of Hallaq, "engendering [meant the] juristic/jural rigidity through *entexting*, and politization through transplantation. Whereas the premodern Sharia and its fiqh operated largely outside dynastic rule, the *entexted* and transplanted fiqh had now come to be lodged within the structures of the state" (Hallaq 2009, 548).[24]

Thus, the *fiqh* and its legal diversity became a uniform law, as the law's dynamism disappeared and was hermetically locked in the mold of *entexting*. This amounts to saying that the *fiqh* was robbed of its capacity to adapt to cases that demanded a study of specific circumstances, and it became obsolete in books and codifications of past cases regarding family status in general unless there was a need to face a new, unprecedented case. In turn, everything that did not belong to this area of family status and that was traditionally covered by Islamic courts was developed by new, foreign legal codes.[25]

Classical Islamic jurisprudence became one of those reminiscences of a glorious time, in which Islamic culture was guided by the sacred texts. Because of this historical evolution, I would later find a call to return to the insertion of Islamic law in the life of Muslims, as part of Islamists' speech. This supported jurisprudence as the necessary and underpinning element in the search for the perfect state. It important to bear in mind that the conception of nation-state in Islamic law was nonexistent. The state was not the one promoting the community (*umma*) throughout Islamic

[23] The methodology of Islamic jurisprudence, known as *usul al-fiqh*. Was applied only in the field of personal status but not in the rest of civil areas.

[24] The word "entexting" that Hallaq uses cannot be found in the dictionary, but we can translate it roughly as "coding."

[25] Some cases belonging to personal status that do not have prior legislation are still in need of *fatwas* (legal opinions) that are issued by legal experts, but these are rare.

history, but the *umma* should create political and religious unity as was established in the Islamic State of Medina and in its written constitution. This kind of Islamic political institution preserved its existence in the form of the Sunni caliphate and the Shiite Imamate. This does not mean, however, that the caliphates were legitimate institutions, since they had not been established in the Quran.[26] But what was legal and provided a certain legitimacy were concepts such as *bay'a*[27] used to elect the caliph and the separation of legal and political spheres, even though the caliphate as a hereditary institution was not set down in the sacred texts.

Islamic history reached the nineteenth century with a *fiqh* that had developed a religious law and methods of reasoning, which together with other Quranic precepts—such as spirituality and morality—composed a culture of daily life. In countries that were dominated by the Ottoman Empire, a government ruled by the enforcement of Islamic law through Islamic courts under the Hanafi school of law, as the official legal school of the Empire. There was the figure of *Shaykh al-Islam*, or the highest religious authority, and the schools of Islamic studies, in addition to secular laws such as the law called *qanun*.[28] Within the

---

[26] The Shi'ites instead testify that the imamate is supported by the original texts.

[27] Once the election of the caliph was consensual, the next step was the *bay'a* or pact—oath of obedience to the caliph—in which the leaders of the *umma* or its members in general took part. This mechanism was already in place during the *jahiliyya* as an unwritten pact in which a commitment to obey the leader by prominent members of the tribe was established in exchange for some responsibilities. Al-Alwani adds to the description of the term that it entailed: "The nomination of the *khalifa* by the leaders of the Ummah, or the seconding of that nomination by the members of the Ummah in general; the covenant the first Muslims of Madinah entered into with the Prophet, giving him their obedience, allegiance, and protection" (Al-Alwani 1994, 23). For Nebot, "etymologically the term comes from the verb *bay'a*, which means to sell, and implies the contractual nature of this elective procedure. The elector sells his quota of participation in power in exchange for management according to the stipulations of the contract. This concept has nothing to do with the general translation of the expression of paying homage (Nebot 2002, 246). Ibn Khaldun comments that it "is a contract of obedience … considered as an action between buyer and seller" (Ibn Khaldun 2005, 166–7).

[28] *Qanun* was also the law produced in the Ottoman Empire by the sultan power. See Esposito (2009, 252). What seems clear is that all systems to adapt Sharia were close to a system of *siyasa shar'iyya* (an attempt is made to apply *siyasa* within the limits of Sharia), in which the law was formulated by the state, although classical law sources were used (Schacht 1996, 54). The author comments that the *qadi* followed the instructions of the sovereign, exercising his power to apply the *siyasa* within the limits of Sharia.

Ottoman Empire, therefore, a more modern legal system had been developed, overlapping with the Sharia.

With the demise of the Ottoman Empire, most Islamic countries would retain Islamic law for Muslim communities in relation to personal status, which fell under the authority of religious courts. Even those countries who had Christian religious minorities, such as Lebanon, would have their courts for religious matters. In countries like Lebanon, Egypt, Sudan, and Morocco, religious minorities can choose whichever faith codes they wish to apply to personal status codes (Davis-Packard 2016).

The new legal codes

The new nationalist project inspired by the European nation-state model imposed codes, as mentioned above, predominantly imitating the French, British, and Egyptian models. Important changes occurred in, for example, Tunisia, where the personal status code of 1957 adopted the Hanafi rules, by which the woman could conclude her own marital contract, polygamy was eliminated, and the woman was considered at the same level as the man when requesting a divorce.[29] Another example is the Iraqi law of 1936, which gave the green light to the hereditary rights of the Shia legal tradition. The Syrian penal statute no longer acknowledged divorce with the mention of "*talaq*" three times in a row, which minimized the control of repudiation by men.[30]

Other personal status codes include the Algerian code of 1984, modified in 2005 and based on the Maliki School; the Egyptian code, promulgated in 1920 and 1929, with the law of successions of 1943 and of testaments of 1946 and legal school of Hanafi;[31] the Iraqi code of 1959, modified in 1994, which does not refer to any specific legal school; the Jordanian code, promulgated in 1976 and repealing the code of 1951, again modified in 1977, which builds on the Hanafi School; the Kuwaiti code of 1984, using the Maliki School; or the code of Lebanon, which maintains the Ottoman law

---

[29] In June 2017, Tunisia overturned a law that banned women from marrying non-Muslims (*BBC News* 2017).

[30] The Syrian government practices the Alawite creed, which is a split from a descendant of the tenth Twelver Imam. Shi'ism does not consider the mention of *talaq* (divorce) three times in a row as effective, as is the case for Sunnism.

[31] Abd al-Rahman al-Sanhuri was the person responsible for the Egyptian civil code of 1949. Other Arab codes, such as the Iraqi, Syrian, Kuwaiti, Qatar, Somalian, and others were inspired by it. He tried to reconcile the European systems with the traditional Islamic system.

of 1917 except for the Druze, Christians, and Jews, and which is based on the Hanafi School. In Libya, the code is from 1984 and does not include any specific legal school, only Islamic law. In Morocco, a 2004 law repealed the 1993 amendment to the personal status code of 1957–8. The Syrian code was promulgated by the decree law of 1953, modified in 1975, and is based on the Hanafi School (Ruiz-Almodóvar, 2005).

According to Amira el-Azhary Sonbol, the codifications of the personal status law diverge in three ways from Sharia practiced in the courts before the reform prior to the nineteenth century. These are the philosophical approach to gender and law, the application of law in courts, and the coding structure itself (El-Azhary Sonbol 2009, 188, 179–260). It is clear that the state would be the one creating and instituting legal codes, since the *ulama* had no recognized role in legislation, having lost their historical monopoly in relation to the interpretation and creation of Islamic jurisprudence (with the exception of the family status laws).

As Hallaq (2009, 500) indicates:

> Arguably, by the middle of the twentieth century the Sharīʿa had been reduced to a fragment of itself at best and, at worst, structurally speaking, to a nonentity. The chipping away by the modern state of the Sharīʿa resulted in: first, the collapse of the financial and *waqf* foundations that sustained the legal profession and its reproductive mechanisms; second, the gradual displacement of this profession by a class of modern lawyers and judges who came from a newly rising bourgeoisie and/or transformed ulama families; third, the replacement of institutional legal structures by modern law faculties and modern hierarchical courts of law; and fourth, the introduction of a massive bulk of commercial, criminal, civil and other laws that either replaced the *fiqh* or were imported in order to accommodate the new legal needs that arose as a result of exposure to the new and open international markets … The totality of these effects, I have argued elsewhere, amounted to the effective structural demise of the Sharīʿa, notwithstanding the continuing viability of the law of personal status, which finds its roots in the *fiqh* but has become transformed in function and modality to a state law.[32]

[32] As an example, the University of al-Azhar underwent great reform since 1961. Its administration was, by Nasserist mandate, placed under the administration of the state; the highest-ranking sheikh was appointed or dismissed under the responsibility of the president's office.

The New Identity Crisis

These changes brought about tension that was reflected not only in the legal field but also at the social level. The duality created by concepts such as modernity and tradition affected the identity of Islamic countries that, accustomed to their traditions, would have to become part of an imposed modernity. Universal values—such as constitutionalism or human rights—became part of the new states. It is not that these did not exist in the world of Sharia, but it was simply another way of life. For example, Sharia observed principles such as limitations on arbitrary detention and values such as the right to life or equality, among others (Esmaeili 2011, 359–61).[33] The possibility of adapting Sharia through its *usul* to other legal codes was not taken into consideration; the new codes were imposed.

The enforced modernity was considered anti-Islamic, mainly by conservative movements. Islamic societies moved between opposing positions, in which both sides struggled to find, among so much confusion, an identity of their own. This identity could be secular, like in Turkey or Tunisia where laws were mostly draw from secular sources, or a return to an original Islam. Many of these positions succumbed to the antithesis between tradition and modernity.

What seems clear is that groups who advocate the Islam of the past tend to forget historical disasters like the *mihna*[34] and the betrayals in the caliph courts, apart from the artificial creation of the hereditary institution of the caliphate, battles like the *fitnas* and Kerbala, or the wear and tear of conquests and bureaucratic problems derived from empires expanding to large areas. The belief in a present that is incapable of providing solutions implies a belief in a sublime past. Islamist radical Salafist movements preconize an Islamic society, and many others a political state, that should

[33] Esmaeili (2011) mentions that some legal principles of traditional Islamic law are similar and somehow precedent to modern legal principles. Under Islamic law, the law should not be applied retroactively, and the principle of legality is recognized. The lives and reputations of individuals are protected, and the presumption of innocence is an important principle of Islamic criminal law. Detention before trial is not allowed, and if allowed, it is for a very limited period only. Similar fundamental theories of the rule of law are human rights and justice.

[34] A kind of inquisition that operated for a few years under the Abbasid caliphate in the ninth century. The end of the *mihna* marked the end of the caliphal claim to religious authority. See footnote 5.

be formed like the society of the times of the Prophet till the third generation of Companions. The political and religious hermeneutic that Islamism carries out rests on a politicization of Islam in general, with its own discursive and communicative techniques that favor the interests of Islamist groups and leaders and that is based on the idea that the main purpose of the Islamic creed is the construction of a political entity. And although in Islam, politics is innate to religion, the reality of religious texts does not clarify this unique and final consequence of this political goal in Islam (Jalloul Muro 2015).[35]

The political situation led to widespread discontent, especially in the Arab world and in Muslim and other religious communities. This was an outcome of the newly imposed State of Israel, the subsequent Arab-Israeli wars, the influence of foreign powers, economic globalization, democratic transformation processes, etc. Muslims in the Arab world perceived the creation of the State of Israel as an attack not only on their geographical and cultural Arabness but also on their Islamic identiy. Jerusalem is one of the sacred cities in Islam, to which prayer was directed before Mecca and where the Prophet's traveled to the heavens on the night of al-Isra' wal-Mi'raj. The discomfort that the creation of the State of Israel created,

---

[35] Islamism, due to the qualities described, is also called political Islam, since there is a political ideologization that separates itself from the political and social tradition, refuting the political authority of the Islamic tradition. This tradition began during the Umayyad caliphate and lasted until the fall of the Ottoman caliphate, with the exception of the time of the Rashidun caliphate. It always takes the Islamic state of the early times of Islam, the one led by the Prophet, as a reference and ideal prototype. However, the term "political Islam" seems controversial to us, since I do not think that the raison d'être of Islam and its goal are political. In any case, the unity of those who are Muslim, or not, decides on the political organization of the community through a common pact or consensus and consultation. Islamism is a novel phenomenon dating from the twentieth century, and its political model does not resemble that of the historical caliphates such as the Umayyad, the Abbasid, the Fatimid, or the Ottoman; although these four were hereditary caliphates, something that Islam never established. After the caliphate of the Rashidun (first four caliphs), in which the caliphs were the political and spiritual heads of the community (which also exceptionally happened with the Fatimid Shiite caliphate in the case of Septiman Shi'ism), in the later Sunni caliphates there would be a separation between the political and the legal sphere. Twelver Shiism, as something new in the history of Shi'ism, established the political representation of religious power through the religious political theory of *wilayat al-faqih* with Khomeini in Iran (Jalloul Muro 2018, 99–121).

together with the loss of Palestine, also affected other, Christian Arab religious communities, many of whose members have been great defenders of the Palestinian cause and Arab nationalism.

The construction of nationalisms implies in many cases the adhesion to a specific culture or archetype that has little to do with reality. Thus, for example, the confrontation between Shia and Sunni Islam made many Shia populations, as is the case in Iran, feel that their identity is Persian, when in fact, as indicated by Hamid Enayat (2004, 124):

> Iranians were free under the Muslim rule to practise their pre-Islamic beliefs, and had therefore no need to fabricate Shīʻīsm to camouflage their ancient traditions. They converted to Islam because there were discontented with the Sassanian autocracy and corruption, and thirsty for a new message of justice and equality. They developed a deep affection for the members of the Prophet's family because they found them the most sincere and most fearless champions of Islamic ideals. There are indeed some Shīʻī traditions which give weight to the contention that the Iranian admiration for the Imāms is connected with the marriage between the third Imām, Ḥusayn, and Shahrbānū, the daughter of Yazdigird, the last Sassanian king. These traditions should be treated with the greatest caution, because, according to Muṭahharī, some of their narrators have been proved, by the standards of the "sciences of tradition," to be unreliable. He indulges in further polemics against European and Iranian exponents of the family link between Shīʻīsm and Iranian nationalism, and says that if inter-marriage were to give rise to sectarian preferences, the Iranians had an equally valid reason for loving the Umayyads, because the Caliph Walīd Ibn ʻAbd al-Malik is also reported to have married Shāh-āfārīd, another descendant of Yazdigird.

Other religious and nationalist communities also claim other ancestral identities, such as the Maronite Christians in Lebanon, who do not consider their identity Arab but Phoenician.

Each nationalist movement has its specificity, depending on the context: while many Arab countries invoke Islam as an indissoluble element of their identity, other, non-Arab countries will exclude or marginalize it, as is the case with Atatürk's Turkey. The pursuit of an independent nation-state was the consequence of colonization: its goal was independence, and the instrumentalization of both political and religious discourses[36] was one of its mechanisms. Moreover, two scenarios will arise: or a new nation-state that will further promote the model of the metropolis, or a new nation-state that will promote its own traditions, which will sharpen the radicalization of the concept of identity, so that to be part of one's own state meant not being part of another one, in addition to the promotion of the identity of belonging to a specific ethnic group.

Benedict Anderson (2006, 6) stated:

> Nation: it is an imagined political community—and imagined as both inherently limited and sovereign. It is *imagined* because the members of even the smallest nation will never know most of their fellow-members, meet them, or even hear of them, yet in the minds of each lives the image of their communion. ... Communities are to be distinguished, not by their falsity/genuineness, but by the style in which they are imagined.

The search for a specific and national identity was created in contradiction to the national realities of other identities, in which, as Edward Said indicates, "The fundamental problem is therefore how to reconcile one's identity and the actualities of one's own culture, society, and history to the reality of other identities, cultures, peoples" (Said 1996, 94). This identity assigned to oneself—by the individual or the group of which he is a member—conditions it in one way or another, and this will always be dependent on the community itself, and on gender, nationality, or ethnicity, among other things. This identity looks to the past in a standardized way, in which history is the one of its nation. Hence, where before, the Islamic world shared the same history without defined borders, now borders delimited the Islamicness of the new nation-states.

The question here is: is Islam reconcilable with the new nationalism that the nation-states tried to impose? The general theory makes these opposites, because Islam not only covers many national states and is not territorially limited, but also does not believe in the ethnic and historical differentiation promoted by nationalisms. However, this has not been an

36 Among other measures, Atatürk permanently abolished the sultanate, replaced the *abjad* with the Latin script, and banned the Islamic veil, harems, the *qadis*' courts, and religious brotherhoods. Although Turkey proclaimed Islam as the state religion, secularism was one of its fundamental pillars.

obstacle for different religions, including Islam, which have adapted within national societies by limiting their spiritual aspirations to a territorial area. Thus, the concept of citizen of the state gained relevance over that of the believer of the *umma*.

The future will entail the continuity of the identity crisis within Muslim societies in their countries of origin, which today continue to be torn between a modernity that implies an Islamic non-religiousness and the rise of Islamist movements claiming an Islamic state with an *umma* and with a politicized historical reading, calling in many cases for the implementation of sharia. In addition, Muslim migratory flows to other countries since the second half of the twentieth century were part of the application of policies such as assimilationism and multiculturalism[37] in the countries of destination, which showed a path that was not exempt from mistakes when integrating Muslim migrants and promoted ghettoization in many cases.

In this context, the interpretation of the religious texts by religious legal personnel who are prepared for its interpretation and the issuing of legal material becomes an essential issue, limiting their area of influence to the Family status code and adapting to modern times.

The Quest for the Right Example

Both the *fatwa* and the figures of the *mufti*, *mujtahid*, and *qadi* emphasize the importance of authority in Islam. The desire to regulate the relationship between God and man created a legal structure over time that tried to equip the religious and the civil spheres with regulatory mechanisms that granted them the necessary legitimacy to stay united and organize the *umma*. This authority comes mainly from God, who showed through the Quran how the community of Prophet Muhammad had to be organized. This would be the legitimate and practical source par excellence, hence the constant effort to identify and approach that example.

Once the Prophet died, *fatwas* were issued by the Companions, who were the guides indicating how Muhammad addressed important

[37]Assimilationism believes that while the first immigrant generations tend to preserve elements of the original culture, subsequent generations assimilate much of the dominant culture. It is intended to transform foreigners into citizens. Meanwhile, multiculturalism advocates the importance of cultural diversity, promoting the value of the new citizenship while preserving the language and culture of origin (Alsayyad and Castells 2003, 31).

issues: any good practice was emulated. Once the Companions were gone, only the *hadith* granted the necessary authority, through the *isnad* or chain of transmission that went back to the authority of the Prophet. The *ulama* would be in charge of these and other sciences throughout the history of law and Islamic legal theory. We have already seen the *fatwa* evolved into a private activity, detached from state control, with the creation of Sunni and Shi'i legal schools with their respective *fatwas* of each school and the bureaucratization of the system inserted into the state apparatus.

The qualities of the *mufti* or *mujtahid* needed to interpret and create *fatwas* must correspond to the Quranic principles of piety, humility, social recognition, etc. This invested them with personal qualities like those that *in illo tempore* the *sahaba* (Companions) had. It was a way of showing personal legitimacy. To prevent the law from suffering from distortion in the hands of any religious authority, there were mechanisms to control interpretation in legal matters besides these characteristics. Thus, one of the first objectives of the *usul al-fiqh* was to regulate the personal *ra'i* (opinion) of some jurists. Moreover, the role of legal schools was to systematize and regulate legal activity, to which the *taqlid* would also contribute.

As we have already mentioned, the Islamic world continues to oscillate between an Orientalist conception originated in the West in relation to the inability to adapt and the stagnation of Sharia, and the activity developed by many Muslim jurists and religious figures who need competent legal adaptation to social demands. I believe that both positions presuppose a negative and unrealistic vision of Sharia and *fiqh*. While the first position denies the capacity for adaptation and dynamism of Sharia and jurisprudence, the second is no less skeptical, because it is the source of many misunderstandings that, in the name of Islamic law, have made interpretation a no less conflictive issue.

Qualities of the *mufti* should resemble more strongly those of *mujtahid* than those of *muqallid*,[38] since *mufti* and *mujtahid* both must exercise *ijtihad* if they wish to find legal solutions to unprecedented cases that needs a new *fatwa*.

---

[38] Authors such as al-Shirazi, Mawardi, Imam al-Haramayn al-Juwayni, Ghazali, al-Amidi, Juwayni, al-Mahalli, and al-Subki speak of the conditions of the *mufti* and the *mujtahid* and their similarities and knowledge necessary for the broadcast of *fatwas*. Hallaq (1996; 2001, 67–71).

Not only is this a problem for the level of professionalization that the religious elite should have, but also, various problems stem from this circumstance. Among these, as already mentioned, is the relationship between the religious sphere and politics, since the latter is involved in the bureaucratic designation of the religious apparatus. To this we must add the proliferation of religious *fatwas* for the justification of political aspirations, which are dangerous not only because of their content but also because they are legitimized with a religious background, far from the original precepts of Islam. The personal interpretation of these men of religion makes Islam an occlusal religion, at the mercy of their ideological elucidation. In addition, they make use of the legal methodology that gives them legitimacy to issue *fatwas*, in the name of concepts such as *maslaha* or *istihsan*.

Multiplicity of opinions is something positive, which involves not only a change or alternative at the legal level but also the ability to adapt the law to different circumstances, what is called *ikhtilaf*. This implies the training of personnel and the religious elite to develop a legal exercise that is consistent with the Quranic precepts, which requires in-depth training in the Islamic legal field. Legal interpreted decisions should not be influenced by personal purposes and ideas of those who issue *fatwas*, whether bureaucratic personnel, leaders, or sheikhs of Islamist parties or religious congregations. *Fatwas* should be a prerogative of official institutions and professional Islamic law personnel.

This controversy is reflected in the existential discussion about authority in Islam, which has been the eternal constant of Islamic legal history since the death of the Prophet. What is clear is that the *ulama*, as guardians of the moral conscience of the community, as well as other religious personnel have been relegated to a status that is not as well considered as in the past. A *fatwa* should be issued based on the plural social reality of the Islamic countries as an instrument of accommodation to current situations.

Nowadays, the system of *fatwa* transmission has different channels, such as international and globalized institutions, *fatwa* committees affiliated with the Islamic World League, the Islamic Academy of Fiqh, the Committee of the *fatwa* of the Organization for Islamic Cooperation, or the Council of the Islamic Ideology of Pakistan. To this we must add many web pages, such as the portal of the General Presidency of Islamic Research and the Issuance of *fatwas*, and many others from recognized sheikhs including al-Qardawi. There are also radio and newspaper features for *fatwa* transmission.

As a result, I consider the *fatwa* somehow a conflictive issue, although we recognize that they are necessary. Conflictive, because of the proliferation of these by, in some cases, unskilled religious personnel, in many cases with general characteristics, which are difficult to apply in specific cases. Also, those that are made for specific cases and that are followed blindly create adherents to many religious movements or religious personalities that are established far from the official or institutionalized Islamic institutions within the state apparatus of each country. On the other hand, these institutions are too embedded in the state apparatus, which makes them less independent in the religious sphere.

In turn, the need for *fatwas* not only highlights the legal dynamism at the time of observing new cases without precedent, but also their ability to adapt to today's society.

On the Proliferation of Fatwa and the Role of Mufti

One of the problems that the Islamic world suffers from is the proliferation of *fatwas*, not only those issued by leaders of some Islamist Suni an Shi'i movements but also those issued through the Internet, television, and radio programs. In many cases, it is unknown whether the authority who issues them has the necessary knowledge to emit and propagate them. I must also add the *fatwa* with a political tone, since many political movements or leaders echo religious *fatwas* to justify their political ideas.[39] The *fatwa* is issued after a research process, taking into account the professional training of the jurist or *mufti*, and after making a permanent effort to apply the *usul al-fiqh* and *ijtihad*, although this function as *mujtahid* is less frequent. A *mufti* can also resort to previous *fatwas* of a legal school, exercising the function of *muqallid*. Searching for information, for example, in the abbreviate manuals of the legal treaties of each school that are called *mujtasar*.[40] The *fatwa* issued is always composed of a question or *istifta'* and an answer.

---

[39] As an example, I can mention the *fatwa* issued by Khomeini against the writer Salman Rushdie, or the one issued against a rap singer for using the name of a Shi'ite religious figure (Erdbrink 2012). See also al-Sistani or al-Zawahiri's political *fatwas*.

[40] It would perform the role of standard pedagogical texts. We must not forget the figure of the *mussanif*, author-jurist in charge of preparing the legal body of the legal school. The collection of *fatwas* of the *muftis* began to appear in the second half of the tenth century. Hallaq mentions that almost all works on *fiqh* consist of three books or chapters, the first

When two *fatwas* are opposed, there must be a legal consultation on them at an Islamic instance or high religious council, which will pronounce which of the two has primacy by consensus. If this is not the case, the person can choose between one or the other, but in general, a Dar al-Ifta' or Dar al-Fatwa seeks to resolve this type of conflict (Knut 2005, 157–61).

There are essential differences between the role of the *qadi* and that of the *mufti*.[41] Essentially, while the *qadi* is appointed by the state, the *mufti's* authority is achieved by his own learning, status, and recognition, not only through the certificate he might have obtained at the *madrasa* but also publicly. The position of *mufti* changed from Ottoman times until the present, where the function of the *mufti* is now more hierarchical and is inserted into the apparatus of the state. This is the case with the *muftis* and sheikhs of the Islamic institutions. It is true that the independence of religious law manifests itself apart from the political apparatus in the sense that those who promulgate *fatwas* are *muftis*, but the responsibility for application in the courts rests with the *qadis*. Both are part of the state apparatus that regulates their functions within religious institutions, in this case Dar al-Ifta' and the *mahkami shara'i* (religious court).

Performing the function of *mufti* implies a series of characteristics. The most important one begins with the moral character that the *mufti* himself must represent. This is based on the pious and fair character that must be inherent in his person. In many cases, the figure of *mufti* is identified with the one of the *mujtahid*, probably because both have the capacity to issue *fatwas*: the latter because of the exercise of *ijtihad* and the former due to the knowledge and promulgation of *fatwas*. The *mujtahid* must be well versed in the Quranic sciences and the attributes that I have mentioned throughout the text in order to carry out the investigative effort that, based on *ijtihad*, will lead to a legal norm. The *mufti* has similar requirements, including knowledge of the Quran, *hadith*, ambiguous and unambiguous verses, the theory of legal schools, and any question subject to consensus, as well as being versed in syntax, grammar, pronunciation,

---

one made up of the *qadi* and his preparation and works, the second dealing with the rights and obligations of the plaintiff, and the third and last one dealing with evidence and testimonies, among others (Hallaq 2009, 342).

[41] The *qadi* was designated by the governors in the Umayyad dynasty, and in the Abbasid by the caliph. Their jurisdiction extended to the court tribunals, the *nazir al-mazalim, qadi al-qudat, al-surta sahib, al-suq sahib*, and *muhtasib*.

the Arabic language, and customs in the time of the Prophet and afterward.

One of the most important manuals on *adab al-fatwa wal-mufti wal-mustafti* was written by Imam al-Nawawe. It describes the conditions established by al-Jatib Abu Baker al-Hafiz al-Baghdadi that one must fulfill to be a *mufti*: qualifications, being trusted, abstaining from debauchery and a life of sin, being a balanced person with correct behavior and procedure, and being able to feel the pain of others such as mute and deaf people, etc. Likewise, Sheikh Abu Amor Bin Salah comments that the *mufti* must be the transmitter, indifferent to enmity and kinship, and not seek benefit or harm. He is not a witness, nor does he impose a binding *fatwa* like a *qadi* does (Imam al-Nawawe 1986, 55–66).

Over time, the figure of the *mufti* has been the subject of various controversies, since his education is questioned and also because some religious personnel believe that this figure should not belong to a hierarchical authority, something that occurred since the time of the Ottoman Empire. The Empire created a body of jurists whose head would be the figure of *Shaykh al-Islam*, the Grand Mufti of Istanbul., as mentioned previously[42] Since then, in many countries of the Arab world, such as in Lebanon, there is a Mufti of the Republic as the highest authority in religious matters. He is responsible for regulating Dar al-Ifta', an institutional part of the state administration that is in charge of issuing *fatwas*. This *mufti* is appointed by the government and a council of *muftis*, which in a way links the religious institution to the political sphere, something unprecedented in Islamic legal history. Their *fatwas* are still not binding, as those of the *qadi* are, and their independence has been compromised, since historically they were outside any kind of government.

An interview with Dr. Tabarah

Throughout the interview with Dr. Annas Tabarah,[43] academic director of the *kulliyat shari'a* (college/institute of Sharia) that belongs to Dar al-Ifta' in Lebanon, he claimed that there are no men of religion (*rijal al-din*) as

---

[42] See footnote 28.

[43] Interviews conducted on October 31, 2012, and May 9, 2013, with Dr. Annas Tabarah, director of the Dar al-Ifta *kulliyat shari'a* in Beirut. I also conducted a telephone interview with him on August 21, 2014.

such, but that there are the *'alim.*[44] When these are able to pronounce a *fatwa,* they give it, and if they are not, they belong to the realm of what is called the family of the *fatwa* (*ahl al-fatwa*). In order to reach this level, it is a must to have a degree obtained at university, although some religious figures have religious certificates obtained in the *kulliyat.* It is important to have experience to be able to teach without directly applying the religion of the books. Sharia advocates teaching religion to true believers, with the goal that religion is not used for personal benefit. Professionals who issue a *fatwa* must be educated for that purpose, or they must be employed by the *mufti.* As an example, he mentioned the *amin al-fatwa,* the person who is responsible for sending the *fatwa* to the *mufti,* should be reviewed and approved by him.

Dr. Tabarah explained to us that in order to become a *mufti,* an election must take place—at least in the Lebanese case—in the *majlis el shara'i Islami al-a'la,* the Islamic High Council of Sharia. This is formed by the president, ministers, and old and new deputies, among others. Around 96 people are responsible for choosing the *mufti.*

The *mufti* is responsible for issuing a *fatwa,* choosing one that is already available and relevant to the case, as those of specialized books on *fatwa,* such as Ibn Taymiyya's *fatwa* collection or *al-fatawa al-kubra.* They are presented with the model: this is the question, and this is the answer; this is the case, and this is the answer.

Dr. Tabarah continued to explain that some books show evidence, or *dalil,* and some do not, while other books refer the reader to others. If the cases are not in the books, the *mufti* issues a new *fatwa* for a new case of which he must have knowledge. This is why it is of vital importance that before becoming a *mufti,* a person has to be an *'alim.* The conditions that should be fulfilled by anyone wanting to become a *mufti* are available in the books on *fiqh* and *usul al-fiqh.* And their *fatwa* is never binding, like those of the judge. Legal opinion is inherent to the principles and application of *ijtihad* and *taqlid,* which ended up being institutionalized in education systems in the religious colleges founded for these exercises.

Dr. Tabarah also commented that some Islamist movements, or *harakat al-islamiyya,* do not take into account the *mufti's fatwas* but the ones of their president, leader, or sheikhs. People of the Shia confession follow the *fatwas* of their religious leaders generally, depending on the *marja',* or source of emulation, they prefer to follow. He also commented that

---

[44] Savant scholar.

Christian priests, when they dictate a *fatwa*, indicate what is good or bad, *halal* or *haram*, and believers follow a course or behavior.

Of equal importance, he commented that the practice of the *ijma'* (consensus) in these times is very complicated, since it needs an agreement or *ittifaq* of the *ulama-mujtahid*. The problem is deciding who is *mujtahid*, since the Islamist movements have their own; as an example, he cited the Islamist party of the Muslim Brotherhood, which has Sheikh al-Qardawi as *mujtahid* and does not accept the presence of a *mujtahid* outside his organization. He also quoted Osama Bin Laden, whose followers also considered him *mujtahid*. From all this, it can be concluded that can conclude the difficulty of reaching the *ijma'* in these times, in which only the *mujtahid mutlaqin* are the ones responsible for *ijma'*.

Dr. Tabarah clarified some doubts about the differences between *faqih* and *mufti*. Although both are authorized to issue *fatwas*, the one that wants to pronounce a *fatwa* or *yufti* must be *faqih*. This implies that the *mufti* must be *faqih*, but that the *faqih* does not have to be a *mufti*. In addition, muftis should have the knowledge of all schools of law to find their differences, or *khilaf*. As an example he clarified that the Shafi'i School imposes the rule of the knowledge of *khilaf*.

References

Al-Mawardi. 1996. *Al-aḥkam al-ṣultaniyya wal-wilayat al-diniyya* (The Ordinances of Government). Translated by Wafaa H. Wahba. Reading: Garnet Publishing.

Alsayyad, Nezar, and Manuel Castells, eds. 2003. *Europa musulmana o Euro-islam? Política, cultura y ciudadanía en la era de la globalización* (Muslim Europe or Euro-islam? Politics, Culture and Citizenship in the Age of Globalization). Translated by Pepa Linares. Madrid: Alianza Editorial.

Alwani, Taha J. al-. 1415/1994. *Source Methodology in Islamic Jurisprudence* (usul al-fiqh al-Islami). Herndon, VA: International Institute of Islamic thought.

Anderson, Benedict. 2006. *Imagined Communities. Reflections on the Origin and Spread of Nationalism*. London: Verso.

Armstrong, Karen. 2001. *El islam* (Islam) Translated by Francisco. J. Ramos. Barcelona: Mondadori.

BBC News. 2017. "Tunisian Women Free to Marry Non-Muslims." *BBC News*, September 17, 2017. https://www.bbc.com/news/amp/world-africa-41278610?__twitter_impression=true.

Coulson, Noel J. 1998. *Historia del derecho Islámico* (History of Islamic Law), Translated by María E. Eyras. Barcelona: Bellaterra.

Davis-Packard, Kent. 2016. "Women's Rights and Family Law in the Middle East and North Africa." *The Arab Gulf States Institute in Washington* (blog). May 23, 2017. https://agsiw.org/womens-rights-and-family-law-in-the-middle-east-and-north-africa/.

El-Azhary Sonbol, Amira. 2009. "The Genesis of Family: How Shari'ah, Custom and Colonial Laws Influenced the Development of Personal Status Codes." In *WANTED: Equality and Justice in the Muslim Family*, edited by Zainah Anwar, 179–207. Selangor, Malaysia: Musawah.

Enayat, Hamid. 2004. *Modern Islamic Political Thought*. New York: I.B. Tauris.

Erdbrink, Thomas. 2012. "Rapper Faces Death Threats in Iran Over Song." *New York Times*, May 14, 2012. http://www.nytimes.com/2012/05/15/world/middleeast/shanin-najafi-iranian-born-rapper-faces-death-threats-over-song.html?_r=0.

Esmaeili, Hossein. 2011. "The Nature and Development of Law in Islam and the Rule of Law Challenge in the Middle East and the Muslim World." *Connecticut Journal of International Law*, 26: 329–66.

Esposito, John L. 2001. *Women in Muslim Family Law*, 2nd ed. Syracuse, NY: Syracuse University Press.

Esposito, John L., ed. 2009. *The Oxford Encyclopedia of the Modern Islamic World*. Oxford: Oxford University Press.

Gellner, Ernest. 1996. "Religion and the Profane." Lecture transcribed by Caroline Schmidt Hornstein. *Internationale Zeitschrift für Philosophie* 1: 7–16.

Gómez García, Luz. 2009. *Diccionario de Islam e islamismo* (Dictionary of Islam and Islamism). Madrid: Espasa Calpe.

Gutierrez de Teran Gomez-Benita, Ignacio. 2003. *Estado y confesión en Oriente Medio: el caso de Siria y Líbano. Religión, taifa y representatividad* (State and confession in the Middle East: the case of Syria and Lebanon. Religion, taifa and representativeness). Madrid: Cantarabia.

Hallaq, Wael B. 1996. "Ifta' and Ijtihad in Sunni Legal Theory: A Developmental Account." In *Islamic Legal Interpretation. Muftis and Their* fatwas, edited by Khalid M. Masud, Brinkley Messick, and David S. Powers, 33–43. Cambridge, MA: Harvard University Press.

Hallaq, Wael B. 2001. *Authority, Continuity and Change in Islamic Law*. Cambridge: Cambridge University Press

Hallaq, Wael B. 2009. *Sharī'a: Theory, Practice, Transformations*. Cambridge: Cambridge University Press.

Hourani, Albert. 1992. *A History of the Arab Peoples*. New York: Warner Books.

Ibn, Khaldun. 2005. *The Muqaddimah. An Introduction to History*. Translated and introduced by Franz Rosenthal. Princeton, NJ: Princeton University Press.

Imam al-Nawawe. 1986. *Adāb al-ʿālim wal-mutaʿalim wal-mufti wal-mustafti wa faḍil talib al-ʿalim*. Beirut: Maktabat al-ṣahaba lil-turaz.

Jackson, Sherman A. 1996. *Islamic Law and the State: The Constitutional Jurisprudence of Shihab al Din al-Qarafi.* Leiden, Netherlands: Brill.

Jalloul Muro, Hana. 2018. "Realidad, ideología y terminología: entre la radicalización, la violencia política y el terrorismo yihadista" (Reality, Ideology and Terminology: Between Radicalization, Political Violence and Jihadist Terrorism). *Revista de Estudios en Seguridad Internacional* 4, no. 2: 99–121.

Jalloul Muro, Hana. 2015. "El islamismo y la utilización del 'fiqh' con fines políticos: el caso del Líbano actual" (Islamism and the Use of 'fiqh' for Political Purposes: The Case of Lebanon Today). PhD diss., Universidad Complutense de Madrid.

Jalloul Muro, Hana. 2016. "Sharia and *fiqh*: Its Meaning as a Legal Corpus." *Anuario da Facultade de Dereito da Universidade da Coruña* 20: 292–320.

Kamali, Mohammad H. 2003. *Principles of Islamic Jurisprudence.* Cambridge: The Islamic Texts Society.

Makdisi, George. 1970. "Madrasa and University in the Middle Ages." *Studia Islamica* no. 32: 255–64.

Masud, Khalid M., Brinkley Messick, and David S. Powers, eds. 1996. *Islamic Legal Interpretation. Muftis and Their* fatwas. Cambridge, MA: Harvard University Press.

Nebot, Nicolás R. 2002. *Religión y política: la concepción islámica.* Madrid: Fundación Sapere Aude.

Ramic, Sukriya H. 2003. *Language and the Interpretation of Islamic Law.* Cambridge: The Islamic Texts Society.

Ruiz-Almodóvar, Caridad, ed. and trans. 2005. *El derecho privado en los países árabes. Códigos de estatuto personal.* Granada: Editorial Universidad de Granada y Fundación Euroárabe de altos estudios.

Said, Edward W. 1996. *Representations of the Intellectual.* Vintage Books: New York.

Schacht, Joseph. 1966. *An Introduction to Islamic Law.* Oxford: Oxford University Press.

Vikor, Knut. 2005. *Between the God and the Sultan: A History of Islamic Law.* London: Hurst & Co.Weiss, Bernard, "The *Madhhab* in Islamic Legal Theory," in *The Islamic School of Law. Evolution, Devolution and Progress*, edited by Bearman, Peri, Peters, Rudolph and Voguel, Frank E. Islamic Legal Studies Program, Harvard Law School. Harvard University Press. Cambridge. Massachusetts.

Part III

Contextual Perspectives

https://doi.org/10.1142/9781800611689_0009

Chapter 9

The Moroccan Family Law between Tradition and Modernity

Mohammed Dahiri

Department of Linguistics, Arabic, Hebrew and East Asian Studies, Complutense University of Madrid, Spain

mdahiri@ucm.es

Introduction

Moroccan women's road to equality has not been easy. It has always been full of restrictions and legal and social obstacles since the approval of the first Personal Status Code (Law 58/1957)—between November 1957 and April 1958—until its latest reform in 2004. Twelve years after the enactment of the new Moroccan Family Code, the *Mudawwana*, in 2004, one of the most important reforms in terms of women's rights in Morocco since independence in 1956 has not yet been implemented, is misinterpreted by judges and court officers, and is considered inadequate with regard to the achievements of Moroccan civil society in the area of equality between men and women laid down in the 2011 Constitution. This chapter proposes an exploration of the difficult path to equal rights for Moroccan women through the particular case of family laws in the Alaouite kingdom.

From the Personal Status Code of 1957–8 to the Family Code of 2004

Forty-seven years of controversy and many initiatives demanding the modernization of the family law system were needed to enact the Family Code of 2004, which went up against those who defended the preservation and consecration of the traditional values of Moroccan families.

The Personal Status Code of 1957–8 was enacted following the doctrine of the Maliki School, the basis for all interpretation of Islamic law in Morocco. Traditionally, it has been the official state doctrine and the only one accepted and practiced by the country's judges and jurists at that time.

Until Moroccan independence in 1956, the family law system was administered by two types of courts: the Sharia courts, competent in matters of Maliki Islamic Law applicable to Muslims in Morocco, and the customary courts created by Dahir (royal decree) in 1930 in the Berber regions (Amazigh), which based their judgments on certain customs and traditions that prevailed in those regions (al-Khamlich 1994, 20).

In 1957, one year after independence, Morocco began a period of profound reforms in all areas, particularly in the legal field. On August 19, 1957, Dahir no. 1-57-190 was published, regarding the creation of a commission to elaborate a "Muslim Rights Code" to avoid "any misinterpretation of a subject that is very delicate and open to many interpretations, which is the case of Islamic Law," as stated in the introduction of the said Dahir.[1] The commission was appointed by King Mohammed V, under the honorary presidency of Crown Prince El-Hassan Ben Mohammed (Hassan II) (Article 1). It was chaired by the Ministry of Justice (or, in its absence, its representative) and was composed of ten members appointed by Dahir at the proposal of the Minister for Justice (Article 2). One of the tasks of the commission was to draw up a Personal Statute based, above all, on Sharia (Islamic Law). In order to facilitate the work of the newly created commission, the Ministry of Justice provided the draft of the Personal Status Code, which contained the doctrine of the Maliki School and certain rules of the Syrian Personal Status Law of 1953.

Between November 1957 and April 1958, the commission produced five texts that together constituted the first Personal Status Code in Morocco. These five laws were : (1) Dahir of November 22, 1957, which includes two chapters: marriage and divorce; (2) Dahir of December 18,

[1] *Bulletin Officiel* no. 2341 of September 6, 1957, 1163.

1957, on birth and its consequences; (3) Dahir of January 25, 1958, on capacity and legal guardianship; (4) Dahir of February 20, 1958, on wills; and (5) Dahir of April 3, 1958, on inheritance.

Despite the aforementioned recommendations made by El-Hassan Ben Mohammed, the text remained true to the interpretation given by the Maliki School at that time. Furthermore, Articles 82, 172, 216, and 297 of the new Personal Status Code referred to the predominant or most common and accepted judicial practice of the Maliki School to resolve what was not expressly included in the new code. In other words, the new Personal Status Code was not adapted to the new social situation in Morocco and to the new circumstances of the Moroccan family of the second half of the twentieth century. Rather, "since its creation, there was a major gap between the real situation of women in Morocco and the new regulations" (Berjawi 1999, 31). This led many critics from different sectors of Moroccan society to consider the new code contrary to the current aspirations of Moroccan women for modernization and equal rights, and it made them feel that the new regulations had not been adapted to reflect the hopes of an entire, newly independent population that aspired to build a new, modern, prosperous, and egalitarian country.

Because of the dissatisfaction of a large part of Moroccan society, several attempts were made to amend the new Personal Status Code. In 1961, the presidents of the courts proposed to extend the application of the code to all Moroccan citizens, except in the area of succession, but the proposal was not accepted (Moulay Rchid 1985, 431). In 1965, under the instructions of the Minister of Justice, a commission was created to amend some provisions of the Personal Status Code, in order to adapt it to the evolution of Moroccan society, but the project did not come to light either. Another attempt was made in 1970, at the suggestion of Mr. Ruott, a French assistant technician in the Ministry of Justice. He presented a new project to amend the Personal Status Code, but it was widely criticized by the conservatives and had the same fate as the previous attempts.

In 1981, a reform project for the Personal Status Code was debated by a number of university researchers and women's associations, most of whom were members of progressive political parties and human rights associations. This debate turned women's issues into a topic for public debate in the country. It gave more visibility to the feminist movement and helped it acquire more autonomy within the associative movement for the defense of human rights in Morocco and left-wing political parties. At the same time as this debate and transformation within the Moroccan feminist movement, many studies conducted by research groups in faculties and departments of sociology, anthropology, law, etc. were published, highlighting the urgent need to amend the *Mudawwana* (Bouayach 2003, 112).

All these initiatives met the same fate, due to the sense of sacredness that conservatives attributed to the provisions of the Personal Status Code of 1957–8. However, all of them, especially the discussions in 1981, succeeded in turning the reform of the *Mudawwana* into a topic for national debate and encouraged reformists to continue proposing initiatives to overcome rigid traditional ideals.

The persistence of these calls for reform began to take shape at the beginning of the 1990s. In 1992, the Union of Women's Action (*Union de l'Action Féministe* (UAF) launched a drive to collect one million signatures to demand the reform of the Personal Status Code. The appeal demanded the prohibition of polygamy, the removal of the legal "guardian," equal rights and obligations for spouses, the establishment of judicial divorce, and guardianship of women over children. This appeal regrouped all feminist and human rights advocacy associations and progressive political parties.

The conservative sector, led by politicians who called themselves Islamists, was quick to reply. It once again expressed its opposition to any attempt to reform the content of the Personal Status Code of 1957–8, considering it "an attack on the Muslim religion and a new attempt to destroy family and social ties, imitating the Western family," which—according to their opinions—"suffers from disintegration and the dissolution of its members to a greater extent than families in Morocco." It also accused the proponents of the "drive to collect one million signatures" of being "pro-Western" that "seek to have children out of wedlock" (Rhiwi 2004, 1).

Faced with the politicization of the matter, King Hassan II took advantage of his annual address in commemoration of the King and People's Revolution Day, on August 20, 1992, to call all these conservatives to order. He made a special mention of the role of the Moroccan woman in the revolution for the country's independence in 1956 by underlining that "the Code has gaps and if it is not being correctly applied, there is injustice and abuse." In this same speech, he announced his decision to reform the Personal Status Code. In response to the demands of the different organizations promoting the "one million signatures" initiative, the king formed a "Committee of Jurists and Wise Men" to reform the 1957–8 code.

For feminist and human rights advocacy groups, the most important achievement of this entire debate was the desacralization of the Personal

Status Code. In fact, the reform was carried out by Decree (Dahir no. 374-93-1 of September 10, 1993[2]), which had the aim of complementing the Personal Status Code. Many positive changes were introduced with this reform. The regulation regarding marriage and the options available to end it, polygamy, guardianship, *ḥadāna* (custody), and family council were amended. The Code of Civil Procedure (Dahir no. 346-93-1 of September 10, 1993) and the Code of Obligations and Contracts (Dahir no. 1-93-165 of September 10, 1993) were corrected as well. A new Law on Abandoned Minors was also passed (Dahir no. 1-93-165, dated September 10, 1993), whereas Books V and VI were not changed.

Moreover, in response to the continuous denunciations of feminist associations and human rights organizations, several texts that discriminated against women were eliminated. This was the case of Article 726 of the Civil Code, which limited the freedom of Moroccan women to conduct commercial activities, since their husbands' authorization was required at that time. Article 336 of the Draft Bill for the Law on Criminal Procedure, which obliged women to first formalize before the court their request for recognition of the injury caused by their husbands. A second request then had to be made before the court, provided that the husband had recognized the cause of the injury, to demand the corresponding compensation. This made it complex for women to exercise their right to obtain compensation for that reason. The regulation that forced women to obtain authorization from their husbands to apply for passports was also repealed (Ouhida 2009, 22).

These reforms were also dictated by the international commitments made by Morocco through its ratification of several international conventions and agreements a few months earlier. On June 21, 1993, Morocco signed the "Convention on the elimination of all forms of discrimination against women" and the "Convention on the protection of migrant workers and members of their families," and it also acceded to the "Hague Conference on Private International Law."

In 1998, a process of political liberalization began in Morocco, ending in the so called "Consensual Alternation Government," which favored progressive opposition parties. One of the projects launched by the new government, one year after its inauguration, was the "*National Action Plan Project for the Integration of Women in Development, PANAFID 1999*" (*Projet Plan d'action national pour l'Intégration de la femme au Développement, PANAFID 1999*). This project was inspired by

[2] *Bulletin Officiel* no. 4222 of September 29, 1993, 1833.

the recommendations of the Fourth World Conference on Women (Beijing 1995) and jointly developed and drafted by civil society organizations (women's associations, human rights organizations, NGOs, experts on development and gender issues) and the government (representatives of all ministries). The Plan was financed by the World Bank and coordinated by the Secretariat of State for Social Protection, Family, and Children (PANAFID 1999).

PANAFID was part of the national measures of the "Alternation Government" to eradicate all forms of discrimination against women and was a response to the historical demands of Moroccan civil society in general and of the feminist movement in particular, in terms of equality and protection of human rights. It comprised four main chapters and regrouped almost all women's demands, which included access to political, economic, and social rights, education, health, and the reform of the Personal Status Code. As regards the Personal Status Code, PANAFID, in its diagnosis of the situation of the Moroccan women, considered it "an obstacle to the participation of women in development" and said that some of its provisions limited "women's civil, political and social rights."

PANAFID was officially presented by the prime minister, Abdurrahman Yussufi, in the presence of the representative of the President of the International World Bank, at a seminar in Rabat on March 19, 1999. After its presentation in March 1999, reactions by conservatives and Islamists soon followed. In May 1999, the "Moroccan League of the Ulama" (Moroccan League of Doctors of Islamic Law), with the support of the minister of Islamic affairs, issued a report that protested against the chapter on the reform of the Personal Status Code contained in PANAFID. They launched an intense public campaign against the government plan, calling it "attacks on the values and faith of Moroccans," accusing PANAFID promoters of being "laymen" and "pro-Western," and calling them "a group of Westernized people who are unfamiliar with Moroccan reality and society." An analysis of the media, conferences, seminars, and discussion meetings at that time made it clear how this debate divided Moroccan society, with two different ideas of what family means. One as progressive and was led by liberal NGOs, women's associations, youth associations, and leftist political parties. The other was conservative, led by the *ulama*, the justice minister, and the Justice and Development Party (JDP), political party of Islamic ideology represented in Parliament since 1997, and its NGOs and related organizations.

This situation, in practice, actually led to the organization of two marches, on Sunday, March 12, 2000: the first in Rabat, which supported

PANAFID and the project for the reform of the Personal Status Code, and the second in Casablanca, against it. The march in Rabat was promoted by civil society organizations and progressive political parties, and the one in Casablanca was organized by conservatives and Islamists. The latter caused an impression in national and international public opinion due to the methods it used to mobilize people, the discipline shown, and the human and material resources available for the organization of the march. Their march brought together more than one million people, mostly women, while less than four hundred marched in Rabat.

In order to save PANAFID and convince opponents regarding the chapter on the reform of the Personal Status Code, the government announced that it will continue with its project, but only the first three sections (political, economic, and social rights, education and health), leaving out the fourth on the reform of the Personal Status Code. Abdurrahman Yussufi, prime minister of the Alternation Government in Morocco at the time, decided to create an "Advisory Committee of Experts, Specialists and Ulama," but the latter did not respond to the invitation. Therefore, the project was put on hold at this stage of the confrontation between democrats and conservatives. Many observers, however, felt that the failure of the government to create a dialogue commission was the failure of its great plan and the end of the PANAFID.

In view of this situation, and as "Commander of the Believers," Mohammed VI, enthroned king of Morocco in July 1999, intervened to reduce the tension between supporters of the reform and its opponents, and to prevent this from adversely affecting relations between the Moroccan people and the stability of the country. His intervention was also conditioned by the proximity of the legislative elections and his desire of avoiding politicization of the subject and its use in the elections.

Nevertheless, the debate continued and on March 5, 2001, he was visited by 40 women from different civil society organizations and political parties, "who presented him with a memorandum for the reform of the Personal Status Code" (Bouayach 2003, 117). A month later, the king appointed the "Royal Commission for the Revision of the Personal Status Code." An interdisciplinary commission was selected. It comprised jurists, researchers, gender specialists, and leading civil society figures, including three women. In his speech to announce the appointment of the aforementioned commission, which was considered a roadmap by some of its members, he emphasized "the need to eliminate all types of injustice suffered by Moroccan women and to consolidate the principles of justice and equality between men and women." Additionally, as Commander of the Believers, he recalled the *hadith* (prophetic traditions) of the Prophet that says "before the law, women are the sisters of men."

The commission was initially chaired by Driss Dahhak, Chairman of the Advisory Council for Human Rights (ACHR). The conservative sector constantly blocked any initiatives, and the commission was unable to move forward in its work or to agree on a reform project for the Personal Status Code. In January 2003, M'Hamed Bucetta, prominent leader and historical figure of the al-Istiqlal Party, replaced Driss Dahhak. Eight months later, Bucetta submitted a reform project for the Personal Status Code to the king. The latter took advantage of his speech to Parliament during the opening session of the second legislative year of the seventh legislature on October 10, 2003, to announce major changes to the Personal Status Code of 1993, which would be presented in the two chambers of Parliament for a vote in early 2004. In the same speech, he defended the reasons for these reforms:

> These reforms, the most important of which I have just announced, should not be looked upon as a victory of one side over another, but rather as benefits acquired by all Moroccan people. We have ensured that they comply with the following principles and references:
>
> …
>
> —It is necessary to draw inspiration from the tolerant designs of Islam, which honor human beings and advocate justice, equality, and peaceful coexistence, and rely on the homogeneity of the Maliki rite, as well as on the *ijtihad* that makes Islam a religion adapted to all places and ages, in order to compile a modern Family Code in line with the spirit of our tolerant religion;
>
> —The Code should not be considered as a law enacted in favor of women alone, but as provisions for the whole family, father, mother, and children. It obeys the will to end the inequality of women, to protect the rights of minors, and to preserve the dignity of man. Would any one of you accept having your family, wife, and children thrown out on the street, or your daughter or sister mistreated?
>
> …
>
> These provisions should not be considered as perfect texts or interpreted with fanaticism. It is rather a matter of approaching them with realism and insight, bearing in mind that they come from an effort by *ijtihad* that

is valid for Morocco today, open to the progress we pursue wisely and increasingly.[3]

Despite resistance and criticism from conservatives and seven MPs from the Justice and Development Party (JDP), the new Family Code (the *Mudawwana*) was unanimously approved by the House of Representatives on January 16, 2004, and by the House of Councilors (upper house of the Moroccan Parliament) one week later, on January 23, 2004. The new Family Code was enacted by Law no. 70-03 of the Family Code of February 3, 2004[4] and repealed the code of 1957–8, amended in 1993, that had been in force until then.

The *Mudawwana* comprises 400 articles, contained in seven books and a preliminary alternative chapter, in which the legislator outlines the scope of application of the new Family Code and introduces the new *ex officio* intervention of the Public Ministry. The latter is defined as the main party in all processes related to personal status and includes information on Jewish Moroccans who, under this code, will be subject to the rules of the Moroccan Personal Hebrew Statute (Articles 1, 2, and 3).

The first book, dedicated to marriage, is divided into six chapters composed of 66 articles (Articles 4 to 69). The second, on the "dissolution of the conjugal pact and its effects," includes eight chapters and eight chapters composed of 71 articles (Articles 70 to 141). The third, on "birth and its effects," is conformed by three chapters made of 63 articles (Articles 142 to 205). The fourth deals with "capacity and legal representation" and consists of three chapters made of 70 articles (Articles 206 to 276). The fifth, on the testament, is divided into six chapters and 43 articles (Articles 277 to 320). The sixth, on succession, contains ten chapters composed of 74 articles (Articles 321 to 395). The seventh features the transitional and final provisions and repeals all others who oppose the new Family Code or repeat it, especially the provisions of the following four royal decrees: Dahir no. 1-57-343 of November 22, 1957; Dahir no. 1-58-019 of January 25, 1958; Dahir no. 1-58-073 of April 2, 1958; and Dahir no. 1-58-112 of April 13, 1958. However, the provisions of the royal decrees referred to above, regarding the laws and regulations in force on the date of publication of the

[3] Author's own translation.

[4] *Bulletin Officiel* no. 5184 of February 5, 2004.

new Family Code, were replaced by the corresponding provisions contained therein (Articles 396 to 400).

The *Mudawwana*: A Step toward Gender Equality and the Recognition and Protection of the Rights of Children

Unlike the Personal Status Code of 1957–8 (Law 58/1957), inspired by Islamic jurisprudence, the *Mudawwana* provided the legal grounds for equality between men and women and ended the legal model of the traditional family, imposed by Law 58/1957, where men were predominant.

The new Family Code assumed that the family would be under the joint responsibility of both spouses. It also increased the legal age for marriage from 15 to 18 years and the guardian figure for the woman. It granted equal rights to both spouses in the case of divorce as well as divorced women the right to retain custody of their children, even if they marry again. It stipulated that children of divorced parents would be free to choose before at and after 15 the parent with whom they prefer to live, or any other person designated by law. Finally, one of the most important reforms of the *Mudawwana* was to define repudiation and divorce as a dissolution of the marriage bonds exercised by both men and women under judicial control. They therefore no longer constitute the sole prerogatives of the male, as they did before.

In short, the new Family Code offered more rights to women, as well as the possibility for them to seek a divorce with new arguments, an increase in the pension a man must pay his wife after separation, or the possibility of reaching another agreement for the distribution of assets.

In conclusion, the *Mudawwana* implemented a great change to Moroccan family law. Children were provided greater protection by putting their interests before those of their parents or relatives. The great differences between the sexes have disappeared, and Moroccan women made a legal breakthrough toward equality with men. A greater role was attributed to justice, thereby eliminating certain abuses by introducing the *ex officio* intervention of the public prosecutor's office. The law also required greater specialization by judges, since it now specifically mentioned the positions of family judge and juvenile judge, instead of referring to any judge. It also finally established that the trials should be before a court instead of a single judge. Consequently, a big step was taken, at least legally, in the transformation of the existing patriarchal family structure.

Twelve Years of the Implementation of the *Mudawwana*: What Is the Outcome?

During the twelve-year period of implementation of the *Mudawwana* (2004–16), evaluations of the same were conducted after three, five, ten, and 12 years.

After three years, the new Family Code had already begun to produce results, according to a report presented by the Moroccan Ministry of Justice in Madrid (Layssar 2008). According to this report, the number of divorces at the request of women shot up in Morocco between 2004 and 2007. In 2007, divorces requested by Moroccan women rose by 44 percent, reaching 27,907, while in 2005, there were only 1,983. On the other hand, divorce cases at the request of men decreased, from 29,668 in 2005, 28,239 in 2006, to 27,904 in 2007. During these three years, the number of marriages increased: 11.5 percent between 2005 and 2006 and 9 percent between 2006 and 2007. The number of agreed divorces between 2006 and 2007 also increased from 6,714 to 8,243. In the application of the new *Mudawwana*, there also was a significant increase in the number of marriages with asset distribution agreements in case of divorce, from 295 in 2005 to 424 in 2006 and 900 in 2007.

According to Ibrahim Layssar, who was Director of Civil Affairs of the Moroccan Ministry of Justice and responsible for presenting the report, "the implementation of the new *Mudawwana* has created conditions that favour the life of the married couple." There are more cases of agreed divorces, "which has a positive impact on the children," and he stressed that "there are more women who marry without a guardian and more marriages have asset distribution agreements in case of divorce" (Layssar 2008). As for divorces in which there was no agreement between the two parties (divorce of discord, *shiqāq*), data from 2015 from the Ministry of Justice showed that in the ten years of application of the *Mudawwana*, this type of divorce multiplied by ten between 2004 and 2014. It went from 4,865 cases in 2005 to 48,376 to 39,826 by December 31, 2013. Specialists believe that the first years of application of the new Family Code in Morocco were positive, and that over time, the law would be fully implemented, contributing to a greater emancipation for women and a stronger consolidation of their rights.

Five years after the law's implementation, feminist organizations in Morocco valued it positively and "agreed that it had fulfilled all their hopes" (Rwadi 2009). Latifa Jebabdy, president of the Moroccan Union of Feminists, believed that "what has been achieved in Morocco in defense of women's rights makes it worthy of receiving the label of 'designation of origin' and the trademark of the important brands 'made in Morocco'" (Rwadi 2009).

Amina Bouayach, head of the Women's Department at the Moroccan Organization for Human Rights (MOHR-OMDH), believed that "the reform of the Personal Status Code is already in itself a bearer of great civilizational symbolism and social change" (Bouayach 2003, 118).

The most striking appraisal was that of some women from the two Islamist parties, who led the Casablanca demonstration against the reform of the Personal Status Code, the Justice and Development Party (JDP), and the Justice and Charity Movement (J&C) (an underground group because it does not recognize the king as "Commander of the Believers"). They welcomed the measures set out in the new Family Code. Nadia Yassine, spokeswoman for J&C, considered "the speech of King Mohammed VI [delivered at the opening of the parliamentary session on October 10, 2003] is inspired by an intelligent reading of the sacred texts" (Yassine 2006).

A delegation of French magistrates from *École Nationale de la Magistrature* (National School of the Judiciary, NSJ-ENM) compiled a report in 2008 on the implementation of the *Mudawwana*, based on a visit in June 2007. One of the conclusions was:

> There is no doubt that this new Moroccan Family Code is part of a desire for modernization and in any case an update on international legal standards on equal rights of men and women and recognition of the interests of the child (ENM 2008, 22).

Tariq Ramadan, a specialist in Islamic Law from Switzerland, analyzes the claim of Muslims in the East and West to "rethink Islamic law and jurisprudence" (*fiqh*) in his book *Islam, La réforme radicale*: *Ethique et liberation* (Islam, radical reform: Ethics and liberation). In the section on the evolution of women's rights in Islamic Law, he dedicates a few lines to the *Mudawwana*, which he considers as one of the best family codes in place in the Muslim Arab world (Ramadan 2008, 324). In a recent interview, "he recommends the rest of the Arab and Muslim countries to follow it as a model" (Ramadan 2009).

American historian and gender studies specialist Margot Badran, speaking at the presentation ceremony of her new book, *Feminism in Islam: Religious and Lay Convergences,* at Georgetown University on December 9, 2009, noted that "the changes made to the Moroccan Family Code represent a model for Muslim societies." She described "the Morocco experience as very interesting .... The reform of the *Mudawwana* in 2004 is totally fascinating and extraordinary." She pointed out that "the most outstanding element of this experience lies in the consecration of equality and the sense of justice within the family unit" because "it is a model for other Muslim societies to the extent that the Moroccan Family Code has been able to reconcile religious and legal aspects and has made changes in favor of equality" (Badran 2009, 1).

Finally, several Iranian feminist organizations gathered in the Institute of Iranian Women were influenced by the various initiatives carried out by Moroccan civil society to amend the former Personal Status Code of 1957–8. They began a campaign to collect one million signatures, similar to the one promoted by the UAF in 1992, to demand that the Iranian government amend the laws related to women in Iran and enact a Family Code similar to the Moroccan *Mudawwana* (Rwadi 2009).

New Social, Cultural, and Normative Changes in Morocco during the Last 12 Years Force a Profound Reform of the *Mudawwana*

Despite all the positive comments the *Mudawwana* received after its approval, Moroccan society is changing at a rapid pace. Twelve years later, the *Mudawwana* has become outdated and overcome by the new developments that have taken place in Morocco since February 2011. It could even be considered unconstitutional if we compare its content with the Introduction and Article 19 of the Constitution enacted in a referendum in July 2011.

In the Introduction to the 2011 Constitution, Morocco "reaffirms its attachment to human rights as they are universally recognized" and commits itself to "protecting and promoting human rights provisions and abolishing and combating all forms of discrimination against anybody, by reason of sex, color, beliefs, culture, social or regional origin, language, disability, or any other personal circumstance." It also grants to "international conventions duly ratified by the country ... primacy over the domestic law of Morocco, and to harmonize accordingly the relevant provisions of its national legislation."

This Introduction is not a separate statement of intent from the Constitution, but "*an integral part of thereof.*" In Title II, concerning "Fundamental Freedoms," Article 19 states that:

> Men and women enjoy the same rights and freedoms of a civil, political, economic, social, cultural, and environmental nature, as set out in this Title and in the other provisions of the Constitution, as well as in the international conventions and agreements duly ratified by Morocco in accordance with the provisions of the Constitution, the Kingdom, and its laws. The State acts to achieve parity between men and women. For this purpose, an Authority for parity and the fight against all forms of discrimination is created.

In addition to the above, according to the current complaints of family lawyers and feminist associations, the 12 years of application of the *Mudawwana* have shown that judges and court officers did not understand the philosophy of the new law and continued to interpret it with a "sexist and patriarchal mentality." "It appears that it bothers them that women have rights" (Mdidech 2014).

A rereading of the wording of the *Mudawwana* today shows the numerous discriminations against women. In addition, if we conduct a comparative study between the Constitution and the *Mudawwana*, we can see how the rights of women guaranteed in the Constitution of 2011 are violated in the *Mudawwana* of 2004. Below are some of the reasons why a number of feminist and human rights organizations in Morocco are demanding an urgent reform of the *Mudawwana* and the revision of several of those articles deemed discriminatory, obsolete, and unconstitutional. These are Articles 20, 40, 41, 42, 43, 44, 45, 46, 106, 173 and 236.

First, Article 20 authorizes the marriage officer (qadi al-nikah) to permit the marriage of minors before the legal age of marriage, 18 years, provided for in Article 19. This "exception" became the norm. Judges have freely interpreted these exceptions and have allowed the marriage of minors, mostly girls. According to data from the Democratic Women's Association of Morocco (DWAM-ADFM) and the National Network of Counseling Centers for Women Victims of Violence, in 2010, judges authorized 34,777 marriages with minors and in 2011, 39,031 an annual increase of 12.2 percent, and the equivalent of 12 percent of all marriages celebrated that year in Morocco.

Regarding articles related to polygamy (Articles 40–6), many men use fraudulent methods to marry a second wife despite the legislator's attempt to make it difficult, according to several feminist associations. Cases of men who married a second wife registered an annual increase of 11.4 percent in the last five years, according to data from the Moroccan Ministry of Justice. As an example, in 2011, 1,104 polygamous marriages were allowed, versus 991 in 2010. These associations demand total prohibition of polygamy in the future reform of the *Mudawwana*.

As regards the legal guardianship of minors, the *Mudawwana* states that "the father is the lawful guardian of his children, as long as the guardianship has not been withdrawn by a court decision. If the father is unable, it will be up to the mother to watch over the urgent interests of her children" (Article 236). According to this article, the mother has the right to tutor her minor children in a secondary position and not on equal terms with the father. The problem is even more complicated in case of divorce. As the father is the legal guardian, for any administrative procedure (enrolment in school, application for a health card, ID or passport, travel abroad, etc.) the authorization of the father is required. For this reason, since 2005, many Moroccan civil society organizations have been demanding reform in order to establish legal equality between the father and the mother and make them both legal guardians of their children on equal terms. These associations have the same objection in relation to Articles 173, 174 and 175, regarding custody of children.

The reform of the *Mudawwana* is being demanded not only by feminist and Moroccan civil society associations but also by several political parties, mainly those of the left wing. At the Seventh Congress of Socialist Women, held in December 2013, the Socialist Union of Popular Forces (SUPF) demanded several changes, including the banning of polygamy and the revising of legislation regarding inheritance distribution (Mdidech 2014).

Conclusion

In conclusion, the *Mudawwana* of 2004 needs profound reform to be adapted to the Constitution of 2011 and all normative, social, and cultural changes that Morocco has witnessed in the last 12 years. However, the reform of the *Mudawwana* will not guarantee the rights of women and equality between men and women without solving the main problem: its implementation on equal terms. Changes are needed to create an independent judiciary, with judges and court clerks trained in the values of human rights and with respect for gender equality.

The new Family Code will only make sense if it is part of a global policy to promote equality between men and women in Morocco. Therefore, not only should the current Family Code be in line with the new Constitution of 2011, but it should also amend the remaining laws that continue to restrict the rights of women and discriminate against them. Otherwise, the legal arsenal will be inconsistent, guaranteeing rights on one side and limiting them on the other.

The future reform of the Family Code should be accompanied by the promotion of educational programs on equality between men and women and the dissemination and teaching of human rights from primary school onward. That will make it possible to eradicate the resistance to the promotion of equality and respect for women's rights, which can be found among many judges and court officers and in a significant part of Moroccan society.

References

Badran, Margot. "Islamic Feminism on the Move," in Margot Badran, Feminism in Islam: Secular and Religious Convergences (Oxford: Oneworld, 2009), pp. 323–38.

Berjawi, Khaled. 1999. *Ishkāliat mudawwanat al-aḥwal al- shakhsia bi al-maghrib bayna al-ḥaraka al-nisā'iyah wa al-ḥaraka al-islāmiya* (The problematic of the Personal Status Code in Morocco between the women's movement and the Islamic movement). Rabat: Maktabat al-shabāb.

Bouayach, Amina. 2003. "Reforma de la 'Mudawwana' en Marruecos" (Reform of the 'Mudawwana' in Morocco). *Afkar/Ideas* 1: 116–9.

Dahir no. 1-57-343 of November 22, 1957 (Marriage and Divorce).

Dahir no. 1-57-379 of December 18, 1957 (Birth and Its Consequences).

Dahir no. 1-58-019 of January 25, 1958 (Capacity and Legal Guardianship).

Dahir no. 1-58-073 of February 20, 1958 (Wills).

Dahir no. 1- 58-112 of April 13, 1958 (Inheritance).

Dahir no. 346-93-1 of September 10, 1993 (The Code of Civil Procedure).

Dahir no. 1-93-165 of September 10, 1993 (The Code of Obligations and Contracts).

Dahir no. 1-93-165 of September 10, 1993 (Law on Abandoned Minors was Also Passed).

Dahir no. 1-04-22 of February 3, 2004 (The Family Code "*al-Mudawwana*").

Dahir no. 1-11-91 of July 29, 2011 (The Moroccan Constitution of 2011).

ENM. 2008. *Le Nouveau Code de la Famille Marocain. Rapport Etabli Par Des Magistrats Français a l'issue d'un voyage d'étude sur l'application de cette législation* (The New Moroccan Family Code. Report prepared by French Magistrates at the end of a study trip on the application of this legislation). Paris: Ecole Nationale de la Magistrature. http://www.jafbase.fr/docMaghreb/EtudeDroitMarocain.pdf.

Khamlichi, Ahmed al-. 1994. *Atta'līq 'ala qānūn al-aḥwal al-shakhsia*, vol. 2 (Commentary on the Personal Status Law, vol 2.). Rabat: Dar Našr Al-Maʿrifa.

Layssar, Ibrahim. 2008. "Balance of the first three years of application of the Moroccan Family Code." Lecture delivered on May 23, 2008 at Casa Arabe, in Madrid.

Mdidech, Jaouad. 2014. "Dix ans après, le code de la famille prend des rides." (Ten years later, the family code is wrinkling) *La Vie Éco,* September 1, 2014. http://www.lavieeco.com/news/societe/dix-ans-apres-le-code-de-la-famille-prend-des-rides-28039.html.

Moulay Rchid, Abderrazak. 1985. *La condition de la femme au Maroc* (The status of women in Morocco). Rabat: Editions de la Faculté des sciences juridiques, économiques et sociales de Rabat.

Ouhida, Jamila. 2009. "Del Código del Estatuto Personal al Código de Familia de 2004." In *La nueva Mudawwana marroquí: entre tradición y modernidad. T.raducción comentada del Código de Familia de 2004* ("From the Personal Status Code to the Family Code of 2004." In *The new Moroccan Mudawwana: between tradition and modernity. Annotated translation of the 2004 Family Code*), edited by Gloria Estaban de la Rosa, 19–33. Sevilla: Junta de Andalucía.

Ramadan, Tariq. 2008. *Islam, la réforme radicale: Ethique et libération* (Islam, Radical Reform: Ethics and Liberation). Paris: Presses de Châtelet.

Ramadan, Tariq. 2009. "Mudawwanat al-usra islāḥ nājih yastaḥiq al-iqtidā' bihi ʿarabiyan" (The Family Code is a Successful Reform that Deserves to be Emulated in the Arab World). *Almassae,* May 25, 2009. https://www.maghress.com/almassae/23108.

Rhiwi, Leïla. 2004. "La réforme du code marocain de la famille" (Reform of the Moroccan Family Code). *Revue-Projet.com,* September 2004. http://www.revue-projet.com/articles/2004-5-la-reforme-du-code-marocain-de-la-famille/#top.

Rwadi, Souad. 2009. "Wadʿiyat al-mar'a fī al-maghrib jams sanawāt min taṭbīq mudawwanat al-usra" (The Situation of Women in Morocco, Five Years After the Application of the Family Code). *Almassae,* June 12, 2009. https://www.maghress.com/almassae/23954.

Secrétariat d'Etat chargé de la Protection sociale, de la Famille et de l'Enfance. 1999. *Projet Plan d'action national pour l'Intégration de la femme au Développement "PANAFID 1999"* (National Action Plan Project for the

Integration of Women in Development "PANAFID 1999"). Rabat: Secrétariat d'Etat chargé de la Protection sociale, de la Famille et de l'Enfance.

Yassine, Nadia. 2006. "Lā yumkin fard al- Sharia bi al-quwwa ʿalā al-mujtama'" (Sharia Cannot be Imposed by Force on Society). *Al-Qantara*, June 7, 2006. https://ar.qantara.de/content/hwr-m-lnsht-lslmy-ndy-ysyn-l-ymkn-frd-lshry-blqw-l-lmjtm.

https://doi.org/10.1142/9781800611689_0010

Chapter 10

The Place of Religious Law in Western Societies

Mathias Rohe

Erlangen Centre for Islam and Law in Europe,
Friedrich–Alexander University Erlangen–Nürnberg, Germany
mathias.rohe@fau.de

Introduction

This chapter takes Europe as an example of Western legal orders. In three parts, this chapter first explains Europe's different systems of organizing the relations between state and religion: state-church systems in a very watered-down version, strictly laicist systems, and secular systems with a positive attitude toward religion. These differences are illustrated by diverse examples of how the wearing of Islamic garments in public space is treated. The second part discusses the application of religious norms under the auspices of freedom of religion (individual and collective), with examples from European legislation and jurisdiction regarding the various fields of law in which and freedom of religion is to be recognized. The third part deals with the application of legal norms based on religious convictions: to what extent can such norms be applied under European laws in the fields of Private International Law (PIL) and dispositive substantive law, and informally among social groups?

Regulations on the Relations between the State and Religions in Europe

In large parts of Europe, Christianity served as the state religion for centuries. In the Western part of Europe, the Roman Catholic church took this role, whereas the Orthodox Church was predominant in the Eastern regions. Religious minorities were sometimes tolerated, sometimes persecuted (particularly Jews and Muslims in the time of the Crusades, the plague epidemic in the fourteenth century, and the Reconquista in Southern Europe), and even expelled. The same goes for "heretics" within Christianity. It was the Reformation in the sixteenth century that caused a fundamental realignment, culminating in the Westphalian order in 1648, after the devastating Thirty Years' War. From this time onward, religious pluralism was increasingly accepted, and became legally fostered in the aftermath of the French Revolution.

In the nineteenth and twentieth centuries, the state-church system broadly lost its political, social, and finally legal basis. The most fundamental breach with the existing system took place in France, where a form of strict separation between the state and religions (*laïcité*) was established by the laws of 1901/1905. A few European states (e.g., the UK and some Nordic states, see e.g., Christoffersen, Modéer, and Andersen 2010) still stick to a state-church system, but in an extremely watered-down shape, leaving only a few legal and ceremonial remnants of the former strong state churches in operation.

For example, in the UK, the ruler still has to adhere to the Anglican High church, since he/she is its worldly representative. In some states, the churches are still entitled to register marriages with civil legal effects, provided that certain administrative prerequisites are met. Nevertheless, such rights are now also granted to other religious communities in some of these states. Most European states chose another option, however: separating religion from state authority but preserving ample space for cooperation and religious public life. These different developments are rooted in different historical experiences and varying socioreligious conditions, resulting in different political and legal assessments of the function of religion(s) in modern states and societies (cf. e.g., Aluffi Beck-Peccoz and Zincone 2004; European Parliament 2007; Ferrari and Bradney 2000; Foblets, Gaudreault-Desbiens, and Dundes Rentel 2010; Potz and Wieshaider 2004; Rohe and Elster 2006). In Eastern and Southeastern Europe, the predominant Christian church was broadly accepted as the major institution for the preservation of native culture under "foreign" (namely Ottoman and Tatar) rule.

In France, after the French Revolution, the predominant Roman Catholic church was suspected of unduly interfering in the increasingly secular political space. France and parts of Switzerland[1] imposed a strict separation between state and religion through the principle of *laïcité*. In Germany,[2] religious pluralism has existed for 500 years. The historical experience of the Nazi state ("Third Reich")—turning the state itself into an instrument of the grossest injustice and crime in world history—resulted in the mobilization of human rights–oriented value systems including religion, which could counterbalance sole state authority in cases of abuse.

At present, we can discern three major models in Europe regarding the regulation of state-religion relations:

1) Watered-down state-church systems granting freedom of religion to all other religions, maintaining a few privileges for the state church;
2) Laicist systems more or less following the French model, establishing a theoretically very strict separation between the state and religions; and
3) Secular systems, including forms of cooperation between the state and religious organizations on the basis of state neutrality toward and equal treatment of religions. Secularity in this sense is in no way anti-religious, as it is misunderstood in some parts of the world. To the contrary, it opens broad space for religions including public space (cf. the next section).

European legal orders reacted to the processes of secularization on different levels. Religious rules were broadly removed from the existing laws or given a new or additional secular meaning. An example is religious holidays, which are now interpreted as common times of rest and social interaction. Criminal law protecting the dominant faith was either abolished or reinterpreted. For example, the rules banning blasphemy are no longer interpreted to protect the dignity of God (who is not in need of human protection), but are restricted to cases in which the freedom of expression is abused to hurt the sentiments of religious persons beyond the broad (!) limits of a legitimate critique of religion, endangering peace

[1]For current developments and debates in a comparative perspective, see Hänni, Heselhaus, and Loretan (2019).

[2]For the current legal system in Germany, see Robbers (2013).

in society. Religiously (and culturally) driven norms restricting sexual activities out of wedlock or between two persons of the same sex were successively abolished as well. The same goes for role of religious authorities in government and administration.

In civil law, Christian institutions served as a blueprint for the legal order regarding personal status and family relations until the twentieth century. During the last five decades, these fields of law were largely de-Christianized: marriage is still restricted to two spouses at the same time and based on lifetime duration as a legal concept. Nevertheless, divorce has been tremendously facilitated: nowadays, in many European legal orders it is easier to terminate a marriage than a rental contract. In addition, a considerable number of states introduced rules for same-sex marriages or partnerships, equating them more or less to traditional marriages. Many states also abolished the former differentiation regarding children being born in- or outside wedlock.

Regarding the freedom of religion[3] granted under state neutrality and through the equal treatment of all religions, Article 9 of the European Convention on Human Rights (ECHR) grants a high common minimum standard in all 47 member states, while certain differences due to different national legal traditions are accepted (margin of appreciation).[4] Freedom of religion is not limited to private worship, but also grants an adequate (but not an unlimited) protection of religious needs in various aspects of public life regulated by public law (Rohe 2007). A particular field of religious norms concerns the internal structure and administration of religious organizations as part of the collective freedom of religion. In the European Union, these rights are granted under Article 17 of the Treaty on the Functioning of the EU (TFEU). Nevertheless, increasing tendencies toward laicism are visible in the jurisdiction of the European Court of Justice with respect to antidiscrimination laws in labor issues.[5] In consequence, the realm of institutional self-determination of religious organizations is challenged to an extent that raises the

---

[3]For a general overview of the various aspects of freedom of religion, see Bielefeldt, Ghanea, and Wiener (2016).

[4]The same kind of protection is granted by constitutions in the Americas and in Australia/Oceania.

[5] Cf. the judgments of April 4, 2018 (http://curia.europa.eu/juris/document/document.jsf?text=&docid=202738&pageIndex=0&doclang=EN&mode=req&dir=&occ=first&part=1&cid=1076599) and of February 2, 2018 (http://curia.europa.eu/juris/document/document.jsf

question whether EU jurisprudence properly respects the scope of Article 17 TFEU. The same is true for religious rights of employees in weighing up their interests against a policy of formal religious neutrality within enterprises.[6]

Conflicts regarding Islam mostly concern its visibility in the public space.[7] The aim of secularity and state neutrality has been translated into severe restrictions on the expression of religion in institutional public space (e.g., concerning civil servants) in all European countries. In common public space (streets, etc.), religion can be expressed to a vast extent. Differences between countries can be explained by different perceptions of the role of the state and religions. In a somewhat simplifying view, countries following the model of strict laicism try to reduce the public visibility and influence of religions, since they are taken to challenge the supremacy of state power. Other countries recognize the potential of religions to positively contribute to society, reinforcing peace and stability in society as well as common human rights values. Such basic elements of political culture certainly influence the scope of religious freedom in the public sphere. Nevertheless, in all European states, a far-reaching minimum standard is granted by Article 9 of the ECHR. In recent years, the ECHR and its main institution, the European Court of Human Rights in Strasbourg, came increasingly under pressure from some member states like Russia or Turkey, who rejected the "interference" in their national religio-cultural heritage, and signalized that they could terminate their membership. In consequence, the Court repeatedly held that the member states may use a relatively broad "margin of appreciation" (Gorzoni 2019)

?text=&docid=205521&pageIndex=0&doclang=EN&mode=req&dir=&occ=first&part=1&cid=1579535) regarding Christian institutions in Germany.

[6] Cf. the judgments Achbita (http://curia.europa.eu/juris/document/document.jsf?text=&docid=202738&pageIndex=0&doclang=EN&mode=req&dir=&occ=first&part=1&cid=1076599) and Bougnaoui (http://curia.europa.eu/juris/document/document.jsf?text=&docid=188853&pageIndex=0&doclang=en&mode=lst&dir=&occ=first&part=1&cid=193217) of March 14, 2017, regarding Muslim employees wearing a headscarf.

[7] Silvio Ferrari has developed a very helpful model by distinguishing between (open) common space, (free and plural) political space, and (neutral) institutional space (Ferrari 2012).Thus, it can make a difference to admit religious symbols for pupils in public schools in order to grant the freedom of expression and the plurality of experiences, whereas it can be problematic to shape this space by the compulsory display of a religious symbol like the crucifix.

with respect to the preservation of their commonly defined sociocultural heritage. Thus, issues such as putting crosses or crucifixes in classrooms[8] or banning the wearing of a face veil in public space[9] were left to the discretion of the member states on the basis of a hardly convincing legal argumentation (see the next section).

In addition to different legal approaches, the social readiness to accept forms of normative pluralism under the law of the land differs in Western European states: British communitarianism often leads to different results than French unitarian thinking (*unité de la Republique*).[10] In consequence, such prelegal concepts have an impact on the interpretation of abstract terms like "neutrality."

In the following, I will concentrate on issues regarding Muslims and the application of Islamic religious and legal norms in Europe[11] for two reasons: First, Muslims are the largest group of "minority religions" in Europe. Second, Islam is much more widely distrusted in European public opinion than any other religion. The treatment of Muslims turns out to be a litmus test for the application of freedom of religion and equal treatment in legal practice, and thus for the credibility of the rule of law system as a whole. In Italy, for example, there exist no clear regulations on establishing religious infrastructure for religious minorities. This consequently makes the building of mosques difficult for Muslim communities.[12] The public debate on Islam and Sharia is still by and large lacking sound information and often serves as a political forum for Islamophobic and Muslim

---

[8] Cf. the judgment of the ECHR in Lautsi of March 18, 2011 (https://hudoc.echr.coe.int/eng#{%22itemid%22:[%22001-104040%22]}).

[9] Cf. the judgment of the ECHR in S.A.S. v. France from July 1, 2014 (https://hudoc.echr.coe.int/eng#{"itemid":["001-145466"]}).

[10] For current debates in Europe and among Muslims worldwide, see, e.g., Shah and Menski (2007); Shah, Foblets, and Rohe (2014).

[11] While Muslim life in Europe is highly diverse and transnational to a considerable extent, the public debate is often very simplistic and based on stereotypes. Moreover, the legal framework for Muslim life is highly dependent on the respective nation-state Muslims live in; see Nielsen (2018). The most comprehensive collection in European libraries on these issues is available at the law library of the University of Erlangen-Nürnberg.

[12] See the regional administrative court of Emilia Romagna judgment no. 792 of November 26, 2009, confirmed by the judgment of the Council of State no. 683 of January 28, 2011; Regional administrative court of Lombardia judgment no. 6226 of December 28, 2009, concerning the establishment of mosques in buildings previously used for commercial purposes.

extremist voices. The heated and poorly informed debate on the speech of the Archbishop of Canterbury Rowan Williams in 2008 on the treatment of some aspects of Sharia in the UK is a striking example (Gaudreault-Desbiens 2010; Milbank 2010; Williams 2008). The same goes for the political propaganda of emerging right-wing populist and extremist parties in large parts of Europe. As a result, the neutral application of the law is all the more crucial for balancing freedom for everyone living in Europe, irrespective of his/her religion, ethnic affiliation, etc., and for the necessary protection of states and societies from all kinds of extremism.

The Application of Religious Norms under European Legal Orders

In applying norms in Europe, states' legal systems fundamentally differentiate between religious and legal issues. In Europe, religious issues are regulated by the European and national constitutional provisions, including Article 9 of the ECHR, which grants freedom of religion and state neutrality toward religions. Thus, from a legal (certainly not a sociocultural) point of view, there are no "foreign" religious norms as opposed to "domestic" ones.

Regarding religious norms, freedom of religion is not limited to private worship, but also grants an adequate (but not an unlimited) protection of religious needs in various aspects of public life regulated by public law, from building mosques and forming religious organizations (for Germany, see Bundesamt für Migration und Flüchtlinge 2010; Rosenow-Williams 2012) to social security issues (Aluffi Beck-Peccoz and Zincone 2004; European Parliament 2007; Ferrari and Bradney 2000; Ferrari and Pastorelli, 2012; Foblets, Gaudreault-Desbiens, and Dundes Rentel 2010; Potz and Wieshaider 2004; Rohe and Elster 2006). Western European countries vary in their application of these provisions due to differing interpretations regarding the desirable degree of distance between the state and religion (for details, see Nielsen *et al.* 2009–current). Thus, the debates and demands regarding visible Muslim religiosity (with respect to, for example, religious garments worn in schools or by state officers) largely differ: whereas in France, even students are not allowed to wear the hijab (Bowen 2009, 2012), in the UK and Germany teachers may do so (Bowen and Rohe, 2014). The Court effectively refused to rule that banning the wearing of headscarves in schools and universities by teachers[13] and students[14]

[13] ECHR, Dahlab v. Switzerland, February 25, 2001, NVwZ 2001, 1389.

[14] ECHR, Leyla Shahin v. Turkey, November 20, 2005, NVwZ 2006, 1389.

violates Article 9 of the ECHR. Thus, the ECHR grants a minimum though considerable European standard of rights, whereas some national constitutions, such as in Germany, provide a broader space for religion in public space.[15] For example, the German Constitutional Court ruled in 2015[16] that schoolteachers are allowed to wear a headscarf during classes under Article 4 of the Constitution (protection of freedom of religion and belief). Restrictions are only possible in cases of "concrete danger," e.g., if a teacher wearing a headscarf were to cause considerable tensions among pupils (see Jones 2015 for background information). A current ban under neutrality laws in the state of Berlin (Schuetz 2018) is likely to be overturned by higher courts.

To some extent, the confrontation with Muslim needs and creeds may help clarify fundamental issues regarding the relation between constituent elements of European states: Often, in debates among Muslims and non-Muslims alike, democracy and the rule of law are simply equated. In reality though, the two might be in conflict with each other. While a broad array of political decisions has to be made in accordance with the will of the majority, human rights—including individual and collective freedom of religion and belief (see Article 18 UNDHR, Article 9 ECHR)—draw firm limits to this will for the sake of legitimate minority rights; the individual being the smallest minority in this sense. Efficient protection of these rights is necessary, not only regarding dictatorial interference but in democratic decisions as well.

The Swiss minaret ban from November 2009 (amendment of the Swiss federal constitution by Article 72 section 3[17]) is an example of a conflict between democracy and the rule of law. While the Swiss political elites, except for the Islamophobic right-populist SVP, were against this ban, a majority of 57 percent voted in support of it. Nevertheless, according to a nearly unanimous conviction among European lawyers, this ban violates Article 9 ECHR, which grants freedom of religion not only in private, but also in public space. The majority is not entitled to infringe

---

[15]For details, see Ferrari (2012) and the other contributions in the same volume.

[16]The text of the German Court decision from January 27, 2015 (1 BvR 471/10; 1 BvR 1181/10) is available at https://www.bundesverfassungsgericht.de/SharedDocs/Entscheidungen/DE/2015/01/rs20150127_1bvr047110.html;jsessionid=D2D17FCBE10EAD375FFFF4C7A15CBEBC.1_cid383.

[17]The text and legal references are available at https://www.admin.ch/opc/de/classified-compilation/19995395/201809230000/101.pdf.

basic rights of the minority. In case of conflict, the rule of law protecting everyone equally supersedes democratic majorities. It is interesting that a considerable number of those supporting the ban had no objections to minarets in particular. Instead, they used the vote to express their unspecific concern about Islam and immigration.[18]

The Swiss example could not have occurred in other democratic European countries since, contrary to the Swiss system of so-called direct democracy, the rule of law is superior to democratic majority decisions. Nevertheless, on the political level, the Swiss debates are far from unique. In Austria, some states have tried to ban or restrict the establishment of mosques and minarets by law, in a formally neutral form but clearly aimed specifically at Muslims. In Germany, according to representative polls in 2010 already, 58.4 percent of the population condoned the idea of considerably restricting Muslims' right to practice their religion (Decker *et al.* 2010, 134). Information and education about constitutionally protected human rights is evidently a never-ending task with respect to society as a whole and not limited to single groups which are under particular suspicion.

Another level where religious norms may have an impact are social relations governed by civil law, specifically (but not exclusively) employment law. In this field, possibly conflicting interests of employers and employees have to be weighed with respect to the employee's religious needs on one hand and the employer's needs on the other (see Alidadi 2005; Hoevels 2003; Rohe 2015a, 461*ff.*). Often, Muslims do not face specific legal problems concerning their employment. For those who need to pray during work hours, acceptable solutions can be found in most cases. Many either pray during regular breaks or concentrate their prayers in the morning and evening. In Britain, a bus driver claiming the right to interrupt his work five times a day for prayer lost his case for obvious reasons (Shadid and Van Koningsveld 1995, 102). On Fridays, employers often allow breaks for Muslim employees to participate in communal prayer at mosques or allow employees to finish working earlier in the day. Muslim workers are also generally allowed to use vacation days during the feasts of Eid ul-Fitr at the end of Ramadan and the Eid al-Adha (Festival of Sacrifice) in the month of pilgrimage. Nevertheless, women wearing headscarves or other religious garments are often discriminated against in Western labor markets. This might pose problems when

---

[18] See the short, but very precise analysis in Schneider (2009).

weighing up the necessity of a labor income and the fulfillment of personal religious needs (Deutsche Islam Konferenz 2012, 16–7; for a broader European perspective regarding religion at the workplace, see Alidadi, Foblets, and Vrielink 2012).

In sum, most Muslims try to live their religion and define their needs within their respective framework. Thus, Muslim life is rather diverse in different Western countries due to such different framing conditions. Nevertheless, far-reaching freedom of religion is the rule in most European countries, not only according to the existing laws, but also in daily practice.

The Application of Islamic Legal Norms in Europe

Introduction

Contrary to religious rules, the application of foreign legal rules does not fall under the freedom of *religion*. Thus, such rules are only applicable if the state law itself provides space for such an application for particular reasons. Major publications on such issues appeared since the 1990s (cf. Ahdar and Aroney 2010; Aldeeb and Bonomi 1999; Allievi and Dassetto 1997; Aluffi Beck-Peccoz and Zincone 2004; Berger 2013; Bernard-Maugiron and Dupret 2010; Büchler 2011; Charnay 2001; Cilardo 2002; Conseil de la communauté marocaine à l'étranger 2010; Ferrari and Bradney 2000; Foblets and Carlier 2005; Foblets, Gaudreault-Desbiens and Dundes Rentel 2010; Fournier 2010; Kahn 2001; King 1995; Malik 2012; Meeusen *et al.* 2007; Mehdi and Nielsen 2011; Nichols 2012; Nielsen 1995; Nielsen and Christoffersen 2010; Pahud de Mortanges and Tanner 2002; Panafit 1999; Pearl and Menski 1998; Potz and Wieshaider 2004; Poulter 1998; Rohe 2015b; Shadid and Van Koningsveld 1995; Shah and Menski 2007; Shah, Foblets, and Rohe 2014; Shah-Kazemi 2001; von Bar 1999).

Islamic law was applied in Muslim realms in Southern Europe, namely in Spain and Southern Italy, until the end of the Middle Ages. In an exceptional case, the German Staufian emperor Frederic II introduced legislation (constitutions of Melfi, 1231), which allowed the non-Christian part of the population (Muslims, Jews) to live under their respective personal laws within his realm (cf. Heinisch 1970, 225*ff*.; Horst 1997, 132). Besides this, the application of foreign laws was usually regulated by bilateral or international treaties. The first prominent example is the treaty between the Ottoman Empire and the Kingdom of France from 1535, which served as an example for numerous later treaties (Rohe 2015a, 202).

Given that after the Reconquista (reconquest of former Muslim territories), the Muslim population came under heavy pressure leading to expulsion, emigration, or forced conversion, Islamic law was applied only in a few exceptional cases regarding diplomats or other persons protected by treaty regulations.

The situation altered significantly after movements of mass immigration to Western Europe, particularly since the 1960s, for various reasons. An example is labor migration or migration to the UK by Commonwealth members before severe immigration restrictions were introduced there. Since then, the application of Islamic legal rules became daily practice in Western European courtrooms and administrations due to the laws of these states, which enabled or even demanded such application in transborder cases. From the very beginning it was clear that the implementation of Islamic legal norms in the existing legal systems or the introduction of a system of personal laws on the basis of religious or ethnic affiliation was not an option for European states. Historically, since the early Middle Ages, European legal systems tended to replace personal law systems with territorial ones (Hattenhauer 1998, 881*ff.*; Rohe 2014, 51*ff.*). Legal pluralism—in the sense of total equality of different legal norms within one state—has no historical precedent and would fundamentally contradict the existing constitutional orders in Europe. Instead, the everlasting necessity to balance legal unity, as a basis of social cohesion, and diversity—as an equally important aspect for granting individual freedom and self-determination—is mastered by creating a frame of compulsory norms applicable to everyone and opening a broad space for individual choice within this frame. The latter includes the application or acceptance of Islamic legal norms or legal relations, which are inspired by Islamic legal thinking (e.g., Islamic investment), under the law of the land (for details, see Rohe 2014, 49, 50*ff.*).

Regarding the application of foreign law—including foreign state law based on Sharia rules—we have to distinguish between different fields of law. Public law, which regulates the legal relations between the state and its citizens/inhabitants, and penal law in particular are nowadays strictly territorial worldwide. Consequently, no foreign legal rules can apply in these fields, with few exceptions regarding freedom of religion.[19]

[19]This is the case of male circumcision on religious grounds among Muslims and Jews alike. Under European laws, it is permitted under the condition that it is executed according to the state of the art. For details, see Rohe (2015b, 458–9).

In contrast, in matters of private law (mainly concerning legal relations between private parties) the situation is different.

In general, the application of Islamic law in the form of modern state law may cause considerable tensions in some fields of private law. Examples are Islamic family and succession law rules, which are not gender neutral or treat adherents of different religions unequally (cf. Hallaq 2009, 271*ff.*; Rohe 2015a, 100*ff.*, 263*ff.*). It is necessary here to distinguish between legal norms enforceable by official state measures on the one hand, and all sorts of norms and acts operating in civil society without validation by the official legal system of enforcement on the other. In the latter field, normative pluralism is indeed widespread. But in case of conflict, compulsory state rules will prevail over social or religiously inspired ones according to the principles of secular legal orders. However, within this framework, the legal system has the flexibility to accommodate pluralism to a considerable extent (Witte 2010, 279*ff.*).

For centuries, personal law systems implementing a kind of legal pluralism have been replaced in Europe by territorially unified laws granting *internal* pluralism, but reserving the right of last decision to state law in case of conflicting norms.[20] This is true despite the normative pluralism within Western societies.[21] Within this scope, legal Sharia norms might be applied to a certain extent under the respective state law. This legal framework is of prime importance for the development of Muslim normativity in Europe: as far as state law leads to or enables such application, Muslims who appreciate this application would be satisfied with the existing system. On the other hand, the readiness of state laws to apply Sharia-based norms leads to criticism among other Muslims and many non-Muslims. Given these controversial attitudes, the existing legal systems, including courts and administrations, have to clarify the scope and limits for the application of Islamic legal norms.

---

[20] For the problems of legal transplants concerning personal law systems into Western legal orders cf. Gaudreault-Desbiens (2010).

[21] See the most informative volume of Nielsen and Christoffersen (2012), namely the chapter on the situation written by Prakash Shah, 117*ff.*; and in particular the models developed by Zucca (2012, 194–6).

Fields of application[22]

Private international law (PIL)

In cross-border cases, such as where foreign citizens are involved, the parties often rely on legal relations created under foreign law. Long-term relations like marriage and the legal aspects of family life deserve legal stability and reliability in particular. Should the legal framework governing their relations necessarily change in cases of changing citizenship or residence? The legal order can accept pluralistic arrangements to a certain extent under the principle of private autonomy but has to grant the amount of unity that is necessary to preserve peace in society. Thus, legal differences can be accepted only to a certain degree.

Private International Law (PIL, which regulates conflicting laws pertaining to civil matters) is the most prominent level at which Islamic legal rules can be directly applied. In primarily private matters with an international dimension, it is desirable to apply the substantive law that has the most significant relationship to the case to be decided. The revolutionary idea underlying this concept is the principal equality of all legal orders; this is why foreign law can be applied.

Nevertheless, it is obvious that sensitive areas of the law, such as family and inheritance law, are highly dependent on social convictions and developments. Hence, substantially different regulations exist all over the world. In such cases, the legal community in a particular country may decide that in certain matters, the same substantive law should be applicable to every resident there. This would be particularly the case in matters touching the roots of legal and societal common basic convictions, like those regulated by family law. When foreign legal norms are applied, the result must comply with the law of the land and public order. This is the necessary limit drawn by every legal system in order to preserve peace in society by maintaining the most important common standards; human rights standards in particular.

Islamic law contains many provisions that do not contradict Western laws (in the area of contract law, for example) and can therefore be easily applied. In the UK, contracts including a choice of law provision

[22]This section is in part based on research in the context of RELIGARE (see www.religareproject.eu), a three-year project funded under the Socio-economic Sciences & Humanities program of DG Research of the European Commission's Seventh Framework Research Program.

("principles of the Glorious Sharia") have been dealt with in courts (Bälz, 2004). The main conflicts between Islamic and European laws concern family matters and inheritance. They arise over constitutional (and human) rights concerns about gender equality and freedom of religion, including the right not to believe, and protection of minors: provisions reflecting classical Islamic law preserve a strict separation between the sexes with respect to their social roles in patriarchal social structures. A far-reaching segregation of religions under the supremacy of Islam is still prevalent, forcing nonbelievers into the application of religiously based family and inheritance laws, prohibiting interreligious inheritance even among spouses, or leading to forced separation of spouses in cases of alleged or real "apostasy" by one of them (Rohe 2015a, 263*ff.*, 292*ff.*, 324*ff.*). In addition, child marriage is abolished in some Islamic countries, but still practiced in others. Moreover, conflicts arise, for example with respect to marriage and inheritance doctrines involving religious difference, polygamy, divorce, and gender-biased rules on guardianship and custody of children.

European legal history is familiar with such religion-oriented and gender-based patriarchal legal structures, but has replaced them with secular and gender-neutral regulations during the twentieth century. This is why fundamental conflicts between Islamic law in its traditional form and current European legal orders arise and have to be tackled in daily legal practice. Again, there is no uniform European approach to this task. The different ways of reasoning within European legal orders will be demonstrated using the most oft-adjudicated issue of divorce (*talaq*) (Büchler 2011; Foblets 2007; Foblets, Marechal, and Nielsen 2001; Gärtner 2008; Koch 2012; Rohe 2015a, 468*ff.*).

According to traditional Islamic law, which is still in force in many Islamic countries despite a number of internal reforms in favor of women,[23] only the husband is entitled to terminate the marriage by a unilateral declaration of repudiation without any reason to be given (*talaq*). This has to be repeated three times, and attempts at reconciliation have to be made; when reconciliation fails, the marriage is dissolved. Such a procedure clearly contradicts the European legal principle of equality between the sexes—since wives only have very limited rights to

[23]For new developments, see Mir-Hosseini (2009), with numerous references; Rohe (2015a, 263*ff.*); Voorhoeve (2012).

divorce[24]—as well as the principle of lifelong marriage, which does not allow the dissolution of the marriage by such easy procedures. Thus, according to regulations in European legal orders, a *talaq* is invalid on European soil[25] (as opposed to the so-called *khul'* or other forms of divorce because of discord[26]). But how to deal with a *talaq* that has become valid abroad? Would European "public order" prevent its recognition in any case or only in those cases where the wife was not able to defend her rights and did not agree to the divorce?

The traditional PIL approach concerning the application of the civil law concept of public order looks at the outcome of the application of the respective foreign law, not at the foreign norm as such. The underlying idea is to concentrate on the individual interests of persons who have to navigate between competing legal orders, not to scrutinize foreign legal orders regarding their compatibility with the law of the land in abstract. In recent years, this pragmatic approach is increasingly challenged by an abstract "human rights approach," which leads to the rejection of foreign norms as such, rather than to first evaluate their concrete outcome (cf. Alidadi 2005; Foblets 2007). German,[27] Italian,[28] and Spanish[29] courts broadly follow the traditional approach. Thus, the recognition of *talaq* would contradict public order in cases where the wife was not able to claim her legitimate interests or was not even informed about the divorce. In other cases, where the prerequisites for divorce according to the law of the land would be fulfilled in a comparable way or where the wife agrees,

---

[24] See Rohe (2015a, 275*ff.*). Courts usually differentiate between these forms of divorce. Foreign decisions are then recognized if the cases meet the prerequisites of an "equal rights" divorce, cf. French Court of Cassation, February 23, 2011, No. 10-14.760.

[25] Cf. e.g., Civil Court Brussels, May 26, 1978; House of Lords, R. v. Secretary of State for the Home Department ex p. Fatima Ghulam, [1986] A.C. 527 (H.L.).

[26] Cf. French Court of Cassation, February 23, 2011, No. 10-14.760, regarding a French-Moroccan case where the spouses had lived separately for three years and the divorce was not qualified as a unilateral divorce by the Moroccan court; Court of Appeals Versailles, March 25, 2010, No. 08/08808; Dutch Supreme Court, July 13, 2001, rechtspraak.nl LJN AB2623 (WPNR 2001 (6470)); Cour d'appel Antwerpen, June 30, 1982, J.D.I. 1982, 740 s.

[27] Cf. e.g., Court of Appeals Düsseldorf, FamRZ 1998,1113; Court of Appeals Köln, FamRZ 2000, 895; Court of Appeals Zweibrücken, NJW-RR 2002, 581; Court of Appeals Hamm 7.3.2006, BeckRS 2007, 00423; Court of Appeals Frankfurt a.M. 11.5.2009, 5 WF 66/09; Rohe, Islamic Law in German Courts, in *Hawwa* 1 (2003), pp. 46–59 (46, 50).

[28] Cf. Court of Appeals Cagliari, May 16, 2008, No. 198.

[29] Cf. Supreme Court, ATS 21.04.1998, RJ 3563.

the legality of such a divorce according to Islamic tenets would be accepted by the legal authority in charge.

Belgium shared this way until 2005, when the courts started to handle recognition more strictly after the enactment of the new law on PIL.[30] The same development can be found in court decisions in France since 2004,[31] whereas in the past, these nations adopted the method used by German courts.[32] In Austria, the Supreme Court[33] has from the beginning refused to accept any kind of *talaq*. Thus, there is an emerging trend in PIL to follow a policy of legal symbolism, which means abstractly defending principles as such instead of deciding concrete cases according to their particularities only. Whereas the abstract "human rights approach" leads to clear results—the rejection of *talaq* in any case—the concrete approach lacks such clarity. This might be one of the main reasons for the increasing popularity of the abstract approach in several European legal orders. In addition, it can be used as a political instrument to demonstrate Western "cultural self-defense" against Sharia-based law.

On the other hand, only the concrete approach might help the divorced wife, e.g., in cases when she herself wants to remarry and therefore needs the recognition of the previous *talaq*.[34] In case of nonrecognition, she would be forced to apply for divorce in European courts. This often turns out to be equally time-consuming and expensive, in particular if the husband is living in a country that is not easily accessible for judicial correspondence or if his

---

[30] Court of Cassation April 29, 2002; after 2005, cf. Court of Appeals Mons, December 20, 2007; Civil court Liège, June 26, 2009; Labor court Brussels, May 27, 2010; but also, Labor court Brussels, January 12, 2011. Cf. Foblets (2007); Koch (2012, 175–8).

[31] Older decisions by the Court of Cassation from 2001, 2002 were overruled since a turn of the same court in 2004 (February 17, 2004, No. 01-11.549, and No. 02-11.618; Court of Cassation, January 3, 2006, No. 04-15.231; Court of Cassation November 4, 2009, No. 08-20.574). The decisions of 2004 were implicitly approved by the ECHR in the decision of November 8, 2005 (Affaire D.D. c France, No. 3/02, available in the French version at the court's website http://hudoc.echr.coe.int), pointing at the relevant new French decisions.

[32] The last decisions in this sense were Court of Cassation July 3, 2001 (Rev. crit. int. privé 2002, 704 note Gannagé).

[33] OGH decision of August 31, 2006 (6Ob189/06), Zeitschrift für Rechtsvergleichung 2007, 35; OGH decision of June 28, 2007 (3Ob130/07z); both decisions available at http://ris.bka.gv.at.

[34] This was the case in the decisions of the German Supreme Court from 2004 (BGH FamRZ 2004, 1952) and from 2007 (BGH NJW-RR 2007, 145, 148*ff.*).

address is unknown. The abstract "human rights approach" would then turn itself against the person it intends to protect;[35] she is punished twice. Inclusive evenhandedness, instead of mere political symbolism to the disadvantage of already disadvantaged parties, would thus require following the traditional approach.[36]

In recent years, the abstract approach gained the support of EU law, namely the Rome III regulation.[37] According to Article 10, gender-biased foreign divorce laws that are in principle applicable are replaced by domestic law. Nevertheless, according to recent jurisprudence, "private" *talaq* procedures are not covered by this regulation and thus left to the discretion of the member states. In Germany, the legislator has subsequently chosen to maintain the concrete approach, now regulated in Article 17 Introductory Act to the Civil Code.[38]

Domestic substantive law

More and more, former "international" cases have turned into "internal" ones because an increasing number of Muslims have obtained citizenship of their country of residence or were simply born there. Usually, the law of the land governs their private transactions and family status and relations. In addition, modern PIL rules in Western Europe now tend to favor the law of residence of the parties over their citizenship; thus, foreign nationals living permanently in Europe are governed equally according to the substantive law of the land (cf. Rohe 2015b, 683–4). Hence, Islamic rules can only be applied under dispositive substantive law—the part of the private law that is not governed by mandatory rules (protective rules that cannot be negotiated by the parties involved, as opposed to dispositive rules). The latter include a number of family law rules, e.g., the sole state competence in deciding on the civil validity of marriages (no private marriages are accepted), or some remnants of Christian heritage within family law, like the prohibition on polygamous marriages.

---

[35] Cf. in this sense the Spanish Supreme Court, ATS 21.04.1998, RJ 3563; Koch (2012, 181).

[36] This part largely corresponds to Rohe (2015b, 677*ff.*).

[37] The English text is available at https://eur-lex.europa.eu/LexUriServ/LexUriServ.do?uri=OJ:L:2010:343:0010:0016:en:PDF.

[38] This is the effect of the regulation in Article 17 sect. 2 no. 5 of the Code; an official translation of the new regulation into English is not yet available.

Regarding economic contracts, there are various methods of investment that do not violate the Islamic prohibition of usury (*riba*, which according to traditional interpretations means not accepting or paying interest; cf. Bälz 2009, with a rich factual background; Zakariyah 2012.). In addition, traditional forms of complex sales contracts (i.e., *murabaha*) are used for the express purpose of circumventing usurious transactions. This form of contract contains at least two sales contracts for one single item, and the margin of profit for the buyer/reseller (usually a bank) is determined in the second contract. With respect to business financing, Islamic law permits the formation of types of companies (i.e., *mudaraba*; cf. Bälz 2004, 117*ff.*; Klarmann 2003). In such companies, gain and loss are shared among the partners according to the success or failure of the company. No usury is present there. None of these transactions would contradict European contract laws (Gassner and Wackerbeck 2010). Similarly, Islamic investments prohibiting engagement in alcohol and pork production, pornography, etc. are now offered in many Western European countries by Islamic or other banks. This is taken to be a kind of ethical economics, which usually does not cause legal problems in principle. Thus, in many European countries, such Islam-based contracts are negotiated and can be enforced under domestic law.

In the field of matrimonial law, the introduction of Islamic norms into marriage contracts has also been addressed in several European legal systems, particularly contractual conditions regulating the payment of dower (*mahr* or *sadaq*) in Muslim marriages (Fournier 2010, 35–100 in particular). It is important to keep in mind that under Islamic law, such payments are due to the bride,[39] not to her father/family, as is customarily the case in countries such as Yemen, Afghanistan, or Pakistan. The latter is not recognizable under European laws.[40] Such payments would indeed be considered a sales price for the bride, which would challenge her human dignity as well as her right to freely decide whether to marry. In contrast, *mahr* paid to the bride would only improve the bride's financial situation and could be used as a "bargaining" tool in case of divorce under Islamic law (for details, see Rohe 2015b, 684*ff.*; Yassari 2014, 34*ff.*) and thus

[39]This was stressed by the French Court of Cassation, November 22, 2005, No. 03-14.961: Therefore, the Mahr cannot be qualified as a "prix de vente."

[40]Cf., e.g., Court of Appeals Hamm, January 13, 2011 (I-18 U 88/10).

cannot be considered as violating her rights.[41] Thus, "false conflicts" in cases where legal institutions are not actually contradictory but wrongly conflated with certain customary practices have to be avoided, and the scope of private autonomy in contract law has to be interpreted in an evenhanded way, irrespective of the origin of the regulation at stake (Rohe 2015a, 488*ff*.).

Consequently, in Britain, according to a court decision in 2010,[42] *mahr* was accepted as a legal norm in marriage contracts. Dutch,[43] French,[44] and German[45] courts have accepted it in principle as well. This could indicate an emerging trend toward the "contractualization" of former "foreign" Islamic legal institutions by simply examining them under domestic dispositive contract law.

Implementation of Islamic law/Islamic legal thinking

A few Western European states have introduced Islamic legal provisions concerning family matters that can be applied in Muslim communities on a voluntary basis. As to the celebration of marriages, in Britain, Muslim institutions can apply to become entitled to register marriages under the Marriage Act 1949 (sect. 46) with civil effects. The British Adoption and Children Act of 2002 amended the Children Act of 1989 by provisions (cf. sec. 115 of the Act) introducing "special guardianship" to enable parental relationships by legal means other than adoption, which is forbidden by Islamic law.[46] This option resembles the Islamic legal institution of *kafala*,

---

[41] The *mahr* was misinterpreted in this sense by Regional court Köln IPRspr. 1980 No. 83; Court of Appeals Lyon, December 2, 2002, reversed by Court of Cassation (1ère civ) November 22, 2005, No. 03-14.961.

[42] Radmacher v. Granatino, [2010] U.K.S.C. 42. The prior decision approving *mahr* (Uddin v. Choudhury, [2009] E.W.C.A. Civ 1205) concerned a case of informal marriage. Dower agreements seem to be taken as contractual in earlier decisions under previous legal rules already (cf. Shahnaz v. Rizwan, [1964] 2 All E.R. 993; Qureshi v. Qureshi, [1971] 1 All E.R. 325).

[43] Rb Alkmaar October 16, 2008; Rb Rotterdam February 22, 2010.

[44] Court of Cassation, December 2, 1997, No. 95-20.026 and November 22, 2005, No. 03-14.961.

[45] German Supreme Court, BGH NJW 1999, 574; OLG Celle FamRZ 1998, 374*ff*.; OLG Saarbruecken NJW-RR 2005, 1306*ff*.; cf. Yassari 2014, 333*ff*.

[46] Cf. Quran 33:4; art. "tabanni" in wizārat al-awqāf, al-mawsū'at al-fiqhīya, vol. 10, Kuwait 1987.

which endeavors to create a stable legal relationship between the child and the persons caring for it while maintaining legal bonds with the biological parents in case they are known.[47] Of course, the new English rule is not formulated on the basis of religion and is thus open to all. In "internal" *kafala* cases, once the child has obtained residence in a EU member state, Dutch legal-anthropological research (Hoekema 2009). indicates that courts and administrations are prepared to integrate *kafala* by analogy: it is classified as a form of caring for children comparable to foster parenthood, and thus integrated into the existing legal rules on child benefit payments. Jurisprudence in other states, namely in Italy, reveals that in immigration cases, *kafala* is usually rejected as a basis for a residence permit for the child. This leads to highly unsatisfactory "limping" legal situations, where a state of affairs is recognized in one legal order but not in others. Recently, the European Court of Justice[48] held that the (Algerian) *kafala* does not meet the legal requirements of an adoption, which would create a parent-child relationship and lead to the right residence; nevertheless, the Court considered the possibility of qualifying the child as an "other family member."

In Spain, Islamic legal norms regulating marriage contracts have been applied to Muslims since 1992 (Mantecón-Sancho 2004, 130*ff*.). However, the Spanish legislator has also amended its international law of divorce (Article 107 of the Civil Code) to enable women living in Spain to get divorced even if matrimonial law in their country of origin or the country in which they married prevents them from doing so. The legislature has stated expressly that this amendment was intended to provide domestic legal remedies for Muslim women in particular.[49] In sum, the formal incorporation of Islamic law is an exceptional case, relating to merely formal legal provisions like the procedural aspects of marriage contracts (though not the substantive ones).

In other European countries, such legislation has not been proposed. Most Muslims of European and Turkish origin would vehemently oppose

[47] There is an obvious lack of information about the different forms of *kafala* in cases where the parents are known or unknown/dead; a PhD thesis by Rabah Mouzaoui supervised by the author is in its final stage.

[48] CJEU Judgment of March 26, 2019, http://curia.europa.eu/juris/document/document.jsf?text=&docid=212226&pageIndex=0&doclang=en&mode=req&dir=&occ=first&part=1&cid=6260333.

[49] BOE 30-09-2003, Ley Orgánica 11/2003, September 29, 4.

the introduction of Sharia legal norms, since Sharia-based regulations were abolished in Turkey and in the Balkans many decades ago. They no longer stick to a personal-law system based on religious affiliation (see Rohe 2015a, 259*ff*. regarding polls on the issue in Turkey). Until now, a broader discussion has emerged only among Muslims in the UK, who mostly originate from the Indian subcontinent, on the (optional) introduction of a Muslim law of personal status and inheritance comparable to the legal situation in their countries of origin (Pearl and Menski 1998, 51*ff*.; for further details, see Rohe 2015b, 691*ff*.). Given the present status of legal developments and evidence from Islamic Sharia councils in Britain, this would lead to forms of legal inequality between sexes and religions (Bano 2012a, 2012b, 24; Malik 2012; Shah-Kazemi 2001). Thus, this would be neither a realistic nor a desirable option for European states.

Alternative dispute resolution (ADR)

All over Western Europe, mechanisms of conflict resolution outside state courts (ADR) are operating in the field of economic disputes. They either work on an informal basis or have the parties agree to engaging arbitration boards or institutions to decide in a legally enforceable way (for the fields and reasons of religiously driven arbitration among Muslims in Europe, see Rohe 2011).

Muslim institutions involved in ADR ("Islamic Sharia Councils") have emerged primarily in the UK, starting in the 1980s. Besides mediating economic disputes, they are mainly engaged in family affairs, divorce issues in particular. In most cases, Muslim wives seek either an "Islamic" divorce in addition to a British state court's divorce decree or the termination of an unofficial "Islamic" marriage, petitioning these councils to convince the husband to agree to an Islamic termination of the marriage by *talaq* or *khul'*. Besides this, British Muslim Arbitration Tribunals (MAT) were established since 2007 in London, Birmingham, Bradford, Manchester, and Nuneaton under the Arbitration Act (1996).[50] Contrary to the informally operating Islamic Sharia Councils, the MAT are entitled to issue formal awards under this act, related to for example commercial disputes, including economic issues arising from family disputes. They have no jurisdiction in family status issues (most notably divorce and the

[50] A broader report on religious laws and legal institutions in England and Wales, including Islamic rules, has been published by Douglas *et al.* (2011).

custody of children; Douglas *et al.* 2011) but aim at providing informal aid, such as in cases of social need for an Islamic divorce,[51] akin to other Sharia courts. Samia Bano (2012b, 24) has stated that the 22 Sharia councils in the UK she contacted seek to avoid any conflict with civil law, by for example requiring the civil divorce of a registered marriage before issuing an Islamic divorce.

Hence, the work of such councils and tribunals seems to serve persons seeking religious support, but also those living a considerable distance from British legal institutions who seek socially acceptable conflict resolutions within their community. This is equally true for cases where divorces under British law are not fully accepted by the parties or in the community unless the Islamic divorce has also taken place. Nevertheless, the price paid is a considerable lack of rights as compared to the standards of the law of the land (Bano 2007, 2012a, 2012b, 24; Bowen 2016; Malik 2012; Shah-Kazemi 2001). It should be mentioned that there are some efforts by small numbers of extremist Islamist groups and the Salafi movement that aim at the construction of an exclusively Muslim normative order opposing the governing rules of the land, based on the concept of *al-wala'wa l-bara'*, which restricts Muslim loyalty to Muslims (Shavit 2012).

Other than in the UK, there is no evidence in countries such as Germany of any kind of institutions (MAT, Sharia councils, etc.) providing Muslim ADR. Instead, in Germany, ADR is mostly performed within informal extended family/clan structures and by some religious actors in family disputes.[52] Only within the extremist Salafi spectrum is there evidence for the establishment of a counterstructure that explicitly ignores German law and legal institutions for being irrelevant instruments of the *kuffar* (infidels) and provides all sorts of "legal" services for those who ask for them. Many imams complained that these Salafistswould for example assist in religious marriages without any regard for the existing laws or the Islamic normative tradition, which leads to legally invalid and Islamically disputed marriages and family bonds.

One of the major reasons that Muslims in Germany are reluctant to use state institutions for resolving legal conflicts is a widespread lack of

---

[51] See the MAT website: http://www.matribunal.com/cases_faimly.html (accessed February 8, 2013).

[52] The first in-depth field study in Germany on these issues was conducted by Rohe and Jaraba (2015). Our research is ongoing.

information about the contents of German law and the ways in which legal institutions operate in daily practice. Many people are not aware of the easily accessible forms of legal aid for those in need, which only require a form available for EUR10 to obtain a lawyer's initial advice. Particularly in family conflicts, including domestic violence, parties are often advised not to make these conflicts public out of a fear of losing their children to state-run shelters. While this is a means of last resort that child protection services apply only in rare cases of massive damages, this fear is still present in broad circles. Others are not informed about the prerequisites for valid marriages concluded in Germany, or lack the necessary documents for this and then resort to merely religious marriages. Until 2009, German marriage law prohibited to have a religious marriage registered before being married under civil law. Since then, purely religious marriages are simply ignored by German law. While there are no representative statistics available for Muslim "religious"[53] marriages in Germany, experts estimate that between 20 and 50 percent of Muslims would conclude a religious marriage, either additionally or solely.

Some imams and organizations declare that German civil marriage (which requires for example the presence of two witnesses chosen by the parties) fulfills the prerequisites of an Islamic marriage, while others disagree. In many mosques, marriage contracts are formulated, some of them in a legally professional manner regarding things such as financial aspects, and others in a way that lacks any sound legal basis.[54] It has to be mentioned here that under German family law, Islamic marriage contracts are in principle accepted with respect to their non-status-related aspects.[55] Nevertheless, some Muslims are uncomfortable with contemporary German family law, which is based on gender equality and individual choices, equal treatment of children born out of wedlock, and the protection of same-sex relations, and prefer to stick to traditional Islamic rules. Others would purposely avoid the legal consequences of a civil marriage and potential costs of a divorce but enter into an Islamic religious marriage

---

[53] Marriage is a civil contract under Islamic law. Nevertheless, it has a "religious flavor," and thus Islamic family law regulations are taken to be part of the religion of Islam by considerable numbers of Muslims, particularly those from Arab countries and from South Asia, but much less by Muslims originating from the Balkans and from Turkey.

[54] In our research projects, we have collected around 2,000, mostly handwritten marriage and divorce documents, which will be evaluated in the future.

[55] Cf. BGH NJW 1999, 147; Yassari (2014).

to make their relationship socially acceptable to their families and communities. An increasing number of polygenic relations on such an informal basis was reported, partly leading to undue payments of social security funds. In cases of both an additional and a sole religious marriage, many have a religious and even more a social need to obtain a religious divorce in cases of fundamental conflicts between the spouses. Otherwise, even in case of a civil divorce, the parties are still seen as married in their social environment. While husbands can make use of the easily obtainable institution of *talaq* and might take more than one wife, wives are in need of mechanisms dealing with their rights to *tafriq* or *khul'* under Islamic law. Here, imams and other representatives of religious associations are frequently consulted for assistance (for details, see Jaraba 2019).

According to many interviewees from Muslim communities in various field studies (see Rohe/Jaraba, 2015; Jaraba 2019), domestic violence, criminal activities, drug addiction, gambling, and the neglect of the family by husbands are the main reasons for divorce pleas of wives. Because of the benefits of the comparatively generous German social security systems, the family gains economic independence from the husband, who is solely responsible for family maintenance under traditional Islamic law. There is a potential for conflicts between wives and immigrated husbands, who maintain their patriarchal convictions and attitudes and compensate for the factual loss of their traditional role by using violence.

Representatives of religious organizations often lack information about the scope limits of German law regarding ADR as well as sound knowledge of Islamic law. According to Jamal Malik and Misbahur Rehman's observations, "most of the leaders of diasporic religious communities are self-made scholars who have been nominated by their communities due to their socio-economic, in seldom cases also religio-cultural capital" (Malik and Rehman 2015, 226). In addition, a lack of cultural sensitivity among members of state administrations and courts and real or perceived discrimination are important factors in the distrust or at least in the reluctance to cooperate. The "culture of shame" might collide with the typically German, very direct and outright mode of conversation, which is unfamiliar to many other peoples within and beyond Europe. In recent years, courses for state officers on religio-cultural factors and needs in communication are increasingly offered and sought in the academies for vocational training.

In sum, regarding family disputes among Muslims regulated by ADR mechanisms, we have to distinguish between cases of professional aid willingly requested by all parties involved within the limits of German mandatory law, and others. The latter cases, which are part of "parallel justice," are relatively rare due to a deliberate rejection of German law and are mostly the work of the Salafist spectrum and criminals. Much more frequently, people make decisions while being ignorant of the existing law, and these decisions lack legal enforceability. Furthermore, many imams complain about an excessive demand by members of the community, which they are not prepared for, neither regarding professional skills nor with respect to resources. There was an attempt to form a common board of Muslim representatives to set up standards for dealing with the aspects of marriage and divorce suitable for ADR, but it failed due to deep internal controversies. Professional aid within the limits of the law of the land is still lacking.

References

Ahdar, Rex, and Nicholas Aroney, eds. 2010. Sharia *in the West.* Oxford: Oxford University Press.

Aldeeb, Sami, and Andrea Bonomi. 1999. *Le droit musulman de la famille* [Islamic family law]. Zürich: Schulthess.

Alidadi, Katajoun. 2005. "The Western Judicial Answer to Islamic Talaq." *UCLA Journal of Islamic & Near Eastern Law*, 5: 1–80.

Alidadi, Katajoun, Marie-Claire Foblets, and Jogchum Vrielink, eds. 2012. *A Test of Faith? Religious Diversity and Accommodation in the European Workplace*. Farnham, UK: Ashgate.

Allievi, Stefano, and Felice Dassetto. 1997. *Facettes de l'Islam belge* [Aspects of Belgian Islam]. Louvain-la-Neuve, Belgium: Bruylant.

Aluffi Beck-Peccoz, Roberta, and Giovanna Zincone, eds. 2004. *The Legal Treatment of Islamic Minorities in Europe.* Leuven, Belgium: Peeters.

An-Na'im, Abdullah A. 2008. *Islam and the Secular State: Negotiating the Future of Shari'a*. Cambridge, MA: Harvard University Press.

Bälz, Kilian. 2004. "A Murabaha Transaction in an English Court." *Islamic Law and Society*, 11: 117–34.

Bälz, Kilian. 2009. "Scharia Jet Set: Islamic Banking." *INAMO Berichte und Analysen*, 57 (Spring): 14–7.

Bano, Samia. 2007. "Islamic Family Arbitration, Justice and Human Rights in Britain." *Law, Social Justice & Global Development Journal*, 1: 2–26. http://www.go.warwick.ac.uk/elj/lgd/2007_1/bano.

Bano, Samia. 2012a. *An Exploratory Study of* Sharia *Councils in England with Respect to Family Law*. Reading: University of Reading. https://www.reading.ac.uk/web/files/law/An_exploratory_study_of_Shariah_councils_in_England_with_respect_to_family_law_.pdf.

Bano, Samia. 2012b. *Muslim Women and* Shariah *Councils: Transcending the Boundaries of Community and Law*. Basingstoke, UK: Palgrave Macmillan.

Bar, Christian von, ed. 1999. *Islamic Family Law and its Reception by the Courts in the West*. Cologne: Heymann.

Berger, Maurits, ed. 2013. *Applying Shari'a in the West*. Leiden, Netherlands: Leiden University Press.

Bernard-Maugiron, Nathalie, and Baudoin Dupret, eds. 2010. *Ordre public et droit musulman de la famille en Europe et en Afrique du Nord* [Public order and Islamic family law in Europe and North Africa]. Brussels: Bruylant.

Bielefeldt, Heiner, Nazila Ghanea, and Michael Wiener. 2016. *Freedom of Religion or Belief. An International Law Commentary*. Oxford: Oxford University Press.

Bowen, John R. 2009. *Can Islam be French? Pluralism and Pragmatism in a Secularist State*. Princeton, NJ: Princeton University Press.

Bowen, John R. 2012. *Blaming Islam*. Cambridge, MA: Boston Review.

Bowen, John R. 2016. *On British Islam. Religion, Law and Everyday Practice in Shari'a Councils*. Princeton, NJ: Princeton University Press.

Bowen, John R., and Mathias Rohe. 2014. "Juridical Framings of Muslims and Islam in France and Germany." In *European States and Their Muslim Citizens*, edited by John R. Bowen, Christophe Bertossi, Jan Willem Duyvendak, and Mona Lena Krook, 135–63. Cambridge: Cambridge University Press.

Büchler, Andrea. 2011. *Islamic Law in Europe? Legal Pluralism and its Limits in European Family Laws*. Farnham, UK: Ashgate.

Bundesamt für Migration und Flüchtlinge. 2010. *Muslim Organisations and the State – European Perspectives*. Nuremberg: BAMF.

Cesari, Jocelyne, ed. 2015. *The Oxford Handbook of European Islam*. Oxford: Oxford University Press.

Charnay, Jean-Paul. 2001. *La Charia et l'Occident* [Sharia and the West]. Paris: L'Herne, Paris.

Christoffersen, Lisbet, Kjell Å Modéer, and Svend Andersen, eds. 2010. *Law and Religion in the 21st Century—Nordic Perspectives*. Copenhagen: Djøf Publishing.

Cilardo, Agostino. 2002. *Il diritto islamico e il sistema giuridico italiano*. Naples: Edizioni Scientifice Italiane.

Conseil de la communauté marocaine à l'étranger, ed. 2010. *Le statut juridique de l'Islam en Europe. Acte du colloque international organize par le Conseil de la communauté marocaine à l'étranger Fès, 14 et 15 Mars 2009*. Rabat: Marsam.

Decker, Oliver, Marliese Weißmann, Johannes Kiess, and Elmar Brähler. 2010. *Die Mitte in der Krise. Rechtsextreme Einstellungen in Deutschland 2010*. Berlin: Friedrich-Ebert-Stiftung. http://library.fes.de/pdf-files/do/07504-20120321.pdf.

Deutsche Islam Konferenz, ed. 2012. *Bessere Integration von Musliminnen und Muslimen in den Arbeitsmarkt* [Better integration of Muslims in the labor market], 2nd ed. Nürnberg: Bundesamt für Migration und Flüchtlinge.

Douglas, Gillian, Norman Doe, Sophie Gilliat-Ray, Russell Sandberg, and Asma Khan. 2011. *Social Cohesion and Civil Law: Marriage, Divorce and Religious Courts*. Cardiff: Cardiff University, http://papers.ssrn.com/sol3/papers.cfm?abstract_id=1940387.

European Parliament. 2007. *Islam in the European Union: What's at Stake in the Future?* Directorate General for Internal Policies of the Union, May 2007 (PE 369.031).

Ferrari, Silvio. 2012. "Religion in the European Public Spaces: A Legal Overview." In *Religion in Public Spaces: A European Perspective*, edited by Silvio Ferrari and Sabrina Pastorelli, 149–52. Farnham, UK: Ashgate.

Ferrari, Silvio, and Anthony Bradney, eds. 2000. *Islam and European Legal Systems*. Aldershot, UK: Ashgate.

Ferrari, Silvio, and Sabrina Pastorelli, eds. 2010. *Religion in Public Spaces: A European Perspective*. Farnham, UK: Ashgate.

Foblets, Marie-Claire. 2007. "The Admissibility of Repudiation: Recent Developments in Dutch, French and Belgian Private International Law." *Hawwa*, 5: 10–32.

Foblets, Marie-Claire, and Jean-Yves Carlier. 2005. *Le code marocain de la famille: Incidences au regard du droit international privé en Europe*. Brussels: Bruylant.

Foblets, Marie-Claire, François Gaudreault-Desbiens, and Alison Dundes Rentel, eds. 2010. *Cultural Diversity and the Law*. Brussels: Bruylant.

Foblets, Marie-Claire, Brigitte Marechal, and Jorgen Nielsen, eds. 2001. *Convergences musulmanes: Aspects contemporains de l'islam dans l'Europe élargie*. Louvain-la-Neuve, Belgium: Bruylant.

Fournier, Pascale. 2010. *Muslim Marriage in Western Courts: Lost in Transition*. Farnham, UK: Ashgate.

Gärtner, Verena. 2008. *Die Privatscheidung im deutschen und gemeinschaftsrechtlichen Internationalen Privat- und Verfahrensrecht: Außergerichtliche Ehescheidung im Spannungsfeld von kultureller Diversität und Integration*. Tübingen, Germany: Mohr Siebeck.

Gassner, Michael, and Philipp Wackerbeck. 2010. *Islamic Finance*, 2nd ed. Cologne: Bank-verlag.

Gaudreault-Desbiens and Jean-François. 2010. "Religious Courts' Recognition Claims: Two Qualitatively Distinct Narratives." In *Sharia in the West*, edited by Rex Ahdar and Nicholas Aroney, 59–69. Oxford: Oxford University Press.

Gorzoni, Paula. 2019. *Der 'margin of appreciation' beim Europäischen Gerichtshof für Menschenrechte: Eine prinzipientheoretische Rekonstruktion.* Baden-Baden: Nomos.

Hänni, Julia, Sebastian Heselhaus, and Adrian Loretan (eds.) 2019. *Religionsfreiheit im säkularen Staat. Aktuelle Auslegungsfragen in der Schweiz in Deutschland und weltweit.* Zürich/St. Gallen: Dike/Nomos.

Hallaq, Wael. 2009. *An Introduction to Islamic Law.* New York: Cambridge University Press.

Hattenhauer, Hans. 1998. *Europäische Rechtsgeschichte*, 3rd ed. Heidelberg: C.F. Müller.

Heinisch, Klaus. ed. 1970. *Kaiser Friedrich II. In Briefen und Berichten seiner Zeit.* Darmstadt,: Wissenschaftliche Buchgesellschaft.

Hoekema, André. 2009. "Does the Dutch Judiciary Pluralize Domestic Law?" In *Legal Practice and Cultural Diversity*, edited by Ralph Grillo, Roger Ballard, Alessandro Ferrari, André Hoekema, Marcel Maussen, and Prakash Shah, 177–98. Aldershot, UK: Ashgate.

Hoevels, Niloufar. 2003. *Islam und Arbeitsrecht* [Islam and Labor Law]. Köln/Berlin/München: Carl Heymanns.

Horst, Eberhard. 1997. *Der Sultan von Lucera: Friedrich II. und der Islam.* Freiburg in Breisgau: Herder.

Jaraba, Mahmoud. 2019. "The Practice of *Khul*ʿ in Germany: Pragmatism versus Conservatism." *ILAS*, 26: 83–110.

Jones, Timothy. 2015. "Constitutional Court Strikes Down Absolute Headscarf Ban." *DW*, March 13, 2015. https://www.dw.com/en/constitutional-court-strikes-down-absolute-headscarf-ban/a-18313377.

Kahn, Philippe, ed. 2001. *L'étranger et le droit de la famille: pluralité ethnique, pluralisme juridique.* Paris: La Documentation française [Mission "Droit et Justice"].

King, Michael, ed. 1995. *God's Law versus State Law: The Construction of an Islamic Identity in Western Europe.* London: Grey Seal.

Klarmann, Reinhard. 2003. *Islamic Project Finance.* Zürich: Schulthess.

Koch, Julia. 2012. *Die Anwendung islamischen Scheidungs- und Scheidungsfolgenrechts im Internationalen Privatrecht der EU-Mitgliedstaaten.* Frankfurt: Lang.

Malik, Jamal, ed. 2004. *Muslims in Europe.* Münster, Germany: LIT.

Malik, Maleiha. 2010. *Anti-Muslim Prejudice: Past and Present.* Abingdon, England: Routledge.

Malik, Maleiha. 2012. *Minority Legal Orders in the UK.* London: British Academy Policy Centre. http://www.britac.ac.uk/policy/Minority-legal-orders.cfm.

Malik, Maleiha, and Misbahur Rehman. 2015. "Islamic Law and Mediation." In *Legal Cultures in Transition*, edited by Werner Gephart, Raja Sakrani, and Jenny Hellmann, 202–30. Frankfurt am Main: Vittorio Klostermann.

Mantecón Sancho, Joaquín. 2004. "L'Islam en Espagne" [Islam in Spain]. In *Islam and the European Union*, edited by Richard Potz and Wolfgang Wieshaider, 109–42. Leuven, Belgium: Peeters.

Meeusen, Johan, Martha Pertegas, Gert Straetmans, and Frederik Swennen, eds. 2007. *International Family Law for the European Union*. Antwerp, Belgium: Intersentia.

Mehdi, Rubya, and Jorgen S. Nielsen. 2011. *Embedding Mahr (Islamic Mahr) in the European Legal System*. Copenhagen: DJ Ø F Publishing.

Milbank, John. 2010. "The Archbishop of Canterbury: The Man and the Theology Behind the Sharia Lecture." In Sharia *in the West*, edited by Rex Adhar and Nicholas Aroney, 43–57. New York: Cambridge University Press.

Mir-Hosseini, Ziba. 2009. "Islamic Family Law and Social Practice: Anthropological Reflections on the Terms of the Debate." In *Family, Law and Religion. Debates in the Muslim World and their Implications for Co-operation and Dialogue*, edited by Siegfried Hass, 37–48. Vienna: Austrian Association for the Middle East Hammer-Purgstall.

Nichols, Joel A., ed. 2012. *Marriage and Divorce in a Multicultural Context*. Cambridge: Cambridge University Press.

Nielsen, Jørgen. 1995. *Muslims in Western Europe*. Edinburgh: Edinburgh University Press.

Nielsen, Jørgen. 2018. "European Islam: Trends and Perspectives." *Oasis*, 14, no. 28 (December): 18–35.

Nielsen, Jørgen, Samim Akgönül, Ahmet Alibašić, Hugh Goddard, and Brigitte Maréchal, eds. 2009–current. *Yearbook of Muslims in Europe*, Leiden, Netherlands: Brill.

Nielsen, Jørgen, and Stefano Allievi, eds. 2002. *Muslim Networks and Transnational Communities in and Across Europe*. Leiden, Netherlands: Brill.

Nielsen, Jørgen, and Lisbeth Christoffersen. 2010. Sharia *As Discourse: Legal Traditions and the Encounter with Europe*. Farnham, UK: Ashgate.

Pahud de Mortanges, René, and Erwin Tanner, eds. 2002. *Muslime und schweizerische Rechtsordnung: Les musulmans et l'ordre juridique suisse*. Freiburg: Universitätsverlag Freiburg.

Panafit, Lionel. 1999. *Quand le droit écrit l'islam*. Brussels: Bruylant.

Pearl, David, and Werner Menski. 1998. *Muslim Family Law*. Lahore, Pakistan: Brite Books.

Potz, Richard, and Wolfgang Wieshaider. 2004. *Islam and the European Union*. Leuven, Belgium: Peeters.

Poulter, Sebastian. 1998. *Ethnicity, Law and Human Rights*. Oxford: Clarendon Press.

Robbers, Gerhard. 2013. *Religion and Law in Germany*, 2nd ed. Alphen, Netherlands: Wolters Kluwer.

Rohe, Mathias. 2003. "Islamic Law in German Courts." *Hawwa*, 1, pp. 46–59.

Rohe, Mathias. 2004. "The Formation of a European Sharīʿa." In *Muslims in Europe: From the Margin to the Centre,* edited by Jamal Malik, 161–84. Münster: LIT.

Rohe, Mathias. 2007. *Muslim Minorities and the Law in Europe: Chances and Challenges*. New Delhi: Global Media Publications.

Rohe, Mathias. 2011. "Alternative Dispute Resolution in Europe under the Auspices of Religious Norms." *RELIGARE* Working Paper No. 6, January 2011. https://patternsofgoverningreligion.weebly.com/uploads/2/7/0/3/27037565/religare_report_alternative_dispute_resolution_in_europe.pdf.

Rohe, Mathias. 2014. "Family and the Law in Europe: Bringing Together Secular Legal Orders and Religious Norms and Needs." In *Family, Religion and Law: Cultural Encounters in Europe*, edited by Prakash Shah, Marie-Claire Foblets, and Mathias Rohe, 49–78. Farnham, UK: Ashgate.

Rohe, Mathias. 2015a. *Islamic Law in Past and Present*, translated by Gwendolyn Goldbloom. Leiden, Netherlands: Brill.

Rohe, Mathias. 2015b. "Sharia in Europe." In *The Oxford Handbook of European Islam*, edited by Jocelyne Cesari, 656–700. Oxford: Oxford University Press.

Rohe, Mathias, and Sebastian Elster. 2006. "Zur öffentlich-rechtlichen Situation von Muslimen in ausgewählten europäischen Ländern." In *Perspektiven und Herausforderungen in der Integration muslimischer MitbürgerInnen in Österreich*, edited by Bundesministerium des Inneren Wien & Sicherheitsakademie. Vienna.

Rohe, Mathias, and Mahmoud Jaraba. 2015. *Paralllejustiz. Eine Studie im Auftrag des Landes Berlin*. Erlangen/Berlin. https://www.boris-weirauch.de/dl/Studie_Paralleljustiz_Rohe_2019.pdf.

Rosenow-Williams, Kerstin. 2012. *Organizing Muslims and Integrating Islam in Germany. New Developments in the 21st Century*. Leiden, Netherlands: Brill.

Schneider, Carola. 2009. "Vier Gründe für das Minarettverbot." *Die Presse*, November 21, 2009. https://www.diepresse.com/525014/minarett-verbot-spaltet-die-schweiz

Schuetz, Jutta. 2018. "Berlin Court Rules Muslim Teacher Cannot Wear Headscarf." *DPA International*, May 9, 2018. http://www.dpa-international.com/topic/berlin-court-rules-muslim-teacher-wear-headscarf-180509-99-241283.

Shadid, Wasif, and Pieter Van Koningsveld 1995. *Religious Freedom and the Position of Islam in Western Europe*. Kampen, Netherlands: Kok Pharos.

Shah, Prakash, Marie-Claire Foblets, and Mathias Rohe, eds. 2014. *Family, Religion and Law: Cultural Encounters in Europe*. Farnham, UK: Ashgate.

Shah, Prakash, and Werner Menski, eds. 2007. *Migration, Diasporas and Legal Systems in Europe*. London: Routledge Cavendish.

Shah-Kazemi, Sonia N. 2001. *Untying the Knot: Muslim Women, Divorce and the Shariah*. London: Nuffield Foundation.

Shavit, Uriya. 2012. "The Wasaṭī and Salafī Approaches to the Religious Law of Muslim Minorities." *Islamic Law and Society*, 19: 416–57.

Voorhoeve, Maaike, ed. 2012. *Family Law in Islam: Divorce, Marriage and Women in the Muslim World*. London: I.B. Tauris.

Williams, Rowan. 2008. "Civil and Religious Law in England: A Religious Perspective." Lecture, Royal Courts of Justice. https://www.cambridge.org/core/journals/ecclesiastical-law-journal/article/abs/civil-and-religious-law-in-england-a-religious-perspective.

Witte, John. 2010. "The Future of Muslim Family Law in Western Democracies." In Sharia *in the West*, edited by Rex Adhar and Nicholas Aroney, 279–92. Oxford: Oxford University Press.

Yassari, Nadjma. 2014. *Die Brautgabe im Vermögensrecht*. Tübingen, Germany: Mohr Siebeck.

Zakariyah, Luqman. 2012. "Legal Maxims and Islamic Financial Transactions: A Case Study of Mortgage Contracts and the Dilemma for Muslims in Britain." *Arab Law Quarterly*, 26: 255–85.

Zucca, Lorenzo. 2012. *Law and Religion in the European Constitutional Landscape*. Oxford: Oxford University Press.

https://doi.org/10.1142/9781800611689_0011

Chapter 11

God as Sovereign; Sovereign as God: An Archeology of the Iranian Constitution

Fatemeh Sadeghi

Institute for Global Prosperity,
University College London (UCL), London, UK
fatemeh.sadeghigivi2@mcgill.ca;
sadegif@gmail.com

> The sovereign represents history. He holds historical happenings in his hand like a scepter. This conception is something entirely other than a privilege of the men of the theater. It is based on ideas about constitutional or state law.
>
> Benjamin, *Trauerspiel*, 48

Introduction

The Iranian Revolution of 1979 was a turning point that was supposed to bring about more equality and freedom for the Iranian people. However, this did not happen. The failure seems to be partially rooted in postrevolutionary developments, particularly in the 1979 Constitution, which is concerned with the consolidation of power and sovereignty rather than with securing the rights of citizens. This Constitution is also a sociopolitical history, in which aspirations, ideals, national imaginations, power relations, and historical trends were articulated. For instance, whereas revolutionary ideals are enshrined in the preamble of the 1979 Constitution, they are gradually eroded in the main document. How was it possible that a Constituent Assembly elected by the people rejected the ideals of equality and justice? More surprisingly, ten years after the ratification of the Constitution, an (un)constitutional assembly—whose members were no longer elected—modified the Constitution in 1989. As a result of this manipulation, people have lost many rights, while the absolute sovereignty of the *vali-e faqih* (the guardian jurist) became lawful. It has to be mentioned though that not all clerics agreed with this. Among them, Ayatollah Kazem Shariatmadari is worth mentioning.

The replacement of "right" (*haqq*) by "judgment" (*hukm*) shattered the weak republicanism of the earlier version of the Iranian Constitution. As a result of this modification, the initial redemptive features of the Iranian Revolution were rejected. In recent years, even the manipulated version was quietly set aside, to be replaced by the Islamic Penalty Code, which contradicts the Constitution in several respects.

Significantly, this trend is by no means exclusive to Iran. More recently, Egypt experienced similar developments, though in a different timeframe and in a variety of forms. There, the new constitution was quickly drafted by the Constituent Assembly following the January Revolution of 2011. Despite massive opposition to Egypt's state of emergency, which lasted for almost half a century (1967–80 and 1981–2011), Article 148 of the 2012 Constitution relegitimized the state of emergency by granting unfettered power to the president, who can suspend the law to his discretion. Similarly, in Turkey, the secular constitution paved the way for the Islamist AKP to take power through the democratic machinery legitimated by the Constitution itself. In 2017, the parliamentary system was replaced by the presidential system through a constitutional amendment by referendum, which greatly increased the power of the president and his control over governmental institutions. Indeed, the phenomenon of constitutional authoritarianism is on the rise in both Iran and much of the Middle East.

The above developments reveal the reappropriation of constitutionalism by sovereignty-oriented forces. The situation is not unprecedented, however. As will be seen, it was recognized and even legitimized by Clinton Rossiter, the historian of constitutional thought, in his classical book *Constitutional Dictatorship* (1948).

This chapter explores the limits of constitutionalism on a universal scale, although the main focus remains on Iran as a symptomatic case. It is argued that the Iranian Constitution is plagued by the notion of sovereignty, which by nature restricts citizenship rights. Nevertheless, sovereignty seems to be rooted in both orthodox religious and secular concepts. Therefore, the issue is not about strengthening constitutionalism or the rule of law against the backdrop of authoritarianism. The issue is that we are dealing with two opposite types of constitutions and constitutionalism: sovereignty-oriented and subaltern constitutionalism. Whereas the first type tends to constitute authority to make the law and preserve the monopoly on violence and coercion to execute the law, the second—subaltern constitutionalism—considers the constitution a platform for citizenship rights. In sovereignty-oriented constitutionalism, the law is the commandment of the sovereign, which itself is not subject to the law. In subaltern constitutionalism (Narain 2016; see also Baxi 2012), however, the constitution is not a fixed ideological text, but is first and foremost a bottom-up democratic, dialogical process with great potential for equality and inclusion. In order to respond to the challenge of a political crisis, it is necessary to revive and focus on the redemptive potential of subaltern constitutionalism, which is in fact a sovereign-less constitution based on justice and a more inclusive understanding of rights.

Dissociating the Iranian Constitution of 1979 from the revolutionary event, this chapter investigates constitutional thought from the perspective of sovereignty as a universal in modern and premodern structures of the polity. It suggests that rather than considering the guardianship of the jurist a particularity of Shi‘ism, it must be studied as a universal framework of sovereignty: in the premodern context in Ash‘arite theology and the Roman legacy; in modern political thought from Jean Bodin all the way down to Carl Schmitt. In the Iranian Constitution, God as sovereign quickly transformed into Sovereign as god, exemplified in the doctrine of the guardianship of the jurist. Nevertheless, this is not peculiar to Shi‘ism or even to religion; in fact, it is hard to get away from sovereignty. As famously formulated by Schmitt (1985, 43), “All vital concepts of the modern theory of the state are secularized theological Concepts.”

Tracking this transformation in the Iranian Constitution, this chapter looks for the sacred and profane *arches* on which such a constitution is possibly built. In doing this, it also reveals the significant limits of the sacred/secular dichotomy for grasping how deeply violence is embedded in both orthodox Sharia and secular constitutional law. The chapter argues, therefore, that the sacred and the secular do not seem mutually exclusive, as it is believed. The ethical task is not to choose between secularism/atheism and religion; they are complementary. Rather, a critical engagement with theology is required, which questions the notion of God as a sovereign ruler and the ultimate source of emulation.

Viewed from an archeological perspective, the sovereignty does not appear as an authoritarian power upon which the law was grounded, but first and foremost as a history that repeatedly and constantly defeated and subjugated the redemptive potentiality of revolutionary events through law-making and law-preserving violence apparatus. Similar to Sharia, which transformed a redemptive theology of justice and equality into command (*hukm*), the Constitution empties the revolutionary movement from its initial redemptive aspirations. In an archaeological approach, the dichotomy of law versus unlawful disappears, since law itself legitimizes the sovereign which stands above the law. In modern Muslim contexts, constitutions play the very role that Sharia played in premodern times: the consolidation of power by all means and in every aspect of life.

Sovereignty is by definition the supreme authority with the particular ability to issue decisions, which are to be observed as law. As Foucault (2003, 240) indicated, the essence of sovereign power is "the right of life and death": "the [absolute] right to kill." For Walter Benjamin (1986, 300), sovereignty is an indisputable mythical authority and an absolute right to kill. Through the notion of sovereignty, the law is in fact constituted by the arbitrary yet law-abiding decisions of the sovereign power with the absolute authority over life and death. Therefore, the problem is not the promotion of the rule of law against lawlessness. The problem is with the sovereign law of exception and the permanent negation of the oppressed. Therefore, "the law's concern with justice is only apparent, whereas in truth the law is concerned with self-preservation. In particular, with defending its existence against its own guilt" (Benjamin 2004, 232).

This chapter argues that since sovereignty is political idolatry, we need to think of a new theology that views God as promise (*bishara*) for the oppressed, instead of viewing God as sovereign and Sovereign as god. In James Martel's words, "given that the staying power of sovereignty comes from a potent mix of political and theological legacies, as I see it, a political theology that tackles such a legacy head-on is required" (Martel 2012, 7).

The Constitution of 1979

The Iranian Constitution of 1979 has been criticized particularly for the notorious concept of the *velayat-e faqih* (the guardianship of the jurist), which has been highly contested every now and then. Seen as an appendix to the revolution, it has also been criticized for being ideological (Arjomand 2007, 8), authoritarian, reactionary, deforming Sharia, and so forth. It seems that the Constitution is intrinsically a schizophrenic document, in which authoritarian forces are at constant war with republican ones. Whereas the *velayat-e faqih* has been sufficiently investigated as being responsible for this condition, it has been hardly inspected in relation to sovereignty.

In recent years, alternative constitutions were drafted by Iranian oppositional groups in which the notion of the *velayat-e faqih* was removed. However, these equally suffer from not adequately taking the issue of sovereignty into account, apart from being undemocratically drafted by mainly a handful of individuals who are not the representatives of the people. This means that even the traumatic experiences of the recent decades are not necessarily sufficient for avoiding them in the future.

In the majority of critical assessments of the Iranian Constitution, a particularistic emphasis is put on the Shia notion of the imamate and the steady development of the theory of the *velayat-e faqih* from the nineteenth century to Khomeini's era, or simply both (notable among them are Adjoudani 2003; Amanat 2009; Arjomand 2013; Farhi 2013; Kadivar 2008; Rahnema 2014; Sabet 2014; Schirazi 1997). Therefore, the Constitution is seen in terms of the Islamic resurgence and the demand for a Muslim nation-state in the postcolonial, post-caliphate era. As Arjomand (2013, 31) indicated,

> In the decades intervening between Iran's two revolutions, a new approach to the reception of constitutionalism in the Muslim world had appeared, when the Muslims of India decided to have their own modern state and created Pakistan. It stemmed from the idea of the "Islamic state" as a distinctive type and was elaborated by pouring the Qur'ān and *hadith* into the framework of a systematic total ideology such as Marxism. The Islamic state was conceived as an ideological state, inevitably making its constitution an "ideological constitution," as I have defined it elsewhere. The confusion of categories entailed by this new approach began with the juxtaposition of the modern constitutional

> notion of national sovereignty to Islamic scriptural texts to prove the superiority of God over the nation, which produced the declaration of God's sovereignty in the 1956 Constitution of Pakistan, the first state in history to be designated "Islamic Republic." Although the declaration had very limited impact on the content of that constitution at first, it generated a new and ideologically powerful idea that the state should be an "Islamic state" and its constitution should be based on the scriptural sources of Islam. This idea of the embodiment of an Islamist ideology in a *Sharia*-based constitution, which had no precedent in the making of Iran's first Fundamental Law and its Supplement, became a major goal of the ideologues of the Islamic revolution in 1979.

It has to be mentioned though that the Iranian Constitution is not the only document into which Sharia was incorporated. The modern law of Iran, crafted during the first Pahlavi government (1925–41), similarly incorporated the Sharia into legislative processes.[1] Moreover, as the Turkish and Egyptian examples demonstrate, secularization alone is unable to prevent the rise of authoritarianism, because arguably, the notion of secular modernity is also deeply rooted in absolute sovereignty. As Mohammad Fadel (2016, 2) pointed out, "the battle that is currently playing out in Egypt is not only between those who would like to see a secular Egypt in contrast to a more religious one, but it is also, and maybe even primarily, a battle between different conceptions of the relationship of religion to the state: a battle between a "republican" form of Islam and a "traditionalist" form of Islam that is sympathetic to authoritarian politics."

Furthermore, if pouring the Quran and *hadith* into the framework of a systematic total ideology such as Marxism was possible, as Arjomand suggests is the case, then pouring it into every other secular ideology is equally possible. Indeed, all constitutions, whether Middle Eastern or not,

[1] See Aqeli 1990, 164–7; 185; 187; 188 passim. Interestingly, Arjomand himself referred to this incorporation of the Sharia into law somewhere else: "The six Majles (1926–8), the last one to be elected relatively freely under Reza Shah, gave Davar extraordinary powers for three months to set up a uniform modernized national judiciary by executive decrees. When the new judiciary was inaugurated in April 1927, a significant number of the clerics (at least six) were among the first appointed judiciary cadre of some forty judges and prosecutors" (Arjomand 2013, 26).

carry certain ideological elements.[2] Even the concept of the *velayat-e faqih* is not that novel, if we consider that *vali* is in fact equivalent to *wali* as guardian, custodian, protector, helper, governor, and friend, all of which has a history in Muslim societies. Khomeini only adds that this governor should be a *faqih* (jurist). Thus, an explanation such as the one above seems inadequate for taking into consideration the universalistic context in which this principle has become possible. Such an analysis seems to reinforce the particularity of this document.

To the contrary, I suggest an archeological approach to identify the constitutional crisis as the problem of sovereignty and of commandment. The task here is to find the "arche" that grounds sovereignty-oriented law. In other words, I seek to demonstrate that the constitutional law does not recognize the Revolution, hence people, as the arche from which the law originates; it is the commandment (of God or a secular sovereign) that makes law. As Agamben (2012) indicates, "In the commandment was the word, not in the beginning. It is in the commandment that law begins. The beginning is also the principle that commands and rules."

From this perspective, the problem is not the fight between ideological, obscure, religious, and lawless forces against the enlightened, secular, and law-abiding ones. Rather, it is the fight between egalitarian democratic forces against inegalitarian, undemocratic ones, whether secular or religious. Drawing on this approach, the question this chapter seeks to answer is: to what extent is the introduction and incorporation of the principle of the *velayat-e faqih* into the Constitution indebted to sovereignty as legitimated by both modern and premodern political thought?

The Principle of the *Velayat-e Faqih*: Article 5

In the Iranian Constitution, the *vali-e faqih* possesses all authorities and forces. He is in fact equivalent to Schmitt's sovereign, who decides on the exception. Article 5 of the Constitution formulates this idea as such:

> During the Occultation of the *vali al-Asr* (may God hasten his reappearance), the *wilayah* and leadership of the Ummah devolve upon the just [*adil*] and pious [*muttaqi*] *faqih*, who is fully aware of the circumstances of his age; courageous, resourceful, and possessed of administrative ability, and who is elected and accepted by the majority of people, and

[2] For a critique on the exceptionality of Middle Eastern constitutions, see Fawcett (2008).

> in case of the absence of such a person, a leader or a leadership council involving *faqih* with the previous conditions will take the responsibilities of this office in accordance with Article 107.

The subject of the *velayat-e faqih* caused a massive dispute and schisms among the members of the Constituent Assembly. Perhaps more than any other aspect of the Constitution, this concept has been analyzed, explained, assessed, and occasionally criticized. It is also partly responsible for the failure of the revolution and its ideals.

In an apparently semiorganized action among the concept's proponents, an obscure member of the assembly unexpectedly raised the issue in the third session. The action was followed by other pro-Khomeini members. The subject completely poisoned the atmosphere of the Constituent Assembly, causing prolonged feuds among members both during and after its suspicious ratification. However, only some discussions around the concept have been published so far, while others are still unknown to the public. Many of the debates and discussions were simply conducted behind closed doors, as pointed out by Yadollah Sahabi (in Majle-se Khobregan-e Ghanun-e Asasi 1985, 383). Due to the dissatisfaction of the majority of its members, the assembly decided to assign a commission to investigate the issue before final ratification in the public assembly. Therefore, disputes took place for months among the members of the commission. The commission, however, proved unable to settle the issue and in fact further intensified the disagreements. Thus, when the subject was brought back to the public assembly, the disputes reached an uncontrollable level, so that in an undemocratic action, vice president of the assembly Beheshti forcefully silenced the opponents—including Bani Sadr, Moghaddam Maraghyi, Makarem Shirazi, and Sahabi—by giving a long rhetorical lecture in defense of the article. The gesture was rapidly followed by a premature vote to ratify the article. Nevertheless, discontent spread outside the assembly among various strata of society, for whom the principle was a hallmark of clerical authoritarianism. Finally, Khomeini himself decided to intervene to silence the critics and opponents. On several occasions, he took the privilege of public sermons to aggressively attack the critics by calling them unaware of Islam and averse to religion and people (Khomeini 1999).

The strong opposition was partially successful in that the final version of this article accepts that the *vali-e faqih* must be "elected" and "accepted" by the majority of the people. Nevertheless, these two key phrases have been omitted from the amendment crafted by another assembly, which was established in 1989 under the direct and unconstitutional command of Khomeini. As expected, the assembly changed the article by omitting the people altogether, granting an absolute power to the *vali-e faqih*:

> During the Occultation of the *vali al-Asr* (may God hasten his reappearance), the *vilayah* and leadership of the Ummah devolve upon the just [*adil*] and pious [*muttaqi*] *faqih*, who is fully aware of the circumstances of his age; courageous, resourceful, and possessed of administrative ability, will assume the responsibilities of this office in accordance with Article 107.

The omission of "people" and their acceptance was a decisive change, though this was by no means exclusive to this article. Parallel manipulations took place in other articles with the aim of a systematic reduction of the people's role.

Negotiations around the concept and its final formulation demonstrate little reference to Sharia. In fact, the final formulation was the realization of a dream that was once articulated by a member of the assembly a few months before the ratification of the article: "the *velayat-e faqih* renders the commands of the government the commands of Allah" (Qorashi in Majle-se Khobregan-e Ghanun-e Asasi 1985, 73). The establishment of the Expediency Discernment Council in 1988 also confirms that government's convenience (*maslaha*) was above Sharia.

Silence as history: Article 2

Those dissatisfied with the *velayat-e faqih* were unsuccessful in invalidating it. This failure can be attributed to the popularity of Khomeini or the organized action of its proponents among assembly members. While this is true, the trend toward authoritarianism was not unprecedented, as mentioned before.

Contrary to the strong debate on the *velayat-e faqih*, the Constituent Assembly is strikingly silent on the contradictory notions of sovereignty as well as on sovereignty's friction with the revolutionary constituent power. It seems that one of the most challengeable and determining concepts was taken for granted without being sufficiently discussed and criticized. As James Martel (2012, 2) pointed out, "sovereignty is so much a part of the fabric of ordinary political life (or what passes for that life, anyway) that we rarely, if ever, question what it is or what it means for us." The question is to what extent this silence contributed to the historically established authoritarian rule. According to the Iranian Constitution, sovereignty belongs exclusively to God. As will be seen, this perception seems crucial for the treatment of the Sovereign as god.

In the 1979 Constitution, sovereignty was mentioned six times: three times in the preamble and three times in the main text. In two of the three instances in the preamble, sovereignty is used to condemn authoritarian and despotic rule. In the third one, "the spread of the sovereignty of God's law" is mentioned among the goals of the army. In the other three places, the term is used in the text of the Constitution: in Article 2, Article 56, and Article 176. The usage of the term in all of these cases is significant, though probably the most significant of all is Article 2, which involves the substance of the Islamic Republic and the description of its nature. This article was ratified after heated debates on the nature of the Islamic Republic. However, discussions around the issue of sovereignty were extremely limited compared to what was expected.

In its ultimate sobriety, Article 2 strongly restricts sovereignty to God. It reads:

The Islamic Republic is a system based on belief in:

1) The single God (as stated in the phrase "There is no god except Allah"), His exclusive sovereignty and the right to legislate, and the necessity of submission to His commands;
2) Divine revelation and its fundamental role in setting forth the laws;
3) The return to God in the Hereafter, and the constructive role of this belief in the course of man's ascent toward God;
4) The justice of God in creation and legislation;
5) Continuous leadership (imamate) and perpetual guidance, and its fundamental role in ensuring the uninterrupted process of the revolution of Islam;
6) The exalted dignity and value of man, and his freedom coupled with responsibility before God; in which equity, justice, political, economic, social, and cultural independence, and national solidarity are secured by recourse to:
    a. Continuous *ijtihad* of the *fuqaha'* possessing necessary qualifications, exercised on the basis of the Quran and the Sunna of the impeccable (*ma'sumin*), upon all of whom be peace;

b. Sciences and arts and the most advanced results of human experience, together with the effort to advance them further;
c. Negation of all forms of oppression, both the infliction of and the submission to it, and of dominance, both its imposition and its acceptance.

In one of the rare occasions when the issue is raised, Hossein-Ali Montazeri reportedly states, as the head of the Constituent Assembly, that by this article the members of the assembly intend to make sovereignty exclusive to God, which means to submit[3] to God and to recognize no other sovereignty than his, and him as the only sovereign. He also added that for the sake of clarification, it is incumbent on the members to discuss this issue. Years later, he expressed his critical assessment of the Constituent Assembly, particularly his own role in the establishment of the principle of the *velayat-e faqih* (Montazeri 2008). Nevertheless, on this occasion, he was equally silent on the authoritarian theology of sovereignty.

The issue of sovereignty was raised on other occasions that were not directly related to this article. They partially represent not only the contradictory positions of the assembly on the issue of sovereignty, but also their inadequacy. On one occasion, the discussion is raised as follows:

> According to the Islamic principles, we assign sovereignty and command to God, and God has granted this sovereignty to the human being. For this reason, people elect us or a group of people with the representative of the Imam or God directly or the *faqih*, following the popular guardianship and as executive force. I have a note on the separation of forces that is accepted also by all Europeans. It is not seen clearly in Islam. However, the tradition of the Prophet shows their interest in it … Therefore, we grant the legislative sovereignty to the hand of the people, while the Imam [Khomeini] has kept the executive sovereignty for himself, which is the same as the guardianship of the jurist, and the jurist in this law is among the most important articles, in which we follow the Prophet and the *ulu al-amr* (the possessors of the rule), that is, the guardianship of the jurist, and we have to follow the guardianship in two practical types, otherwise with a slight deviation a great deviation takes

[3] "*Taslim*" is equivalent to Islam, with similar connotations.

> place from the Islamic principles, which would endanger the *umma*'s interests. First, at the top of the executive force is the Imam, but he is not a dictator, because a dictator rules according to his personal interests, while one who represents God does not. So, it is not a problem. And if this is not a practical problem, the second type [of the guardianship] is that with the clear supervision of them and their sovereignty right in primary issues, first the election of the president and the prime minister should be directly based on law and with the consideration of the *vali.* Second, this must be particularly elucidated given the circumstances and conditions, since every country has a special condition and, considering that condition, granting too much power and authority to one single person clearly has the risk of dictatorship. For us, fourteen centuries' experience of Islam is sufficient [to conclude] that whenever the principles are violated, the dictatorship took over. Later, there must be principles to proportionately divide the revolution [sic], meaning the president with lesser power and the prime minister with more power, so that the people's interests are guaranteed (Mohammad Khamenei in Majle-se Khobregan-e Ghanun-e Asasi 1985, 54).

In response, another member of the assembly warns against the consolidation of power by recalling the tradition of the Prophet and his distribution of power among his people (Ali Akbar Parvaresh in Majle-se Khobregan-e Ghanun-e Asasi 1985, 56). Nevertheless, the opposition remained ineffective. Instead, the warning was immediately rejected by another member, who pointed out that the *vali-e faqih* as *hakim* (sovereign) should have full control over all the government's forces (Monir al-Din Hashemi in Majle-se Khobregan-e Ghanun-e Asasi 1985, 59–60).

Further investigation of this article exhibits the deadlock that the opponents of the *velayat-e faqih* faced. According to Article 2, since God created the world; he commands it. God is the lawgiver. Put differently, law originates neither from the people nor from the Constituent Assembly; it is rooted in God's will. One can, therefore, reasonably wonder: if God is the sovereign of the world and if he exclusively has the right to legislate, then where does the authority of the Constituent Assembly to make law come from? In other words, by ratification of this article, the Constituent Assembly invalidates itself. More grotesque in this article is that it discredits the popular event of the revolution and the people as the main constituent power. Finally, according to this article, law is not the origin of power. Rather, it is the (primordial) power (arche) that constitutes law and makes it possible. It seems therefore that this article is the beginning of a procedure resulting in the absolute sovereignty of the *vali-e faqih* and the metamorphosis of popular demand for justice and equality to empty words.

Ten years later, when Khomeini unconstitutionally appointed a group to revise the Constitution, similar unscrupulous silence was repeated. Interestingly, he even preassigned the framework of the discussions of the members of this group. Some of the members of this group became political dissidents in the post-Khomeini era, though at the time, they did not criticize the undemocratic and unlawful procedure of the revision.

Popular sovereignty

Whereas Article 2 attributes absolute sovereignty to God, Article 56 grants it to the people:

> Absolute sovereignty over the world and man belongs to God, and it is He Who has made man master of his own social destiny. No one can deprive man of this divine right, nor subordinate him to the vested interests of a particular individual or group. The people [*millet*] are to exercise this divine right in the manner specified in the following articles.

Similar to Article 2, Article 56 was ratified by the majority of the assembly members without any further discussion (Majle-se Khobregan-e Ghanun-e Asasi 1985, 835). For instance, it does not elucidate through which processes popular sovereignty is to be exercised. In fact, this article enunciates the contradictory nature of the Iranian Constitution.

National sovereignty

The final occasion where sovereignty is mentioned is Article 176 of the Constitution. Here, sovereignty implies "national sovereignty":

> In order to safeguard the national interests and preserve the Islamic Revolution, territorial integrity, and national sovereignty, a Supreme Council for National Security presided over by the president shall be constituted to fulfill the following responsibilities:
>
> 1) Determining the defense and national security policies within the framework of general policies determined by the Leader.

2) Coordination of activities in the areas relating to politics, intelligence, social, cultural, and economic fields in regard to general defense and security policies.
3) Exploitation of materialistic and intellectual resources of the country to face internal and external threats.

Drawing on these cases, one can conclude that in the 1979 Constitution, sovereignty was portrayed as three, intertwined types: God's sovereignty (Article 2), popular sovereignty (Article 56), and national sovereignty (Article 176). However, popular sovereignty is significantly overshadowed by God's sovereignty, as articulated in Article 2. This article seems grotesque, considering that by granting exclusive sovereignty and legislation to God, it dispossesses and disregards the people. Moreover, it debunks the Constituent Assembly and its qualification for legislation. This is a fatal flaw, from which the unconstitutionality of the Constitution originates. This article paves the way for authoritarianism, including the guardianship of the *faqih* of Article 5 that was ratified later. Here, constitutionalism and authoritarianism collide. However, this contradiction remained unnoticed. It seems that for the members of the assembly, sovereignty and God's sovereignty were taken for granted as a normal situation. Such silence reminds us of what Hent Kalmo and Quintin Skinner (2010, 11) indicate: that sovereignty does not have a history; it is a history.

The Divine Command theory

Sovereignty historically developed before becoming itself history. In the early Muslim community, "*hakim*" and "sultan" as synonyms for sovereign had pejorative meanings. In fact, at one point in the early Muslim community, emir, imam, and later on God's caliph were the common words used to refer to the principal of society. Contrary to sultan and *hakim*, imam initially had some spiritual and moral connotations, whereas emir implied both spiritual/moral and profane leadership of the community (*umma*).

The replacement of spiritual leadership with absolute sovereignty did not take place overnight. It has a long history, during which the expansion of the Muslim territories required a profound development in Muslims' morality, power relations, authority, and government. The transformation from earlier to later attitudes is perhaps best exemplified in a story narrated by Ibn Khaldun (1994, 530):

> Then Mughirah b. Shu'ba [the messenger of the Muslim army] arrived. When he reached them [Persian army], they [Persian elites] were in their own particular suits, while their seat was set below the seat of Rostam [i.e., Rostam Farrukhzad, the commander of the Persian army]. He approached Rostam and sat on the throne. They took him away from the throne. He said: "I haven't seen people more imprudent than us Arabs. Yet, we do not worship our fellows. I thought you're the same. You had better inform me that some of you are the slaves of others, I wouldn't have come to you then, although you have invited me. Now, I am sure that you will be defeated. No kingdom will sustain this way." The subordinates said, "By God, this Arab tells the truth." The superiors said, "By God, he said things that please our servants."

The story might be fabricated. Yet, it demonstrates that the idea of sovereignty was not as widespread in the early Islamic community as in later periods. In fact, the early eschatological egalitarian message of Islam successfully contested the Persian and Roman notions of Sovereign as god (Donner 1998).

The steady yet decisive replacement of the Prophet's successor by emir, sovereign (*hakim*) and sultan was partly caused by the imperialist tendency of the Muslim community, which increasingly inclined toward conquering lands, slaves, and wealth. Whereas in earlier times, the head of society was referred to as the Prophet's caliph, this was gradually replaced by emir, which discloses Sassanian and Roman influence. As Kristó-Nagy remarks, emir seems to be the Arabic equivalent of the Latin *imperatur*; both words are linked to the idea of command:

> The term *amr* (or its derivative *imāra*) was not used to describe a territory either, but to indicate the power of a commander (*amīr*). Thus the Arabic term *amīr* and the Latin term imperator (emperor) both mean 'commander,' and the term used for the supreme leader of the Muslim community after the death of Muḥammad was *amīr almuslimīn* ('the commander of the Muslims'). The Latin imperium also designated power vested in a person, and only by extension the territory over which he had this power (Kristó-Nagy 2016, 60).

I will return to the Roman effect later.

The development of emir to sovereign (*hakim*) seems to be largely rooted in the Ash'arite *kalam* as the imperial theology of the Muslim caliphate. This development has had huge impacts on both Sunni and Shia Islam, with certain moral, political, and legal outcomes. To begin with, it is worth mentioning that according to Ash'arite theology, God is the author of moral law, but he himself is not subject to it (Legenhausen 1988, 259). God stands outside of his own rules beyond the sphere of morality. Whereas Mu'tazilites believe that the good is good, and hence he commands it, the Ash'arites believe that what God commands is good regardless of it being good in itself. The outcome is that it is not wrong for God to do evil. The idea was contested by John of Damascus (cited in Legenhausen 1988, 260):

> If you say that both good and evil are from God, you would make him unjust, which He is not. And if you were to say that God had ordained the adulterer to commit adultery, the thief to steal, and the murderer to kill, they would in that case be worthy of respect for doing God's will. You would thus belie your lawgivers and pervert your Books, since they command that the adulterer and the thief be flogged, and the murderer killed, who should rather be honoured for having done God's will.

The Ash'arite assault on Mu'tazilite ethics had been revolved around the preservation of divine sovereignty: the idea that God is beyond all restrictions; that God's own activity does not fall within the scope of any decree (Legenhausen 1988, 259). God's exceptionality seemed simply the translation of the voluntarist approach into the moral sphere and vice versa. As Sherman A. Jackson (1999, 197) indicates,

> The destruction of Mu'tazilite objectivism would bring a number of significant byproducts in its train, among the most important of which being the removal of ethics from the realm of reason and the endorsement of the unreflexive view of the self, according to which reason was propelled in every first instance by desire. Meanwhile, the establishment of scripture as the only legitimate source of value necessitated the adoption of the view that the scope of revelation was infinitely expandable.

Muslim jurisprudence is heavily indebted to Ash'arite theoreticians, methodologically as well as doctrinally (Jackson 1999, 187). In defense of the principle of *maslaha* (expediency), famous Ash'arite theologian al-Qarafi, for instance, points out that everyone who practices *qiyas* (syllogism) "inevitably indulges subjective judgments based on what is perceived to promote personal or group interest" (Jackson 1999, 198). "The only difference between one preference and another was the degree to which its advocates had mastered the art of expressing themselves in scriptural terms" (Jackson 1999, 187). Other Ash'arite theologians, such as Fakhruddin Razi, similarly denied free will and good and evil in actions; a position that effectively negates the moral responsibility of human beings. According to Razi, "while we as humans are legally responsible in that our actions entail Sharia consequences in the form of reward or punishment, we are not morally responsible, because we are not really the authors of our acts" (Jackson 1999, 191).

Obviously, there is a difference between God and a human sovereign ruler. Whereas God is the lord of all creatures, the sovereign is not. Nevertheless, the Ash'arite God as the arbitrator creature is a source of inspiration for a decisionist sovereign. As the possessor of all creatures, God supposedly governs them the way he wills. If, the Ash'arites suggested, all creatures are taken to heaven or to hell, he is right, simply because he is the absolute possessor. This is quite the opposite of the Mu'tazilite *kalam*, in which God is rational and keeps his promises.

The Ash'arite *kalam*—with its approach toward a decisionist God whose commands are the only measure of good and evil and who decides on good and evil voluntarily—was partly a natural response to the tyrannical, immoral context in which it grew. This age was characterized by terror, torture, violence, tyranny, and chaos that had spread increasingly since the rule of Mutawakkil, the Abbasid Caliph (AD 822–61) who was famous for encouraging irrationality, violence, and immorality. As Tabari (1996, 5998) reports, Mutawakkil's rule was contested from the beginning. Ultimately, he was chopped into pieces at his son Muntasir's orders. The latter then became caliph. This chaotic era (Bonner 2011), when God and sovereign rulers governed the world arbitrarily, was remote from the previous notions of a moral and just ruler as the ideal of the early Islamic community.

The Ash'arite *kalam* has had a significant impact on the formation of the Muslim perception of God and mundane sovereignty. As Bielik-Robson (2016, 4) points out,

> the voluntaristic God of the Ash'arite and the then nominalistic teaching constituted the farthest possible development of the logic of power: he does what he pleases and there is no other explanation for what he does

> apart from what "He pleases" (quod libet), or the famous Ockhamian quia voluit [because He wanted it that way].

Via the triumph of the Ash'arite over the Mu'tazilite theology, the decisive dissociation of morality from justice was completed. Morality was no more the origin of law; the origin of law was the arbitrary decision. This split of morality and law has had a decisive impact on Muslim theology and polity.

According to Bielik-Robson, the Ash'arite *kalam* affected the secularized notion of sovereignty. Quoting Hans Blumenberg, she indicates,

> all modern political concepts were indeed secularized theological notions (which Blumenberg in fact does not endorse), there is no reason to suggest that the most "vital" or "significant" of them derive from this particular strain of the theology of sovereignty, which, according to Blumenberg, develops from the late-medieval nominalistic school, itself deeply influenced by the Ash'arite version of the Islamic kalam.[4]

The Roman Effect: The Prince Is Not Bound by the Laws

The glossators of Roman law are divided on whether it is the origin of Western constitutionalism or the origin of the state of exception and absolute sovereignty. Both groups, however, share mainly in praising mighty Rome and its significance for the modern world. For instance, Clinton Rossiter, who also coined the term "constitutional dictatorship" to refer to a certain category of government rooted in Roman law, while admiring Rome, observes that "only in the republican Rome, was the

[4]Bielik-Robson 2016, 2. She adds, "The Ash'arite structure, which took the Aristotelian notion of potentiality but transformed it radically, by attributing it not to the passivity of matter but to the highest activity of God as his infinitely willful potency/potentiality, maintains itself through the whole modern philosophy as this or another form of a master superstructure: the Real, Life, Nature, Capital. Potentiality opposed to actuality—as power opposed to passivity, subject opposed to object, energy opposed to matter—creates a powerful organizing scheme in which the former is granted the advantage of infinity and originality against the finite, derivative, and merely relative status of the latter. With this one revolutionary move, potentiality, so far characteristic of the lowest forms of existence, got translated into an infinite power/potency" (7).

constitutional dictatorship recognized as a regular instrument of government" (Rossiter 1948, 15). According to him, "the dictatorship could be used as an instrument of class warfare" (22). Rossiter points out that the Roman dictatorship

> was primarily a military office, instituted to save the state from the threat of foreign or rebellious arms, but the power of the dictator extended out from the army and its camp and embraced the entire state. The resort to the dictatorship converted the Roman Republic and its complex constitution into the simplest and most absolute of all governments an armed camp governed by an independent and irresponsible general (25).

Moreover,

> in addition to the general powers which attach everywhere to absolutism, the dictator had other and peculiarly Roman functions. He could convoke any of the assemblies and preside over them, and this power extended to the Senate. In the realm of judicial power his jurisdiction extended to all criminal cases affecting the safety of the state. To this end he possessed the power to execute summarily and without appeal, as well as to fix fines. His power of arrest overrode the intercession of the sacrosanct tribune. He could coin money, take the highest auspices, and freely dispose of booty and honors. According to Roman constitutional law the dictator could not legislate, that is, initiate and promulgate a lex; but he had the *ius edicendi*, and his decrees were, for the duration of his power, as good as laws and were published as such (25).

Against this somewhat healthy image, recent studies depict a deeply violent picture of this era. As Welborn (2015, 26) points out,

> the sole sovereignty of the successors of Augustus was an ongoing "state of exception" in which politics perished, a new structure of power constituted and reconstituted by the imposition of various degrees of dependent subjecthood and, in the last instance, by terror. The wealth of the emperor and his syndicate depended upon the vigorous exploitation of the resources of the provinces and upon the enslavement of a significant portion of the population—the latter institution maintained by the cruelty of crucifixion. By the age of Nero, spectacle had become an all-encompassing feature of social experience, which not only blurred the

> boundary between the real and the representational but threatened the expropriation of human sociality itself. The mass burials uncovered by archeological excavations outside the gates of Rome are a grisly testimonial to the dehumanization of precisely that segment of the population from which Paul [the Apostle] and other evangelists recruited the members of their messianic assemblies.

Furthermore, the state of exception was not provisional or coincidental; "the phenomenon was structural: terror was the means by which sole sovereignty was constituted and reconstituted in the Roman Empire" (Welborn 2015, 26). The emperor's power was of divine origin (Tierney 1963, 386), entailing certain rituals such as the extremely violent gladiatorial shows that were closely associated with the worship of the sovereign emperor.[5]

Modern sovereignty

"*Sovereignty is that absolute and perpetual power vested in a commonwealth which in Latin is termed* majestas" (Bodin 1955, 25). These are the Bodin's words at the beginning of his famous *Six Books of the Commonwealth.* Bodin pioneered the modern concept of sovereignty, in which the sovereign king and prince replace the emperor. However, his definition of sovereignty is more or less the replication of the Roman and Ash'arite traditions. The main common feature is that the sovereign is not bound by the law, whether the previous laws or his own:

> If the prince is not bound by the laws of his predecessors, still less can he be bound by his own laws. One may be subject to laws made by another, but it is impossible to bind oneself in any matter which is the

[5] Welborn 2015, 27. Cf. Buijs (2003, 242): "Shortly after his assassination on March 15, 44 BC Julius Caesar was already declared to have been divine. Augustus quickly arranged to be called 'son of the divine Caesar' and actually established a cult of worship centered around his own *genius*, which spread rapidly throughout the empire. However, as *pontifex maximus* the emperor, notwithstanding his own divinity, still had the sacred duty to ensure the proper worship of all the traditional deities. Later on, emperor worship more and more functioned as the one overriding public cult for the entire empire (while at the same time allowing ample room for local and private cults). This development was enhanced strongly by the growing influence of the East in the empire: the city of Rome experienced an influx of Eastern religions and simultaneously the gravitation point of the empire moved toward the Eastern regions."

> subject of one's own free exercise of will. As the law says, "there can be no obligation in any matter which proceeds from the free will of the undertaker." It follows of necessity that the king cannot be subject to his own laws. Just as, according to the canonists, the Pope can never tie his own hands, so the sovereign prince cannot bind himself, even if he wishes. For this reason, edicts and ordinances conclude with the formula "for such is our good pleasure," thus intimating that the laws of a sovereign prince, even when founded on truth and right reason, proceed simply from his own free will (Bodin 1955, 28).

Also, similar to both the Ash'arite and the Roman traditions, Bodin's sovereign is decisionist and decides on what is and is not law:

> On the other hand, it is the distinguishing mark of the sovereign that he cannot in any way be subject to the commands of another, for it is he who makes law for the subject, abrogates law already made, and amends obsolete law. No one who is subject either to the law or to some other person can do this. That is why it is laid down in the civil law that the prince is above the law, for the word law in Latin implies the command of him who is invested with sovereign power (Bodin 1955, 28).

Finally, his sovereign is godly:

> Because there are none on earth, after God, greater than sovereign princes, whom God establishes as His lieutenants to command the rest of mankind, we must enquire carefully into their estate, that we may respect and revere their majesty in all due obedience, speak and think of them with all due honour. He who contemns his sovereign prince, contemns God whose image he is (Bodin 1955, 40).

Carl Schmitt, who praises the decisionist attitude as the most prominent juristic thinking, summarizes the idea as such:

> Not only in Calvin's absolutist concept of God, but also in his teaching of predestination, theological notions make their appearance whose inherent decisionism has also exercised an influence on sixteenth century notions of state sovereignty, particularly those of Bodin … The classic case of decisionist thinking first appears in the seventeenth century with Hobbes. All Recht, all norms and statutes, all interpretations of

> laws, and all orders are for him essentially decisions of the sovereign, and the sovereign is not the legitimate monarch or established authority, but merely the one who decides in a sovereign manner. Recht is the statutes and statute is the deciding command in the conflict over Recht … The sovereign decision is, therefore, juristically explained neither from a norm nor from a concrete order, not incorporated into a sphere of a concrete order, because for a decisionist, it is on the contrary, the decision which first establishes the norm as well as the order. The sovereign decision is the absolute beginning, and the beginning (also in the sense of Arche), is nothing but sovereign decision (Schmitt 2004, 61–2).

In these words, Schmitt not only summarizes decisionism, but also the premodern and modern history of sovereignty.

The Ash'arite, Roman, and modern attitudes might be different in Weltanschauung. However, they share the treatment of human beings as impotent creatures unable to reach salvation. They also portray human nature as sinful and violent, similar to the wolf-like picture of human beings provided by Hobbes in *Leviathan*. Thus, sin and violation become the origin of law, which are to be avoided only via the absolute will of the sovereign/God. Whereas modern theories of sovereignty treat the sovereign ruler as the origin of law, premodern legal systems such as Sharia also see the sovereign God as the originator of law. The latter substitute theology with theocracy. If theology is considered an unending endeavor, in which God is not to be defined as a brutal sovereign but as a promise stimulating hope for the possible salvation of human beings as they approach their God, theocracy on the other hand implies the fixation of God, the impossibility of justice, and the futility of any such endeavor. It in fact closes the door of salvation by portraying God as a violent sovereign, whose only promise is to punish the violators of the canon. Furthermore, such a picture results in the inalterability of human creatures, who should only be ruled violently by means of authoritarian governments. Obviously, this is not congruent with the universal message of Islam and its God. Theocracy in fact imposes nature over history, starkly contrasting with the political endeavors of people to improve their situation throughout human history.

Conclusion

Demands for equality and inclusion played a vital role in Middle Eastern revolutionary movements, including the 1979 Iranian Revolution. These demands have been systematically defeated by postrevolutionary constitutions, as the cases of the Iranian Constitution and Arab Spring clearly demonstrate. In the Iranian Constitution, the *vali-e faqih* as the sovereign ruler is bestowed absolute authority above the law.

Furthermore, according to this document, sovereignty belongs exclusively to God. Sovereignty-oriented law, including Sharia, and constitutions constitute a paradox by being unable to function as law, simply because they do not represent the subjects that are expected to obey the law. The introduction of the principle of the *velayat-e faqih* best represents this paradox. As a result, the Constitution became itself a conflict zone, where sovereignty is at constant war with countersovereign republican forces. The Iranian Constitution provides a basis for rethinking the legal constellation in which sovereignty is an unquestionable authority that abides by no law except arbitrary decisions. This notion was legitimized by both Sharia and secular attitudes.

Sovereignty-oriented constitutions and constitutionalism are in constant conflict with subaltern constitutionalism, which considers law not as the solid commandments of a sovereign but first and foremost as a collective, multilogical process with a potentiality of inclusion (Narain 2016). Here, to constitute is a verb rather than a noun. Whereas as an unending process, the constitution is open to becoming, as a codex it implies solidity and fixation. Subaltern constitutionalism is an attempt to go beyond sovereignty as the commandments of God or human beings.

It is strongly believed that in order to democratize the Constitution, the concept of the velayat-e faqih needs to be wiped out altogether and the Constitution needs to be secularized.[6] However, as has been argued in this chapter, the problem of sovereignty cannot be solved by secularization alone. I attempted to argue that in order to have a more democratic society, instead of desperately accepting Sharia and its commanding apparatus or simply relinquishing the notion of God altogether and becoming atheist, questioning the theology of God's sovereignty seems inevitable. This position is not only necessary but ethical. The problem in fact lies with sovereignty and commandment; a demonology that is rooted as much in the legacy of Muslim theocratic thought perceiving God as a voluptuous

[6] In recent years, different constitutions were drafted by Iranian oppositional groups in which the notion of the *velayat-e faqih* is removed. Yet, they equally have not taken the issue of sovereignty into account.

sovereign of the world as it is in Roman and modern notions of sovereignty. In other words, the very demonology is to be problematized.

The theocratic notion of sovereignty depicts God as a masculine sovereign. This personified patriarchal God can effectively be questioned by a theology in which God is neither masculine nor sovereign; it is rather a vision that promises the capacity of human beings to constitute a more equal and freer community.

References

Adjoudani, Masha'allah. 2003. *Mashrouteh Irani*. Tehran: Aktaran.

Agamben, Giorgio. 2011. "The Archaeology of the Commandment." European Graduate School Video Lectures. Uploaded January 31, 2012. https://www.youtube.com/watch?v=JVV94Fi5ChI.

Amanat, Abbas. 2009. *Apocalyptic Islam and Iranian Shiism*. London: I.B.Tauris.

Aqeli, Baqer. 1990. *Davar va adlieh* (Davar and the Judiciary). Tehran: Elmi.

Arjomand, Saïd A. 2007. *Constitutionalism and Political Reconstruction*. Leiden, Netherlands: Brill.

Arjomand, Saïd A. 2013. "Shi'ite Jurists and the Iranian Law and Constitutional Order in the Twentieth Century." In *The Rule of Law, Islam and Constitutional Politics in Egypt and Iran*, edited by Saïd A. Arjomand and Nathan J. Brown, 15–56. New York: State University of New York Press.

Baxi, Upendra. 2012. "Postcolonial Legality: A Postscript from India." *Verfassung und Recht in Übersee/Law and Politics in Africa, Asia and Latin America*, 45, no. 2: 178–94.

Benjamin, Walter. 1986. "Critique of Violence." In *Reflections: Essays, Aphorisms, Autobiographical Writings*. New York: Schocken Books.

Benjamin, Walter. 2004. "The Right to Use Force." In *Selected Writings 1: 1913–1926*, edited by Marcus Bullock and Michael W. Jennings, 231–4. Cambridge, MA: Belknap Press.

Benjamin, Walter. 2019. *Origin of the German Trauerspiel*, translated by Howard Eiland. Cambridge, MA: Harvard University Press.

Bielik-Robson, Agata. 2016. "Beyond Sovereignty: Overcoming Modern Nominalistic Cryptotheology." *Journal of Cultural Research*, 20, no. 3: 295–309.

Bodin, Jean. 1955. *Six Books of the Commonwealth*. Oxford: Basil Blackwell.

Bonner, Michael. 2011. "The Waning Empire." In *New Cambridge History of Islam*, vol. 1, edited by Chase Robinson, 305–59. Cambridge University Press.

Buijs, Govert. 2003. "Que les latins appellant maiestatem: An Explanation into the Theological Background of the Concept of Sovereignty." In *Sovereignty in Transition*, edited by Neil Walker, 229–60. Oxford: Hart Publishing.

Donner, Fred. 1998. *Narratives of Islamic Origins: The Beginnings of Islamic Historical Writings*. Princeton, NJ: Darwin Press.

Fadel, Mohammad. 2016. "Islamic Law and Constitution-Making: The Authoritarian Temptation and the Arab Spring." *Osgoode Legal Studies Research Paper*, 53, no. 2: 472–507.

Farhi, Farideh. 2013. "Constitutionalism and Parliamentary Struggle for Relevance and Independence in Post-Khomeini Iran." In *The Rule of Law: Islam and Constitutional Politics in Egypt and Iran*, edited by Saïd A. Arjomand and Nathan J. Brown, 123–52. New York: State University of New York Press.

Fawcett, Louise. 2008. "Neither Traditional nor Modern: Constitutionalism in the Ottoman Empire and its Successor States." *Journal of Modern European History / Zeitschrift für moderne europäische Geschichte / Revue d'histoire européenne contemporaine*, 6, no. 1: 116–36.

Foucault, Michel. 2003. "Society Must be Defended." In *Lectures at the Collège de France, 1975–1976*, edited by Mauro Bertani and Alessandro Fontana, translated by David Macey. London: Allen Lane.

Ibn Khaldun. 1994. *Al-ibar fi mobtada'e va al-khabar* (The book of allusions), vol. 1. Tehran: Pajouheshgah-e Olum-e Ensani.

Jackson, Sherman A. 1999. "The Alchemy of Domination? Some Asharite Responses to Mutazilite Ethics." *International Journal of Middle East Studies*, 31, no. 2 (May): 185–201.

Kadivar, Mohsen. 2008. *Hokumat-e velayi*, 5th ed. Tehran: Ney.

Kalmo, Hent, and Quintin Skinner, eds. 2010. *Sovereignty in Fragments: The Past, Present and the Future of a Contested Concept*. Cambridge: Cambridge University Press.

Khomeini, Ruhollah. 1999. *Sahife-ye Emam Khomeini* (Ayatollah Khomeini's Collected Speeches), vol. 22. Tehran: Mo'assey-e Tanzim va Nashr-e Asaar-e Emam Khomeini.

Kristó-Nagy, István T. 2016. "Conflict and Cooperation between Arab Rulers and Persian Administrators in the Formative Period of Islamdom, c.600–c.950 CE." In *Empires and Bureaucracy in World History: From Late Antiquity to the Twentieth Century*, edited by Peter Crooks and Timothy H. Parsons, 54–80. Cambridge: Cambridge University Press.

Legenhausen, Gary. 1988. "Notes towards an Ash'arite Theodicy." *Religious Studies*, 24, no. 2 (June): 257–66.

Majles-e Khobregan-e Ghanun-e AsasiShoray-e Eslami. 1985. *Sourat-e mshrouh-e mozakerat-e majles-e barrasiy-e nahayi-e qanun-e asasiy-e jomhouriy-e eslamiy-e Iran* (The Detailed Reports of the Negotiations of the Assembly of the Experts of the Constitution), vol. 1. Tehran: Majles-e Shoray-e Eslami.

Martel, James R. 2012. *Divine Violence: Walter Benjamin and the Eschatology of Sovereignty*. Milton Park, UK: Routledge.

Montazeri, Hossein-Ali. 2008. *Enteqad az Khod: Ebrat va vasiyat* [Self-criticism: Lessons and last will]. https://amontazeri.com/ayatollah/censure/336.

Narain, Vrinda. 2016 "Postcolonial Constitutionalism in India." *Southern California Interdisciplinary Law Journal*, 25, no. 107 (January): 107–33.

Rahnema, Ali. 2014. "Ayatollah Khomeini's Rule of the Guardian Jurist: From Theory to Practice. In *A Critical Introduction to Khomeini*, edited by Arshin Adib-Moghaddam, 88–114. Cambridge: Cambridge University Press.

Rossiter, Clinton. 1948. *Constitutional Dictatorship: Crisis Government in the Modern Democracies*. Princeton, NJ: Princeton University Press.

Sabet, Amr G. 2014. "Wilayat al-Faqih and the Meaning of Islamic Government." In *A Critical Introduction to Khomeini*, edited by Arshin Adib-Moghaddam, 69–87. Cambridge: Cambridge University Press.

Schirazi, Ashghar. 1997. *The Constitution of Iran: Politics and the State in Islamic Republic*, translated by John O'Kane. London: I.B.Tauris.

Schmitt, Carl. 1985. *Political Theology: Four Chapters on the Concept of Sovereignty*, translated by George Schwab. Cambridge, MA: The MIT Press.

Schmitt, Carl. 2004. *On the Three Types of Juristic Thought*, translated by Joseph Bendersky. Westport, CN: Praeger.

Tabari, Muhammad Ibn Jarir. 1996. *Tarikh ar-russul va al-molouk* (The History of the Prophets and Kings), vol. 14. Tehran: Asatir.

Tierney, Brian. 1963. "The Prince Is not Bound by the Laws: Accursius and the Origins of the Modern State." *Comparative Studies in Society and History*, 5, no. 4 (July): 378–400.

Welborn, L. L. 2015. *Paul's Summons to Messianic Life: Political Theology and the Coming Awakening*. New York: Columbia University Press.

https://doi.org/10.1142/9781800611689_0012

Chapter 12

Private Inequality and Public Religion: A Comment on Shayara Bano, India's Triple *Talaq* Decision

Vrinda Narain

Faculty of Law, McGill University,
Montréal, Canada
vrinda.narain@mcgill.ca

Introduction

Muslim women in India are subject to discriminatory personal law that regulates their status within the family and the community. They are unequal relative to Muslim men and other Indian women. Personal laws regulate family relations and are the only laws that apply to individuals on the basis of their religious identity. Whereas all religious personal laws disadvantage women, the postcolonial Indian state has reformed some of the most egregious gender discrimination in the personal law of other religious groups while Muslim law remained unreformed. The public regulation of Muslim women's inequality is a consequence of the contradiction between constitutional guarantees of equality and state-sanctioned discrimination against them under Muslim personal law (Narain 2014). Simultaneously included and excluded from equal citizenship, Muslim women are located at the intersection of public-sphere equality and private-sphere discrimination, facing discrimination within the family in the "private sphere" and being denied the constitutional guarantee of equality (Narain 2017).

The family is where women's everyday life is lived. When this is termed private, it is deemed beyond the reach of the law or constitutional guarantees, and the state absolves itself of any responsibility (MacKinnon 1993, 116–7). Together with the state, religious leaders have blocked Muslim women's claims to equality and their call for the reform of personal law. The judiciary, for its part, has dealt with specific claims to equality by sidestepping constitutional guarantees, choosing instead to decide such cases on technical matters of law. While the judiciary has enforced substantive equality in the public sphere, in the private sphere of the family, the Supreme Court has deferred to the legislature (Narain 2017).

This chapter is a comment on *Shayara Bano,* the 2017 decision in which the Supreme Court of India declared instantaneous divorce under the triple *talaq* (*talaq-e-biddat*) unconstitutional.[1] The triple *talaq* is an unregulated, unilateral right of divorce enjoyed by Muslim men. A husband pronounces *talaq* (divorce) thrice, and at the third pronouncement, the divorce becomes final and irrevocable. The legal validity of triple *talaq* in India is a controversial issue, implicating minority rights, religious freedom, and gender equality. It also implicates the issue of the Uniform Civil Code (UCC) provided for as a Directive Principle in the Constitution under Article 44, itself a matter of great controversy and debate.[2]

Soon after the decision was given, the government introduced the Muslim Women (Protection of Rights on Marriage) Bill (2018, Bill No. 181 of 2018). In May 2019, with a majority in Parliament, the newly reelected government of Prime Minister Modi succeeded in passing the Muslim Women (Protection of Rights on Marriage) Act (MWMA) (2019, No. 20 of 201).[3] The Act makes instant triple *talaq* illegal and void and provides for up to three years' imprisonment for the husband and/or a fine.

---

[1] *Shayara Bano v. Union of India*, [2017] AIR 4609, 9 Supreme Court Cases 1 (India). Hereafter referred to in the text as "*Shayara Bano*" or "*Shayara Bano v. Union of India.*"

[2] Article 44 in *The Constitution of India*, 1950. 44. Uniform civil code for the citizens: "The State shall endeavor to secure for the citizens a uniform civil code throughout the territory of India." *Mohammed Ahmed Khan v. Shah Bano Begum*, [1985] AIR 945 (Supreme Court of India). Hereafter referred to in the text as "*Shah Bano*."

[3] While the Bill was finally passed by the Lower House on December 27, 2018, with strong support, it failed in the Upper House. Since the Bill failed to pass, the government issued an Ordinance, the Muslim Women (Protection of Rights on Marriage) Ordinance, which remained in effect until the passage of the Bill. See the Muslim Women (Protection of Rights on Marriage) Ordinance, 2019 (No 1 of 2019), *The Gazette of India, Extraordinary*, January 12, 2019.

The chapter is organized in the following manner. The next section contextualizes the situation of Muslim women and describes the multiple axes of discrimination they face. The following section sets out the legal framework governing Muslim women's rights in the family and the constitutional provisions regulating minority rights. Next, the chapter details the facts of the *Shayara Bano* case, identifying the issues considered by the Court. It assesses the Court's analysis of key issues, including the constitutional status of personal law, women's equality rights under Muslim personal law, the validity of the triple *talaq*, and the issue of whether the religious freedom guarantee disallows reform of personal law. The final section discusses the consequences and future implications of *Shayara Bano* for Muslim women's rights.

Context

Historically, the postcolonial state has been committed to a policy of secularism in the public sphere but has refused to reform religious personal laws in the private sphere, using arguments of secularism, religious freedom, and minority rights, even when these laws conflict with constitutional guarantees (Narain 2017, 192). The state premised its policy of multiculturalism and legal pluralism on cultural difference while neglecting crucial questions of structural inequality (Narain 2017, 207). It reinforced Muslim religious leaders' control over women of the community, acquiescing in their refusal to reform personal law to address women's disadvantage. Premised on the public/private binary, Muslim women are caught between two patriarchies, the state's and religious leaders', with the state legitimizing their continued subordination through patriarchal interpretations of personal law by religious leaders (Narain 2008, 64). Governments were reluctant to reform religious personal laws for fear of an electoral backlash, as invariably the claims of culture are pitted against women's equality (Khilnani, Raghavan, and Thiruvengadam 2013). Within this complex negotiation that raises questions of group identity and representation, the possibilities of reform were politically fraught.

Over the years, the Supreme Court of India has ruled on conflicts between secular and personal law, culminating in the famous *Shah Bano* case, which raised serious constitutional issues concerning spousal support provisions for Muslim women in the context of a conflict between Muslim personal law and the secular law of spousal support and the issue of the UCC, a uniform family law. While a uniform family law in the form of a UCC was a longstanding demand of the Indian women's movement, feminists have now come to the position that rather than a universal family law, incremental change and targeted reform in all laws relating to women is a better way to engender sustainable law reform (Narain 2017, 192). The women's movement initiated and achieved legal reform in areas such as violence against women and sexual harassment in the workplace (Narain 2017, 203).[4] It continues to push for reform in personal laws of all communities to ensure conformity with constitutional guarantees of equality and non-discrimination (Narain 2017, 203–4).

Today, the issue of Muslim women's marginalization has gained even greater public prominence. The publication of two high-level government reports exposed the state's failure to address the stark inequality of the Muslim minority (Government of India 2006, 2007). These reports showed the state's failure to address structural inequality and systemic discrimination and provided empirical data demonstrating that the state's focus on cultural difference rather than structural inequality has failed Indian Muslims (Thakur 2013, 581). The *Sachar Report* blames the state for neglecting the social, economic, and political aspects of inequality experienced by Muslims across India. Excluded from democratic participation and marginalized, Muslims are politically and economically disempowered (Government of India 2006, 187).[5] While India has achieved significant growth and development, Muslim communities in India have not benefited from this economic progress. The report notes that "the Muslims, the largest minority community in the country, constituting 13.4 percent of the population, are seriously lagging behind in terms of most of the human development indicators" (2).[6] Muslim women are in even worse shape. Disadvantaged also compared to other Indian women

---

[4]The Protection of Women from Domestic Violence Act, 2005 (India), No. 43 of 2005, *The Gazette of India Extraordinary*, Part II, Section 1, September 13, 2005. The Sexual Harassment of Women at Workplace (Prevention, Prohibition and Redressal) Act, 2013 (India), No. 14 of 2013, *The Gazette of India Extraordinary*, Part II, Section 1, April 22, 2013.

[5]According to the *Sachar* Report, Muslims have not benefited from affirmative action programs. One of the main causes the report suggests is the lack of political participation of Muslims—they are excluded from governance structures. In the 2007 lower house of 543 candidates only 36 were Muslim.

[6]The Muslim population in 2018 was reported to be 14.2 percent, or just over 182 million. See Index Mundi 2018.

with regard to employment, participation in the workforce, literacy and education levels, and political participation, they also live in a greater degree of poverty (Hasan 2010, 951; see also Government of India 2006, 151–7; Narain 2014). Muslim women have been deeply disadvantaged by a state that permits their subordination by accepting religious leaders as the sole representatives of the community and accepting these leaders' contention that adherence to an unyielding personal law is the defining feature of group identity, ignoring women's subordination through patriarchal interpretations of religious norms (Government of India 2006).

The 2017 *Triple Talaq Report*—released by the Muslim women's rights organization Bharatiya Muslim Mahila Andolan (BMMA, or Indian Muslim Women's Movement)—identifies the unilateral right of Muslim men to extrajudicial, unregulated, instantaneous divorce as the biggest problem facing Muslim women (Soman and Niaz 2015). This report on the triple *talaq* was part of a larger project on the reform and codification of Muslim personal law (Soman and Niaz 2015, 2). This study was carried out in eight states: Karnataka, Maharashtra, Madhya Pradesh, Odisha, Rajasthan, Tamil Nadu, Uttar Pradesh and West Bengal (5). It reveals the harsh conditions that women divorced through the triple *talaq* face (24). For example, 79 percent of the women respondents did not receive any spousal support or maintenance after the divorce (9). The report characterizes the triple *talaq* as an "atrocity" that goes against Quranic provisions and as a denial of Muslim women's rights as guaranteed by the Quran (31). It asserts that the lack of reform and codification of Muslim law at a time when other personal laws were being reformed and codified has led to the high incidence of triple *talaq*, whereby men are not subject to any regulation in this matter and the religious judges, or *qazis*, continue to support men rather than address women's vulnerability in marriage and divorce (32).

Challenging the protection of triple *talaq* by religious leaders as an aspect of religion that cannot be reformed or regulated, the report boldly calls out community leaders for justifying women's oppression in the name of religion. It urges them to address the suffering caused by the triple *talaq* and to recognize Muslim women's rights (Soman and Niaz 2015, 24). The report ends with the recommendation to reform personal law to address women's disadvantage and specifically recommends a ban on instantaneous triple *talaq*. Significantly, rather than calling for the enactment of a UCC, the BMMA calls for the reform of Muslim personal law within the framework of religion and culture. Any reform made must, however, withstand the test of constitutionality and the fundamental right to equality for all women. In doing so, it rejects a single-axis construction of Muslim women's identity, insisting on their claim to both religious and constitutional equality (Soman and Niaz 2015).

A significant aspect of Muslim women's inequality is the state's lack of acknowledgment of the multiple axes of discrimination experienced by Muslim women (Narain 2017, 199). The nature of citizenship for Muslim women is premised on a single-perspective politics that is in turn premised on a dichotomous construction of women's equality rights versus minority rights (Narain 2017). This understanding is perpetuated both by the state and by religious leaders, serving to preserve each other's sphere of authority. For Muslim women, this is a tricky position to occupy, as community leaders see any claim to equality and call for reforming personal law as a threat to religion. This single-axis framing of discrimination against Muslim women has resulted in absolving the state of any responsibility to address systemic inequality (Narain 2017, 198). It has absolved religious leaders of any responsibility to seriously examine disadvantage perpetuated by religious personal law. It further serves to immunize personal law from constitutional scrutiny (Narain 2017).

It would be wrong to frame Muslim women as victims, disempowered and without agency. Indeed, Muslim women have been organizing, challenging their inequality under personal law (Narain 2017, 201). There has been a rise of Muslim women–led organizations contesting their disadvantage under personal law (for more on these organizations, see Narain 2017). Challenging the *ulema*'s monopoly on the interpretation of religious law, Muslim women have set up Women's Personal Law Boards and women-run community courts. Just as important, they have continued to approach the courts using secular law to challenge their inequality and seek legal remedies for inequities in personal law (Bhaskar 2014). Awaaz-e-Niswaan (AeN, or Women's Voice) was founded in 1985 by Shehnaaz Sheikh, who had personally experienced discrimination under personal law (Awaaz-e-Niswaan 2020). Significantly, AeN focuses not only on the reform of Muslim personal law but also on the reform of all unequal personal laws affecting all Indian women, and it explicitly recognizes the impact that unequal legal status has on other aspects of women's inequality: education, economic empowerment, or violence against women (Awaaz-e-Niswaan 2020). Recognizing the need to build alliances and form coalitions, AeN formed an advocacy platform, the pan-Indian Muslim Women's Rights Network, to campaign for the rights of not only

Muslim women but all Indian women suffering discrimination under the personal law system (Awaaz-e-Niswaan 2020). More recently, in the mid-2000s, a number of Muslim organizations that confronted the *ulema* and countered their misogynistic interpretations of religious law arose. These include the All India Muslim Women's Personal Law Board (AIMWPLB), the BMMA, and a number of women's Shariat courts and Jamaats across the country (Narain 2017, 201–2).

All of these organizations were formed in response to the continued refusal of the *ulema* and the All India Muslim Personal Law Board (AIMLPB), to issue a call for reform in Muslim personal law and in particular to listen to women's calls for reform of the triple *talaq* and polygamy (Narain 2008, 153). The AIMPLB's primary focus is the preservation of personal law (Narain 2017, 200). Over the years, it has intervened in various court challenges mounted by Muslim women against inequities in personal law, including *Shah Bano* and *Shayara Bano*, to categorically reject any reform of the law (Narain 2017, 200–201).

Although until *Shayara Bano* and the passage of the MWMA there had been no reform of personal law, Zoya Hasan notes that "the presence of Muslim women-led networks marks a significant shift in the Indian social landscape" (Hasan 2014, 269). The strong presence of these groups challenges the discourse of the state and the *ulema*, which pits women's equality rights against religion and holds that religion is being safeguarded through the denial of women's rights. This uneasy relationship between women's rights and the secularism/religion and public/private binaries are problematized and unsettled by Muslim women's challenging of their inequality.

In the current political context of India's majoritarian democracy, there is a crisis of secularism as minority rights are seriously threatened (Narain 2017, 203). With a Hindu Right government in power since 2014 and its landslide victory in the May 2019 general election, these issues are even more urgent, as minority anxiety increases in the face of the government's legitimization of Hindu hostility. The government's initiation of legislation consequent on the *Shayara Bano* decision demonstrates a break from the stance of previous governments, where electoral politics and a symbiotic alliance between the state and the *ulema* resulted in a refusal to reform personal law. The Modi government, with its Hindu nationalist agenda, is no longer committed to noninterference in Muslim personal law as its majoritarian politics no longer require Muslim votes. It seized the opportunity to ban the triple *talaq*, citing concern for Muslim women's welfare. While Muslim women's organizations welcomed the ban, this action has also been seen as disingenuous, given the Hindu Right's hostility to Muslims in general and Muslim personal law in particular. Women's groups need to remain attentive to this political context while welcoming progressive legislation that addresses women's disadvantage.

Legal Framework: Muslim Personal Law and Constitutional Provisions

Muslim personal law is based on the Shariat and the Quran. It includes uncodified religious law as well as legislative enactments. The governing laws include the Muslim Personal Law (Shariat) Application Act, 1937, and the Dissolution of Muslim Marriages Act, 1939, both of which were enacted during the British colonial rule.[7] The former made the Shariat applicable to all Muslims in India and disallowed the use of customary law. The latter provided the grounds on which a Muslim woman could seek the dissolution of a marriage.[8] Since India gained its independence in 1947, two more laws have been enacted, the Muslim Women (Protection of Rights on Divorce) Act (MWDA) (1986, Act No. 25 of 1986) and more recently, following *Shayara Bano*, the MWMA.

There are constitutional provisions guaranteeing fundamental rights. Article 14 ensures equality before the law and equal protection by the law. Article 15 prohibits discrimination on the grounds of religion, race, caste, sex, and place of birth. Article 21 provides that no person shall be deprived of his life or personal liberty except through the procedure established by law. Article 25 ensures freedom of conscience and the right

[7]The Muslim Personal Law (Shariat) Application Act, No 26 of 1937, India Code, indiacode.nic.in. Section 2 of the Shariat Act is relevant: "2. Application of personal law to Muslims. Notwithstanding any customs or usage to the contrary, in all questions (save questions relating to agricultural land) regarding intestate succession, special property of females, including personal property inherited or obtained under contract or gift or any other provision of Personal Law, marriage, dissolution of marriage, including *talaq*, *ila*, *zihar*, *lian*, *khula* and *mubaraat*, maintenance, dower, guardianship, gifts, trusts and trust properties, and *wakfs* (other than charities and charitable institutions and charitable and religious endowments) the rule of decision in cases where the parties are Muslims shall be the Muslim Personal Law (Shariat)."

[8]The Dissolution of Muslim Marriages Act, No. 8 of 1939, India Code, http://indiacode.nic.in. *DMMA*, Section 2.

to freely profess, practice, and propagate religion. Article 26 ensures the right to manage religious institutions and religious affairs, subject to public order, morality, and health. Article 13(1) states that all laws in force must conform to the fundamental rights provisions of the Constitution. Article 13(1) is very important in the context of personal law reform because much of the controversy in Indian jurisprudence revolves around the applicability of this constitutional provision to personal law. Until *Shayara Bano*, Indian courts ruled that personal law, and particularly the practice of triple *talaq*, were not "laws in force" for the purpose of Article 13 and therefore did not have to conform to fundamental rights. Consequently, personal law could not be subject to a constitutional challenge for violating the fundamental right to equality. The interpretation of Article 13(1) is key to understanding the constitutionality of discriminatory personal law.

Under Muslim law, there are different modes of divorce for men and women. Whereas men enjoy the unilateral, unregulated right to divorce, women may divorce only on certain limited grounds. Men can divorce their wives either through the instantaneous triple *talaq* where they utter the words "I divorce you (*talaq*)" thrice, consecutively or over a three-month period during which they pronounce the divorce at one-month intervals. Triple *talaq* is considered sinful in Muslim law and is not favored by religious leaders; however, it is a recognized mode of divorce among Sunni Muslims in India.

Under uncodified Muslim personal law, women can initiate divorce (*khula*) only with the consent of the husband, or if the husband delegates the right to divorce to her, usually at the time of signing the marriage contract; alternatively, a woman could obtain a divorce through a decree by a religious judge. Otherwise, the Dissolution of Muslim Marriages Act provides certain limited grounds for divorce. However, women rarely can exercise the right to initiate divorce; the social, cultural, and financial context makes it near impossible. Whereas in most Muslim-majority countries men no longer enjoy the unilateral right to divorce, in India the right remains, despite Muslim women's calls for change and appeals to both the state and religious leaders. Muslim women have a very limited right to spousal support. Furthermore, should a husband regret uttering the instant triple *talaq*, the couple cannot simply remarry. Under personal law, the divorced wife must marry another man, consummate the marriage, and be divorced by him. Only then can she remarry her former husband (*nikah halala*). Not surprisingly, this practice has also been challenged by

Muslim women. Moreover, while bigamy is punishable under the criminal law, exceptionally, polygamy is permitted for Muslim men under Muslim personal law.

Over the years, the judiciary has made some moves to respond to women's disadvantage under the arbitrary triple *talaq*. *Shah Bano* was the culmination of a trilogy of cases dealing with similar issues regarding the status of personal laws and discrimination against women. Women's precarious situation and vulnerability under divorce laws are exacerbated by the fact that divorce is often conveyed in the absence of the wife via text messages, fax, or email (Mandal 2018, 91). It is noteworthy that when women challenge their husbands or when wives are deserted by their husbands and ask for spousal support under India's secular law, men typically respond by either divorcing their wives immediately or else by claiming in court to have divorced under personal law, thus avoiding paying any support. This was the situation in *Shah Bano*.

Following the Supreme Court's decision awarding spousal support to Shah Bano, a 73-year-old divorcee, the government passed the MWDA. This Act was aimed at reversing *Shah Bano*, circumscribing Muslim women's rights by specifically excluding them from the application of secular laws of spousal support they had thus far enjoyed. In effect, the Act absolved the former husband of a divorced wife from the duty of spousal support beyond the *iddat* period prescribed by Muslim personal law.[9] The Act, bitterly opposed by Muslim progressives, reformists, and feminists, was successfully challenged in *Danial Latifi*.[10] The Supreme Court in *Danial Latifi* reaffirmed its decision in *Shah Bano* and upheld the spousal support provisions under *Shah Bano*. Subsequently, in *Shamim Ara*, the Supreme Court ruled that the triple *talaq* was unconstitutional, thereby settling the case law with regard to the constitutional and legal status of triple *talaq*.[11] Although triple *talaq* was not at issue, Shamim

[9]According to Section 2(b) of the MWDA, the "*iddat* period" varies depending on several factors: if the woman is menstruating at the time, three menstrual cycles after the date of divorce; if she is not menstruating at the time, three lunar months after her divorce; or if she is pregnant at the time, the period between the divorce and childbirth or termination of pregnancy, whichever comes first.

[10]*Danial Latifi v. Union of India*, [2001] 7 Supreme Court Cases 740, Criminal Law Journal 4660 (India). Hereafter referred to in the text as "*Danial Latifi*."

[11]*Shamim Ara v. Uttar Pradesh* (State of), [2002] AIR 3551 (Supreme Court of India). Hereafter also referred to in the text as "*Shamim Ara*" or "*Shamim Ara v. Uttar Pradesh*."

Ara's husband refused to pay her spousal support on the ground that he had divorced her under Muslim personal law, which did not require him to pay support beyond the *iddat* period. The Supreme Court held that the mere statement by a husband that he had divorced his (ex-)wife was insufficient. It was in this context that the Court considered the validity of the triple *talaq*. This decision has been understood as invalidating triple *talaq* and has been relied on by courts across India as precedent (Mandal 2018, 92). It is important to acknowledge, however, that court rulings have a limited impact on the lived reality of Muslim women, since much of the regulation of family relations takes place in a non-state-law context of community courts, religious courts, and individual *qazis* issuing rulings or *fatwas* (see, for example, Narain 2014).

Shayara Bano v. Union of India

Shayara Bano's husband divorced her under the triple *talaq*, and she filed a constitutional challenge to this practice on the grounds of Article 14, equality; Article 15, nondiscrimination on the basis of gender; Article 21, right to a life with dignity; and Article 25, religious freedom. Her petition was joined by similar challenges to the triple *talaq* laws, polygamy and the practice of *nikah halala* by four other Muslim women, all of whom had been divorced by their husbands under the triple *talaq* law. They were supported in their challenge by a number of civil society organizations and Muslim women's rights advocacy organizations, including the AIMWPLB, the BMMA and the Bebaak Collective, a coalition of several Muslim women's groups who were intervenors in the petition. Muslim women's challenge to the triple *talaq* and their call to reform personal law were strenuously opposed by Muslim religious leaders, the AIMPLB and the Jamiat Ulema-i-Hind—a national organization of Islamic religious scholars. The AIMPLB was a respondent opposing the challenge to triple *talaq*, and the Jamiat was an intervenor. The federal government was the main respondent. The Attorney General supported the constitutional challenge to personal law, asserting that these aspects of personal law violated constitutional guarantees because they discriminated against Muslim women who were disadvantaged compared to non-Muslim Indian women, Muslim men, and Muslim women in Muslim-majority countries where these practices had been reformed.[12]

[12] Mukul Rohatgi, Attorney General of India, as quoted in *Shayara Bano v. Union of India*, [2017] AIR 4609, 9 Supreme Court Cases 1 (India), para 65.

In an unrelated case concerning Hindu women's right to property, taking judicial notice of the Court's consistent efforts to uphold social reform legislation where personal laws disadvantaged Muslim women, the Supreme Court decided to *suo motu* register a Public Interest Litigation petition (Mandal 2018, 93). The case was duly registered and was entitled Muslim Women's Quest for Equality. The Court added the Jamiat-Ulema-i-Hind and the AIMPLB as parties to the case. Both organizations refuted the challenge, arguing that personal laws were exempt from constitutional scrutiny (Mandal 2018, 93). This petition was heard together with *Shayara Bano*.

The Court confined itself to the issue of triple *talaq* and considered the following questions. First, can religion-based personal law be tested against the fundamental right to equality and nondiscrimination under Articles 14 and 15 of the Indian Constitution? Second, are personal laws "laws in force" under Article 13 of the Constitution, and do they therefore have to conform to the fundamental rights to equality?[13] Third, is the triple *talaq* an essential religious practice protected by the right to religious freedom under Article 25? Finally, do India's obligations under international law require it to recognize and enforce gender equality?

The crucial question before the Court was the relationship between personal law in general, triple *talaq* in particular, and fundamental rights. How should the Court balance gender equality with religious freedom? The legal status of the triple *talaq* determined its constitutional status inasmuch as the dispute in the courts revolved around whether triple *talaq* could be understood as being a part of the Muslim Personal Law (Shariat) Application Act. If it was understood as having been codified pursuant to the Shariat Act, then for constitutional purposes, it was statutory law and therefore subject to the fundamental rights of the Constitution. On the other hand, existing jurisprudence held that uncodified personal law was not subject to fundamental rights or constitutional scrutiny. Therefore, if the Court decided that the Shariat Act did include triple *talaq* within its purview, then it would be subject to constitutional scrutiny and would have to conform with fundamental rights. The Court could either rely on precedent and hold that triple *talaq* was exempt from constitutional conformity, or

---

[13] See Article 13, Laws inconsistent with or in derogation of the fundamental rights in *India Constitution*: Article 13(1), "All laws in force in the territory of India immediately before the commencement of this Constitution, in so far as they are inconsistent with the provisions of this Part, shall, to the extent of such inconsistency, be void." See also Narain (2001).

break from precedent and rule afresh, insisting on constitutional compliance (Bhatia 2017). Another important question was what constituted the "essential" aspects of religion that are insulated from state legislative regulation? Depending on whether triple *talaq* was considered an essential aspect of religion, what was the scope of the Supreme Court's authority to subject it to constitutional scrutiny, and did the religious community or the legislature have the authority to amend the personal-law system?

The Court split 3:2. The majority of three judges—with Rohinton Fali Nariman J. and Uday Umesh Lalit J. delivering the majority opinion, and Kurian J. concurring—ruled that the triple *talaq* was unconstitutional and declared it invalid and illegal. The minority of two judges, Chief Justice of India Jagdish Singh Khehar and S. Abdul Nazeer J., held that the triple *talaq* was constitutional. To complicate matters, the concurring judge disagreed with the majority on some issues and agreed with the dissent on others, while ultimately concurring with the majority on the question of the constitutionality of the triple *talaq*. Despite the landmark ruling that triple *talaq*, as an aspect of personal law, is subject to constitutional scrutiny under fundamental rights, key questions remain unanswered in the area of personal law. As a result, personal law remains a contested terrain, where religious freedom continues to be seen as oppositional to gender equality and is inextricably linked with questions of identity, nationalism, modernity, and secularism.

The majority and concurring opinions

Majority

Writing for the majority, Nariman J.'s opinion confined itself to the narrow issue of the validity of instantaneous triple *talaq* and not of all forms of divorce, nor that of other discriminatory practices under personal law. Nariman J. considered the meaning of equality under Article 14 the Constitution. Citing *EP Royappa* and *Maneka Gandhi*, he asserted the centrality of equality to constitutionalism and the rule of law, underscoring that arbitrariness is the denial of equality.[14] Nariman J. struck down

[14] See *Shayara Bano v. Union of India*; see also *EP Royappa v. Tamil Nadu (State of)*, [1974] AIR 555 (Supreme Court of India); *Maneka Gandhi v. Union of India*, [1978] AIR 597 (Supreme Court of India). Hereafter also referred to in the text as "*EP Royappa*" and "*Maneka Gandhi.*"

triple *talaq* for being manifestly arbitrary and precluding any possibility of reconciliation that would preserve the institution of marriage. He also rejected its validity because it does not follow any of the procedures required for divorce in the Quran, such as attempts at reconciliation or presenting a good reason. He noted that the practice of instantaneous triple *talaq* enables the marital tie to be "broken capriciously and whimsically by a Muslim man without any attempt at reconciliation to save it. This form of *talaq* must, therefore, be held to be violative of the fundamental right contained under Article 14 of the Constitution of India" (*Shayara Bano v. Union of India*, para 57, 262–3).

Significantly, Nariman J., in considering whether personal law is exempt from constitutional scrutiny by virtue of the definition of laws in force as provided in Article 13(1) of the Constitution, decided that triple *talaq* must be subject to constitutional scrutiny. Boldly overturning the precedent set in *Narasu Appa*, he held that personal law is included under the term "laws in force" under Article 13(1) of the Constitution because personal law is recognized and enforced by the 1937 Muslim Personal Law (Shariat) Application Act and, as such, is subject to fundamental rights.[15] This is of critical importance in the religious freedom doctrine, as hitherto the Supreme Court had rejected the contention that personal laws fall within the definition of "laws in force" and thereby excluded them from the fundamental rights provisions of the Constitution.

Nariman J. rejected the argument that the triple *talaq* was an essential aspect of religion protected under religious freedom provisions in the Constitution (*Shayara Bano v. Union of India*, para 23, 234). He was careful to point to jurisprudence that affirms the protection of only essential aspects of religion (para 24, 235).[16] Next, Nariman J. considered whether the Supreme Court could refuse to adjudicate on the challenge to the constitutionality of the triple *talaq* and instead "send the matter back to the legislature to remedy such a wrong" (para 26, 237). He cited Supreme Court decisions to affirm that the right of citizens to approach the courts under Article 32 of the Constitution to protect their fundamental rights is a fundamental right in itself (para 27, 237). Finally, the majority stated that India is committed to gender equality through its various international commitments.

---

[15] See *Bombay (State of) v. Narasu Appa Mali*, [1952] AIR 84 (Bombay High Court, India).

[16] See also *Javed v. Haryana (State of)*, [2003] 8 Supreme Court Cases 369 (India).

Ultimately, Nariman J. held that the triple *talaq* violates the Constitution and must be struck down. He reasoned that it does fall within "laws in force" under Article 13(1) of the Constitution, that it must therefore conform with the fundamental rights provisions, and that it thus must be struck down for violating the right to equality. Finally, he held that triple *talaq* was not an essential aspect of religion and was not protected by the right to religious freedom.

Concurrence

Agreeing with the majority on the outcome but differing in the reasoning, Kurian J concurred that triple *talaq* was unconstitutional. Significantly, he disagreed with the majority on the possibility of testing triple *talaq* on the grounds of violating Article 14 of the Constitution—equality and arbitrariness. Kurian J., noted that the only question to be considered by the Court was "whether triple talaq has any legal sanctity."[17]

For Kurian J., the answer was clear; it lay in the precedent set in *Shamim Ara* that triple *talaq* lacks legal sanctity (*Shamim Ara v. Uttar Pradesh*). Kurian J. also relied on *Fuzlunbi v. K. Khader Vali*,[18] wherein the Court expressed skepticism as to whether something can be "good in law, though bad in theology" (para 26, 221). Holding that the provisions of the Quran on triple *talaq* are unambiguous and that it is against the tenets of the holy text because it precludes reconciliation and revocation, whereas the Quran attributes sanctity and permanence to matrimony, he concluded that the practice violates the 1937 Shariat Act, and therefore cannot be constitutionally valid. Ultimately, Kurian J. held that the fact that triple *talaq* was contrary to Quranic principles meant that it could not attract constitutional protection under the religious freedom provisions (*Shayara Bano v. Union of India*, para 26, 221).

Kurian J., based on a long line of precedent, disagreed with the Chief Justice that the practice of triple *talaq* could be considered an integral part of religious practice (*Shayara Bano v. Union of India*, paras 23–4, 220–1). According to him, "Merely because a practice has continued for long, that by itself cannot make it valid if it has been expressly declared to be impermissible" (para 24, 221).

---

[17] See Kurian J. in Shayara Bano v. Union of India, para 1.

[18] *Fuzlunbi v. K Khader Vali*, [1980] 4 Supreme Court Cases 125, 3 Supreme Court Reporter 1127 (India).

However, he agreed with the dissent that in considering the scope of religious freedom under Article 25, in this context, only issues of public order, health, and morality, and other constitutional provisions dealing with fundamental rights permit the state to regulate religion. He went on to state that the discourse pits religious freedom against other constitutional rights. He was reluctant to privilege one over the other but rather, hoped for reconciliation and harmonization. Significantly, however, he asserted that this was best left to the legislature, while stating that religious freedom must be balanced with other constitutional rights.

The dissent

Disagreeing with the outcome reached by the majority, Chief Justice of India Jagdish Singh Khehar and S. Abdul Nazeer J. held that triple *talaq* was constitutional. They found that personal law did not constitute "laws in force" under Article 13(1) of the Constitution and therefore could not be tested against fundamental rights (*Shayara Bano v. Union of India*, para 159, 163). They stated that courts should not interfere with personal law and should exercise a lot of restraint when assessing personal laws that are challenged simply because they conflict with modern-day concepts (paras 161–6, 173–81). The dissenting judges also found that because the instant triple *talaq* had been in use for 1,400 years and was part of the personal laws of the community, it was protected by religious freedom clauses in the Constitution (para 127, 159). They held that Article 25 guarantees religious freedom protections to all faiths and provides that religious practices, including those under personal law, are subject to state regulation only if they are contrary to the interest of public order, health and morality (para 193, 208). Thus, according to the dissent, triple *talaq* "transcends the barriers of constitutional morality" (para 194, 208). They did not, however, provide rigorous analysis or reasoning for these assertions.

With regard to compliance with India's obligations under international law, the dissent held that personal law prevailed over any conflict between it and international law. Furthermore, the dissent reasoned that the Constitution guaranteed equality and therefore there was no need to draw on international law (*Shayara Bano v. Union of India*, paras 186, 189). Finally and somewhat contrarily, although the dissent held that triple *talaq* was constitutional, it called on the state to enact legislation to ban it. The dissent, deferring to the legislature, ruled that the state alone was competent to prohibit triple *talaq* as per Article 25(2), but nevertheless called on the government to enact such a law within six months.

Critical analysis

Shayara Bano is a landmark decision because it advances the law in certain crucial ways and enlarges Muslim women's rights. First, although by a razor-thin majority, it ruled that personal law is statutory law and is therefore subject to fundamental rights (Jaising 2017). Second, the Court held that the practice of triple *talaq* was not protected by the right to religious freedom. For the first time, personal law was tested on the ground of constitutionality, and it was held that women's inequality within the family, with the triple *talaq* understood as arbitrary, cannot be shielded by religious freedom protection. Since the 1950s, the Supreme Court avoided the question of whether personal law is subject to the fundamental rights guarantees, and so, in the evolution of Indian jurisprudence, these are two highly significant advances. This decision interrupts the public/private dichotomy, where the private inequality of Muslim women is an aspect of public regulation (MacKinnon 2006). *Shayara Bano* has profound implications for women's equality, the nature and scope of the religious freedom guarantee, the tension between women's equality rights claims and minority rights, the interpretation of religion accepted by the state, the notion of secularism, and equal citizenship.

The *Shayara Bano* decision was welcomed by Muslim women, civil society groups, and women's rights activists across the country. Yet, it cannot be simplistically understood as a victory for Muslim women's rights. On the contrary, it underscores the need for a complex, nuanced analysis of women's vulnerability in marriage and divorce. Arguably, the *Shayara Bano* decision demonstrates the Supreme Court's continued reluctance to fully reform family laws and the persistence of a conflicted approach to discrimination under personal law. The basis of the ruling that the triple *talaq* was unconstitutional was a strained constitutional interpretation rather than a robust justification of women's substantive equality rights. Although the majority struck down triple *talaq* as unconstitutional, it confined itself to the issue of the instant triple *talaq*, and did not examine the broader context of discrimination under Muslim personal law. On the one hand, the Supreme Court asserted its authority to ban the instant triple *talaq*, while on the other, it left the graduated triple *talaq* right intact, albeit it must be pronounced over a three-month period in three instances and not in three simultaneous pronouncements. So, in practice, not much will change for Muslim women, who are still subject to unilateral, unregulated divorce. While the dissent painstakingly detailed the reforms in Muslim family law across the world, signaling the need for reform in India, it held that triple *talaq* was permissible and could not be regulated by the state, and yet directed the legislature to enact a law banning it.

Shayara Bano squarely placed triple *talaq* within the purview of the equality provisions and fundamental rights. However, the Supreme Court insisted on locating the unconstitutionality of triple *talaq* in its arbitrariness and lack of possibility of reconciliation rather than in women's fundamental right to equality and non-discrimination on the basis of gender (Redding 2017). None of the five judges discussed discrimination on the basis of sex, illustrating their reluctance to engage in a jurisprudential analysis that treats Muslim women as equal citizens equally worthy of rights protection (Kapur, 2017). The Court, instead, framed its judgement around privileging the preservation of the institution of marriage.

Nariman J. held that triple *talaq* violated equality by invoking arbitrariness under Article 14 rather than invoking discrimination on the basis of sex under Article 15. Once he found triple *talaq* to be manifestly arbitrary and thus violative of equality, he "[did] not find the need to go into the ground of discrimination in these cases" (para 57, 263). In Kurian J.'s concurrence as well, the opportunity to build a robust jurisprudence on gender equality was missed, as women's claims were relegated to the sidelines. Rather than analyzing the triple *talaq* in the context of women's rights, Kurian J. chose to anchor his decision in the religious interpretation of the Quran and the assertion that because the triple *talaq* precludes efforts for reconciliation and revocation it violates Quranic rules and therefore was unconstitutional.

Gender justice was even less evident in the dissenting opinion. The issue of women's equality rights was not a matter of consideration for the Chief Justice, who largely ignored the jurisprudential tradition around religious freedom and demonstrated a complete disregard for women's disadvantage under personal law. It is unsettling that the dissent shielded the triple *talaq* from constitutional scrutiny by virtue of its long-standing practice, asserting that the state could interfere only for matters of public order, health or morality. The dissent focused on discussing the nature of religion and interpretations of Quranic verses, confining the debate to theological parameters. However, as Indira Jaising points out, the duty of the Court is to interpret the Constitution, not religious dogma and faith (Jaising 2017). Furthermore, Khehar C.J.I. referred to a line in the Quran that compares the relationship between a husband and wife to that of a man's tilth and fertile soil. He stated that marital sex is tantamount to a man sowing his fields "in order to reap a harvest, by choosing his own time and mode of cultivation, by ensuring that he does not sow out of season, or cultivate in a manner which will injure or exhaust the soil" (para 18, 17). Clearly such opinions are, as Kapur notes, "unacceptable from the standpoint of feminist jurisprudence, they also reflect the Court's continued inability to comprehend women, Muslim and non-Muslim, as bearers of rights entitled to full equality as Indian citizens" (Kapur 2017).

Although *Shayara Bano* ruled triple *talaq* to be unconstitutional, the Court did not meaningfully engage with the systemic disadvantage of women in the personal law system nor with the lived reality of Muslim women and the gender discrimination perpetuated by personal laws. There was a serious lack of reflection on the meaning of substantive equality. None of the judges discussed ancillary matters such as the lack of spousal support beyond the prescribed *iddat* period, child custody, or guardianship—which automatically passes to the father in Muslim personal law. Furthermore, in contrast to the Supreme Court's earlier receptiveness to India's obligations under international law, in *Shayara Bano*, claims of gender equality under Article 15 of the Constitution as well as India's international legal obligations to uphold women's equality rights were not adequately addressed by the majority and simply dismissed by the dissent.[19]

In this respect, the decision provides little jurisprudential guidance for future rights claimants with implications not just for Muslim women but indeed for all Indian women. This refusal of the Court to engage in a discussion of women's disadvantage under personal law represents a rupture in the jurisprudential narrative of progress in acknowledging and enforcing women's substantive equality. Notwithstanding the crucial fact that this constitutional challenge was initiated by Muslim women demanding change, and despite the majority's reliance on constitutional equality protections in the private sphere, there was little effort to elaborate this as sound legal jurisprudence based on the intersectionality of gender and minority religious identity.

With regard to the constitutional status of personal law, while Article 13(1) of the Constitution explicitly calls for striking down all laws not in conformity with fundamental rights, historically, courts have

[19] See, for example, *Vishaka v. State of Rajasthan*, [1997] AIR 3011 (Supreme Court of India) on the adherence to CEDAW in the absence of domestic legislation.

somewhat unconvincingly argued that personal laws are exempt from this constitutional provision, a stance that implies its reluctance to strike down legislation as unconstitutional and preference for a more conciliatory approach.[20] In this context, it is a major development that the majority in *Shayara Bano* broke with precedent and categorically asserted that triple *talaq* must be considered as a law in force under Article 13(1) of the Constitution and must therefore be subject to constitutional conformity. Scholars speculate that with *Shayara Bano*, the Supreme Court signaled a new approach to personal law and an emphatic move away from the previous hands-off approach using the excuse of judicial deference to the legislature (see, for example, Herklotz 2017). However, it is important to note that the dissent continued to favor judicial deference to the legislature and a hands-off approach to personal law. Though the dissent directed the state to consider banning triple *talaq* by enacting new legislation, it nevertheless upheld its constitutionality.

Shayara Bano demonstrates the importance of locating agency in individual acts of resistance challenging the institutional and legal structures of postcolonial India. It is noteworthy that the AIMPLB originally asserted the position that the court had no jurisdiction over personal law, then later modified its position in its affidavit to the Supreme Court to state that triple *talaq* was against the Shariat and calling on the Muslim community to ostracize those who practiced it (Mandal 2018, 104). Further, it even undertook the project of issuing guidelines to *qazis* to include a clause that excludes triple *talaq* as a mode of divorce (Mandhani 2017). When the Court finally handed down its decision, the AIMPLB stated that the court's pronouncement on the status of triple *talaq* was in line with its own position (Mandal 2018, 104). This change in the AIMPLB's position could be seen as a response to the challenge posed by Muslim women's activists to its authority (104). The increasing visibility and authority of women's organizations was finally having an impact on religious leaders (104). This in itself is of tremendous importance and demonstrates a break from the past: Muslim women's interests were no longer defined within the discourse of either state or community interests and *Shayara Bano* served to move beyond a discourse of protectionism.

---

[20] See for example *Bombay (State of) v. Narasu Appa Mali*, [1952] AIR 84 (Bombay High Court, India); *Mary Roy v. Kerala (State of)*, [1986] AIR 1011 (Supreme Court of India); and *Madhu Kishwar v. Bihar (State of)*, [1996] AIR 1864, 5 Supreme Court Cases 125 (India).

Despite *Shayara Bano*'s lack of meaningful acknowledgment of women's equality rights, the jurisprudence emerging in the area of personal law suggests that the Supreme Court is more willing now to strengthen its argument upholding women's rights in personal laws by connecting equality within the family to the wider constitutional context of fundamental rights (Dam 2005; Iyer 2004; Rao 1997; Sathe 2001, 2003). *Shayara Bano* ultimately illustrates the potential of the Constitution to forward women's equality in the family (Baxi 2000, 540; MacKinnon 2006, 202). Balancing equality with religious freedom and responding to the call for change from within the Muslim community, *Shayara Bano* is an important milestone in the evolution of India's religious freedom jurisprudence. It demonstrates the persistence of the difficulties around the constitutional status of the personal-law system and its continued discriminatory impact on women. As important, this judgment underscores the significance of subaltern constitutionalism in strengthening women's rights, democratic citizenship, and the rule of law. The Constitution is open to an interpretation that upholds and reinforces social justice (Baxi 2009, xiii). Despite the disappointing lack of gender analysis in *Shayara Bano*, the Supreme Court's acknowledgment of the impact of inequitable personal laws on the status of women is, on the whole, promising.[21]

Conclusion

Consequent upon the *Shayara Bano* decision, the Hindu nationalist government of Prime Minister Modi enacted the MWMA in 2019, making triple talaq illegal and providing for ancillary reliefs for divorced women including spousal support, child custody and guardianship, first issuing it as an Ordinance. By introducing the law to ban triple *talaq*, the postcolonial state has intervened for the first time to enlarge the rights of Muslim women, opposing religious leaders' objections. The enactment of the MWMA represents a shift in the state's stance on legislating in the area of Muslim personal law, demonstrating a willingness to reform Muslim personal law in comparison to a historical refusal to do so, and must be set within the political context of the Hindu Right's anti-Muslim agenda and hostility to Muslim personal law. Under this law, any pronouncement of triple *talaq*, whether spoken, written, or in electronic form such as a text

---

[21] See, for example, MacKinnon (2006, 189). See also Austin (1966); *Kerala (State of) v. N M Thomas*, [1976] AIR 490 (Supreme Court of India).

message is void and illegal (MWMA, Section 3). The wife is entitled to an allowance from the husband both as spousal support and child support and she retains custody of minor children (MWMA, Sections 5 and 6). Finally, the Act criminalizes triple *talaq*, making it a bailable offense, punishable by imprisonment and/or a fine.

This law has also resulted in hardening the stance of the Hindu right wing, as the Modi government has attempted to criminalize the pronouncement of *talaq* with imprisonment. While Muslim women and women's rights advocates welcomed the decision to ban triple *talaq*, the move to criminalize it has not met with the same enthusiasm: criminalization is deemed to be harsh and disproportionate. Arguably, this will have unintended consequences for the women and children involved. Most importantly, it has been criticized as misidentifying the problem. Mandal argues that "criminal law is an ineffective and disproportionate response to the problem (106). And it might well face a constitutional challenge on the grounds of being manifestly arbitrary" (106). However, others, like Safia Niaz, have asserted that a law without deterrence will not have any impact.

Shayara Bano is a huge step forward for women's equality rights with its ruling that personal laws must conform to constitutional guarantees of equality. It is significant that the practice of triple *talaq* was struck down by the majority as being *ultra vires* the Constitution and declared invalid. While it provides hope for future rights claimants that the Constitution remains a critical site of transformative struggle for Muslim women's equality, there are certain critical ways in which *Shayara Bano* serves as a caution to the Supreme Court and its jurisprudence on women's equality and religion.

Shayara Bano appears to interrupt the narrative of progress in Supreme Court jurisprudence on women's rights under personal law through its lack of rigorous reasoning and the absence of analysis of women's equality rights. This is worrying in terms of India's jurisprudential evolution on the relationship between religious freedom and women's equality. Going forward, it is important that the Court acknowledges women's equality rights specifically and puts women at the center of its analysis. Shayara Bano's plea to the Court was not simply about the triple *talaq* but more fundamentally about the systemic discrimination entrenched in personal law that fundamentally and profoundly disadvantages women. The Court had the responsibility not simply to strike down the instant triple *talaq* but to subject the unilateral *talaq*, and the discrimination under personal law in its entirety, to constitutional scrutiny. Further, going beyond Muslim personal law, all religious personal law must be subject to constitutional scrutiny and judged in the bright light of the fundamental right to equality. Finally, the Court must move away from binary categories of analysis that perpetuate women's inequality justified in the name of religious freedom. It is time for the Supreme Court of India to enforce the fundamental right to equality for all citizens, including Muslim women.

References

Austin, Granville. 1966. *The Indian Constitution: Cornerstone of a Nation.* Oxford: Clarendon Press.

Awaaz-e-Niswaan. 2020. "Milestones" and "Campaigns and Advocacy." http://niswaan.org.

Baxi, Upendra. 2000. "Postcolonial Legality." In *A Companion to Postcolonial Studies*, edited by Henry Schwarz and Sangeeta Ray, 540–55. Malden, MA: Blackwell.

Baxi, Upendra. 2009. *Human Rights in a Posthuman World: Critical Essays.* New Delhi: Oxford University Press.

Bhaskar, Srinivas. 2014. "Progressive Muslim Women Call for Personal Law Reform." https://webcache.googleusercontent.com/search?q=cache:T3l14C1Eq7YJ:https://www.newageislam.com/islam-women-and-feminism/srinivas-bhaskar/progressive-muslim-women-call-for-personal-law-reform/d/97826+&cd=1&hl=en&ct=clnk&gl=pk.

Bhatia, Gautam. 2017. "The Supreme Court's Triple Talaq Judgment." *Indian Constitutional Law and Philosophy*, August 22, 2017. https://indconlawphil.wordpress.com/2017/08/22/the-supreme-courts-triple-talaq-judgment/.

Cossman, Brenda, and Ratna Kapur. 1993. "Communalising Gender/Engendering Community: Women, Legal Discourse and Saffron Agenda." *Economic and Political Weekly*, 28, no. 17 (April): 35–44.

Dam, Shubhankar. 2005. "Lawmaking Beyond Lawmakers: The Little Right and the Great Wrong." *Tulane Journal of International and Comparative Law*, 13, no. 1: 109–40.

Government of India. 2006. *Social, Economic and Educational Status of the Muslim Community: A Report.* New Delhi: Prime Minister's High Level Committee, Ministry of Minority Affairs, Government of India. https://sabrang.com/sachar/sacharreport.pdf.

Government of India. 2007. *Report of the National Commission for Religious and Linguistic Minorities.* New Delhi: Ministry of Minority Affairs, Government of India. http://www.minorityaffairs.gov.in/sites/default/files/volume-1.pdf.

Hasan, Zoya. 2010. "Gender, Religion and Democratic Politics in India." *Third World Quarterly*, 31, no. 6: 939–54.

Hasan, Zoya. 2014. "Religion, Feminist Politics and Muslim Women's Rights in India." In *Women and Law: Critical Feminist Perspectives*, edited by Kalpana Kannabiran, 264–73. New Delhi: SAGE Publications.

Herklotz, Tanja. 2017. "Walking a Tightrope: Balancing Law, Religion and Gender Equality in the Aftermath of the Indian Supreme Court's Triple Talaq Ban." *Journal for Law & Islam*, 9: 179–204.

Index Mundi. 2018. "India Demographics Profile 2018." January 20, 2018. www.indexmundi.com/india/demographics_profile.html.

Iyer, V. R. Krishna. 2004. "Judicial Activism: A Democratic Demand." 31 *Indian Bar Review*, 1.

Jaising, Indira. 2017. "SC Strikes Down Triple Talaq, But Does Little for Gender Justice." *The Quint*, August 24, 2017. https://www.thequint.com/voices/opinion/indira-jaising-triple-talaq-gender-justice-judgement.

Kapur, Ratna. 2017. "Triple Talaq Verdict: Wherein Lies the Much Hailed Victory?" *The Wire*, August 28, 2017. https://thewire.in/gender/triple-talaq-verdict-wherein-lies-the-much-hailed-victory.

Khilnani, Sunil, Vikram Raghavan, and Arun K. Thiruvengadam. 2013. "Introduction: Reviving South Asian Comparative Constitutionalism." In *Comparative Constitutionalism in South Asia*, edited by Sunil Khilnani, Vikram Raghavan, and Arun K. Thiruvengadam, 1–22. New Delhi: Oxford University Press.

MacKinnon, Catharine A. 1993. "Reflections on Law in the Everyday Life of Women." In *Law in Everyday Life*, edited by Austin Sarat and Thomas R. Kearns, 109–22. Ann Arbor, MI: University of Michigan Press.

MacKinnon, Catharine A. 2006. "Sex Equality under the Constitution of India: Problems, Prospects and 'Personal Laws'." *International Journal of Constitutional Law*, 4, no. 2: 181–202.

Mandal, Saptarshi. 2018. "Out of Shah Bano's Shadow: Muslim Women's Rights and the Supreme Court's Triple Talaq Verdict." *Indian Law Review*, 2, no. 1: 89–107.

Mandhani, Apoorva. 2017. "Men Resorting Triple Talaq to Face Social Boycott: AIMPLB in its New Affidavit in SC." *LiveLaw*, May 22, 2017. www.livelaw.in/men-resorting-triple-talaq-face-social-boycott-aimplb-new-affidavit-sc-read-affidavit.

Narain, Vrinda. 2001. *Gender and Community: Muslim Women's Rights in India*. Toronto: University of Toronto Press.

Narain, Vrinda. 2008. *Reclaiming the Nation: Muslim Women and the Law in India*. Toronto: University of Toronto Press.

Narain, Vrinda. 2014. "The Supreme Court of India and Maintenance for Muslim Women: Transformatory Jurisprudence." In *Routledge Handbook of Gender in South Asia*, edited by Leela Fernandes, 97–114. London: Routledge.

Narain, Vrinda. 2017. "Law, Gender, and Nation: Muslim Women and the Discontents of Legal Pluralism in India." In *Islam, Gender, and Democracy in Comparative Perspective*, edited by Jocelyne Cesari and Jose Casanova, 188–210. Oxford: Oxford University Press.

Rao, Makani N. 1997. "Judicial Activism." *Supreme Court Cases Journal*, 8, no. 1. http://www.ebc-india.com/lawyer/articles/97v8a1.htm.

Redding, Jeffrey A. 2017. "Shamim Ara and the Divorce Politics of a Secular and Modern India." *SHARIA source, Harvard Law School*, October 8, 2016. https://papers.ssrn.com/sol3/papers.cfm?abstract_id=2849917.

Sathe, Satyaranjan P. 2001. "Judicial Activism: The Indian Experience." *Washington University Journal of Law and Policy*, 6, no. 1: 29–109.

Sathe, Satyaranjan P. 2003. *Judicial Activism in India: Transgressing Borders and Enforcing Limits*. New Delhi: Oxford University Press.

Soman, Zakia, and Niaz, Noorjehan S. 2015. "No More 'Talaq Talaq Talaq': Muslim Women Call for A Ban on an UnIslamic Practice." *Bharatiya Muslim Mahila Andolan*, November 21, 2015. https://www.academia.edu/25297601/No_MORE_TALAQ_TALAQ_TALAQ_NO_MORE_TALAQ_TALAQ_TALAQ_Muslim_Women_Call_for_a_Ban_on_an_UnIslamic_Practice.

Thakur, Manish K. 2013. "Democracy, Pluralism and the Religious Minorities: The Muslim Question in India." *Social Change*, 43, no. 4 (December): 581–94.

https://doi.org/10.1142/9781800611689_0013

Chapter 13

Constitutionalism and Sharia in Pakistan: A Debate on the National Narrative and the Identity of the State

Ana Ballesteros Peiró

Barcelona Centre for International Affairs (CIDOB), Barcelona, Spain
ana.ballesterospeiro@gmail.com

Introduction

Pakistan's origins are still a subject of debate, especially when the question of national identity arises. As a home for the Muslims of colonial India, important issues were not considered. This was either deliberate—as a political strategy—or because of the pressure that hastened the process of the Partition. The ambiguities with which the state was born, such as what kind of state it would be or how it would integrate the many different groups under its flag, have damaged the construction of a national identity. The leaders of the Muslim League represented modernity. Islamists, while opposing Pakistan in the first place, joined the fray to demand an Islamic state under Islamic laws. These two positions agreed on one thing: the territory's cultural and geographical heterogeneity presented a danger rather than a strength.

How to reconcile modern and Islamic as the two models of a state was to occupy an important space in the national debate. Building a country from scratch was not easy. The basis was a theory (Two Nation Theory, TNT) that considered Muslims and Hindus to be different nations.

The TNT, as will be further developed, considered Muslims to share common codes, values, and traditions. Thus, they were to have their own state in order to protect them from being ruled by a Hindu majority. Building the state on religious arguments merged Islam with national identity. But Islam, even as a religion, is not homogeneous. Nor were the peoples that made up the new state.

The ideological construction of Pakistan was developed during the struggle for the independence of British India. Its ideological origins can be traced back to 1920s–30s: with the separational political awakening in India. Muhammad Ali Jinnah[1] was the leader of the All India Muslim League (AIML), the political party that championed the independence movement for Muslims. Jinnah went from defending Hindu-Muslim unity under the Indian National Congress Party to asking for an independent state with the AIML, having passed through demanding all shades of self-government for Muslims.

We will have a look at three speeches with which Jinnah constructed Muslim nationalism and at how its contents served its purpose, namely, being the basis on which the state of Pakistan would be built. The legacies of this ideology, known as the "ideology of Pakistan," explain the troubles of finding an identity other than that of Islam. Religion, it was claimed, provided homogeneity to otherwise plural ethnic, linguistic, ideological, and regional Muslim cultures. The source of Jinnah's discourses can be found in Muhammad Iqbal's ideas on Muslim nationalism. Although critical of democracy and its different practices in other countries, Iqbal wrote:

> The best form of government for such a community would be democracy, the ideal of which is to let a man develop all the possibilities of his nature by allowing him as much freedom as practicable. The Caliph of Islam is not an infallible being like other Muslims, he is subject to the same law; he is elected by the people and is deposed by them if he goes contrary to the law. An ancestor of the present Sultan of Turkey was sued in an ordinary court of law by a mason who succeeded in getting him fined by the town Qazi. *Democracy, then, is the most important aspect of Islam as a political ideal* … Though the principle of election was not quite original

[1]Although he was not alone in this struggle, he rose to become the sole leader of the party. Ideologically, others also contributed to the components of the Pakistan demand, such as Chaudhry Rahmat Ali, the person who coined the acronyms that would name Pakistan; Sir Sayyed Ahmad Khan; or Muhammad Iqbal, the poet and philosopher who continued to inspire AIML and Jinnah ideologically in this demand.

> in Asia … yet somehow or other it was not suited to the nations of Asia in the early days of Islam. It was, however, reserved for a Western nation to vitalise the countries of Asia politically (italics added).[2]

Iqbal dealt with the contradictions between democracy and his society and saw none in establishing a democratic system. According to him, democracy and Islam could not be separated. Religion had to play a role in the state. The Muslim intelligentsia represented by the members of the Muslim League "tried to enlarge Islam into a comprehensive system through integration of Western concepts, terms and values and thus to legitimize the existing (colonial) system" (Malik 1998, 16). In Macaulay's[3] *Minute on Education* view, they were a class "made of Indians by blood and colour, but English in taste, in opinion, morals and intellect" (Cutts 1953, 825).

On the Road to Partition: Muslim Nationalism

Ever since the British began the devolution of power to Indian nationals, this Muslim intelligentsia worried about their future as an elite in an independent India ruled by an overwhelmingly Hindu majority. They felt that their Muslim political identity was threatened. Two parties claimed to represent Indian subjects on the road to self-government: Congress, with Jawaharlal Nehru as its leader and Gandhi among one of its defining figures, and the AIML, which attempted to represent all Muslims. The AIML did not get much recognition from Congress, which considered itself the only representative of India. To facilitate self-rule, the British passed the Government of India Act (1935), which served as a constitution. After this law was passed, elections took place. The Congress party won overwhelmingly. The AIML failed to get representation in the Muslim-majority provinces, while it retained a fair share of seats in those where they were a minority (United Provinces or Assam).

If there was to be some sort of confederation on the principle of Muslim self-rule in Muslim-majority areas, efforts had to focus on gaining the trust

---

[2]Iqbal's first speech in English in Lahore, April 1908, in Hashimy 1955, 53–101.

[3]Thomas Babington Macaulay introduced Western learning in India. He considered English to be superior, and Indian education to be backward. Macaulay was behind the government's decision to introduce education in English and abandon local languages that were the medium of instruction in government schools. He attempted to create an Anglicised class of Indians.

of their leaders. In the 1937 elections, these leaders failed to follow an all-India policy. Indeed, they were more concerned with local politics. In Bengal and Punjab, Muslim politicians who won the elections were not members of the Congress Party or AIML. In Bengal, the Krishak Praja Party (KPP) led by Fazlur Haq formed a coalition with the Muslim League and smaller parties, although Congress was the first force.[4] In Punjab, the Unionist Party led by Fazl Hussain was composed of Muslims, Hindus, and Sikhs. In the North West Frontier Province (NWFP), the Khudai Khitmatgar (Servants of God, a Pashtun nationalist party) formed a coalition with Congress.

Thus, Jinnah bargained with leaders of those Muslim-majority areas that were to become Pakistan. He emphasized the need of a separate government (not yet a homeland). In his address to the AIML in Lahore, 1940, otherwise known as the Lahore Declaration, Jinnah expressed:

> They are not religions in the strict sense of the word, but are, in fact, different and distinct social orders, and it is a dream that the Hindus and Muslims can ever evolve a common nationality, and this misconception of one Indian nation has troubles and will lead India to destruction if we fail to revise our notions in time. *The Hindus and Muslims belong to two different religious philosophies, social customs, literatures. They neither intermarry nor interdine together and, indeed, they belong to two different civilizations which are based mainly on conflicting ideas and conceptions.* Their aspect on life and of life are different. It is quite clear that Hindus and Mussalmans [Muslims] derive their inspiration from different sources of history. They have different epics, different heroes, and different episodes. Very often the hero of one is a foe of the other and, likewise, their victories and defeats overlap. To yoke together two such nations under a single state, one as a numerical minority and the other as a majority, must lead to growing discontent and final destruction of any fabric that may be so built for the government of such a state (Moore 2001, 180; italics added).

In this discourse, Jinnah refers to the complex relations between religion and the social order of Islam and Hinduism. The social construction of Muslim and Hindus around caste and occupation served more as a base

---

[4] Muslim and Hindu peasants supported KPP. Its popular base was mainly located in East Bengal.

for policymaking than religion per se.[5] This speech is also known as the Pakistan Resolution, and it is considered the basis for the reclamation of a separate state. The flaws of the discourse are not lost. Jinnah purposefully overlooked those episodes of history where coexistence was more the rule than the exception, as well as everything that Muslims and Hindus still had in common: religious rituals and practices, mixed marriages and wedding traditions, Bengalis' (Muslim and Hindu alike) devotion to their national literary hero (Rabindranath Tagore), and languages indifferently spoken by Hindus and Muslims, to name just a few.[6]

Redoubling his bargain to demand a separate homeland for Muslims, in his Eid message in 1945, two years before the Partition, Jinnah delivered a speech that stressed Islam as a complete code of conduct that regulates the daily lives of Muslims:

> The Quran is the general code for the Muslims, a religious, social, civil, commercial, military, judicial, criminal and penal code. It regulates everything, from the ceremonies of religion to those of daily life, from the salvation of the soul to the health of the body, from the rights of all to those of each individual from morality to crime; from punishment here to that in the life to come, and our Holy Prophet Mohammad (Peace be upon Him) has enjoined on us that every Mussalman should posses [sic] a copy of the Quran and be his own priest. Therefore, *Islam is not merely confined to the spiritual tenets and doctrines or ritual and ceremonies. It is a complete code regulating the whole Muslim society*, every department of life, collective and individual (italics added).

Certainly, the moment cannot go unnoticed. This speech sounds like a plea for Islam to become law. In it, Jinnah says that Islam is not a private issue, relegated to personal practice, but a code with a Quranic source. It sounds like an Islamist positioning. Was this not odd for Jinnah, as he was closer to a secular leader than an Islamist one? The instrumentalization of Islam done by Jinnah, known as Quaid-e-Azam (Great Leader), had a purpose, which was achieving self-government for the Muslims of India.

[5] It became impossible to separate ethnicity, occupation, caste, and religion from politics.

[6] In fact, Tagore would be the author who composed *Amar Shonar Bangla*, the hymn of Bangladesh.

Only two years later, once Pakistan was born and became an independent state, his address to the Constituent Assembly (August 11, 1947) was framed in entirely different terms:

> I cannot emphasize it too much. We should begin to work in that spirit, and in course of time all these angularities of the majority and minority communities, the Hindu community and the Muslim community—because even as regards Muslims you have Pathans, Punjabis, Shias, Sunnis and so on, and among the Hindus you have Brahmins, Vaishnavas, Khatris, also Bengalese, Madrasis and so on—will vanish … You are free; you are free to go to your temples, you are free to go to your mosques or to any other place or worship in this State of Pakistan. *You may belong to any religion or caste or creed—that has nothing to do with the business of the State*. As you know, history shows that in England conditions, some time ago, were much worse than those prevailing in India today. The Roman Catholics and the Protestants persecuted each other. Even now there are some States in existence where there are discriminations made and bars imposed against a particular class. Thank God, we are not starting in those days. We are starting in the days where there is no discrimination, *no distinction between one community and another, no discrimination between one caste or creed and another*. We are starting with this fundamental principle: that we are all citizens, and equal citizens, of one state (italics added).

This discourse made more sense, given Jinnah's personality, private life, and the values he defended, but as Stephen Cohen (2004, 43) stated: "A few speeches could not erase four decades of emphasis on the differences between Hindus and Muslims, and the threat to Muslims from the larger community." Pakistan was born on the basis of Islam, under the TNT, and Muslims now had their land.

From Partition, a Partitioned Pakistan

The Muslim-majority areas of India (Punjab, NWFP, Balochistan, and Sindh on the west side; Bengal on the east side),[7] except Kashmir, became Pakistan on August 14, 1947. A Pakistan born from the great trauma of

---

[7] Punjab and Bengal were divided on the basis of Muslim-majority districts and geographical contiguity.

Partition (it inherited a divided Punjab and a divided Bengal without Calcutta) had to build its institutions from the very beginning. It also had to, in ideological terms, build a national narrative; its heroes, its foes, its history. Partition took more than 500,000 lives and displaced around 14 million people. The scars were to endure and mark the evolution of the new state. Besides, with Kashmir as a disputed territory that marked the first Indo-Pakistani war (1947–8), the stage was set for defense to be high on the agenda. Jinnah died one year after independence, leaving an ideological void that others could not fill, as they lacked his authority and legitimacy.

The Government of India Act (1935), enacted by the British, became the provisional constitution until the Constituent Assembly reached a consensus about the future laws of the land. The Independence Act 1947 provided a guideline for the Constitution of Pakistan. Among other matters, it required the continuity of previous legislations, including the legal description of religious identity: a Muslim was defined as the one who abided by the law of Islam. From the passing of the Objectives Resolution (1949) till the first constitution of 1956 was approved, the debate progressed toward the role that Islam should have. As Jawed (1999, 53) describes, there were four main issues in the debate of an Islamic state: (1) the functions of the state; (2) democratic values; (3) the character and form of government; and (4) the law and legislation. The Objectives Resolution (1949) marked the first step toward a constitution. It was important because it established the place of Islam in Pakistan:

> Sovereignty over the entire universe belongs to God Almighty alone and the authority which He has delegated to the state of Pakistan through its people for being exercised within the limits prescribed by Him is a sacred trust.
>
> …
>
> Wherein the principles of democracy, freedom, equality, tolerance, and social justice as enunciated by Islam shall be fully observed.
>
> Wherein the Muslims shall be enabled to order their lives in the individual and collective spheres in accordance with the teachings and requirements of Islam as set out in the Holy Quran and the Sunnah (Khan 2001, 91).

The Resolution carries on, emphasizing the fundamental rights of all citizens, including "equality of status, of opportunity and before law, social, economic and political justice, and freedom of thought, expression, belief, faith, worship, and association, subject to law and public morality." Liaqat Ali Khan, the first prime minister of Pakistan, explained at the Constituent Assembly that the authority was therefore with the state through the chosen representatives of the people. That is, through elections. The concepts of freedom, equality, democracy, tolerance, and social justice were considered within the framework of Islam. These fundamental rights were emphasized considering Pakistan's minorities, not just other religions (Hindus and Christians) but also other ethnicities (Pashtun, Baloch, Bengali, Sindhi) and different interpretations of Islam. Even so, the Resolution blends fundamental rights with religion. We are to remember Jinnah's August 1947 discourse where he said that religion had nothing to do with the business of the state. Unsurprisingly, the first ones to object to this preamble of the Constitution were Hindu members of the assembly. To that purpose, Sris Chandra Chattopadhyay made reference to Jinnah's 1947 speech. In the debate that followed, Birat Chandra Mandal, another Hindu member of the assembly, mentioned that Jinnah meant for Pakistan to be a secular state. Others argued that Islam was not meant to be a private affair but a public one, and that the Resolution was only a preamble to an Islamic constitution. In support of the Resolution, Maulana Shabbir Ahmed Osmani made references to Jinnah's Eid 1945 discourse. Jinnah's discourses had different interpretations. The debate, thus, was served.

A contentious part of the Resolution was: "Muslims shall be enabled to order their lives in the individual and collective spheres in accordance with the teachings and requirements of Islam as set out in the Holy Quran and the Sunnah" (Khan 2001, 93). The question with these "requirements of Islam" is: who is to interpret what is required and what is not? The same debate surfaces when considering Sharia in Pakistan: whose Islam? Jinnah and the leaders of the League were well aware that the plurality of Muslim groups in Pakistan could be a threat to unity, if one vision was to be imposed on others. Although a big majority of Muslims in Pakistan are Sunnis, this does not mean that they all follow the same schools of thought (see Figure 1). The Hanafi *madhhab* is the prevalent *fiqh* school, but there are minorities who do not accept it, such as the Shia or the *Ahl-e Hadith*. Even those who are Hanafis, such as the Deobandis and Barelvis, have different interpretations of the same *madhhab*. As illustrated in Figures 1 and 2, Sunnis and Shia have different interpretations of Islam. Then, what is the meaning of an Islamic system?

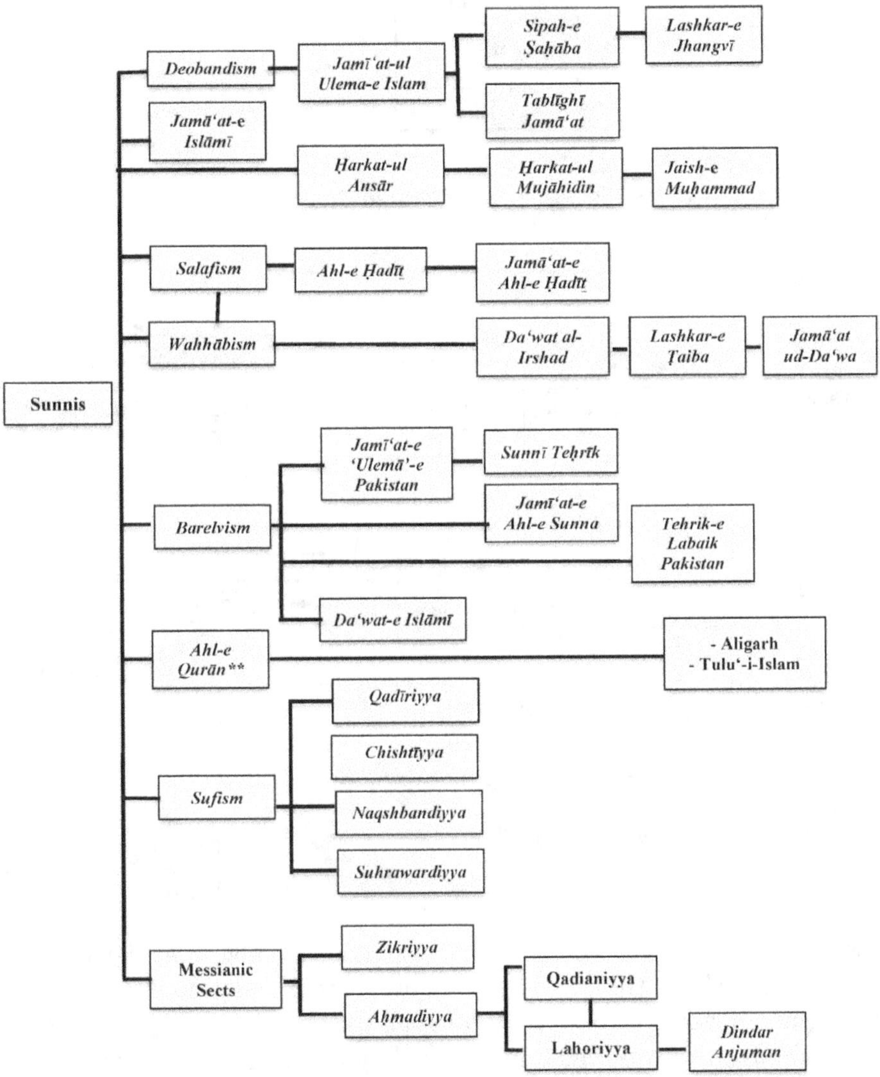

Figure 1: Sunni schools of thought, political parties, and other groups in Pakistan.
*Source: Author's elaboration based on Ahmad (1999); **Qasmi (2011).*

The Objectives Resolution was passed, regardless of minorities' concerns for their safety. At the same time, while the TNT saw a threat to Islam in the Hindu majority, Pakistan began to see the enemy within in "bad" Muslims or wrong interpretations of Islam. After the Resolution

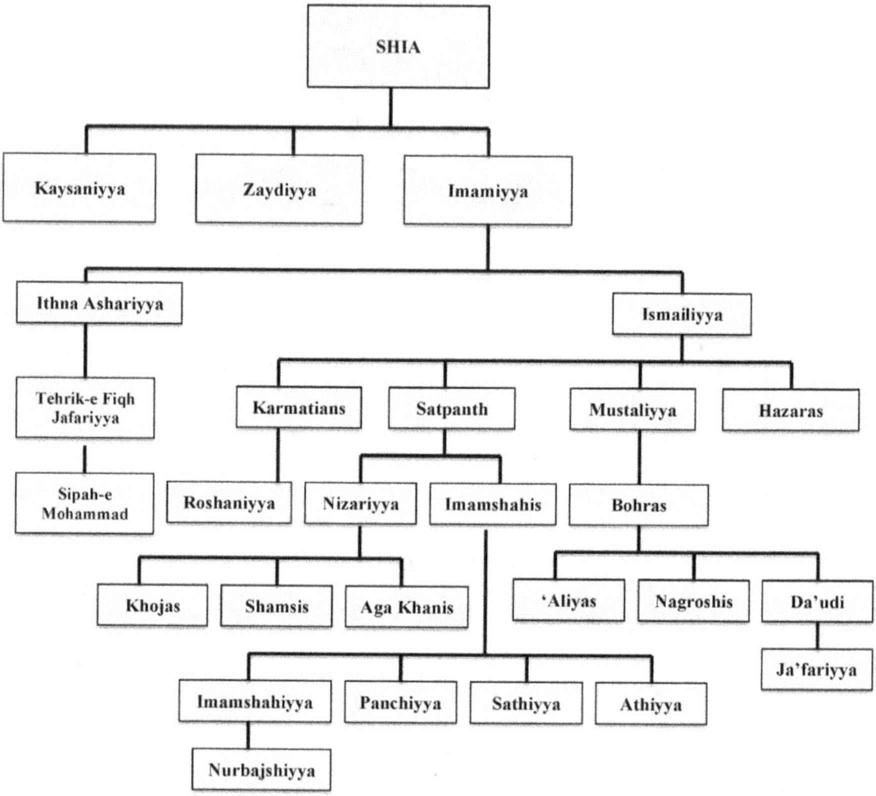

Figure 2: Shia groups/parties.

Source: *Hollister (1979); Ballesteros Peiró (2013); author's elaboration.*

was passed, some still considered it was not enough. More Islam was needed; true Islam. The debate slowly progressed to defining who was a (true) Muslim and who was not a Muslim.

Defining who was Muslim further divided Pakistan. As mentioned, Islam—as the main source of identity ("Muslims are a nation")—had to be further described, defined, or demarcated. Reform movements had evolved during the nineteenth and twentieth centuries, and they never lost momentum. Religion proved to be an easy way to rally support and mobilize the population. The first target was the Ahmadiyya community. In 1953, there were unprecedented protests against Ahmadis. Those who had opposed the creation of Pakistan—such as the members of the Jamā'at-e Islāmī (JI) and the Ahrar (former members of the Congress party who broke away from it in the 1920s)—found a cause to attack a better-off community and try to take their place (in politics, business, education). Thus, they faulted them for lacking loyalty to the new state in the past and for lacking patriotism. From the 1930s, the Ahrar had been demanding Ahmadis to be declared non-Muslims, due to their belief that their leader, Mirza Ghulam Ahmad, was a *nabi* (albeit a lower one, only outranked by the Prophet Muhammad). This campaign led impoverished and famished people (because of the hike in basic product prices and food shortages) to fall prey to hate speeches made by Ahrar leaders. The result was looting, attacks, the destruction of property, and murders of Ahmadis. Former patterns of Hindu-Muslim communalism had been adopted to purge Pakistan of those who were considered to be untrue Muslims.

An example of the nature of this problem is the investigation conducted by members of the Supreme Court on the causes of the riots. In 1954, a court of inquiry published the results, also known as the Munir Report (after chief Justice Muhammad Munir, who led the investigation). The committee found that not a single *ulama* (Deobandi, JI, Barelvi, *Ahl-e Hadith*) they interviewed gave the same definition of who is a Muslim, and they fell short of using *takfirism* against each other. Had they all followed their ideas of denouncing *kuffar* and declaring them *murtad*, there would not have been a single Pakistani left. The judges who authored the report expressed (Khan 2001, 121):

> Keeping in view the several definitions of a Muslim given by the ulema, need we make any comment except that no two learned divines are agreed on this fundamental. If we attempt our own definition as each learned divined has done and that definition differs from that given by any one of the ulema, *we remain Muslims according to the view of that alim but kafirs according to the definition of everyone else* (italics added).

The Constitution was passed in 1956, soon to be abrogated and followed by the imposition of martial law. It was based on a Westminster system of government: power was divided between executive, legislative, and judicial branches. It provided for the creation of a federal state, with a bicameral Parliament (National Assembly and Senate), a president as head of the state, Provincial Assemblies, and a Supreme Court (see Figure 3). It also declared Pakistan an Islamic state. It emphasized the implementation of measures that could facilitate Muslims "to order their

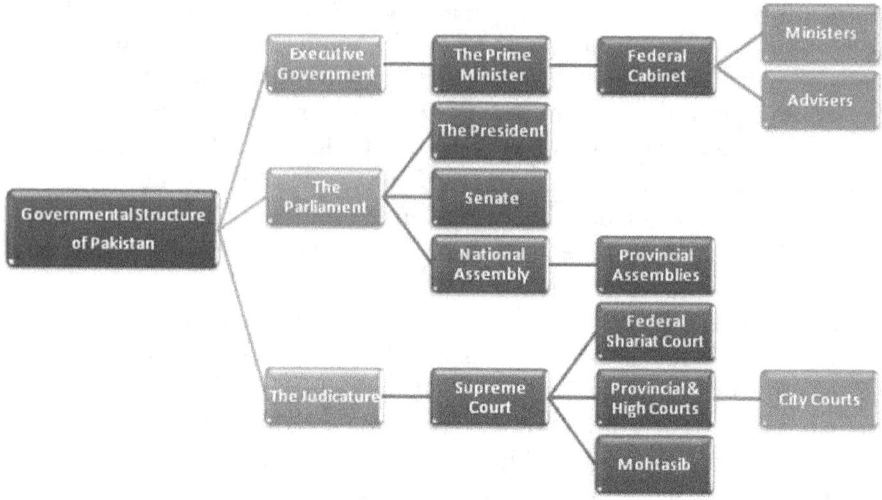

Figure 3: Government structure of Pakistan.
Source: National Democratic Foundation.

lives in accordance with the Quran and *Sunna*," and a few objects of debate were introduced, such as the prohibition of drinking, gambling, and prostitution. Other issues introduced in the principles of the state policy had to do with discouraging "parochial, tribal, and racial feelings among Muslims." These last elements refer to provincial affiliations, especially between Bengalis (who were a numerical majority of the population), Balochis, and Pashtuns, and to a lesser degree Sindhis; virtually everyone except Punjabis. Thus, by discouraging local affiliations, the government considered that it had strengthened the centralization of power and reduced divisions. It nonetheless alienated centuries-old traditions that predated Pakistan and the arrival of Islam. Instead of convincing Bengalis, Balochis, or Pashtuns to integrate with the state, it sent them the message that their other sources of identity were problematic. Nationalism was popular with these groups, and the feeling that the central government was fragile still prevailed.

It was not surprising that the Constitution was abrogated in 1958 and martial law was imposed. A real democracy meant that power would be transferred to the eastern side, to East Pakistan. Bengalis constituted around 53 percent of Pakistan's population, and the leaders of

West Pakistan were obsessed with neutralizing that majority. The western half concentrated power: the capital was in Karachi and the administration was in the hands of those who migrated from India (also known as *mohajirs*). Pluralism was made into a real threat by marginalizing communities. One of the main steps toward the alienation of provinces was the imposition of Urdu as the official language, with English being co-official. Both languages were not indigenous to any of the peoples that inhabited Pakistan. In the process of providing a national identity—or, as Talbot (1998) names it, the process of "Pakistanisation"—"the adoption of Urdu as a common *lingua franca* was less effective promoting a national Pakistani identity than Bengali, Sindhi, Pashto, Saraiki or Balochi have been in articulating ethnic identity" (Talbot 1998, 26). Bengali was not recognized as co-official until 1956. Apparently, for leaders in West Pakistan, Bengalis were not Muslim enough. Some suspicions arose from the fact that their language was not written in the Perso-Arabic alphabet but in Nagari script, from left to right, sharing this language with Hindu Bengalis not only in East Pakistan but in India as well. Although other languages were recognized in the 1973 Constitution, it took a long time to accept Pashtu, Balochi, and Sindhi as state languages.

Progression: Evolution of Islamic principles in the Constitution

One of the Islamic features of the Constitution (1956) is Article 198: "no law shall be enacted which is repugnant to the injunctions of Islam as laid down in the Holy Quran and the Sunna," and that existing laws "shall be brought into conformity with such injunctions." This clause remained in the 1962 and 1973 Constitutions, contained in Part IX: Islamic Provisions. The evolution of the state and conflicts between communities were finally reflected in the last Constitution of Pakistan, acknowledging the sectarian differences. Currently, Article 227 of the Constitution 1973 states[8]:

> Article 227: Provisions relating to the Holy Qur'an and Sunnah.
>
> All existing laws shall be brought in conformity with the Injunctions of Islam as laid down in the Holy Quran and Sunnah, in this Part referred to as the Injunctions of Islam, and no law shall be enacted which is repugnant to such Injunctions.

[8] Constitution of Pakistan: http://www.pakistani.org/pakistan/constitution/part9.html.

[Explanation: In the application of this clause to the personal law of any Muslim sect, the expression "Quran and Sunnah" shall mean the Quran and Sunnah as interpreted by that sect.]

In order to help with the interpretation of Islamic laws, given that the big majority of members of Parliament were not *ulama*, the government created different institutions to consider the laws redacted and passed by the legislative body (National Assembly). Different successive governments provided for different institutional bodies. Parliament is the institution that legislates, and the Islamic bodies recommend or advise on the suitability of laws according to their Islamic interpretation. Legislators can either accept or refuse these. Constitutional guarantees from 1956 on provided for the creation of an Islamic Council.[9] The president of the state nominates its chairman, and its functions are included in Article 230:

(1) The functions of the Islamic Council shall be,
   a. to make *recommendations* to the—Majlis-e Shoora (Parliament)—and the Provincial Assemblies as to the ways and means of enabling and encouraging the Muslims of Pakistan to order their lives individually and collectively in all respects in accordance with the principles and concepts of Islam as enunciated in the Holy Quran and Sunnah;
   b. to *advise* a House, a Provincial Assembly, the President or a Governor on any question referred to the Council as to whether a proposed law is or not repugnant to the Injunctions of Islam;
   c. to make recommendations as to the measures for bringing existing laws into conformity with the Injunctions of Islam and the stages by which such measures should be brought into effect; and
   d. to compile in a suitable form, for the guidance of—Majlis-e Shoora (Parliament)—and the Provincial Assemblies, such Injunctions of Islam as can be given legislative effect (italics added).

The president was to nominate whomever he deemed suitable for the Council (for a period of three years) and would also be able to dismiss any member he considered unsuitable. Thus, the advisory council was

[9]The 1962 Constitution would name it the Advisory Council of Islamic Ideology. The 1973 Constitution named it the Council of Islamic Ideology.

subordinated to the executive, legislative, and judiciary bodies.[10] This subordination of Islamic bodies has been at the root of Islamist demands. A section of Islamic scholars does not agree with the primacy of the Constitution (irrespective of it containing Islamic clauses). Protests demanding the introduction of Sharia soon followed, especially when the different governments failed to provide the basic means for the population.

1973 Constitution: Islamic socialism

Pakistani leaders did not have any qualms about using religion for political purposes. Even the first military dictator who imposed martial law in 1958, Mohammed Ayub Khan—known for his secular leanings and his contempt for religious figures (known as *mullas* or *maulanas*)—used religion as a tool in times of unpopularity. He ruled Pakistan until 1969 and was followed by another military dictator: Yahya Khan. The first general elections in Pakistan took place in December 1970. The two main leaders were secular and presented socialist leanings: Zulfikar Ali Bhutto was a native of Sindh province and founder of the Pakistan Peoples Party (PPP); and Sheikh Mujibur Rehman was the Bengali nationalist founder of the Awami League (AL). East Pakistan's AL won a majority of the seats (160 of 300) in the National Assembly, and 288 of 300 seats in the Bengali provincial assembly (Talbot 1998, 201). PPP got 81 seats in the National Assembly, and all parties of the western part combined, 138 seats. Western leaders did not want the Bengali party in the central government. The military had changed the capital to Islamabad, so power could be closer to their headquarters in Rawalpindi. The inability of Yahya Khan, then president, and Ali Bhutto to share power with the winners of the elections led to rising tensions in the East. Eventually, circumstances precipitated a civil war that led to the independence of Pakistan's eastern half and the creation of Bangladesh at the end of 1971.

[10] The powers of the president have varied, depending on the form of government adopted. Pakistan has gone from a hyperpresidential to a presidential to a parliamentary system. The executive was concentrated in the president through the introduction of Article 58.2(b) in the 8th Amendment of the Constitution, 1985. Presidentialism is more usual in military governments, while parliamentarism was reinforced in 2008, when President Zardari devolved power to the prime minister and approved the 18th Amendment.

In what was left of Pakistan, leaders could not come to terms with the fact that the division proved the TNT to be wrong. Muslims of India were not a nation. Islam (or rather, its instrumentalization) failed to provide cohesion in Pakistan. The country had become two different nations that had fought a terrible war. But instead of trying to establish a different base for future generations and look for other sources of identity, Bhutto turned toward the Middle East, and the answer was "more Islam." The identity of Pakistan was still considered as being in danger, even without the Bengali majority. There were parallel nationalist and separatist claims in Balochistan and the NWFP that were brutally crushed. These perpetuated the fear of insecurity, of further divisions and enhanced the power of the military, which took it on itself to protect the physical and ideological frontiers of Pakistan. Islam would thus be heavily relied on, and Islamism was the ideology to counterbalance nationalism. Bhutto, the socialist leader, was not unaware of the power that religion could have to gather support, especially in times of economic recession. While he was a secular man, his government approved the third Constitution (1973), which did not essentially change the Islamic clauses included in the previous ones. Islam was still the official religion and the president and prime minister were to be Muslims.

Talbot (1998) identified the main troubles with Bhutto's government that were shared by civilian leaders all along. That is, "how to assert the authority of the elected institutions of the state over the military and bureaucracy, establish a functioning federal system and resolve the role of Islam in constitutional theory and practice" (Talbot 1998, 217). But Bhutto could not break the old dynamics of patronage networks. Ideology proved to have a weaker appeal to Pakistani crowds. People voted for politicians who could deliver services, locally and in the short term. The only ideas that seemed capable of mobilizing the masses had more to do with tradition and Islamic causes. The opposition and Islamists were quick to manipulate people's legitimate claims (food shortages and a dearth of education, health, water, or electricity) to attack the government. Bringing about a revolution such as land reform, however attractive, met with the opposition of those entrenched in the system. It was extremely difficult to go against the landowning elite, to which Bhutto belonged, and divide their lands and enforce taxes. They were extremely powerful and constituted the basis for the perpetuation of economic and political patronage at local, provincial, and national levels. Also, India had conducted nuclear tests in 1974, and Pakistan was brought to the brink of recession to pursue its own nuclear agenda to match India's capabilities. The search for nuclear parity had a negative economic effect on development.

Bhutto witnessed countrywide protests by the end of his tenure and before, during, and after the 1977 elections. Mobilization, headed by Islamists (with the backing of the military), denounced socialism as un-Islamic and demanded more Islamic laws. Bhutto, under pressure, made several concessions that were more cosmetic than real efforts to establish an Islamic state. Among them was his acceptance of the ban on alcohol consumption and of the closure of nightclubs. These measures were half-hearted, as alcohol was still available.

The 1974 anti-Ahmadi riots were led once again by Ahrar (organized in a political party called the Majlis-e Ahrar-e Islam) and the JI. But they were not alone. Other parties, such as Tehrik-e Istiqlal, and bar associations joined the protests. Death and chaos took over different areas, especially Rabwah, where the Ahmadiyya has its Pakistani base. Initially, Bhutto opposed the demand to declare Ahmadis non-Muslims. He tried to buy some time by referring the issue to the Advisory Council of Islamic Ideology. The question was brought to the National Assembly by mid-June. Although the PPP had a majority in the assembly, most opposition parties (except the National Awami Party) joined hands in demanding the declaration of Ahmadis as a (non-Muslim) minority. Bhutto tried to give it time and debate the issue outside Parliament (on the basis that it was a religious matter; Paracha 2013). But the opposition argued that it had to be debated in the National Assembly because "they told him that the constitution had declared Pakistan as an Islamic Republic so how could he claim that a religious issue had no place in the National Assembly?" (Paracha 2013) The result of the pressure on the government was the adoption of the Second Amendment to the Constitution, which declared Ahmadis a minority and imposed sanctions on their behaving as Muslims. A clause was added in Article 260 (3), negatively specifying who is a Muslim. While no one seemed to be able to define who was a Muslim, at least they had agreed on who was not:

(3) In the Constitution and all enactments and other legal instruments, unless there is anything repugnant in the subject or context

a. "Muslim" means a person who believes in the unity and oneness of Almighty Allah, in the absolute and unqualified finality of the Prophethood of Muhammad (peace be upon him), the last of the prophets, and does not believe in, or recognize as a prophet or religious reformer, any person who claimed or claims to be a prophet, in any sense of the word or of any description whatsoever, after Muhammad (peace be upon him); and

b. "Non-Muslim" means a person who is not a Muslim and includes a person belonging to the Christian, Hindu, Sikh, Buddhist or Parsi community, a person of the Quadiani Group or the Lahori Group who call themselves "Ahmadis" or by any other name or a Bahai, and a person belonging to any of the Scheduled Castes.

The definition of Muslim was a choice made in a way that excluded a community due to its beliefs. Even if the Lahori Ahmadis do believe in the finality of Prophet Muhammad, it made no difference. Exclusion would from then on be the key to defining who is a true Muslim. But protests did not stop there; excluding Ahmadis from Islam was not enough. The following group to be targeted was the Zikris, a minority group on the Baloch coast of Makran. Protest and violence marked the way with which untrue Muslims would be revealed.

Zia ul-Haq's Islamization process: The power of polarization

Zia ul-Haq headed the coup of July 1977 that ousted Bhutto from power. He promised to hold elections within 90 days, which he failed to do. In order to gain legitimacy, he was set to establish an Islamic system he called *Nizam-e Islam*. Zia imposed the interpretation of the majority, that is, the interpretation of a few selected scholars of Hanafi law. As a military and religious leader, Zia considered it necessary to preserve Pakistan's character as an ideological state and thus protect the ideology based on Islam from those who could harm it from within and without.

In addition, the beginning of his rule coincided with the Iranian Revolution, the Iran-Iraq war, and the Soviet invasion of Afghanistan. The polarization of different confessions was unprecedented. Violence increased to limits never witnessed before. The imprint of Saudi aid to Afghanistan affected Pakistan. A proxy war was fought between Saudis and Iranians, taking advantage of the widely held belief that indigenous practices were not Islamic enough. Policies were oriented towards Arabization[11]; towards making Pakistan less South Asian and more Middle Eastern.

[11]There were differences between those considered noble (*ashraf*) and the converts from Hinduism and Buddhism, usually from low castes (*ajlaf*), considered polluted.

As Malik (1998, 7) describes, all religious groups in Pakistan "hold different ideological and theological positions … they recruit their members from different social strata and can be identified with different regions." The two groups in Pakistan that are followers (*muqallidun*) of the Hanafi *fiqh* are Deobandis and Barelvis. Both groups consider themselves to be *ahl-e sunna wa-l-jama'at*. Some Deobandis, though, are close to Salafist positions. The main bone of contention between both groups (Deobandis and Barelvis) is the nature of the figure of Prophet Muhammad. JI is a Sunni avant-garde group. It distinguishes itself from others through an organization that does not rely on traditional institutions but that selectively recruits members among the best university graduates. In South Asia, traditional institutions are *auqaf* (religious endowments), *madaris* (religious schools), and *khanqah* (hospices). JI follows an Islamist ideology that refuses tradition as represented by Deobandis and Barelvis. An imposition of Hanafi law also left out the *Ahl-e Hadith*, who refuse all *madhahib*; Wahhabis, who are closer to a Hanbali interpretation of law; the Shia Twelvers, who follow Ja'fari law; and all Ismaili groups.

Zia's Islamization polarized the population, and nationwide protests followed. He found special opposition from the reinvigorated Shia, who had the Iranian Revolution as a source of inspiration. Islamization was conducted on four fronts: (1) judicial reforms; (2) economic programs "Islamizing" economy through the introduction of more Islamic taxes; (3) the introduction of an Islamic criminal code; and (4) Islamic education.

Zia endorsed Presidential Order 3 (1979) that established Sharia benches at the High Courts. In 1980, a parallel body of the Federal Sharia Court was created in Islamabad, with the capacity to declare invalid any law or provision of a law it deemed repugnant to the principles of Islam as laid down in the Holy Quran and the Sunna. For the first time in its history, the *ulama* were appointed as judges to this court. Likewise, the composition of the Council of Islamic Ideology (CII) was changed. Members with more "secular" education were replaced with members with "Islamic" education from among the traditional religious elites. Several visits of international Islamic organizations, especially from Saudi Arabia, also contributed to an increased presence of *ulama* with Salafi inclinations. A pro-government council issued a ruling that condemned "elections through political parties" and considered that the most

---

Impurity was henceforth to be considered something to fight with "pure" Islam, that is, Arab Islam.

Islamic system of government was presidentialism. This provided Islamic legitimacy to Zia's rule. Between 1977 and 1984, resignations of CII's Shia, Barelvi, secular, and JI members followed, as they disagreed with those selected by Zia. *Qazi* courts were also established, with *ulama* with a basic madrassa degree acting as judges (*qazis*) (Talbot 1998, 274).

On the economic front, the *Zakat* and *Ushr* ordinance (1980) was imposed on savings, gold, silver, jewels, properties, bank accounts, insurance policies, investments (2.5 percent to be levied annually on the first day of *Ramadan*), and land (5 percent of produce) without prior notice. From voluntary alms, *zakat* and *ushr* were made into compulsory taxes. Shia (between 10 to 15 percent of the population) held a protest in Islamabad in September 1980. It was the biggest mobilization of Shia in Pakistan's history. They succeeded, and the tax was withdrawn. Some Sunnis even posed as Shia to avoid paying taxes, so the law was amended to adapt it to Shia law. Nonetheless, these taxes failed to curb poverty.

For Zia, the main thrust was to control the institutions. He approved the *Hudood* Ordinances, which introduced penal codes inspired by an interpretation of *hadd* and *tazir* laws. The penalties introduced included stoning to death and flogging (for the consumption of alcohol and *zina* offenses: adultery and fornication), the amputation of hands (for theft), and an extension of the death penalty to a wider range of crimes. Ahmadis were to be punished with death if they were found to pose as Muslims (see Table 1). They could go to jail for simply saying "*as-salam-u aleikum*."

The reform of the education boards (*dini madaris*) introduced changes in traditional religious schools to bring them under government control. These boards were organized according to ideological schools: JI, Deobandis, Barelvis, *Ahl-e Hadith*, and Shias. Each had their own board of madrassas that they administered independently. Each group controlled the content of their education, which was key to maintaining their position and ideological preeminence, and to gaining devotees. The government tried to homogenize the schools' curricula in order to bring uniformity and officially finish with religious differences. In January 1979, a Committee for *Dini Madaris* was formed with 27 members: 16 nominated by the Ministry of Religious Affairs (four Barelvi maulanas, two Deobandis, one Shia, and one *Ahl-e Hadith*, five deans of universities, two members of the Ministry of Religious Affairs, and another member of the Ministry of Education), six members nominated by the government (three *Ahl-e Hadith* and a Deobandi, a pedagogue, and a scientist), and five members nominated by the Committee (three teachers, of which two were Deobandis and one Shia, plus a government worker and a pedagogue)

Table 1: Summary of offenses related to religion.

Section of the penal code	Year of introduction	Offense	Sentence	Bailable and cognizable?
Art. 295	1860	Injuring or defiling place of worship, with intent to insult the religion of any class	Up to two years' imprisonment, rigorous or simple, or fine, or both	Bailable and cognizable
Art. 296	1860	Disturbing religious assembly	Up to one year of imprisonment, or fine, or both	Bailable and cognizable
Art. 297	1860	Trespassing on burial places, and other offenses	Up to one year of imprisonment, rigorous or simple, or fine, or both	Bailable and cognizable
Art. 298	1860	Uttering words, etc., with deliberate intent to wound religious feelings	Up to one year of imprisonment, rigorous or simple, or fine, or both	Bailable and noncognizable
Art. 295-A	1927	Deliberate and malicious acts intended to outrage religious feelings of any class by insulting its religion or religious beliefs	Up to ten years' imprisonment, rigorous or simple, fine, or both	Nonbailable and noncognizable

(*Continued*)

Table 1: (*Continued*)

Section of the penal code	Year of introduction	Offense	Sentence	Bailable and cognizable?
Art. 298-A	1980	Use of derogatory remarks in respect of holy personages	Up to three years imprisonment, fine, or both	Bailable and cognizable
Art. 295-B	1982	Defiling the Holy Quran	Mandatory imprisonment for life	Nonbailable and cognizable
Art. 298-B	1984	Misuse of epithets, descriptions, titles, etc., reserved for certain holy personages or places	Up to three years and fine	Nonbailable and cognizable
Art. 298-C	1984	"Person of Quadiani group or the Lahori group (who call themselves 'Ahmadis' or by any other name)" who "directly or indirectly" pose as Muslim	Up to three years imprisonment, rigorous or simple, and fine	Nonbailable and cognizable
Art. 295-C	1986	Use of derogatory remarks, etc., in respect of the Holy Prophet	Mandatory death sentence	Nonbailable and cognizable

Source: *International Commission of Jurists 2015, 13.*

(Malik 1998, 133). The composition rendered the Committee basically dysfunctional, as it was difficult for a group of such disparity to agree on common Islamic tenets.

Certain Deobandi groups and Barelvis also opposed the administration of the distribution of funds through the department of *auqaf*. Religious schools closer to the government received more funds, while those ideologically or religiously opposed to Zia's policies were marginalized. There were violent clashes between different members of different schools. Even Sufis, who usually stayed away from political involvement, held countrywide protests. The Islamization program thus proved to be more divisive than any other policy implemented before.

Other measures to control behavior were also approved. The 1981 Ramadan Ordinance made eating, drinking, and smoking during the holy month punishable by law. Some *ulama* wanted to impose dress codes on women, while beards and the *salwar-kameez* (instead of Western suits) were encouraged for men. Government workers were compelled to stop working and pray. All these measures did not make Pakistan more Islamic or Pakistanis better Muslims. Theft, alcoholism, rape (with women ending up in jail because they were considered adulterous under *zina* law) still occurred, and wide corruption still marred the different courts. Justice was not easier to find, the juxtaposition of jurisdictions brought chaos, and the "[c]ourt was vulnerable to manipulation in order to reach politically desired results" (Khan 2001, 641).

One of the most controversial laws approved during Zia's era was the law on blasphemy. Although the British first introduced the concept (see Table 1), Pakistani leaders did nothing to revoke it. Zia's government introduced harsh criminal charges against those accused of having blasphemed, including the death penalty. The punishments (Articles 295, 295-A and 298) where feelings are involved open the door to irrational and random accusations, as proof of such a crime cannot easily be objective. Similarly, "intent" is also difficult to prove. Some of the punishments in place during Zia's era particularly targeted the Ahmadis. However, Christians have also been victims of religious zealots, whose feelings' protection seems to be high on the government's agenda.

Conclusion

During Zia's period, several sectarian groups were formed, basically fighting either to make Pakistan a Sunni state (according to their particular

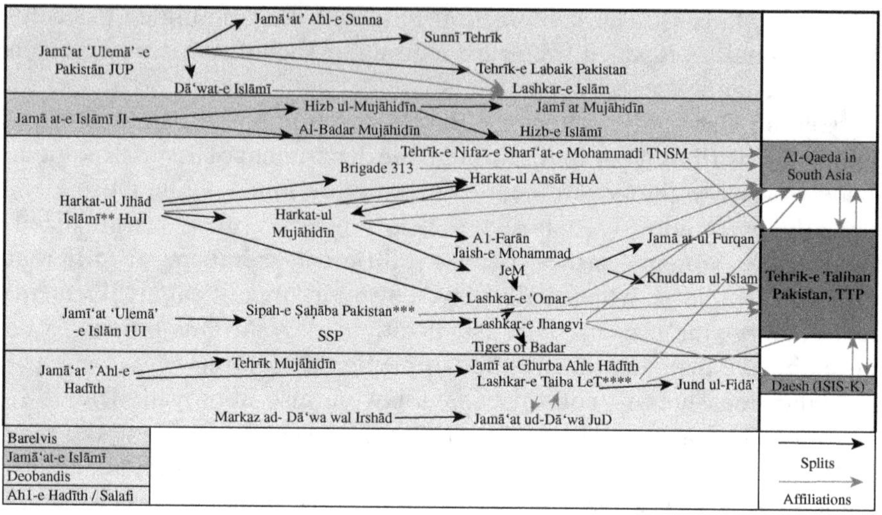

*Figure 4: Splits and ideological radicalization of politico-religious parties.**

Source: *Author's elaboration.*

Note: *Degrees are approximate. Groups have been ordered according to ideological affinities **HuJI/HuM/HuA are also ideologically close to Deobandism ***SSP took the name Ahl-e Sunna wa-l-Jamā'at (ASWJ) **** LeT latest name is Pasban-e Ahl-e Ḥadīth.

interpretation) or to impose and defend Shia rights. Some of these groups (*Sipah-e Sahaba* Pakistan, *Lashkar-e Jhangvi*, *Tehrik-e Jafariyya*) have evolved and continue to pursue divisive policies. Pakistan, as seen in Figure 4, is plagued by a myriad of groups claiming to represent true Islam and fighting (with different degrees of violence) to establish their utopian visions of a perfect Islamic society. As there are as many ideas on what an Islamic society looks like as there are Muslims, divisions are to be expected. These disagreements are a consequence of the legacies of Partition as much as of leaders' policies throughout Pakistan's history. The repudiation of dissent, though, has its origins in the Pakistan movement. By linking Islam to the state, identity was interrelated to religion. Thus, discord was turned into an anti-state and anti-Islamic threat. This condemned other identity affiliations (linguistic, ethnic, provincial, religious) as being against the nationalist narrative. Unsurprisingly, local nationalism and separatism became an alternative for marginalized groups.

Different leaders used Islam as a distraction from their own failures, resulting in a widespread lack of governance and legitimacy. Every government, instead of providing basic welfare, competed to preserve its elite interests. The military, in turn, goes against the interests of Pakistan's real security concerns. Regardless of who governed after Zia, his legacy was almost impossible to erase. Religious scholars entered the institutions and each one, following their different agendas, perpetuated divisions. Every attempt to unite Pakistanis using religion has backfired. Today, repealing the Blasphemy Law is a delicate issue, one that can bring death to those espousing this cause. Few judges dare try blasphemy cases without fearing for their lives, if the accused was to be acquitted. Cases remain unresolved forever. Accusers, as they are unable to testify to the blasphemy (as they themselves would commit the crime), cannot bring a proper testimony to court.

There is a lack of a free national debate. Identity feels constantly threatened, not only because Sharia has been interpreted in myriad ways, but also because few agree on what an Islamic state should look like, where to set the limits, or what role morality should play in the state's government, policies, and laws. The question that Malik asks in his masterly work on the *Colonialization of Islam* in Pakistan gains a renewed meaning: "what is to be Islamized in a country which, by its *raison d'étre*, is supposed to be Islamic and has been created for the Muslims of the subcontinent?" (Malik 1998, 289). For Islamists, everything must still be Islamized, and Sharia is always the answer to Pakistan's problems. Meanwhile, minorities and even the mainstream population bear the brunt of an obsession that has turned anyone into a bad Muslim. Pakistan still finds it necessary to link national identity to Islam, thus never giving up on its search for the perfect citizen, the perfect Muslim.

In the meantime, few have really tried good governance for a change.

References

Ahmad, A. 1999. *Studies in the Islamic Culture in the Indian Environment*. New Delhi, India: Oxford University Press.

Ballesteros Peiró, A. 2013. *Comportamientos religiosos y sectarismo en el islam pakistaní. Estudio de la comunidad pakistaní en España [Religious Behaviors and Sectarianism in Pakistan's Islam. A Study of the Pakistani Community in Spain]*. PhD diss., Universidad Autónoma de Madrid.

Cohen, Stephen P. 2004. *The Idea of Pakistan*. New Delhi, India: Oxford University Press.

Cutts, Elmer H. 1953. "The Background of Macaulay's Minute." *American Historical Review*, 58, no. 4 (July): 824–53.

Hashimy, S. Y. ed. 1955. *Islam as an Ethical and a Political Ideal: Iqbal's Maiden English Lecture*. Lahore, Pakistan: Orientalia.

Hollister, John N. 1979. *The Shi'a of India*. New Delhi: Munshiram Manoharlal Publishers.

International Commission of Jurists. 2015. *On Trial: The Implementation of Pakistan's Blasphemy Laws*. November 2015, Geneva. https://www.icj.org/wp-content/uploads/2015/12/Pakistan-On-Trial-Blasphemy-Laws-Publications-Thematic-Reports-2015-ENG.pdf.

Jawed, Nasim A. 1999. *Islam's Political Culture. Religion and Politics in Predivided Pakistan*. Karachi, Pakistan: Oxford University Press.

Khan, Hamid. 2001. *Constitutional and Political History of Pakistan*. Oxford: Oxford University Press.

Malik, Jamal. 1998. *Colonization of Islam: Dissolution of Traditional Institutions in Pakistan*. First published 1996. Delhi, India: Manohar Publishers & Distributors.

Moore, Robin J. 2001. "Jinnah and the Pakistan Demand." In *India's Partition. Process, Strategy and Mobilization*, edited by Mushirul Hassan, 160–97. New Delhi, India: Oxford University Press.

Paracha, Nadeem F. 2013. "The 1974 Ouster of the 'Heretics": What Really Happened? *Dawn*, November 21, 2013. https://www.dawn.com/news/1057427.

Qasmi, Ali Usman. 2011. *Questioning the Authority of the Past. The Ahl al-Qur'an Movements in the Punjab*. Karachi, Pakistan: Oxford University Press.

Talbot, Ian. 1998. *Pakistan. A Modern History*. New Delhi, India: Oxford University Press.

https://doi.org/10.1142/9781800611689_0014

Chapter 14

Learning from the Sharia Debates

Muhammad Khalid Masud

Shariat Appellate Bench,
Supreme Court of Pakistan, Islamabad, Pakistan
khalid.masud@gmail.com

Academic studies mostly label public discourses on Islamic legal issues in the twenty-first century as "Sharia debates" (for instance, Kogelmann 2006 and Mahdi *et al.* 2006 on Nigeria and Africa; Ghobadzadeh 2010 and Aftab 2019 on Australia; Reda 2015 and Korteweg 2006, 2008, 2012, Selby and Korteweg 2012, Selby 2013 on Canada; Mfumbusa 2014 on Tanzania; and Schroter 2014 on Indonesia). Even though there are no more than 15 countries in which Sharia is the state law or source of law, Sharia is still the source of Muslim personal law in most Muslim societies. The Sharia debates began with the rise of nation-states in the twentieth century. They differ contextually, but they reveal visible shifts in their focus from local to global concepts and universal values in the present century. Toward the end of the twentieth century, Sharia had become the most prominent subject of intense, and even violent debates in some Muslim countries, such as Afghanistan, Iran, Nigeria, and Pakistan (Masud 2019). Muslim minorities in some countries—such as India, Great Britain, and Canada—also called for recognition, application, and arbitration of Islamic personal laws. A comprehensive study of these Sharia debates in the globalizing world is important but cannot be done in a short chapter. The subject is so vast that *Sharia Incorporated* (Otto 2010), an unbelievably brilliant analytical book-length survey of Sharia laws in modern Muslim states, had to limit its overview to 12 countries only.

This chapter focuses on South Africa because while interpreting the universal values of freedom, equality, and justice, the four South African legal traditions—indigenous customary, common, civil, and Sharia law—have raised some basic issues. Sharia debates on the issue of the "recognition of Muslim marriages" are deeply contextualized in this country.[1] While the public debate is greatly diverse and the Constitutional Court is dynamically open, judicial reasoning seems highly inflexible and politically rigid. This chapter explores what we can learn from a contextual study of Sharia After a brief note on the 'Sharia debates,' the chapter offers a contextual analysis of these debates in three sections. The first section 'South African Context' overviews the local social and legal conext and the second offers an analysis of the development of 'Muslim Personal Law' and focuses on the issue of the 'recognition of Muslim marriages' based on case law, constitutional court, and law reform commissions. The fourth section analyzes the five perspectives of debates on this issue: local politics, legal positivism, Muslim tradional and secular views and gender justice.

Sharia Debates in South Africa

Franz Kogelmann, a social anthropologist and expert in Islamic law in Africa, was probably the first to use the term "Sharia debate," for his research project at the University of Bayreuth, Germany, in 1999. Dissatisfied with the academic approaches to Sharia debates—which framed them as a conflict between Islam and the West or a clash between Muslim and Christian religious identities—he studied them as a movement of independence from colonial rule, in which formation of nation-states and unified legal systems faced the challenges of ethnic and religious diversity. These challenges differed in "character and scope from country to country" and, therefore, required a multidisciplinary and critical approach to political and legal development (Kogelmann 2008). According to Ebrahim Moosa, a South African public intellectual and presently Professor of Islamic Thought and Muslim Societies at the University of Notre Dame, United States, the colonial legacy introduced a significant shift by making the state an integral player in the construction of modern Muslim laws. "The traditional ulama preferred to sustain

---

[1] I am grateful to Professor Abdulkader Tayob, Chair in Islam, African Publics and Religious Values at the University of Cape Town, South Africa, for reading the early draft of this chapter and for his valuable comments.

the presumptions of the pre-colonial imaginary of Muslim law, irrespective of the resultant anachronism" (Moosa 2009, 176).

Sharia debates provide us with the opportunity not only to look critically at Sharia as a legal system in a modern secular nation-state context, but also to examine how Sharia and common and civil law systems interacted in the face of religious diversity and multiculturalism in the modern political context. In the words of Patrick Glenn, a leading comparative law expert at McGill University, Canada, "These debates have had Islamic thinkers responding to Western ideas, and Western ideas have also had to respond to Islamic ideas, though that has happened more in informal debate in the so-called 'developing countries' than in Western literature" (Glenn 2014, 224).

Studies on South Africa never fail to remind the reader that recognition of Muslim marriages is the most complicated debate in South Africa (Abduroaf 2013, 6, 2020; Amien 2010; Bakker 2009; Gabru 2004, 2; Manjoo 2007, 5; Moosa 1996; Moosa 2014; Rautenbach 2000). As recently as June 1, 2020, MP Ganief Hendricks, the leader of the al-Jama-ah Party, invited the attention of the South African Parliament to the predicament of Muslim families who lost their members in the COVID-19 pandemic. Families of those who were married under Islamic rites could not resolve legal issues because the courts refused to recognize the deceased as being validly married and their spouses and children as legal heirs. They were left without legal protections or safeguards. Responding to the question, Aaron Motsoaledi, Home Affairs Minister, said that the government had no powers to legalize Muslim marriages and, therefore, had no plans to amend the law about *nikah*, even temporarily. Hendricks protested, asking how a wife was supposed to feel when her husband died of coronavirus and the official death certificate stated that he was never married (Nkosi 2020). This impasse on the recognition of Muslim marriages needs to be critically explored. It is imperative to provide a contextual overview, even a brief one, of the development of South African law and politics as well as the history of Muslim communities in the country, and the development and role of religious authority in these communities.

South African Context

For more than five hundred years, South Africa has attracted seafarers, traders, and settlers from all over the world as a cape of hope. The land was a battleground for occupation between white settlers from European countries and indigenous tribes from other parts of Africa. Long wars during 1770–95 ended with the British occupation of the Cape. Another long war between the British and the Boer during 1899–1902 ended with the victory of the Boers, the South African descendants of the Dutch, German, and French settlers called Afrikaners. The South Africa Act (1909/1910) brought the colonies and republics of Cape, Natal, Transvaal, and Orange Free State together as a self-governing dominion within the British Commonwealth. The dominion was granted to the white minority, excluding the others from political participation. The South Africa Act (1910) declared independence under the name of the Union of South Africa (for different perspectives on this point, see Hansard 1931; O'Malley n.d.).

The Afrikaners united themselves to form the National Party (NP) and unified their colonies to establish the Union of South Africa. The African National Congress (ANC) was formed in 1912 to bring all African people together. In 1948, NP enforced white supremacy and racial segregation under the legal doctrine of apartheid, a codified system of racial stratification. This doctrine restricted citizenship rights to white people, and rest of the population was divided into the categories of colored, Indian, and Black; a defining hierarchy of legal status. Marriage between white people and people of other races was disallowed by the Prohibition of Mixed Marriages Act 55 of 1949, and property and voting rights of nonwhite people were denied in 1950. The ANC was banned in 1960 and its leaders were exiled or sent to prison.

In 1961, the South Africa left the Commonwealth after a referendum and had its first constitution, which declared South Africa a republic and restricted the right to vote to white people. The Republic of South Africa Constitution Act, 1983, created the Tricameral Parliament, with separate houses representing white, colored, and Indian people; the Black vote was limited to their homelands. ANC's long struggle to introduce democratic majority rule for all succeeded in 1991. Apartheid ended, and elections were announced. The ANC won the elections in 1994, and South Africa got its first constitution after apartheid. The 1994 interim Constitution declared the right to vote for all. It is also known as the declaration of rights or a charter of rights, because it lists the basic and fundamental rights and guarantees in place to protect people against infringement from public officials and private citizens. Constitutional law played a significant role in law reforms, which could not be initiated before 1994. Law reforms, nevertheless, faced technical and procedural difficulties.

One of these was the issue of recognition of Muslim marriages. The issue has been shaped by the peculiar development of South African law.

South African legal system

South African law developed as an integral part of the colonial history of the country. Social customs and norms constituting the law of indigenous societies were either explicitly cast aside or ignored, except where they were recognized as part of the colonial administration of native peoples (Klug 2002, 1485a). South African common law is a mixed system of civil and common law. The origin of South African civil law is traced to the Roman Dutch law that arrived in South Africa with the Dutch East India company in 1652. The British occupation of Cape in 1806 and British settlers brought English common law to South Africa. The Charter of Justice of 1827 and 1832 transformed the judicial system with codes of procedure and a professional judiciary. The civil law, however, was not replaced. The colonial principle was that the colonies retained their old laws unless they were repealed. According to Klug, "Racial discrimination and segregation became embedded in South African society from the earliest days of colonial penetration"; not introduced in 1948, even though the policy of apartheid is usually identified with the NP government (Klug 2002,1486a). Extending the franchise to Indians and "colored" and the exclusion of the African majority increased resistance to this segregation. The ANC adopted a Bill of Rights in 1990 and made it enforceable through the courts by making it part of the 1996 Constitution (Klug 2002, 1486b).

This duality allowed judges and courts to play a significant role in South Africa, as legislative reforms were comparatively slower. They relied on the Constitution as an authoritative source of law to fill gaps and reconcile contradictions between statutory and customary laws. They subjected both of them to the Constitution (Bakker 2009, 397, 403). Muslim and Jewish religious laws are treated as customary laws, but not authoritative unless they fulfill the requirements of South African law (Du Bois 2004, 5–8, 19–20, 48–9).

The significance of statutory law was enhanced by the doctrine of parliamentary sovereignty. Klug clarifies that the doctrine was however misused to justify the absolute authority of the white minority and, with reference to the philosophy of legal positivism, "Their[judges'] deference to the will of the sovereign and strict distinction between law and morals framed their interpretation of the law" (Klug 2002, 1487a). This tension in the legal system was redressed by the introduction of constitutional review, for which a new constitutional court was created. The Constitution adopted a "deep and substantive understanding of equality," which provided for affirmative action as a mechanism "to deal with the legacy of inequality and discrimination" (Klug 2002, 1487b). The Constitutional Court symbolizes constitutional supremacy as the highest court for all constitutional matters, whereas the Supreme Court of Appeal and Special Appellate Courts deal with other matters. The High Courts are sources of legal interpretation as superior courts at the provincial level, hearing appeals for lower courts in the country. Debate over the supremacy of Parliament was summed up by the former chief justice at the Truth Reconciliation Commission in 1998, who said that the courts had no power to question the validity of the laws that Parliament made. Lawyers associations argued that lawyers and courts mostly cooperated with the unjust political order under apartheid. The Commission concluded that one of the reasons for the longevity of apartheid was the superficial adherence to the "rule of law" (Klug 2002, 1490a).

Muslims in South Africa

Muslims in South Africa are a small minority (1.46 percent of the population, 2001 census), yet they feature prominently in the country's representative institutions since 1994. Having multiple identities and Islamic voices, Muslim communities are ethnically complex and sociologically diverse (Vahed 2004, 252, 278–9). South African Muslims consist of three ethnic groups who are concentrated in different regions in South Africa. The Southeast Asians—the Malays and Indonesians—came earlier in the seventeenth century and mostly settled in Western Cape. They speak the local common language, Afrikaans, and are generally well integrated into the local population. The South Asians, who arrived from India mostly in nineteenth century and settled in the Eastern regions of Natal and Transvaal, are educated and are well established in their professional fields, but not completely integrated with the local people. On the contrary, the Arabic-speaking Muslims who arrived from other regions of Africa are very well integrated (Esack 1997; Günther 2004; Tayob 1996, 2002; Vahed and Jeppie 2005, 253–70).

During the late 1970s and early 1980s, a number of Black youth embraced Islam as they found it to be a nonwhite, non-Christian and non-oppressive religion with a clear statement on the equality of all human beings. They adopted it as an ideology to resist apartheid. This might have encouraged the idea of an increasing number of Black Muslims in South Africa (Günther 2004).

Günther explains this multiplicity from the perspective of existing demographic phenomena of settlement that result from different historical and geographical roots of migration. The nature of the differences between the communities of the Western Cape and those of Natal and Transvaal seems to be cultural, ethnic, and linguistic, but closer examination reveals that there are considerable differences with regard to the questions of theology and religious practices. Both the cultural background and the historically rooted different social statuses shaped and still shape the corresponding religious institutions, rituals, and symbols (Günther 2004). Günther also noted that Muslim communities with a Southeast Asian background in the Western Cape developed a unique culture with a particular cultural flexibility. On the contrary, the cultural particularism in the Muslim communities with a South Asian background in Natal and Transvaal prevented the processes of acculturation. Apartheid reinforced this cultural difference further. It served as the basis for the "racial classification" of the apartheid ideology, according to which Indians and colored were privileged as a category between white and Black (Günther 2004).

Tayob extends this exclusivity to both Asians, from South as well as Southeast Asia. During apartheid, they were classified as Indian and colored, respectively. He argues that statistics do not reflect this qualitative difference between Black and other Muslims. The exclusivity for Indians and Southeast Asians was largely due to their residential concentration in racially segregated urban areas. They lived closer to mosques and *madrasas* and had a strong sense of being Muslim. Also, African Muslims were a further minority among Muslim minority communities until 1991. It was only later that African Muslims became the fastest growing segment of the Muslim population (Tayob 1996).

According to Farid Esack, there was no difference between the "colored" or "Indian" Muslims in their sociopolitical attitude under apartheid. This small community of Muslims survived as a distinct religious and cultural community against tremendous odds. It was their sense of exclusivity, even superiority vis-à-vis non-Muslims that led to their survival. Muslims often identified themselves with other "superior groups," including the ruling class in South Africa. The *ulama* of all communities—who shared a conservative political attitude with little willingness to change and a considerable loyalty to the government in power—were able to establish orthodoxy, despite several differences.

Esack illustrated this attitude with the example of the Muslim Judicial Council (MJC), which was established in 1945 in order to create a judicial umbrella body. Most *ulama* joined the MJC, believing that it guaranteed the protection of the principles of Islam. Through the MJC, they could claim to speak for the entire Muslim community as sole guardians of the Islamic doctrine and its values. It is no exaggeration to describe them as being complacent, silent, even a-political with regard to the political landscape, especially in the course of the 1960s and 1970s (Günther 2004). The MJC corresponded to the *ulama's* professed ideal role as guardians of classical Muslim personal law. They were not happy with the court judgments.

Muslim Personal Law

As explained above, South African law developed as an integral part of the colonial legal system. In colonial systems, where applied, Islamic law was restricted to personal matters such as marriage, divorce, inheritance; it was called Muslim personal law (MPL), or family law. Even so, it was applied within the framework of common or civil law. Local Muslim histories maintain that Muslim marriages were not formally recognized; they created no rights and Muslims had no legal status under South Africa law (Mahida 1993, 17). Nevertheless, as Ebrahim Moosa argues, the application of MPL in South Africa is documented to have occurred from the seventeenth century onward. The Dutch East India Company Commander Courts during 1652–1795 recognized and applied this law to Muslims (Moosa 1996, 132). This recognition of law for Muslims must have created a need for Muslim Law experts, but it had no impact on the development of South African law until 1994, as will be explained below.

The Dutch and British brought Muslims as political prisoners, convicts, bonded labor, and slaves from their other colonies to South Africa during the seventeenth century (Mahida 1993; Moosa 1996). Among these prisoners were learned Muslims like Sheikh Yusuf (d.1699), exiled from Indonesia to the Cape in 1652, and reputed scholars of Sharia and *qadis* such as Tuang Guru Imam Abd Allah b. Qadi Abd al-Salam (d.1807) and Abu Bakr Afandi (d.1880) (Moosa 1996, 133). These and other *ulama* established mosques and religious schools, formed *ulama* organizations and councils that regulated marriage, divorce, and succession, and settled family disputes (Mahida 1993, 67). MJC Natal, founded in 1963, settled disputes between Muslim individuals and families without either party taking recourse to courts. Problems were solved according to Islamic law (Mahida 1993, 95).

By 1828, the *ulama* had developed a system of dual legal authority in Muslim communities: they recognized the authority of civil courts for the settlement of their disputes about the mosque and leadership in prayers and the religious authority of the *ulama* bodies in personal law matters (Moosa 1996, 133–40). Consequently, eight *ulama* bodies were established during 1935 and 1994, which had divisions dealing with marriage, divorce, custody, and succession (Moosa 1996, 136–40).

In the 1970s, several *ulama* bodies, educational institutions, and individuals called upon the government to recognize MPL. According to Ebrahim Moosa, the Law Commission dismissed that call, explaining that such a recognition would cause "confusion" in South African law (Moosa 1996, 135). Moosa discussed in detail how the shifting politics between 1970s and 1980s affected Muslim communities. MPL, however, became contested when in 1983 the NP government introduced a Tricameral Parliament and promised limited recognition of Muslim marriages to entice Muslims of Asian origin. The traditional *ulama* accepted this offer in 1985, but Muslim groups who were part of the freedom struggle against apartheid opposed this offer (Moosa 1988). Eventually, the community rejected it as an apartheid design.

Political transformation in South Africa began with the Constitution in 1994, which introduced the Bill of Rights that recognizes diversity and religious freedom. The provision of basic rights in the 1994 Interim Constitution tempted the *ulama* to call for an exemption of MPL. An MPL Board was constituted to draft a law. The *ulama*, however, disassociated themselves from the Commission's Draft Law 1995; it was against their expectations. They, again, welcomed the developments between 1996 and 2003 and expected that MPL would be part of the legal system (Moosa 1996,136). Draft Bill 2003 was received with both negative and positive reactions. MPL became controversial, because it was not clear if it recognized Sharia as an ethnic customary law recognized by South African law, or as a religious law.

Muslim marriages: Statutory recognition

Arguably, Muslim marriages enjoyed some statutory recognition after 1965, although the law subjected them to South African civil marriage laws. The Marriage Act of 1965 recognized marriages solemnized with Mohammedan rights as follows: "The Minister and any officer in the public service authorized by him may designate any minister of religion of, ... a marriage officer for the purpose of solemnizing marriages, according to Christian, Jewish or Mohammedan rites or the rites of any Indian religion" (Marriage Act 25 of 1965, 3[1]). Günther (2004) refers to some other statutes that use broader definitions of the terms "marriage," "spouse," and "survivor," assuming inclusion of Muslim marriages, even though for allowing for some specific purpose. The Criminal Procedure Act 1977 defined "marriage" as "any marriage concluded under any system of religious law" (Criminal Procedure Act 51 of 1977, 195). The Children Act 2005 interpreted marriage as "concluded in accordance with a system of religious law subject to specific procedures" (Children Act 38 of 2005, 1[1]). The Intestate Succession Act 81 of 1987 and the Maintenance of Surviving Spouses Act 27 of 1990 use the term "spouse" to include survivor. The Reform of Customary Law of Succession and Regulation of Related Matters Act 11 of 2009 defines the term "survivor" as "the surviving spouse in a marriage dissolved by death, and includes a spouse of a customary marriage which was dissolved by a civil marriage contracted by her husband in the customary marriage to another woman" (Art. 4, Section 1). As we shall discuss shortly, the courts were reluctant to consider this indirect and limited recognition as a valid and full formal and valid recognition of Muslim marriages. The issue remained under discussion with the South African Law Reform Commission.

Judicial interpretations

The following cases are cited frequently as landmark cases on the issue of Muslim marriages.

Seedat's Executors v The Master (Natal) 1917 302 (AD)

This judgment belongs to the period before the Marriage Act 1965. In this case, the court declined to recognize a widow of a Muslim marriage as a "surviving spouse," because a Muslim marriage was "reprobated by the majority of the civilized peoples, on grounds of morality and religion" and because it was "repugnant to the policy and the legal institutions both of Holland and England" (Seedat's Executors v The Master (Natal) 1917 AD 302, 307, 308).

Ismail v Ismail 1983 (1) SA 1006 (A)

Christa Rautenbach (2000, 42–6) summarized the facts of the case (1983 1 SA 1006 [A]) as follows.

(1) The Court of Appeal interpreted the provisions of the Marriage Act 53 in Ismail v Ismail.

(2) H. and W. were married in terms of Islamic law. Their marriage was at all material times monogamous. Approximately four years after their marriage, H. divorced W. by means of *talaq* (MPL method of divorce). W. claimed for arrear maintenance [She alleged that H. did not maintain her during the last two years and ten months of their marriage], delivery of deferred dowry, payment of certain jewelry in W.'s possession, and maintenance for the period of *iddat* [MPL requires a waiting period after the divorce, mentioned by the Moulana, expert in MPL in his "judgment"]. The Moulana gave judgment in favor of W. H. neglected to abide by the judgment and W. instituted action in the Transvaal Provincial Division.

(3) To begin with, H. raised a point against her particulars of action "inasmuch as the customs relied upon by the plaintiff [W.] are contra bonos mores, unreasonable and in conflict with law, alternatively are in conflict with rules of law which are unalterable by agreement" (Ismail vs Ismail 1983, 1019E–F).

(4) The Court found that the marriage was polygamous and therefore void on the ground of public policy and argued, that to "entertain the plaintiff's [W.'s] claims would be tantamount to recognizing the illegal union entered into by the parties and that would be to fly into the face of all authority in this country" (Ismail vs Ismail 1983, 1019F–G).

(5) W. lodged an appeal against this decision. In order to decide whether the Court *a quo* erred in upholding the starting point of H., the Appellate Division investigated the validity of the marriage between H. and W.

(6) W.'s council agreed that the marriage was not valid, because it was potentially polygamous and did not comply with the formalities of the Marriage Act (Marriage Act 1965, Sections 2, 3, 11 and 29[2]). He pleaded that W.'s cause of action was based on certain Muslim customs and a marriage contract and not on the marriage between the parties. The question that had to be considered was whether the

Muslim customs and a contract arising from them are contra bonos mores and not whether the marriage was valid or void.

(7) The Court did not agree with this approach and found, "In my view the claims should not be viewed in isolation. The tenets of the Muslim faith appear to govern all aspects of the marriage relationship. … the Court must have regard to the very close and intimate connection between the customs and contract in question and the underlying conjugal union" (Ismail vs Ismail 1983, 1020D–F).

(8) The second argument submitted by W.'s council was the change in the attitude of society toward polygamy. First, the provisions of sections 3(1) and 11 of the Marriage Act afforded Muslim marriages some form of recognition (Ismail vs Ismail 1983, 1020H et seq.). Section 3(1) reads, "The Minister and any officer in the public service authorized thereto by him may designate any minister of religion of, or any person holding a responsible position in, any religious denomination or organization to be, so long as he is such a minister or occupies such position, a marriage officer for the purpose of solemnizing marriages according to Christian, Jewish or Mohammedan rites or the rites of any Indian religion."

(9) The Court held, however, that Section 3(1) did not afford any recognition to Muslim marriages. It found that the emphasized words related to the form of the marriage ceremony and not to the requirements of the marriage as such (Ismail vs Ismail 1983, 1021B–D).

(10) The Court added that Section 3(1) enables Muslims to conclude their marriages according to Islamic rites by an imam (leader of the Muslim community). If, however, they want their marriages to be valid monogamous marriages in terms of South African law, the imam must be a designated marriage officer who has to comply with the formalities applicable to the solemnization of marriages in terms of the Act (Ismail vs Ismail 1983, 1021D–E).

(11) W.'s council argued that Section 11 gave some form of recognition to Muslim marriages, because such marriages do not "purport to effect a valid marriage" in terms of subsection 3. Section 11 reads as follows:

> A marriage may be solemnized by a marriage officer only. Any marriage officer who purports to solemnize a marriage which he is not

> authorized under this Act to solemnize or which to his knowledge is legally prohibited, and any person not being a marriage officer who purports to solemnize a marriage, shall be guilty of an offence and liable on conviction to a fine not exceeding four hundred rand or, in default of payment, to imprisonment for a period not exceeding 12 months, or to both such fine and such imprisonment.

Nothing in subsection (2) contained shall apply to any marriage ceremony solemnized in accordance with the rites or formularies of any religion, if such ceremony does not purport to effect a valid marriage.

(12) The Court evaluated Section 11 and found that there was nothing in the provisions that gives some form of recognition to Muslim marriages. It held that the mere fact that the Legislature has not prohibited polygamous unions, recognized as marriages under the tenets of the Muslim faith, does not mean it also approves of such unions or that the consequences thereof are legally enforceable (Ismail vs Ismail 1983, 1021H–1022A).

(13) The third point by W.'s council about the recognition of polygamous marriages in England and Zimbabwe was dismissed, as it referred to foreign polygamous marriages and [which] were, therefore, distinguishable from the facts of this case (Ismail vs Ismail 1983, 1022B–1023H).

(14) The fourth point by W.'s council was that the legislature, in a number of statutes, gave recognition to polygamous marriages (Ismail vs Ismail 1983, 1023H–1024C). The Court concluded that the existence of such legislation was not indicative of recognition (or "tolerance" as the Court called it) of Muslim marriages in general (Ismail vs Ismail 1983, 1024C–D).

(15) Finally, the Court concluded that the marriage of W. and H. was contra bonos mores (Ismail vs Ismail 1983, 1024D–1026B), and thus void on the following grounds:

   a. There was no justification to deviate from the long line of decisions in which the courts had refused to give recognition to Muslim marriages.
   b. The concept of polygamous marriages would undermine the monogamous status of civil marriages (Ismail vs Ismail 1983, 1024D–1026B).
   c. The recognition of Muslim marriages should be in conflict with the principle of equality between marriage partners.

d. Muslim marriages were "contrary to the accepted customs and usages that were regarded as morally binding upon all members of society" (Ismail vs Ismail 1983, 1026B).

Ryland v Edros 1996 (4) All SA 557 (C), and Ryland v Edros 1997 (2) SA 690 (CC)

In this case, the court held that since a Muslim marriage is a contract from which certain proprietary obligations flow, it provided reason enough to impose some of the consequences of civil marriage on a Muslim marriage, chiefly the obligation of maintenance. The court did not recognize Muslim marriage as a valid contract but allowed the obligations that this contract had created.

Amod v Multilateral Motor Vehicle Accidents Fund
1999 (4) SA 1319 (SCA)

In this case, Hafiza Ismail Amod (born Peer) claimed damages in the High Court against the Multilateral Motor Vehicle Accidents Fund for loss of support arising out of the death of her husband in a motor vehicle collision in 1993. The Court held that even though the right of a spouse married according to African customary law to claim damages for loss of support has since been provided for, subject to certain conditions (Section 31 of the Black Laws Amendment Act 76 of 1963), no equivalent statutory provision existed in respect to a spouse married according to Islamic law.

The court held that a legally enforceable duty of support would arise from a marriage in accordance with the tenets of a recognized and accepted faith, and that the "inequality, arbitrariness, intolerance and inequity" that would result from not following this approach was inconsistent with the new ethos of a constitutional democracy. In this case, the crucial question was whether the relationship between the deceased and the dependent was recognized by common law. The court relied on Ismail v Ismail, holding that marriages contracted in accordance with Islamic law were not lawful marriages in terms of common law because such marriages were potentially polygamous.

In the Court's view, the 1996 Constitution did not authorize the courts to eliminate established rules from the common law; this, [the Judge] held, was the responsibility of the legislature. The Court dismissed the appeal because it was premature. The Court would consider the leave to appeal after the matter had been dealt with by the Supreme Court of Appeal, or if leave to appeal to the Supreme Court of Appeal was not granted by the High Court or the Chief Justice.

Khan v Khan 2005 (2) SA 272 (TPD)

In 2005, the Pretoria High Court held that partners in Muslim marriages (whether monogamous or not) owe each other a duty of support, just as in civil marriages and, therefore, have the right to claim maintenance from one another in terms of the Maintenance Act 99 of 1998, 20 (Khan v Khan, 19).

Ismail v Ismail and Others (86) (2007) ZAECHC 3;
2007 (4) SA 557 (E) (8 February 2007)

This is a complicated case involving rights to property and validity of Muslim marriage.

The applicant, Toufeeqah Ismail, was Yusuf Ismail's second wife, whom he married with Islamic rites in 1992. He had married his first wife Nafisah through civil marriage. Toufeeqah had been living in a house with her two children from a previous marriage. She ran this house as a home for children to maintain herself and the children. After marriage, Yusuf provided Toufeeqah with a flat as her home. She continued occupying her previous house after marriage with Yusuf Isma'il. Yusuf and his first wife purchased Toufeeqah's house. Soon after, marriage estrangement occurred between Toufeeqah and her husband. She came to know that Yusuf had placed her house on sale. She applied to the court for interdiction of the sale. On July 7, 2006, notice was served to Yusuf Isma'il accordingly. Toufeeqah received a paper from her husband on July 17, 2006, terminating the marriage unilaterally.

Hassam v Jacobs No & Others, July 18, 2008, Case 5704/2004 (C)

In this case, the applicant, Fatima Gabie Hassam, was married to Ebrahim Hassam according to Muslim rites. He married a second wife, Miriam Hassam, also according to Muslim rites, without the knowledge or consent of the first wife. He had three minor children from his second wife Miriam Hassam. He died intestate in August 2001.

According to the South African legal system (Administration of Estates Act 66 of 1965), a deceased's estate is administered by a person officially called the "executor," who must abide by the laws of testate and intestate succession. Normally, this person is named in the deceased's will. In special cases, they are appointed by an official of the Department of Justice, mostly with the rank of a magistrate, and designated as Master who is responsible to the minister of justice. The executor must meet with the family of the deceased in order to obtain all relevant information and documentation needed, such as the death certificate and a list of the deceased's assets and liabilities. The deceased's estate must be reported to the Master of the High Court in the area where the deceased lived. The executor must provide notice to the creditors and request them to institute their claims. In this case, Mr. Johan Hermanus Jacobs was the executor for Hassam's estate. He reported to the court that Hassam's death certificate showed that he was "never married."

The applicant Fatima Hassam approached the High Court seeking an order entitling her to be recognized as a spouse and surviving spouse of the deceased for the purposes of maintenance (Maintenance of Surviving Spouses Act 27 of 1990). The executor questioned the validity of the applicant's marriage with the deceased; if valid, then marriage with the second wife made it polygamous, also invalid. The High Court found that except for the executor, no one disputed the validity of the marriage and that it was extant at the time of the deceased's death. The applicant also maintained that the word "spouse" in Section 1(4) of the Act should include a husband or wife married in terms of Muslim rites, regardless of whether the marriage is monogamous or polygynous. By excluding her from the definition of "spouse" on account of a polygynous union, the Act unfairly limited her right to religious freedom and equality before the law.

The High Court held,

> Marriages concluded under Muslim private law are potentially polygynous as the male in such a union, subject to compliance with the onerous prescripts of the Qur'an, is permitted to marry more than one woman. Unless the concept "spouse" … [is] construed to encompass also widows of polygynous Muslim marriages, the practical effect would be that the widows of such marriages will be discriminated against solely because of the exercise by their deceased husbands of the right accorded them by the tenets of a major faith to marry more than one woman. Such discrimination would not only amount to a violation of their rights to

> equality on the basis of marital status, religion … and culture but would also infringe their right to dignity. … [D]iscrimination of that kind is presumptively unfair unless valid grounds exist under Section 36 of the Constitution for limiting their rights as regards equality and human dignity.

Later, in the case of Hassam v Jacobs NO and Others 2009 (5) SA 572 (CC), the Constitutional Court went further and held that this right extended to polygamous Muslim unions as well.

Between the High Courts and Constitutional Courts

Different approaches to statutory provisions between the courts, especially High Courts of Appeal and Constitutional Court, are a significant development in twenty-first century South Africa. While the latter argued that, through applying the constitutional principles of diversity and equality, the courts could provide recognition to Muslim marriages, the courts insisted on clear legislation. Consequently, Muslim marriage was given only limited recognition in exceptional cases, for specific purposes or relief, even after constitutional recognition. The South African Law Reform Commission observed that, "While indigenous polygamous marriages were declared legal, Muslim marriages, even monogamous, were disallowed as potentially polygamous, children from these marriages had no rights or legal status." In Brown v Fritz Brown (1860 3 Searle 313 at 318), the Court recognizes Islamic marriage as "concubinage" (SALR Commission Report 2003, 5, n. 9). The following case illustrates this judicial debate more substantively.

Daniels v Campbell NO and Others 2004 (5) SA 331 (CC), Daniels v Campbell and Others 004 (7) BCLR 735 (CC)

In this case, Juleiga Daniel, the applicant, was married to Robin Grieve Campbell in 1977, with Muslim rites but without a "marriage officer." Their marriage was monogamous. Robin Campbell, who was the applicant's second husband, died in 1994 without bequest. The applicant went to the court for maintenance against her husband's estate. She had no children with Campbell. However, the husband and wife both had children from previous marriages. The court investigated her claim about being a "surviving spouse" who deserved maintenance from the estate.

Regarding the estate, it is important to mention that Juleiga had a small house before her first marriage in 1969. After marriage, the first husband applied for and got the Council accommodation. He divorced her in 1976. She and the children continued living in the Council house until her second marriage in 1977. According to the rules, the Council transferred the allotment of the house in the second husband's name. Campbell purchased the house on long-term installments in 1990. Even though Juleiga also contributed to the purchase and signed the deed with her cross mark, the Council wrote off the rest of the installments and transferred property ownership to the deceased husband in 1998 when the husband died in 1994. The master (the state official, see above in Hassam v Jacobs) told the applicant that according to the law (Marriage Act 1965), her marriage was not valid due to Muslim rites without a marriage officer. She, therefore, did not qualify as a surviving spouse for the purpose of maintenance under the Intestate Succession Act 81 of 1987 and the Maintenance of Surviving Spouse Act 27 1990 (8).

Judge Van Heerden at the High Court ruled that "The interplay between the applicant's belief and the cultural practices in the community—and the failure of South African law to properly accommodate such beliefs and practices—resulted in the applicant being denied relief. Such omissions violated the rights of equality until Muslim personal law of succession was recognized by the legislators. … There was no justification for limitation of equality rights." The omission is unconstitutional in the Act of 1987. The Judge recommended that the definition of spouse be amended to add: "Spouse shall include a husband or wife in accordance with Muslim rites in a de facto monogamous union" (11, 12).

Judge Sachs at the Constitutional Court clarified that the exclusion of Muslim marriages was due to "culturally and racially hegemonic appropriation of the interpretation of "spouse" (19). Discriminatory interpretation was injurious to the affected person. Constitutional values of equality, tolerance, and respect for diversity favor broader inclusive meaning. The issue is to remove the strain imposed by past discriminatory interpretations in favor of ordinary meanings. The purpose is to provide relief for a particularly vulnerable section of the population. Statutory protection is necessary for illiterate and vulnerable women like the applicant. A narrow focus on the legality of marriage does not protect the rights.

The judge held that a Muslim spouse in a monogamous marriage had the right to inherit and the right to claim maintenance from a deceased spouse who had died intestate. It was further determined that the word "spouse," as contained in the two Acts, should apply to "spouses" married in accordance with Muslim law. Judge Sachs set aside the Order of the High Court about the invalidity of marriage and declared the word "spouse" in the Intestate Succession Act 81 (1987) and "survivor" in the Maintenance Act 1990 to include monogamous Muslim marriages. The Court ruled that no leave to appeal was required for this judicial interpretation.

The other judge at the Constitutional Court, Judge Moseneke, held that this "persisting invalidity of Muslim marriages is, of course, a constitutional anachronism. It belongs to our dim past. It originates from deep-rooted prejudice on matters of race, religion, and culture. True to their worldview, judges of the past displayed remarkable ethnocentric bias and arrogance at the expense of those they perceived different. They exalted their own and demeaned and excluded everything else" (74). Judge Moseneke, however, agreed with the High Court that "Normal canons of statutory construction dictate that where the legislature recognises that a definition needs to be explicitly widened for a statute to apply to Muslim spouses, the opposite would also be true. The narrower common law definition would apply whenever there is no expanded definition (79).

South African Law Reform Commission (SALRC)

Established under the SALRC Act 19 of 1973, the South African Law Reform Commission did not include the issue of Muslim marriages in its list of reforms. Discussions began with the recognition of customary and other marriages, but even in that area, actual reform was made legally possible only after the Bill of Rights was included in the 1996 Constitution as Chapter 2. Section 9 on equality declared that this principle protects ethnic, cultural, and religious diversity and prohibits discrimination on such grounds. As mentioned above, even though Section 15(3) recognized "marriages concluded under any tradition or system of religious, personal or family laws," substantive reformative legislation on customary marriages was made only in 1998.

It was in 2000 that the SALR Commission established Project Committee 59 to examine the issue of Islamic marriages. The Committee's report was published in 2003. The report observed that the 1996 Constitution, Section 15, "does not prevent legislation recognizing—(i) marriages concluded under any tradition, or a system of religious, personal or family law; or (ii) systems of personal and family law under any tradition, or adhered to by persons professing a particular religion, (b) Recognition in terms of paragraph (a) must be consistent with this section and the other provisions of the Constitution" (SALRC 2003, 3 [a], [b]) .

The report examined the court cases and observed, "Historically, and until the landmark 1999 Supreme Court of Appeal decision in Amod v Multilateral Motor Vehicle Accidents Fund, a marriage contracted according to Islamic law was regarded by our courts as null and void *ab initio*, and contrary to public policy, with the result that the marriage and its consequences were not legally recognised in any form" (SALRC Report 2003, 2.4). Exploring the reason for the refusal to recognize these marriages, the report noted that "The apparent rationale for not recognizing Islamic marriages was because they were regarded by our courts as being polygynous" (SALRC Report 2003, 2.4, n. 9).

The report added, "The Appellate Division reaffirmed this in Ismail v Ismail 1983 (1) SA 1006 (AD) when it stated that an Islamic marriage was 'contra bonos mores in the wider sense of the phrase' i.e., as being contrary to the accepted customs and usages which are regarded as morally binding upon all members of our society" (SALRC Report 2003, 2.4, n. 9). "This approach may be traced back to as early as 1860 (Brown v Fritz Brown's Executors and Others [1860 3 Searle 313 at 318]) which described an Islamic marriage as 'recognized concubinage'." It was the Draft Bill 2003 that began addressing this issue.

Muslim Marriages Draft Bills 2003, 2011

Legislation has been passed recognizing and regulating marriages concluded under Islamic law. Draft Bill 2003 clarified that "A Muslim marriage to which this Act applies and in respect of which all the requirements of this Act have been complied with, shall for all purposes be recognized as a valid marriage" (Draft Bill 2003, 113, 2(5)). The Draft Bill also provides recognition to all Islamic marriages concluded before and after the enactment of the Bill. In fact, the recognition is conditional subject to complying with the provisions prescribed under the heading "Application of the Act" (Article 2, subsections [1] to [5]) and under the heading "Requirements for Muslim Marriages" (Article 5, subsections [1] to [10]). A Muslim marriage will have to comply with all these requirements after the commencement of the Act. Muslim marriages concluded before the commencement of the Act will have the option to elect out of these requirements, but then the Act would not apply to them and only limited recognition for certain purposes will be afforded (SALRC Report 2003). The reason for this option was that most Muslims conclude a Muslim marriage and shortly after enter a civil marriage to have legal recognition (Bakker 2009, 400).

Sharia debates ensuing after this Bill raised issues with these conditions. Consequently, the Draft Bill 2011 added a number of important definitions and clarifications, mostly based on MPL, to provide for the recognition of Muslim marriages; to specify the requirements for their validity; to regulate their registration; to define the status and capacity of spouses; to regulate the proprietary consequences; to regulate their termination and the consequences thereof; and to provide for matters connected therewith. The Bill defined "Muslim marriage" simply as a marriage between a man and a woman contracted in accordance with Islamic law only.

Analytical Perspectives on Sharia Debates in South Africa

Politics of recognition

The politics of recognition was shaped by the ideas of power and supremacy that believed in sovereignty rather than equality based on diversity. South Africa remained a battleground for political supremacy between the indigenous tribes, the British, and the other European settlers. The foundation of ANC in 1912 and NP in 1914 reflected the continued political tension surrounding the recognition of diversity. The ANC stood for the right of vote for all Africans, and the NP restricted the right to vote to white people only. The apartheid doctrine ignored diversity and restricted citizenship rights to white people. The recognition of marriages became the benchmark of this doctrine. White people were not allowed to marry people of other races, as explained above. The South African Law Commission (SALC) was founded in 1987 to assess the need for law reforms. It did not include the issue of the recognition of marriages.

The Bill of Rights in the 1996 Constitution provided the necessary legal framework for reform. Soon after, the Recognition of Customary Marriages Act (RCMA) in 1998 defined "customary law" as the customs and usages that were traditionally observed among the indigenous African peoples of South Africa and recognized "customary marriage" as a valid marriage concluded in accordance with customary law. For a customary marriage, indigenous African traditions and customs were the norms.

Marriage was a family matter and did not require the approval of an officiator. It had certain other requirements for validity. A ceremony of a union was not concluded by a single event; the rituals continued for some time (SAHO 2019a, b). Due to our focus on Muslim marriages, we need not go into debates on the recognition of customary marriages. It is, however, relevant to understand how the politics of recognition now shifted from customary to Muslim marriages. Interestingly, whereas the RCMA recognized "polygamy" without using that term, most courts refused to recognize Muslim marriage because it was potentially polygamous. The Draft Bill for Muslim marriages from 2003 insisted that a Muslim marriage was not valid unless it conforms to South African law.

Legal positivism

The British and other European settlers had both developed legal systems based on the philosophy of legal positivism. The British followed the common law tradition and the others civil law; the British accommodated custom and religion, but the others did not. Three reasons may be discerned from the debates on this issue: (1) common law restraints about custom; (2) negative perception of diversity as a threat to the modern state and the ensuing politics of law; and (3) positivist debate on the restrictive normativity of customary law.

Legal positivism had moved away from the classical positivist concept of normativity that insisted that a custom becomes a law only when a legislature enacts a rule legalizing it or a court applies it to a dispute. H. L. A. Hart (d. 1992) set out an argument supporting that a custom can be a law in its own right. A community's respect for a custom might be sufficient reason for the custom to operate as law (Duxbury 2017, 2). A.N Allot (d.2002), the founder of African law as an academic discipline at SOAS, observed that British judges in African courts considered English law as the basic law and regarded customs as deviations (Allott 1957, 245). The common law doctrine of "ascertainment of usage and custom" and the criteria of antiquity, repugnancy, applicability, and incompatibility developed in English law posed difficulties in Africa (Allott 1957, 244–57). Allot argued that local African customs "might be 'foreign' and 'unknown' to English judges, but not to the Africans who practiced it" (Allott 1957, 244–57). He argued that the binding force of custom ultimately rests on the fact that it was the assent of the community that gave custom its validity (Allott 1957, 258). British judges in African courts recognized Islamic law also as "native customary law," even though it was written and available in books, and experts were there to ascertain its existence and validity." Hence, it could qualify as statutory, but it was not legislated or codified by political authorities (Allott 1957, 244–57).

Heinz Klug notes that reforms were superimposed on a legal system that was fundamentally colonial and based on the philosophies of sovereignty and legal positivism (Klug 2002, 1487). He suggested that reform in customary laws within the classical framework of legal positivism produced patchworks where reconstruction was required.

Muslim personal law politics

A number of Muslims registered their marriage as civil marriage after the Islamic ceremony of *nikah*. Some *ulama* discouraged civil marriages as un-Islamic. Therefore, Muslims generally concluded only *nikah* marriage (Amien 2013, 360). This dual practice was in accordance with the Muslim Marriages Act 25 (1961).

Historically speaking, interpretations and tensions within Islamic law have political roots, in addition to their other sources. Ebrahim Moosa warned that if MPL did not consider the sociopolitical realities of South Africa, it would become repressive instead of liberating (1988, 24).

Commenting on the politics of recognition, Moosa mentioned that in 1975, the Director of the Institute of Islamic Sharia Studies told the Prime Minister of South Africa that some aspects of Islamic law—such as divorce, succession, and so on—may be recognized. SALC disagreed, because such recognition would create confusion in South African law (Moosa 1988, 32). Several *ulama* bodies jointly issued a statement that they hoped to see MPL as part of the legal system of the Republic of South Africa (Moosa 1988, 34). The Islamic Council of South Africa (ICSA) also proposed establishing Muslim family law courts, appointing judges recommended by ICSA's judicial committees.

This was the period when the NP was politically active, winning the support of the Muslim population for their policies. The Muslim Youth Movement warned about the legitimacy crisis that the NP was facing and called upon Muslims to unite and discuss the issues publicly. Some *ulama* bodies were taking decisions without a public mandate (Moosa 1988, 35). Ebrahim Moosa (1996) argued that the Sharia debate began with the historical political change introduced by the 1996 Constitution. The *ulama* welcomed drafting initiative by SALC and expected MPL to be part of the legal system (Moosa 1996, 136).

Sheikh Muneer Abduroaf, a religious scholar, trained lawyer, and academic, represents the MJC, whose main functions relate to religious guidance, education, *fatawa, da'wah, halal* certification, and marriage counseling. According to the sheikh, MPL does not cover all Sharia laws. He finds that court judgments were at times in total conflict with the "classical and majority understanding of MPL." He explained that the real issue was that instead of legislation, the court was bound by precedents. The judges proceeded in the common law framework. In the absence of clear statutory laws, the courts could not provide relief. The Muslim community was asking to enact laws as Acts of Parliament (Abduroaf 2013, 6–10).

Secular perspective

Waheeda Amien, a learned lawyer, observed three social approaches to the recognition of Muslim marriages: assimilation, accommodation, and integration. None of the legal systems protects gender equality, including MPL. She argued that nonrecognition has impacted Muslim women disproportionately (Amien 2010, 363). As a secularist, she forcefully argues that South African secularism can protect gender equality, because it does not support strict separation between religion and state. Rather, it promotes collaboration between religion and state. The South African secular state respects the Muslim minority community and can apply religious freedom without negatively impacting gender equality. Applied without reference to religious law, the Bill of Rights could better guarantee female members' right to equality (Amien 2010, 361). Also, since the Constitution does not use the phrase "in force" for laws that need reforms, the Bill of Rights might not be restricted by the term "in force"; this means that all "laws" may be scrutinized. According to Amien, "in force" should not mean that "unrecognized law is not law" (Amien 2013).

The *ulama* opposed the Draft Bill 2010 because it required compliance with civil marriage terms and proposed the inclusion of Islamic law experts as assessors with the judges. Mostly, Muslims registered their marriages as civil marriage in accordance with Marriage Act 25 (1961) in addition to *nikah* marriage. Deeply religious people did not register civil marriages, and the secular did not register *nikah* marriage. Usually, the *ulama* discouraged civil marriages; some of them declared civil marriage un-Islamic. In all cases, Muslim women suffered (Amien 2013, 360).

Gender perspective

The Sharia debates exposed paradoxes in the legal systems and MPL's reluctance to reform. *Ulama* generally argued that Sharia could not be subjected to reforms. According to Rashida Manjoo, the majority of Muslims contended that MPL discriminated against women's rights. She argued that the 1996 Constitution specially aimed at reversing the effects of racial discrimination under apartheid, whereas the Draft Bill 2003 disregarded it (Manjoo 2007, 8). Although the South African Commission for Gender Equality had proposed an alternative draft bill based on the principle of gender equality, the Bill did not consider gender equality a basic constitutional right (Manjoo 2007, 3, 4). Rashida Manjoo's main criticism relies on the challenge in balancing equality rights and rights to religion. Complexity in the South African context is also faced by individuals who are culturally and legally tied to both the group and the state. She proposed that a legislative solution lay in recognizing religious marriage while avoiding codifying laws in accordance with one particular religion (Manjoo 2007, 28).

Manjoo and Amien both stress the need for exploring *fiqh* provisions and a broader interpretation of the Quran and other sources to find solutions. A critical reading of Islamic sources is necessary. Their main critique is that legislators consider civil law normative for both customary and Muslim institutions of marriage. Civil law does not consider marriage as communal bond between two families but between two individuals.

Conclusion: Learning from Sharia Debates

Debate as a formal discourse on a particular matter is one of the characteristic processes in discursive traditions. Sharia is no exception. Academic studies notice a shift in the Sharia debates from an interpretive to a discursive approach to Sharia in the present century. Fascinated by the textual sources of Islamic law, Western Orientalist scholarship considered the growth of Islamic law as a significant departure and focused on gaps between classical Islamic theory and practices, and between modernist and Islamic essentialist debates on Sharia in the last two centuries.

In the twentieth century, the focus of Sharia debates began shifting from pan-Islamism to the nation-state. In his brilliant analysis of Muslim political thought in this period, in his work entitled *Islam in a World of Nation-States*, political scientist James Piscatori studied the phenomenon as "territorial pluralism." He noted that in the beginning, Muslim thinkers like Sayyid Abu l-Ala Mawdudi and Muhammad Iqbal were opposed to the idea of a territorial nation for Muslims. However, by the mid-twentieth century, Iqbal began defining Pakistan in terms of territorial nation-state, and when Pakistan came into existence, Mawdudi also adopted the idea of a nation-state as an essential component of an Islamic state. Traditionally, Sharia—which had been regarded as personal—also came to be formulated in territorial terms of application. Mawdudi argued, "Indeed, over centuries of historical experience and the evolution of theory, Muslims have largely freed themselves of a model which denigrates territorial pluralism and demands monolithic unity" (Piscatori 1986, 150). Sharia has faced some other serious problems in the world of nation-states. Some academic studies even concluded that the Islamic state is impossible (Hallaq 2013, 7). Academic studies have, however, noted that the idea of the nation-state has also been a subject of debate in the context of international law (see Cavanaugh, this volume).

In South Africa, Sharia debates on Muslim marriages emerged in 1993 and focused on two points: the status of Muslim women and the normativity of Sharia in South African law. Customary marriages came to be recognized in 1998 but religious, especially Islamic, law is not recognized. Sharia debates are often associated with legal pluralism that challenges the process of the unification of laws in a modern state. Legal pluralism in premodern societies was commonly practiced on account of local ethnic, political, and religious diversity and plurality. The rise of modern states was coeval with colonialism that introduced the modern concepts of unified law and absolute state authority.

The legality or invalidity of Muslim marriages has been the main issue of Sharia debates since the mid- twentieth century and is still under discussion. In order to understand this legal issue, one must explore the historical background of the impact of ideas of racial segregation determining legal capacity, development of constitutional law defining citizenship, fundamental rights and legal system informed the framework for legislation and codification of personal laws in modern states. Several chapters in this volume explore these themes.

The analysis of Sharia debates points not only to the fault lines in the debate process but also to the politics of law that prevents revisiting the theological and legal essentialism, an apparent cause of this impasse. The focused contextual approach that places the study of these debates in the required historical, social, and legal contexts reveals that debates have a political context as well. Two significant conclusions emerge from this chapter.

Discretionary judicial power always existed but, as Du Bois argues, "today there clearly is a greater willingness to use this power to modernize the law than there had been for a long time, as well as greater openness about its existence and the manner of its use" (Du Bois 2004, 6). Consequently, Sharia debates in South Africa (MJC, see Abduroaf 2013), Britain (Sharia Council, see Bano 2012), Canada (Dar al-Qaza, see Ali 1991; Blackstone 2005), and Pakistan (Tahreek Nifaz-e Shariat Muhammadiyah, Shar'i Nizam-e-Adl Regulation 1999, see NCSW 2014, 18) remained more focused on the institutions of judiciary and judicial authority powers than on reforms through parliamentary legislation and *ijtihad*.

References

Abduroaf, Sheikh Muneer. 2013. "Evolution of Muslim Personal Law in the South African Constitutional Dispensation." *Nederduitse Gereformeerde Teologiese Tydskrif*, 54, no. 1: 6–11.

Abduroaf, Sheikh Muneer. 2020. "An Analysis of the Rationale behind the Distribution of Shares in Terms of the Islamic Law of Intestate Succession: Recent Case Law." *De Jure*, 53, no. 1: 115–22.

Aftab, Amira. 2019. "Religious Freedom and Gender Equality: The Sharia Debates and Gendered Institutions in Australia and Britain." *Australian Journal of Human Rights*, 25, no. 2: 281–98.

Ali, Syed M. 1991. "Why Was the Institute Formed?" *Muslim Canada*. http://muslimcanada.org/IICJ.html. Accessed June 19, 2020.

Allott, Anthony N. 1957. "The Judicial Ascertainment of Customary Law in British Africa." *Modern Law Review*, 20, no. 3: 244–63.

Amien, Waheeda. 2010. "A South African Case Study for the Recognition and Regulation of Muslim Family Law in a Minority Muslim Secular Context." *International Journal of Law, Policy and the Family*, 24, no. 3: 361–96.

Amien, Waheeda. 2013. "Reflections on the Recognition of African Customary Marriages in South Africa: Seeking Insights for the Recognition of Muslim Marriages." *Acta Juridica*, 2013, no. 1: 357–84.

Amod v Multilateral Motor Vehicle Accident Fund 1997 (12) BCLR 1716 (D). http://www.saflii.org/za/cases/ZACC/1998/11.html.

Bakker, Pieter. 2009. "Towards the Recognition of Diversity: Muslim Marriages in South Africa." *Journal of Contemporary Roman-Dutch Law*, 72 (2009): 394–406.

Bano, Samia. 2012. *An Exploratory Study of Shariah Councils in England With Respect to Family Law*. http://www.reading.ac.uk/web/files/law/An_exploratory_study_of_Shariah_councils_in_England_with_respect_to_family_law_.pdf.

Blackstone, Laureve. 2005. "Courting Islam: Practical Alternatives to a Muslim Family Court in Ontario." *Brooklyn Journal of International Law*, 31, no. 1: 207–51.

Constitution. 1996, 15(3). Government of South Africa website. https://www.gov.za/documents/constitution/chapter-2-bill-rights#15.

Customary Marriages Act of 1998. https://www.sahistory.org.za/article/customary-marriages-south-africa-understanding-recognition-customary-marriages-act-1998. 27 August 2019. Accessed August 25, 2020.

Daniels v Campbell and Others (CCT 40/ 03) [2004] ZACC 14; 2004 (5) SA 331 (CC); 2004 (7) BCLR 735 (CC) (11 March 2004). Accessed on September 10, 2020. ww.saflii.orgw/za/cases/ZACC/2004/14.html. Accessed November 11, 2020. https://collections.concourt.org.za/handle/20.500.12144/3577#:~:text=Synopsis%3A,with%20a%20preliminary%20point%20only%20%3F.

Du Bois, Francois. 2004. "Introduction to South African Law: History, System and Sources." In *Introduction to the Law of South Africa*, edited by Cornelius G. Van der Merwe and Jacques E. Du Plessis, 1–53. Dordrecht, Netherlands: Kluwer.

Duxbury, Neil. 2017. "Custom as Law in English Law." *Cambridge Law Journal*, 76, no. 2: 337–59.

Esack, Farid. 1997. *On Being a Muslim: Finding a Religious Path Today*. Oxford: OneWorld.

Fatima G. Hassam v J.H. Jacobs, 2009. "http://www.saflii.org.za/za/cases/ZACC/2009/19.html" https://elce.co.za/categoty.press-release October 1.

Gabru, N. 2004. "Dilemma of Muslim Women Regarding Divorce in South Africa." *Potchefstroom Electronic Law Journal/Potchefstroomse Elektroniese Regsblad* 7, no. 2: 44–56.

Ghobadzadeh, Naser. 2010. "A Multiculturalism–Feminism Dispute: Muslim Women and the Sharia Debate in Canada and Australia." *Commonwealth & Comparative Politics*, 48, no. 3: 301–19.

Glenn, H. Patrick. 2014. *Legal Traditions of the World*. Oxford: Oxford University Press, 2014.

Günther, Ursula, and Inga Niehaus. 2002. "Islam in South Africa: The Muslims' Contribution in the Struggle Against Apartheid and the Process of Democratisation." *Islam in Africa*: 69–90. Accessed September 15, 2020. https://mesbar.org/islam-in-south-africa-muslims-contribution-to-the-south-african-transition-process-and-the-challenges-of-contextual-readings-of-islam/"https://mesbar.org/islam-in-south-africa-muslims-contribution-to-the-south-african-transition-process-and-the-challenges-of-contextual-readings-of-islam/#.

Hallaq, Wael B. 2013. *The Impossible State: Islam, Politics and Modernity's Moral Predicament*. New York: Columbia University Press.

Hansard, the Official Report of Debates in Parliament. STATUTE OF WESTMINSTER BILL.HC Deb 20 November 1931 vol 259 cc1173-224. Accessed November 11, 2020. https://api.parliament.uk/historic-hansard/commons/1931/nov/20/statute-of-westminster-bill#S5CV0259P0_19311120_HOC_27.

Isma'il v Isma'il 1983. Accessed November 11, 2020. http://www.saflii.org/cgi-bin/LawCite?cit=1983%20%281%29%20SA%201006.

Ismail v Ismail and Others (86) (2007) ZAECHC 3; 2007 (4) SA 557 (E) (8 February 2007). Accessed November 11, 2020. http://www.saflii.org/za/cases/ZAECHC/2007/3.html.

Klug, Heinz. "South Africa." In *Legal Systems of the World: A Political, Social, and Cultural Encyclopedia*, edited by Kritzer, 4: 1483–91.

Kritzer, Herbert M. 2002. Editor. *Legal Systems of the World, A Political, Social and Cultural Encyclopedia*. Oxford: ABC. CLIO Incorporation.

Kogelmann, Franz. 2006. "The 'Sharia Factor' in Nigeria's 2003 Elections." In *Muslim-Christian Encounters in Africa*, edited by Benjamin F. Soares, 6: 256–74. Leiden, Netherlands: Brill.

Kogelmann, Franz. 2008. "Sharia Debates and Their Perception by Christians and Muslims in Selected African Countries." In *Sharia Debates in Africa. An International, Comparative and Multidisciplinary Research Project at University of Bayreuth*. Volkswagen Stiftung. Last updated February 24, 2008; Accessed August 21, 2019. http://www.sharia-in-africa.net/.

Korteweg, Anna C. 2006. "The Sharia Debate in Ontario." *ISIM REVIEW* 18: 50–1.

Korteweg, Anna C. 2008. "The Sharia Debate in Ontario: Gender, Islam, and Representations of Muslim Women's Agency." *Gender & Society*, 22, no. 4: 434–54.

Korteweg, Anna C. and Jennifer A. Selby. 2012. *Debating Sharia: Islam, Gender Politics, and Family Law Arbitration*. Toronto: University of Toronto Press.

Mahdi, Hauwa, Maria Cavallin Ajmer, Göran Malmstedt, Adam von Scheéle, and Monica Weikert. 2006. "Sharia in Nigeria: A Reflection on the Debates." In *A World in Transition: New Challenges for Gender Justice*, edited by Mahdi, Hauwa. "Sharia in Nigeria: A Reflection on the Debates." A World in Transition: New Challenges for Gender Justice, Indian International Centre, New Delhi (2006): 13–15. New Delhi: Indian International Centre.

Mahida, Ebrahim M. 1993. *History of Muslims in South Africa: A Chronology*. Durban: Kat Bros.

Manjoo, Rashida. 2007. "The Recognition of Muslim Personal Laws in South Africa: Implications for Women's Human Rights." Islamic Law and Law of the Muslim World Paper No. 08–21, July. https://dx.doi.org/10.2139/ssrn.1115987.

Marriage Act 1949. Accessed April 15, 2019. http://www.legislation.gov.uk/ukpga/Geo6/12-13-14/76/contents.

Masud, Muhammad K. 2019. "Modernizing Islamic Law in Pakistan: Reform or Reconstruction?" *Journal of South Asian and Middle Eastern Studies* 42, no. 2 (Winter): 73–97.

Mfumbusa, Bernardin. 2014. "Chaos Will Never Have a Chance: Sharīʿa Debates and Tolerance in a Provincial Tanzanian Town." In *Sharīʿa in Africa Today*, edited by … 241–58. Leiden, Netherlands: Brill.

Moosa, Ebrahim. 1988. "Application of Muslim Personal and Family Law in South Africa: Law, Ideology and Social Implications." MA thesis, University of Cape Town.

Moosa, Ebrahim. 1996. "Prospects for Muslim Law in South Africa: A History and Recent Developments." *Yearbook of Islamic and Middle Eastern Law Online*, 1: 130–55.

Moosa, Ebrahim. 2009. "Colonialism and Islamic Law." In *Islam and Modernity, An Introduction to Key Issues and Debates*, edited by Muhammad K. Masud, Armando Salvatore, and Martin van Bruinessen, 158–81. Edinburgh: Edinburgh University Press.

Moosa, Najma. 2014. "Faskh (Divorce) and Intestate Succession in Islamic and South African Law: Impact of the Watershed Judgment in Hassam v Jacobs and the Muslim Marriages Bill." *Acta Juridica*, 2014, no. 1: 160–191.

Muslim Marriages Act 25. 1961. https://www.gov.za/sites/default/files/gcis_document/201505/act-25-1961.pdf.

Muslim Marriages Draft Bill. 2003. Accessed September 2, 2010. https://static.pmg.org.za/bills/110117muslim-marriages-bill.pdf.

National Commission for the Status of Women. 2014. *Litigation Related to Women under Nizam-e-Adl (Malakand Division)*. Islamabad: NCWS.

Nkosi, Bongani. 2020. "We Can't Legalise Muslim Nikah Marriage, Says Home Affairs Minister." *Star*, June 2. https://www.iol.co.za/the-star/news/we-cant-legalise-muslim-nikah-marriage-says-home-affairs-minister-48851280.

O'Malley Archives. *1909 [Union of] South Africa Act*. Accessed November 19, 2020. https://omalley.nelsonmandela.org/omalley/index.php/site/q/03lv01538/04lv01646/05lv01735.htm.

Otto, Jan M. 2010. *Sharia Incorporated, A Comparative Overview of the Legal Systems of Twelve Muslim Countries in Past and Present*. Leiden, Netherlands: Leiden University Press.

Piscatori, James P. 1986. *Islam in a World of Nation-States*. Cambridge: Cambridge University Press.

Rautenbach, Christa. 2000. "The Recognition of Muslim Marriages in South Africa: Past, Present and Future." *Recht van de Islam* 17: 36–89.

Reda, Nevin. 2015. "From the Canadian Sharia Debates to the Arab World: Developing a Quran-Based Theology of Democracy." In *Religion and*

Democracy: Islam and Representation, edited by Ingrid Mattson, Paul Nesbitt-Larking, and Nawaz Tahir, 78–100.

SAHO, South African History Online. 2019b. "Recognition of Customary Marriages Act of 1998." Last updated August 27, 2019.

SAHO, South African History Online. 2019c. "A History of the South African Constitution 1910–1996. Last updated August 27, 2019.

South African Law Reform Commission, Project 59, Islamic Marriages and Relater Matters Report. July 2003. https://www.justice.gov.za/salrc/reports/r_prj59_2003jul.pdf.

Schroter, Susanne. 2014. "Between 'sastra angi' and 'pedal sharia': Debates over Gendered Citizenship in Post-Authoritarian Indonesia." *Review of Indonesian and Malaysian Affairs*, 48, no. 1 (2014): 67.

Selby, Jennifer A. and Anna C. Korteweg, eds. 2012. *Debating Sharia: Islam, Gender Politics and Family Law Arbitration.* Toronto: University of Toronto Press.

Selby, Jennifer A. 2013. "Promoting the Everyday: Pro-Sharia Advocacy and Public Relations in Ontario, Canada's 'Sharia Debate'." *Religions*, 4, no. 3: 423–42.

South Africa Bill of Rights 1994. https://static.pmg.org.za/bills/110117muslim-marriages-bill.pdf.

Tayob, Abdulkader. 1996. "Counting Muslims in South Africa." *Annual Review of Islam in South Africa*. Cape Town: Centre for Contemporary Islam, UCT. http://www.cci.uct.ac.za/usr/cci/publications/aria/download_issues/1998/1998_9.pdf.

Tayob, Abdulkader. 2002. "The South African Muslim Communities Response to September 11th." *Annual Review of Islam in South Africa*. Cape Town: Centre for Contemporary Islam, UCT. http://www.cilt.uct.ac.za/usr/cci/publications/aria/download_issues/2002/2002_M2_tayob.pdf.

Tayob, Abdulkader. 2005. "The Struggle over Muslim Personal Law in a right-based Constitution: A South African Case study." *Recht van den Islam*. 22: 1–16.

Vahed, Goolam, Jeppie, Shamil. 2004-2005. "Multiple Communities: Muslims in post apartheid South Africa." In John Daniel, Roger Scuthall and Jessica Lutchman (eds.) *State of the Nation: South Africa 2004–2005*. Pretoria: Human Science Research Council.

https://doi.org/10.1142/9781800611689_bmatter

Glossary

'ādil	just
ADR	Alternative Dispute Resolution
aḥkām, fatāwā	legal elaborations
ajārakum	"...granted you protection..." This refers to the following statement by Prophet Muhammad, "Allah has granted you protection from three things: Your Prophet lays no curse upon you, lest you utterly perish; the party of falsehood among you will never triumph over the party of truth; you will never agree on a false doctrine." Muttaqi, *Kanz al-'ummal* (Hyderabad 1312–14, 6:233)
ajlāf	low caste, riff raff
amāna	trust
amīr	commander
amīr al-muslimīn	the commander of the Muslims
amīr al-mu'minīn	commander of the faithful
amr, imāra	the power of a commander
'aql	reason
arche	primordial power
ashrāf	nobility
auqāf	religious endowments

bid'ah, biddat	unapproved religious act added as legal obligation
al-birr	right conduct, doing good/charity
cadí	see, Qāḍī
civil law tradition	characterized by written legal codes and a unique set of judicial procedures
common law tradition	developed in England from the local corpus of judgments, doctrines implicit in those decisions, and customary practices
consensus ecclesiae	consensus of the Church and papal infallibility
capitatio	capitation or poll tax
dahir, dhahir, al-Ẓahīr	decree by the Moroccan king
ḍarar, al-ḍrār	harm
dhawu' l-farḍ, dhawi'l farā'iḍ	Quranic heirs
dhimma	protected status of conquered people, legal superiority of Muslims over non-Muslims
dīnī madāris	schools for religious education
dogma	a set of undisputed mandatory beliefs for the followers of a given religion
DWAM	Democratic Women's Association of Morocco
emir, amīr	commander
faqīh	experts in Islamic jurisprudence and law
fatwā, fatwās, fatāwā	legal opinion
fiqh al-aqalliyyāt	jurisprudence on Muslim minorities
ghuluww fi'l din	religious extremism
gizya	see, Jizya
ḥaḍāna	custody

ḥadd, Ḥudūd, Hudood	fixed punishments generally prescribed for six offences, Quranic punishments
ḥadiṭh	Prophetic traditions, reports about the Prophet Muhammad's sayings and actions
ḥākim	sovereign, ruler, decision-maker, arbiter
ḥalāla	intermittent marriage by a divorced wife with another man who divorces her after consummation to enable her to remarry her former husband
ḥalaqas	circles of learning
ḥaqq	truth
harag, kharāj	real estate contribution
ḥirābah	armed robbery or rebellion
ḥisbah	public order, promotion of good and prevention of evil
ḥuqūq al-insān	human rights
'iddat	three months period of waiting
iḥsān	kindness and benevolence
ijmā'	consensus
ijtihād	juridical reasoning
ikhtilāf	difference, plurality of legal opinions
īmān	belief, faith
imam	leader in group prayer, religious leader
imāra	conclusive power
imperium	absolute power
iṣlāḥ	reform
jizya, jizyah	gizya, historically, a tax paid by non-Muslim populations to their Muslim rulers, based on the conditions of the pact between them.
jus cogens	a principle of international law that is based on values taken to be fundamental to the international community and that cannot be set aside

kadi	see also, Qāḍī
*kāfir*s	disbelievers
kālam	theology
khalīfah	caliph, vicegerent, successor
khanqah	hospices
kharāj	real estate contribution, land tax
al-khayr	beneficial, good
khiyār al-'ayb	option of defect
khul', khula'	procedure for women to obtain divorce from their husbands in exchange for payment of money incentive to husband, usually by wife renouncing her entitlement to *mahr*
lex	law, legal system
ma'rūf	good and approved
madāris	religious schools
madhāhib	schools of Islamic jurisprudence
madrasa	institutionalized colleges
mahr	dowery, bride gift
makrūh	reprehensible
maqāṣid	higher purposes, objectives
maṣlaḥat	convenience, interest
al-maṣlaḥa al-'āmma	common good, public interest
ma'ṣūm	impeccable, infallible
mawlāna	our master, title of a religious leader
miḥna, miḥnah	inquisition
milla, millah	religious group

millet	system of organizing religious minorities
millī	religious courts, judicial system for non-Muslims to settle their personal status disputes outside state regulation
mohajir, muhājirs	migrants, immigrants, who migrated from India to Pakistan and Bangladesh
mu'allafat al-qulūb	influential people, not necessarily poor, non-Muslim, who have helped Islam
mubāḥ	merely optional, neutral, one of the five legal values of obligation
muḍāraba	business financing, a permitted type of formation of finance companies in Islamic law
Mudawwana	family law code in Morocco
muftī	jurist, scholar, legal scholar
al-mujtahid al-muqayyad	one for whom legal opinions are tied to a particular juridical school
al-mujtahid al-muṭlaq	one who extracts legal rulings from scriptural sources without reference to a particular juridical school
mukhtaṣar	digest, a compendium of law
mukus	civil taxes
mullāhs, mullā	religious scholar (sometimes pejorative usage)
murābaḥa	traditional forms of complex sales contracts
murtad, murtadd	apostate
muttaqī	pious
nabī	prophet
Niẓām-e Islām	Islamic order
PANAFID	Plan of Action for the Integration of Women into Development, *Plan d'Action pour l'Intégration des Femmes au Développement*
qāḍī	judge

qānūn	law, Emperor's law, civil law
qaṭ'iy, qaṭ'ī	categorical, definite
qazi	see also, Qāḍī
qiṣāṣ	retaliation, retribution
qiṣṭ	fairness, justice, full measure
qiwāma	authority, male authority over women
qiyās	reasoning by analogy, syllogism
Quaid-e-Azam	title of the founder of Pakistan, Muhammad Ali Jinah
quia voluit	because he wanted it that way
quodlibet	as one pleases, arbitrary, whatever
reislamization	restoring Islamic system, decolonizing
ribā	usury
riddah	apostasy
ṣadāq	dower
sariqah	theft
sharb al-khamr, shurb al-khamr	consuming alcoholic drink
shiqāq, Šiqāq	discord
shūrā	consultation
siyāsa	governance, executive power, punishment, privilege of the ruler
al-siyāsa al-shar'iyya, siyasa shar'iyya	Sharia compliant governance, principle that gives rulers more leeway to determine punishments and admits less complicated procedural and evidentiary rules
stipendaria, civitas stipendaria, stipendio multitude	tributary community, the lowest and most common type of towns and communities under Roman rule
sulṭān	power, army ruler, absolutely powerful

sultanic, *maẓālim*	courts of complaints not restricted by Sharia procedural laws
suo motu	on its own motion, an act of authority taken by government or court without prompting the court
tajdīd	renewal
takfirism, *takfīr*,	alleging a Muslim for committing an act of disbelief, declaring a person apostate
takhayyur	selecting the best, selecting the view from a school of law other than one's own, choice between two or more juristic views, principle of selectivity
ṭalāq	divorce, repudiation, end of marriage contract
talaq-e-biddat, ṭalāq bid'ī	contrary to the divorce procedure prescribed in the Qur'an and Sunnah
talfīq	combining parts of the doctrines of different schools or jurists into a new doctrine, borrowing across *madhhab* boundaries
tanzimat	reorganization, reforms, Ottoman reforms
tawātur	continuous acceptance
ta'zīr	punishment not fixed as *ḥadd*, discretionary punishment by the judge or ruler of the state
tazkiyat al-anfus	inner purification
topos	a standard form of rhetorical argumentation or a variably expressible literary commonplace (Oxford), a traditional or conventional literary or rhetorical theme or topic
triple talaq	divorce formula uttered three times
UAF	Union of Women's Action
Ulamas, ulema, 'Ulamā'	scientists, scholars, religious scholars
ultra vires	without legal authority
ulū l-amr, *ulī'l amr, walī al-amr*	the possessors of the rule, ruler, executive authority

'urf	custom
uṣūl	sources
uṣūl al-fiqh	sources of law or methodology, methodologies of interpretation
vali al-Asr, Walī al-'Aṣr, Imām Zamān, Mahdi	the Messiah prophesied to appear at the world's end and establish a reign of peace and righteousness. In Twelver Shia belief, the 12th Imam, who is expected to emerge from occultation to fulfill this role
velayat-e faqih	the guardianship of the jurist
vinculum iuris	legal tie, a bond of law, legal obligation that makes one party becomes legally bound to another to do something according to law
voluntaristic	the principle that individuals are free to choose goals and how to achieve them within the bounds of certain societal and cultural constraints, as opposed to actions that are coerced or predetermined
wakil	spokesman
walā' wa l-barā'	restricts Muslim loyalty to Muslims
waqfs	religious endowments
Weltanschauung	worldview
wilāyah	sovereign power; power delegated by the sovereign
zakāt	fixed amount of alms. Islamic tax on savings
ẓannī	suppositional
Zikrīs	followers of Mahdawism in Pakistan
zinā	fornication

https://doi.org/10.1142/9781800611689_bmatter

Index

G

K

L

www.ingramcontent.com/pod-product-compliance
Lightning Source LLC
LaVergne TN
LVHW011659200926
848484LV00004B/999